Evolutionary economics

Evolutionary economics

Applications of Schumpeter's ideas

Edited by
HORST HANUSCH
University of Augsburg

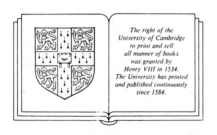

The right of the
University of Cambridge
to print and sell
all manner of books
was granted by
Henry VIII in 1534.
The University has printed
and published continuously
since 1584.

CAMBRIDGE UNIVERSITY PRESS

Cambridge
New York   New Rochelle   Melbourne   Sydney

Published by the Press Syndicate of the University of Cambridge
The Pitt Building, Trumpington Street, Cambridge CB2 1RP
32 East 57th Street, New York, NY 10022, USA
10 Stamford Road, Oakleigh, Melbourne 3166, Australia

First published 1988

Printed in the United States of America

Library of Congress Cataloging-in-Publication Data

Evolutionary economics.

Bibliography: p.

Includes index.

1. Schumpeter, Joseph Alois, 1883–1950 – Contributions
in economics. I. Hanusch, Horst.
HB119.S35E95   1988   330′.092′4   88–6050

British Library Cataloguing in Publication Data

Evolutionary economics: applications of
Schumpeter's ideas.
1. Economics. Theories of Schumpeter, Joseph A. (Joseph Alois), 1883–1950
I. Hanusch, Horst
330.1

ISBN 0 521 36220 2

Contents

vi   **Contents**

Acknowledgments

This volume consists of papers and discussions presented at a congress held in Augsburg, Federal Republic of Germany, in September 1986. During this congress, the International Joseph A. Schumpeter Society (ISS) was founded with an impressive response by scholars and practitioners from all over the globe. It is a pleasure for me to thank all those who contributed to make both events resounding successes.

My special thanks go, first of all, to my friend Wolfgang Stolper for his personal engagement and his manifold support in founding the ISS and in planning the Augsburg congress. Without his contacts with international scholars in the field of Schumpeterian economics, the society would not have come into existence.

Establishing an international society and organizing a congress cannot be accomplished without financial support. In this matter, I express my gratitude to the German Science Foundation, the University of Augsburg, the City of Augsburg, the Augsburg Chamber of Commerce, the German Bundesbank, and a number of business firms.

The statutes of the ISS provide for the position of a general editor, responsible for all publications of the society. Mark Perlman was in charge of this volume. I would like to express my cordial thanks to him and to Naomi Perlman, who assisted in the editorial work.

The founding of the ISS and the organization of the congress have also led to a heavy burden on some of my co-workers at the University of Augsburg. I am especially indebted to Uwe Cantner and Thomas Kuhn for their devoted and competent assistance.

Horst Hanusch

Contributors

Moses Abramovitz
Department of Economics
Stanford University
Stanford, CA 94305

Reinhard Blum
Universität Augsburg
Memminger Strasse 14
D-8900 Augsburg
Federal Republic of Germany

George Catephores
Department of Political Economy
University College, London
Gower Street
London WC1E 6BT
England

Gunnar Eliasson
Industrial Institute for Economic and
   Social Research
Grevgatan 34
114 53 Stockholm
Sweden

Franz Gehrels
Volkswirtshaftliches Institut Univer-
   sität München
Ludwigstrasse 28
D-8000 München 22
Federal Republic of Germany

Karl-Dieter Grüske
Universität Erlangen-Nürnberg
Lange Gasse 20
D8500 Nürnberg 1
Postfach 3931
Federal Republic of Germany

Horst Hanusch
Universität Augsburg
Memminger Strasse 14
8900 Augsburg
Federal Republic of Germany

Arnold Heertje
Laegieskampweg 17
1412 ER Naarden
The Netherlands

Dirk Ipsen
Fachgebiet Politische Ökonomie
Technische Hochschule Darmstadt
Fachbereich 1
Residenzschloss
6100 Darmstadt
Federal Republic of Germany

Peter M. Jackson
University of Leicester
Leicester LE1 7RH
England

Burton H. Klein
P.O. Box 28446
San Diego, CA 92128

Eduard März
Deceased

Alfred Maussner
Volkwirtshaftliches Institut
Friedrich-Alexander-Universität
Erlangen-Nürnberg
Postfach 3931
8500 Nürnberg
Federal Republic of Germany

viii

Michio Morishima
The London School of Economics
Houghton Street
London WC2A 2AE
England

Richard A. Musgrave
University of California
Santa Cruz, CA 95064

Mark Perlman
Department of Economics
University of Pittsburgh
Pittsburgh, PA 15260

Rolf-Dieter Postlep
Fachbereich Wirtschaft-
  swissenschaften
Philipps-Universität Marburg
Am Plan 2
3550 Marburg
Federal Republic of Germany

Fritz Rahmeyer
Universität Augsburg
Memminger Strasse 14
8900 Augsburg
Federal Republic of Germany

Kurt W. Rothschild
Döblinger Hauptstrasse 77A
A-1190 Wien
Austria

Frederic M. Scherer
Department of Economics
Swarthmore College
Swarthmore, PA 19081

Friedrich Schneider
Department of Economics
Institute of Economic Policy
Johannes Kepler University of Linz
A4020 Linz-Auhof
Austria

Yuichi Shionoya
Department of Economics
Hitotsubashi University
Kunitachi, Tokyo
Japan

Wolfgang F. Stolper
Department of Economics
The University of Michigan
Ann Arbor, MI 48109

Raphael Valentino
SQS 111 – Bloco F – Apt 302
Brasilia-D.F.
Brazil-CEP: 70374
Brazil

Henri J. Vartiainen
Vidobackavaegen 4 C 15
00700 Helsinki
Finland

Heinz-Dieter Wenzel
Ludwig-Maximilians Institut
Universität München
D-800 München 22
Federal Republic of Germany

Horst Zimmermann
Public Finance Group
Faculty of Economics and Business
  Management
University of Marburg
Am Plan 2
D-3550 Marburg
Federal Republic of Germany

Introduction

HORST HANUSCH

In economic theory, as well as in economic policy, the work of Joseph A. Schumpeter has come into a remarkable renascence during the last decade. Perhaps the next quarter of the century will even be called the era of Schumpeter. The crisis of neoclassical theory is evidently one reason for this development. The critical situation in which Keynesian policy has found itself in the seventies and eighties is certainly the other reason. More and more economists are searching for more appropriate explanations of the economic problems of our day. Evolutionary economics, of which Shumpeter is regarded as the spiritual father, provides an appropriate framework for theoretical and empirical analysis of a larger number of these problems.

From the point of view of evolutionary economics, Schumpeter copes with one major problem: dynamic growth of the potential aggregate supply. But contrary to neoclassical theory, he is not at all interested in optimization and pure equilibrium economics. For him, the driving forces of economic development are dynamic entrepreneurs and dynamic competition. It is the role of the entrepreneur to create innovations and to destroy old equilibria by establishing new combinations. Along with this process of "creative destruction," progress in productivity will be achieved. In addition, dynamic competition, forced by innovation, provides the necessary transfer of productivity gains to consumers, resulting in an increase in social welfare.

On the other hand, in his mainly market-oriented framework, Schumpeter does not neglect the legitimate role of government. It certainly has to supply society with the desired public goods and has to finance this supply in such a way that it does not interfere with growth, productivity, and taxable capacity.

With this short characterization of evolutionary economics, the focus of this volume is already delineated. Most of the contributions deal with one of the following issues: the dynamic entrepreneur, the dynamic competition, and the role of the state in a dynamic economy. The volume contains important and remarkable chapters on these subjects, as well as original and convincing comments. In my introductory

1

remarks, however, I shall try to summarize only the chapters' most essential arguments. To comment on the discussions would go too far into detail. At the end of this Introduction, I shall also outline some directions for further research.

Entrepreneur and innovation

In the evolutionary process, as it is normally conceived in Schumpeterian economics, innovations are at the root of cyclical movements. The principal economic agent is the entrepreneur, who establishes new combinations by introducing new products as well as new production methods.

In addition, or perhaps even contrary to this view, Michio Morishima and George Catephores try to demonstrate that Schumpeter's greatest contribution was to assign to the banking sector an explicit role as the fifth constituent in the general equilibrium system. It is through the bankers' creation of credit that savings are made flexible and are adjusted to investment. "Banker" and "credit," rather than "entrepreneur" and "new combination," should therefore be considered the key words in Schumpeter's economics. This is certainly an inspiring interpretation of Schumpeterian ideas, but it is also open to question. So let me return to the more traditional path of reasoning, to the role dynamic entrepreneurs do play in an evolving economy.

In mainstream economics, the notion of a "dynamic entrepreneur" is completely unknown. Keynesian theory, on the one hand, looks primarily at the demand side of the economy and has no microeconomic foundation at all. Neoclassical theory, on the other hand, is based on a capable microeconomic system; however, it is primarily concerned with static efficiency, ignoring problems of dynamic equilibrium and of risk taking. The necessity to develop models of the firm more fully specified than the determinate and mechanistic models of neoclassical theory is emphasized in the chapters by Burton Klein and Frederic M. Scherer.

Burton H. Klein examines the ability of firms to act in a dynamically flexible manner, that is, to adapt immediately to a changing environment. Flexibility of this kind is of eminent importance, because it is a main prerequisite for firms' improvement in productivity. These gains, however, cannot be achieved without losses in static efficiency, as firms are not able to produce at minimum costs at any time. Empirical studies have shown that flexibility depends to a great degree on specific characteristics of the microeconomic production process: The less the process is specialized and routinized, the more a firm can be dynamically flexible and productive. To explain this relationship, one has to look into organizational and behavioral theories. But these theories are banished to a "black box" by traditional microeconomics.

Frederic M. Scherer shows that ownership patterns of firms have changed basically over the past century. The corporation has come to be the dominant organizational form for conducting business. In addition, control of corporations by financial intermediaries has experienced some resurgence during the past two decades. This whole development may have had remarkable consequences for the firm's behavior. To a certain degree, it might provide for both the restriction of risk taking and the extinction of a creative entrepreneurial spirit. From a Schumpeterian point of view, we are forced to ask whether or not these events will have severe implications for the industrial strength of Western nations.

Dynamic competition and economic targets

Competition among firms is a necessary condition for achieving efficiency in the allocation of resources. In particular, the neo-Schumpeterian concept of *dynamic efficiency* plays a crucial role when one tries to understand how the allocation process really works in market economies. This concept essentially means that competition among only a few oligopolistic firms will generate a substantially greater increase in the welfare of society than perfect competition with numerous enterprises would ever accomplish. But how does this concept come to its astonishing conclusion?

First, it is assumed that innovation is the driving force of competition and does not reflect the mere numbers of actors in the supply side of the market. Innovations depend heavily on the capacity of firms to invest in R&D expenditures. This investment is correlated with the sizes and market shares of firms.

Second, firms involved in dynamic competition are supposed to be unable to completely internalize the gains accruing to them. They have to transfer part of the gain to consumers in the form of low prices. To use Burton Klein's terminology, in this respect we are confronted with a positive-sum game.

This reasoning also seems to be quite obvious in a situation where the labor market is characterized by rigid or increasing wages. Then, improvement in productivity via process innovations is the only way to reduce unit labor costs. Corresponding to that, firms have to reduce prices in order to preserve their ability to compete. Decreasing prices usually will cause an increase in demand and bring about greater output. So innovations in the process of production need not lead naturally to unemployment or to a decline in growth.

Results obtained by Gunnar Eliasson in his simulation studies confirm this thesis and also emphasize the relationship between innovative behavior on the microeconomic level and macroeconomic targets. In his chapter, he concludes that significant variations in performance and price structures of individual agents have to be present continuously to generate stable macroeconomic performance. "Because competition makes low performers exit, this can be achieved only through vigorous innovative entry."

Theoretical reasoning within the frame of evolutionary economics obviously can cope not only with growth and employment but also with inflation, as Fritz Rahmeyer's chapter shows. Using a behavioristic approach and starting with the idea that firms always act on cost-based pricing, his analysis points out the relationship among wages, productivity, and the development of prices. Because wages do not vary substantially among different sectors in the economy, the main determinant of price formation in industry is productivity. Relative prices and productivities are negatively correlated. This can even be proved empirically. The general price index, at any point in time, reflects a weighted structure of relative prices; its development represents not only the dynamics of productivity but also the process of inflation. The relationship between productivity development and relative prices may thus be considered as the core of an evolutionary treatment of inflation.

The role of the state

We have seen that innovation is of essential importance for the economic growth process. This process is always accompanied by structural change. Evolution consists of innovations and adaptions. Innovation in one sector occurs along with distortion and displacement in other sectors. In this situation, society has to decide whether to accept the uncertainty incidental to these dynamic changes or to implement an institutional frame that regulates structural change with all its negative influences on innovative activities.

We all know how this conflict is solved in the European industrialized nations: By accepting the dynamics of capitalism and structural change, comprehensive social systems and government interventions were established. These institutions ultimately evolved into the so-called welfare state.

The best expression of this development is the public sector's share of GNP, which has already reached extremely large proportions in many industrial nations. Financing governmental expenditures by tax revenues as well as public debt, however, seems to have reached its limits. In the private sector, the increasing public burden creates disincentives to innovation, labor input, and investment, as well as to the level of performance. In the public sector, growing budgets have the immanent tendency to contribute to fiscal pressure because of their reduced contribution to GNP and future revenues, as Horst Zimmermann concludes in his chapter. So the ideal of a self-financing public budget cannot work in reality. On the contrary, extending governmental expenditures not only imposes fiscal pressures but also hinders the private sector's ability to adapt to structural change.

Behind these processes we also have to recognize an essential driving force: the big trade-off between equity and efficiency. But these two goals are not only to be found in an antagonistic relationship; they also form a special kind of jointness, as Okun has stated: "They need each other – to put some rationality into equality and some humanity into efficiency" (Okun, 1975, p. 20). This way of looking at dependencies may even have inspired Schumpeter. In any case, Peter M. Jackson in his chapter demonstrates that Schumpeter acknowledged the legitimate role of government and the necessity for social policy in a capitalistic economy. But he has also drawn attention to the disincentive effects of taxation and the possibility that government interventions may distort the price system of the market. A slowdown in the dynamics of the growth process must then be the inevitable consequence.

How a country solves the conflict between efficiency and equality is also of great importance for its ranking on the international productivity scale, as Moses Abramovitz and Mark Perlman found out in their studies. Perlman states that social reform policies have destroyed the capacity of the United States to match other nations' productivity gains. For Abramovitz, different institutional settings are the main reasons that the catch-up process between advanced and backward nations is not self-limiting in every case.

Prospects for further research

Now let me come to the prospects for further research. Wolfgang Stolper and Arnold Heertje have contributed greatly to this subject. I would like to discuss only one aspect, that which I consider most important for the future of evolutionary economics. I am thinking primarily of methodological improvements, both in empirical research and in model building. As economic history shows, Keynes finally achieved an intellectual victory over Schumpeter, because Keynes's work is characterized by a mathematical formalism. It therefore provides a far greater appeal to rationality than does the descriptive analysis of Schumpeter, which appeals more to intuition. But if we look at the current state of the art, we need not be too pessimistic. In microeconomics and in macroeconomics, quite a number of economists are already working successfully to enhance the ideas of Schumpeter.

On the microeconomic level, "industrial economics" is making extraordinary efforts to embrace the model of the neoclassical firm. The innovative activities of firms, especially, are studied with great energy. In this field, we already possess sophisticated econometric investigations. Recently, even some outstanding theoretical approaches have been presented, such as that of Dasgupta and Stiglitz (1980). In their model, the innovative activity of firms, as well as the optimal degree of market concentration, can be determined endogenously. But this model still clings too much to neoclassical tradition, using the methods of welfare economics and concentrating on allocative efficiency alone. The role of innovation as a strategic instrument in dynamic competition and the resulting process of creative destruction have not yet been treated analytically in a convincing manner.

In mainstream macroeconomics, innovations, as they are seen by Schumpeter, have little relevance. Attempts to endogenize technological progress in growth theory and in business-cycle theory are not appropriate for models that should be set up to describe the evolutionary process. First, such models have to be based on an adequate theory of the firm. Second, they have to concentrate on the process of creative destruction and have to explain that process by a formalized theory of dynamic equilibria. Simulation studies like those of Eliasson in this volume and of Nelson and Winter (1982) are one possible way of dealing with these demands.

Perhaps theoretical analysis should also be influenced much more by other disciplines that have worked on the processes of structural change and on evolution for a far longer time than economics. Modern physics and mathematical biology, in particular, come to mind. Knowledge already gained in these sciences may also contribute to a better understanding of the mechanisms that determine the generating, selection, and adaptive behavior of firms, as well as the nature of dynamic macroeconomics.

Schumpeter was, as we know, a creative and independent scholar, self-consciously committed to scientific truth alone. Those who had the good fortune to know him personally report that he was always interested in a more precise and formal version of his theory. Competition among those trying to formalize and/or extend his theories is certainly in harmony with his desire.

References

Dasgupta, D. S., and Stiglitz, J. F. (1980). "Industrial Structure and the Nature of Innovative Activity," *Economic Journal,* 90:266–93.

Nelson, R. R., Winter, S. G. (1982). *An Evolutionary Theory of Economic Change.* Cambridge University Press.

Okun, A. M. (1975). *Equality and Efficiency – The Big Tradeoff.* Washington, D.C.: Brookings Institution.

CHAPTER 1

Development: theory and empirical evidence

WOLFGANG F. STOLPER

The major points in my brief remarks will be addressed to the purpose of the new International Schumpeter Society. I have been told by a friend that we are acting contrary to all of Schumpeter's views by founding a society in his name, for Schumpeter was against the founding of a Schumpeter school, which, in his words, should never exist. Another friend expressed the fear that we might degenerate into yet another sect, another group defending special interests in the name of science. Schumpeter, in a letter to my father, Gustav Stolper, that Seidl and I published in our introduction to the collected political and economic policy writings of Schumpeter (1985, p. 85), expressed his fear that special interests would be seen to be behind much policy discussion and that he intended to counteract this by trying to teach that mysterious beast, the intelligent layman, how to think economically rather than how to misuse economics to defend special interests. If we ever should degenerate into a school, or worse, a sect, it would be much better that this society had never been founded, and it will deserve to die if it ever forgets its mission to find and defend truth, whatever its nature.

There are thus certain pitfalls to be avoided. The society has chosen this name to honor Schumpeter and to try to devote itself to the topics of investigation that he raised and that seem important to us. To be effective, the society must remain nonideological, divorced from politics and any schools.

Our field of scholarship has made enormous strides in the present century, with scholars like Jan Tinbergen, Ragnar Frisch, John R. Hicks, Simon Kuznets, Gottfried Haberler, Paul Samuelson, and Tjalling Koopmans making significant contributions, to name just a few giants of the older generation. Any impression to the contrary is due to a strange kind of myopia, fostered, I sometimes suspect, by the deliberate wish to eliminate any professional criticism of whatever policy is in fashion. It is similar to that seen in criticism of the fluoridation of water, the kind of myopia that sees in any temporary change in movement a trend, and proof of failure or success, as the case may be.

9

The fact is that the first years following World War II were years of a historically unprecedented increase in prosperity for the great majority of people, not only in the North Atlantic and Mediterranean areas but also in many areas of the underdeveloped world. Economists can, I believe, take some credit for these developments. Usually the name of John Maynard Keynes springs to mind. But economists of a more classical persuasion also have contributed significantly: insisting on not repeating the errors of the first war (not to burden the world economy with reparations payments, which would have poisoned the atmosphere), insisting on giving freer markets a chance, insisting on free trade and convertibility of currencies against a vocal minority who believed that only "planning" and administrative decision making would solve Europe's problems, insisting on opening the way not just for entrepreneurs but particularly for workers, for new men and methods. Much less of this is ideological than it might appear, as the more recent reforms in Hungary and China show.

I mention this because Hungary and China do not become capitalist because they engage in decentralization, and even more because these developments point to one of Schumpeter's major interests and contributions: what he called "economic sociology" and what is nowadays referred to as "political economy."[1] I shall return to this complex of topics later.

Of course, much remains to be done. From our standpoint, the important fact is that when economists deal with microeconomic issues, they do in fact and for all practical purposes speak with one voice. Disagreements appear primarily with respect to macroeconomic issues and policies. But this is really not the central point of my remarks. Among the economists who stand out like Mt. Everest alongside lesser peaks, surely Schumpeter comes to mind. Why?

The basic reason is his "vision," more than any individual contribution. Like Marx (perhaps only Marx), he saw the economy essentially not as an equilibrium but as a dynamic phenomenon. Schumpeter put it concisely in his introduction to the Japanese translation of *The Theory of Economic Development:*

I was trying to construct a theoretical model of the process of economic change in time, or perhaps more clearly, to answer the question how the economic system generates the force which incessantly transforms it. [1951, pp. 158–59]

[1] The term "political economist" is now occasionally preempted by so-called radical economists or political scientists, though originally it seems to have denoted one who studies what we today call economics, as, for example, in Ricardo's title *Principles of Political Economy and Taxation.*

This differs from most economic theory, including most growth models. Schumpeter mentioned that Walras told him that

the course of economic life is essentially passive and merely adapts itself to the natural and social influences that may be acting on it, so that the theory of a stationary process constitutes really the whole of theoretical economics and that as economic theorists we cannot say much about the factors that account for historical change but must simply register them. [1951, pp. 159–60]

Schumpeter described the function of economic theory to be, in addition to Marshall's "machine for organizing facts," a method of investigating how particular institutions work, how they evolved, and how one might want to change them to achieve certain aims. Some of this is similar to the "new institutional economics," which thus might claim Schumpeter as one of its patron saints, at least up to a point.

Even as late as the 1930s it was by no means uncommon to consider the business cycle a sort of mistake, one that would not occur if only we had perfect competition and/or if only government and/or the central bank were behaving properly, which all too often meant if only they would get out of the way. Government was to refrain from interfering, and the central bank was to pursue a policy of monetary neutrality.

In my way of looking at things, and that of most of us who are influenced by Schumpeter, this obviously is not so. With all due respect we must have for the achievements of growth theory, it is still true that these theories do not ask the question that was decisive for Schumpeter: how the investments that bring about growth arise from inside the system.

None of this makes Schumpeter a Marxist, nor is it all clear how much he was really influenced by Marx. He read and admired Marx, of course, as he did many others. None of those authors had answered the questions that concerned Schumpeter, and few had even asked the questions.

It can be answered that many economists have viewed the entrepreneur as a central figure. Nowadays it seems to be sufficient to occasionally mention entrepreneurship to be considered a Schumpeterian. There is even a Pavlovian reaction to this word, which has become a kind of shorthand for finding fault with anything the government does and giving a free hand to any shenanigans that greed might devise. To be sure, not only is much fault to be found with what governments and central banks have done; there is even a Mephisto-like quality in the capitalist process that turns greed into social welfare, much as Goethe's spirit that creates by denial and destruction. Or, to paraphrase Mancur

Olson (1982), greed is directed to income-creating activities rather than income-distributing activities.

Nothing could be further from what Schumpeterian theory is about. To be sure, Marshall (1925) has sung the praises of the entrepreneurs even more rhapsodically than Schumpeter, but neither in his writing nor in that of anyone else does one find an attempt to spell out what this means theoretically in terms of connecting it with general equilibrium theory. There is nowhere else an attempt to show what happens when an equilibrium is destroyed, or why or how it is destroyed.

This formulation applies necessarily to the classical formulation. There are two points I wish to make. First, the great contributions of most of the scholars I have named relate to refinement and further development of equilibrium theory or a working out of aggregative theory. Samuelson's magnum opus may serve as an example. But the same is true also for the contribution of Hicks and Koopmans, although not quite for Kuznets. Their dynamics are defined essentially by the time subscripts of the variables, but the basic parameters of the system do not change, or their changes are introduced from outside without further explanation.

Second, the investigation of the Schumpeterian dynamics – which implies that fundamental parameters change at discrete intervals – has begun. Perhaps – I am not absolutely certain – the beginning may be found in Ragnar Frisch's contribution (1933) to the Cassel Festschrift on impulse and propagation problems. In this classic article, Frisch gives a hint of how this noble purpose may be achieved, and he states that after lengthy correspondence with Schumpeter, the latter agreed that what Frisch had in mind was a fair presentation of Schumpeter's views.

Briefly, Frisch's article first dealt with introducing and considerably refining the acceleration principle. He showed that the acceleration principle as developed by A. Aftalion (1913) and J. M. Clark (1917) would lead to fluctuations in the economy, and he presented ballpark estimates concerning the magnitudes of the different parameters that seemed plausible to him (although not really based, in that article at least, on specific statistical investigations), but that actually produced short cycles, later dubbed by Schumpeter Kitchin cycles, and the ordinary or Juglar cycle.

The problem was, of course, that although this formulation might explain why, in Wicksell's rocking-horse analogy, the economy would react to shocks in a fluctuating manner, it still required an impulse to set the horse rocking. This led Frisch to go back to Slutsky (1927), who had shown that random shocks could produce regular cycles.

In the correspondence, Schumpeter must have objected to this. Schumpeter and Frisch were friends and admired each other greatly. I have tried to locate the Frisch-Schumpeter correspondence, which, if found, should be of considerable interest to scholars in general, not only to scholars interested in the history of thought. So far, my search has not been successful. The University of Oslo has not yet sorted out the many boxes of Frisch material; neither has Harvard University performed the task for the Schumpeter papers.

As I see it, there are two problems with this approach of combining Aftalion and Clark, and Frisch and Slutsky. The first is that it could account for cycles, but not for an upward trend. It is no accident that the long-wave Kondratieff cycle or wavelike trend is never mentioned.

There is also a point suggested to me by Professor Lawrence Blume. Irving Fisher (a student of Willard Gibbs), Koopmans, Samuelson, and in fact virtually all good theorists since the 1930s have developed models similar to those developed in physics. Schumpeter admired this point of view, but his paradigm is really along different lines. In physics, there is no such thing as a perpetuum mobile. Nonetheless, he was looking for a social science equivalent to just that concept, and in social sciences there is such a possibility. Perhaps he was, in a physical analogy, looking for a controlled chain reaction. I hasten to add that although this does not imply any rejection of the mathematical method or of physical analogies, it does suggest to me that for Schumpeter, the latter methods have definite limitations as far as the explanatory value of the workings of the economy is concerned.

The second problem is that in Schumpeter's view, random shocks do not go to the heart of the problem. In his view, the shocks come from inside the economic system; they are produced by the capitalist economy itself. Schumpeter believed that the facts of economic history showed a fair regularity in the appearance of these shocks, though I heard him remark several times that this regularity was not required by his theory. Whether or not this made him uncomfortable I do not know.

Frisch's response to whatever question Schumpeter might have posed in their correspondence was another analogy, as follows: Assume the possibility that innovations occur in a regular stream over time. How can we explain that the actual innovations occur in a discrete fashion, that they are bunched? I believe that the question as usually posed (Why should clusters of innovating entrepreneurs appear only periodically?) is wrongly put. The question really should be this: Why do they have a chance only at discrete intervals? Schumpeter's answer was in general terms – that creative destruction had to have proceeded sufficiently to establish the neighborhood of new equilibrium.

Frisch suggested the analogy of a pendulum that would receive an impulse every so often by a gadget attached to it. This gadget was continuously being filled with water – the stream of innovative possibilities. But only when it was sufficiently full would it snap and thus trigger a shock to the pendulum, which would then start to swing, with diminishing amplitude, to be restarted by the next impulse.

An ingenious idea, and Schumpeter, according to Frisch, accepted this analogy as appropriately depicting his basic idea. Frisch also stated that the problem was easily worked out mathematically, but he did not do so. I find it difficult to visualize how such a model (which indeed internalized what previously had been outside random shocks) could lead to ever higher equilibrium levels in an economy. Only a more explicit model can do so. Lawrence Blume has suggested to me that a model involving different kinds of innovations complementary to each other might do the trick. I must leave it to my mathematical betters to work out and judge such an idea.

We now have such a possible model by Nelson and Winter (1982), and models on other levels by Eliasson (1983) and Scherer (1984). I do not want to speak about them, partly because of hesitation about my qualifications to do so, and partly because Gunnar Eliasson and F. M. Scherer are here to speak for themselves. The reason I mention this is that whereas Schumpeter never succeeded in working out a precise mathematical formulation of his approach, a failure for which he has been criticized (Niehans, 1981), Nelson and Winter (1982) and perhaps Richard Goodwin (1986) and others have at least started formulations of precisely such a model. I suspect, though I do not know for sure, that Schumpeter's failure probably was rooted as much in his attempts to work along classical lines as in his inadequate knowledge of mathematics. As should be expected, such a model is likely to be radically different from the classical equilibrium paradigm, which nevertheless would be a part of it. As also might be expected, there is in Schumpeter's approach a great deal more than the mention of entrepreneurs.

On the monetary side, less progress has been made. How a theory of money should be integrated with microeconomic theory, in the Schumpeterian meaning of the terms, still awaits investigation. Schumpeter's *Wesen des Geldes* (1970), posthumously published from a manuscript he considered not ready to be published, is of little help here, though his early article "Das Sozialprodukt und die Rechenpfennige" (1952) is, and there are lengthy discussions to be found in his *Theory of Economic Development* and in his *Business Cycles.* Schumpeter's was not a monetary theory of the cycle, although money played an essential part in it. In his policy prescriptions he was decidedly not a deflationist, and he certainly was not a quantity theorist. The quantity theory has a full meaning only in equilibrium, in which case the supply of money is largely irrelevant; its basic function is to supply the missing equation in the Walrasian system needed to convert relative prices into "absolute" (i.e., money) prices, a point made originally, I believe, by Gunnar Myrdal (1939). Nor has anyone attempted to come to terms with the normative aspects of Schumpeterian dynamics with their unorthodox policy implications. None of the monetary theorists have tried to spell out what precisely the entrepreneurial function is, nor how it relates to industrial structure and evolution. It does not belittle Milton Friedman's work to say that he stresses that changes in the quantity of money will eventually lead to price increases if they outrun the increase in output, while being essentially "agnostic" about what actually causes the increase in output and its fluctuations. Of course, he is interested primarily in the control of inflation, but this is not really the subject of the Schumpeterian view of money.

The Schumpeterian dynamics are concerned with how the economic system and its variables change endogenously in a historical and political context. Obviously, the idea did not fall from heaven nor, like Pallas Athena, spring fully grown from the head of Zeus. Scholars like Marshall and those interested in the theory of stages, a typically German phenomenon, represent attempts to come to grips (by essentially unsuitable means) with the very real problem of how an economic system evolves or, more specifically, how one economic system or type of organization evolves from another (i.e., how a system continuously changes its essential character). I say "unsuitable" because these scholars remained essentially descriptive and static, if we allow that latter term in this context, because of their failure even to consider how one stage develops into another higher stage. We have present-day equivalents of the theories of stages. What I have in mind I can perhaps illustrate best by reference to the work of Chenery (1960), who has investigated and found regularities in the industrial structure of an economy and the level of per capita income. I have always admired his work; so if I express some doubts, I trust that my audience will at least grant me that I am not dealing with a straw man. The "new institutional economics" is to some extent also a present-day equivalent of the theory of stages.

Suppose we find that per capita income of *x* dollars is, on the average, associated with y percent of GNP originating in manufacturing and z percent in agriculture and that GNP from manufacturing is positively related to per capita income and GNP from agriculture is negatively related to per capita income. Or suppose we find that, as Martin and Lewis (1956) have found, that a country will not really get anywhere until investment (measured by cost) is 15 percent of GNP. The specific numbers do not matter in the present context. It remains nevertheless true that if we reverse the procedure and neglect agriculture in favor of manufacturing, as has all too often been the case in less developed countries (LDCs) for far too long, we do not necessarily increase per capita income. Yet this has precisely been the policy pursued in many LDCs. Even a crude investigation of the history of developed countries would have been an important corrective to this procedure. Yet if we had asked the question how our economy works and what policy we should pursue, we would almost invariably come out with a Schumpeterian answer.

To be sure, it is not the fault of Chenery or Martin and Lewis that their interesting finding has been stood on its head by insisting that if only an LDC will practice sufficient austerity and invest 15 percent of its GNP, it will become developed. But it illustrates the weakness of this approach that it is so easily stood on its head.

Studies by other scholars, particularly Arthur Spiethoff's (1933) discussion of "economic styles" and Colin Clark's ([1940] 1957) and Simon Kuznets's (1971) empirical investigations into structural changes, have given more precise and quantitative answers to what in the earlier literature was essentially impressionistic. (I deliberately avoid the term "historical" in this context.) I mention these scholars because I have always admired them. Yet it is fair to say that, for example, Spiethoff's attempt was, by its very nature, static in proposing to construct, as it were, any number of possible economic systems by combining 20 variables in all possible ways.

Schumpeter could not have been more different. Those of us who have been trained by him or at least influenced by his ideas have the same respect for facts and for history. It is no accident that Schumpeter was a founding member of the Econometric Society. Schumpeter never wavered in his conviction that economics had to become not only quantitative but also numerical. Nor did he waver in his conviction that economic analysis consists of theory, history, and statistics.

Abramovitz has suggested to me that Schumpeter contributed more to explaining why long-term development should proceed in a wave-like fashion than to explaining the problem of why some countries should lead at some times and decline at others. I wish it were totally clear in my mind how to react to this comment. Basically, I am in agreement. My response lies along the following lines.

One approach that I have spelled out in more detail elsewhere (Stolper, 1982) suggests that some innovative changes lead to others; they change parameters in the economy at large and produce effects greater than themselves. This is Schumpeter's own point: Railroads are his prime example. They opened new territories and markets and thus led to new possibilities throughout the economy. In this view, it is really no criticism to say that railway investment declined long before the railway Kondratieff cycle was finished. It is too easy an answer to say that there are some investments so important that they take more than one Juglar cycle to complete.

The second approach leads me to Mancur Olson (1982), who explains why there should be endogenous cycles of growth and ossification, why there should be periods in which (if he will forgive my excessive brevity) income-distributional considerations dominate and others in which income-creating considerations push an economy forward. I find his work exciting and convincing, original in the best sense of the word – adding a new dimension to a foundation that surely is Schumpeterian.

As I see it, true historical research into problems of growth and evolution must consist of more than the finding of past regularities and the use of these regularities to project the future, important though both those processes are.

My problems depend on two aspects of history: that history deals with unique events in addition to common factors, and that in many actual instances choices are to be made, what theologians call freedom of will. It is readily granted that there are historical regularities. What happened did so because it could happen and is therefore logical, though not necessarily determinate ex ante. It is also granted that there are what Knut Borchardt (1979) has called *Zwangslagen,* in which it may be increasingly difficult and occasionally impossible to have a choice, that is, moments in which history does become determinate. But the approach of econometricians and cliometricians, although valuable, nevertheless gives to the sequence of events an inevitability that may be exaggerated. The outcomes of choices are explicable, but it nevertheless is true that what did occur was not the only event that could have occurred. A beautiful example of explaining history in such a somewhat different manner is the work of Borchardt or, again quite differently, the work of Mancur Olson.

So I would argue that the Schumpeterian view of economic history goes beyond showing the uniqueness of parameters and their changes.

It is a view of looking at historic developments ex ante, as it were, from the standpoint of the moment in which decisions had to be made by people, what the actual decisions were, and why and how they were made. This would add another historical and political dimension to the investigation, very much in sympathy with Schumpeter's way of asking questions, and I believe that it would enrich much of economic history research. It would explain why we find so many exceptions to the rules, as, for example, Abramovitz finds in his study (see Chapter 10), or why this historical approach makes some decisions more understandable than appears in prospect. Examples of the latter are the studies of Borchardt (1979) and James (1984, 1986) on developments during the Weimar Republic.

It is this attention to detailed facts in a theoretical context that is characteristic of Schumpeter and that, I believe, unites all of us who feel ourselves influenced or attracted by his work. Perhaps someone will energize the Walrasian system along Schumpeterian lines on the abstract level of the "greatest of all economists," as Schumpeter thought, as well as the "luckiest," as Samuelson added, because there was only one general equilibrium to be discovered. Certainly Ragnar Frisch's attempt (1933) and, more recently, Richard Goodwin's attempt (1986) belong in this category.

Beyond this, however, the developments that gave rise to and furthered our knowledge of how the real economy works have been advanced by quantitative work based on Shumpeterian ideas and on questions his suppositions and statements raised.

I have already mentioned Sidney Winter, who has modeled Schumpeterian questions on the macroeconomic level, simultaneously based on microeconomic considerations, that is, on assumptions about decision making by individual firms. Gunnar Eliasson's Swedish econometric model (1983) is explicitly based, at least in part, on Schumpeterian ideas and is built up from data on individual firms. I find Mancur Olson's analysis (1982) of the rise and decline of nations both Schumpeterian and convincing. No one has done more than F. M. Scherer (1984) to follow up the Schumpeterian question in the context of industrial organization, examining such questions as the most suitable organization of the market for stimulating innovation and development, the relation between R&D spending and productivity, the different types of R&D spending in their relation to development, and the relation between invention and innovation. We have a whole range of gifted scholars who have made important contributions – even to a nonspecialist in this field, like myself, two names come to mind immediately, Jacob Schmookler (1966) and Edwin Mansfield (1969) – and who perhaps will succeed in producing a better version of how the economy works than the pure competitive model.

In addition to Scherer's work, there has been a spate of quantitative models on a partial economic basis (I must avoid the term "partial equilibrium"), based explicitly on Schumpeterian questions. I mention a most recent example that has come to my attention, a study by Edward Montgomery and William Wascher, "Creative Destruction and the Behavior of Productivity over the Cycle" (1986). And there are many more scholars who are working along these directions, who are trying to answer the questions raised by Schumpeterian analysis – not only how the real economy developed but also where it might be heading. When Horst Hanusch and I asked in our original questionnaire what the prospective members of the Schumpeter Society thought the focus of the society-suggested research might be, Scherer appropriately argued that only the scholars themselves were entitled to define their research interests, an observation entirely in the spirit of Schumpeter.

Still, there is a common bond, if not a common focus. There are economic historians and historians of economic thought. There are those interested in the development of theories of bureaucracy and of public choice, the latter claiming Schumpeter as an ancestor, the former trying to work out his ideas. I have already mentioned imaginative theorists like Winter, model-builders like Eliasson, and historians like Olson who are bravely and, I believe, successfully working on reformulating Schumpeter's vision in more precise terms and thereby developing them further. There are the superb studies of Scherer within the framework of industrial organization. The list is long, and omission of further names does not imply a low estimation. There can be no doubt that they, among others, have contributed significantly to our knowledge of how the real economy works.

The last point raises important questions and indicates misunderstandings to be avoided. Stressing the real economy emphatically does not imply antitheoretical overtones, nor does stressing the importance of historical research imply an antimathematical bias. Quite the contrary: As the Bible indicates, there are many mansions in a father's house. As Winter has somewhere remarked, one has to admire Schumpeter's taste in raising questions, even, I may add, when one need not always be satisfied with his answers. Real progress, as Niehans (1981) and, of course, Schumpeter pointed out, normally comes by working out successive problems step by step as they arise in the course of solving problems. Each problem solved usually raises, hydra-like, seven new ones. Quantum jumps are rare and far between. All of us here believe that Schumpeter made such a quantum jump.

Abstraction and selection are necessary for any theory, as for any historical analysis. Only reality is real, and the demand for a theory that would mirror reality completely is a chimera that, in the nature of things, cannot exist. However, the assumptions made may legitimately eliminate only those matters that are not essential for the problem at hand; they must not eliminate the problem itself.

The fact that many mathematical models are trivial or worse is not an argument against the method itself. After all, Mother Nature is very profligate. A fish lays thousands of eggs so that a few may survive. Developments in economics will surely eliminate in a quasi-Darwinist manner contributions that made a splash for a day. But contributions of lasting value will lead to rigorous formulations, and that will be real progress. Let us not forget that economics viewed in Schumpeterian terms as a science also implies that we can build on the contributions of our intellectual ancestors, slough off what turns out to be untenable or unimportant, add and develop, until after a while a structure will emerge that possibly only very learned historians of thought can fully trace back to its origins.

There is, finally, the danger of ideological bias. Schumpeter did not write the Koran or the Bible. He did not say, nor did he claim to have said, everything that was to be said. So although exegesis has a role – my own work has become that sort of thing to establish "what he really thought" – it is a very minor role. "Ideological bias" has nothing to do with our ultimate moral and ethical views, or even with what we would like developments to be. Everyone agrees that these matters are not subject to scientific evaluation, though their internal consistency certainly is. Ideological bias is, rather, in Schumpeter's definition, the inability to see facts (and, I add, logical relationships) as they are rather than as one wishes them to be (Schumpeter, 1984). What unites us are not the specific problems in which we are interested individually, nor a specific method of approach. What unites us is a general view of economics as a widely conceived ("imperialistic," as it recently has been put) social science of economic and social evolution, and above all a scholarly commitment to the search for truth.

References

Aftalion, Albert (1913). *Les crises periodicues de surproduction*. Paris: M. Riv-
ere et cie.

Borchardt, Knut (1979). "Zwangslagen und Handlungsspielraume in der grossen Wirtschaftskrise der frühen Dreissigerjahre. zur Revision des ueberliefenten Geschichtsbildes." *Jahrbuch der Bayerischen Akademie der Wissenschaften*, 85–112.

Chenery, Hollis (1960). "Patterns of Industrial Growth." *American Economic Review*, 50:624–54.

Clark, Colin [1940] (1957). *The Conditions of Economic Progress* (3rd ed.). London: Macmillan.

Clark, John M. (1917). "Business Acceleration and the Law of Demand: A Technical Factor in Economic Cycles." *Journal of Political Economy*, 25:217–35.

(1935). *Strategic Factors in Business Cycles*. New York: National Bureau of Economic Research.

Eliasson, Gunnar (1983). "The Swedish Micro-Macro Model. Idea, Design Application." Industriens Utrechningsinstitut, Working Paper No. 103, Stockholm.

Frisch, Ragnar (1933). "Propagation Problems and Impulse Problems in Dynamic Economics," in *Essays in Honour of Gustav Cassel* (pp. 171–206.) London: Allen & Unwin.

Goodwin, Richard M. (1986). "The M-K-S System. The Functioning of Capitalism," in H. J. Wagener and J. W. Drukker (eds.), *The Economic Law of Motion of Modern Society. A Marx-Keynes-Schumpeter Centennial* (pp. 14–21). Cambridge University Press.

James, Harold (1984). "The Causes of the German Banking Crisis of 1931." *Economic History Review*, 37:68–87.

(1986). *The German Slump. Politics and Economics 1924–1936*. Oxford: Clarendon Press.

Kuznets, Simon (1971). *Economic Growth of Nations. Total Output and Production Structure*. Cambridge Mass.: Belknap Press, Harvard University Press.

Mansfield, Edwin (1969). *The Economics of Technical Change*. New York: Norton.

Marshall, Alfred (1925). "Possibilities of Economic Chivalry," in A. C. Pigou (ed.), *Memorials of Alfred Marshall*. New York: Macmillan.

Martin, Alison, and Lewis, W. Arthur (1956). "Patterns of Public Revenues and Expenditures." *The Manchester School of Economic and Social Studies*, 3:203–34.

Montgomery, Edward, and Wascher, William (1986). "Creative Destruction and the Behavior of Productivity Over the Cycle." Board of Governors, Federal Reserve System, Economic Activities Section, Division of Research and Statistics, No. 60.

Myrdal, Gunnar (1939). *Monetary Equilibrium*. London: Hodge.

Nelson, Richard R., and Winter, Sidney G. (1982). *An Evolutionary Theory of Economic Change*. Cambridge, Mass.: Harvard University Press.

Niehans, J. (1981). "Economics: History, Doctrine, Science, Art." *Kyklos*, 2:165–77.

Olson, Mancur (1982). *The Rise and Decline of Nations.* New Haven: Yale University Press.

Scherer, Frederic M. (1984). *Innovation and Growth. Schumpeterian Perspectives.* Cambridge, Mass.: M.I.T. Press.

Schmookler, Jacob (1966). *Invention and Economic Growth.* Cambridge, Mass.: Harvard University Press.

Schumpeter, Joseph A. (1951). *Essays* (R. V. Clemence, ed.) Cambridge, Mass.: Addison-Wesley.

[1934] (1961). *The Theory of Economic Development* (translated by Redvers Opie). New York: Oxford University Press.

[1939] (1955). *Business Cycles.* New York: McGraw-Hill.

(1952). "Das Sozialprodukt und die Rechenpfennige." *Archiv für Sozialwissenschaft;* reprinted in *Ausätze zur Öhnpischen Theorie.* Tubingen: J. C. Mohr.

(1970). *Das Wesen des Geldes* (F. K. Mann, ed.). Gottingen: Vandenhoeck & Rupprecht.

(1984). "The Meaning of Rationality in the Social Sciences." *Zeitschrift für die gesamte Staatswissenschaft,* 140:577–93.

(1985). *Aufsätze zur Wirtschaftspolitik* (W. F. Stolper and C. Seidl, eds.). Tübingen: J. C. Mohr.

Slutsky, Eugen (1927). "The Summation of Random Causes as the Source of Cyclical Processes," in *Conjuncture Institute of Moscow,* Vol. 3, No. 1 (Russian and English summary), as quoted by Frisch (1933).

Spiethoff, Arthur (1933). "Die allgemeine Volkswirtschaftslehre als geschichtliche Theorie. Die Wirtschaftsstile," in A. Spiethoff (ed.), *Festschrift für Werner Sombart.* Munchen: Duncker & Humblot.

Stolper, Wolfgang F. (1982). "Aspects of Schumpeter's Theory of Innovation," in H. Frisch (ed.), *Schumpeterian Economics* (pp. 28–48). New York: Praeger.

CHAPTER 2

Anti–Say's Law versus Say's Law: a change in paradigm

MICHIO MORISHIMA and GEORGE CATEPHORES

2.1   Introduction

It is generally believed that in the period of about 120 years from Ricardo's *On the Principles of Political Economy and Taxation* (1817) to J. M. Keynes's *The General Theory of Employment, Interest and Money* (1936) (works that marked a new era), the most important development in economic thought was replacement of the paradigm of classical economics by a paradigm based on the use of marginalist methods in economic analysis. Whatever the merits of the prevailing opinion, it seems to us that the marginalist revolution does not exhaust the range of paradigm changes that took place in economics in the period under consideration. Hence, the intention of this chapter is to put forward another aspect of the transition: to examine the change from classical economics as a shift from a paradigm incorporating Say's Law to one in which Say's Law is not fulfilled. This shift is signposted by the works of Ricardo and Keynes, the latter having constructed his own theories on an Anti–Say's Law.[1]

A first version of this chapter was presented by Professor Morishima under the title "Marx, Schumpeter, Keynes" at the 1983 conference of the AUTE in Oxford. Subsequently, the two current authors worked together in exploring the original ideas further, and they report the results of their joint research.

[1] In spite of Leijonhufvud's claim that Keynes's target was "not the best thought that Classical economics could offer, but a stereotyped, cliché-ridden version of received doctrine" (Leijonhufvud, 1968, p. 34), Keynes gave a clear definition of "classical economists" at the commencement of this attack. Like Marx, Keynes gave the name of "classical economists" to the group of economists comprising "Ricardo and James Mill and their predecessors, that is to say for the founders of the theory which culminated in the Ricardian economics" and accurately saw the division between these men and himself as resting on whether they accepted or rejected Say's Law. Where problems are more likely to arise is with Keynes's inclusion of the post-classicists, such as "J. S. Mill, Marshall, Edgeworth and Professor Pigou" among the "classical economists" (Keynes, 1936, p. 3, fn. 1).

It is true that Keynes gave documentary proof for his claim that J. S. Mill and Marshall accepted Say's Law (Keynes, 1936, pp. 18–19), but Hicks made it clear that in

The crucial significance of accepting or rejecting Say's Law has been asserted by Keynes himself.[2] Ricardo, on the other hand, is well known to have gone on record as a strong believer in Say's Law of the markets. He refers to J. B. Say's *Traité d'économie politique* in the preface to his *Principles,* and in a footnote he states that "Chap. XV, part i 'Des Débouchés,' contains, in particular, some very important principles, which I believe were first explained by this distinguished writer" (Ricardo, [1817] 1954, p. 7). Ricardo based this chapter, "The Effects of Accumulation on Profits and Interest" (the most important chapter in the whole of the *Principles*), on Say's Law of *Débouchés,* which he endorsed.

Say's own exposition of this law is not clear. It permits various interpretations and has given rise to multiple confusions (Baumol, 1977, pp. 146–61; Baumol and Becker, 1952, pp. 355–96; Schumpeter, 1954, pp. 616–18). However, for the purposes of this chapter, an enquiry into what Say himself regarded as comprising the law of *Débouchés* is immaterial. What is important is how Ricardo and Keynes each interpreted this law and how they formulated it. Furthermore, in order to interpret the evolution of economics from Ricardo to Keynes, it is also important to clarify the modes of thought of those theorists who fall in between Ricardo and Keynes, who tried to advance economics by criticizing Ricardo, though at the same time influenced by him – theorists who stepped outside the Ricardian canon. As outstanding exam-

---

his *Essays on Unsettled Questions* (1844), Mill recognized the possibility of a postponement of the demand for goods as a result of the hoarding of money. It may well be the case that, as Sowell has stated, Mill in his essays still recognized the existence of the law for the barter economy only and that, as Sowell again has pointed out, the fairest judgment probably is to say that Mill trod the narrow path between acceptance and rejection of the law. Schumpeter has pointed out that both J. S. Mill and Marshall recognized that people may desire to hold money rather than spend it on goods and services (Hicks, 1983, p. 62; Schumpeter, 1954, pp. 529, 621–2; Sowell, 1972, pp. 146–9). In any case, there is no question concerning what Keynes meant by classical economics and on what point he attacked it.

[2] In recent years, many economic theorists, such as E. Malinvaud, have compared Keynes's equilibrium theory with that of Walras in works that claim to provide the microeconomic foundations of Keynesian economics. However, among the points of difference between these two theorists noted by such writers, little emphasis is laid on the question whether or not the system of Keynes or Walras fulfills Say's Law. As will become clear, our view, in contrast to the view generally held, is that Walras's general equilibrium theory was premised on Say's Law, and it was because of this that full employment could be achieved under his general equilibrium situation. To disregard this fact and to emphasize other differences between the economics of Keynes and Walras, as recent economic theory has tended to do, is an interpretation that we cannot accept.

ples of this group, we consider Walras and Marx.[3] We also ask why it was that these economists were unable to carry their argument through to the point of rigorously stating an Anti-Say's Law such as that reached by Keynes.

In the development leading to Keynes, a special place must be reserved for J. A. Schumpeter. Despite the fact that he was Keynes's contemporary, in terms of publications he can be treated as a forerunner. His book *Theorie der wirtschaftlichen Entwicklung* was first published more than 20 years before Keynes's *General Theory*. It was translated into English in 1934, based on the second German edition of 1926. The English version is much shorter than the original German. In German, the book, probably under the influence of Karl Marx, contains an exposition of a dual accounting system (i.e., separate value and price calculations). It also contains lengthy historical notes on the economic literature that are very useful, particularly with regard to Schumpeter's attitude toward Say's Law. All of these have been excised from the English translation, but the essential part of the work, which has been retained, constitutes an admirable synthesis of Walras and Marx. Later, Schumpeter will be seen to have adopted from Walras the idea of the entrepreneur, the idea of technological progress, the idea of profit creation in the process toward a new equilibrium after the previous equilibrium had been disturbed by the introduction of innovation, and the idea of the disappearance of profit after a new equilibrium has been reached. From Marx, he took over the idea of banks as the crucial agents in the process of capital accumulation (i.e., of saving and investment); this is a Marxian influence less obvious but far more important than that of the dual accounting system, because it leads directly to the formulation of an Anti-Say's Law.

Say's Law is frequently summarized in the expression "supply creates its own demand." The corresponding summary of Keynes's Anti-Say's Law would consist in a statement about the emergence of a deficiency of effective demand. Behind such deficiency lies the discrepancy between savings and investment and the consequent adjustment of savings to investment (not vice versa). It is argued here that such discrepancy develops not as a result of abstract human psychology but in the context of a specific structure of society and its institutions that tend to support or undermine Say's Law. In particular, it will be suggested that it rests on two closely interrelated conditions: (1) the rise

---

[3] Marx and Walras are classified as "transition" economists only with respect to one part of their work; otherwise, they both stand at the heads of distinctive schools of thought that followed their respective original contributions.

of two distinct social groups, the owners of capital, specializing in saving, and the entrepreneurs, specializing in investment, and (2) the existence of investment functions that describe the behavior of entrepreneurs with regard to investment, as independent of the decision of capital owners with regard to saving.[4]

These conditions, constituting the substantive content of Anti–Say's Law, are explored in this chapter, in their emergence and development in the works of Ricardo, Marx, Walras, Schumpeter, and Keynes, and they are contrasted with a more detailed examination of Say's Law itself. It will be seen that Schumpeter's contribution on the bankers' role of coordinating savings and investment was a decisive departure from the world of Say's Law; he almost completely prepared the way for the Keynesian revolution.

2.2   Keynes

"Supply creates its own demand" does not necessarily mean that when the supply of a good is increased, the demand for that good will increase by the same amount; it is an assertion that the demand for some goods will increase. In the case of those goods for which supply has been increased, there is overproduction, but because in the case of those other goods for which demand has increased there is underproduction, under Say's Law the overproduction exists only for certain goods, and overproduction can never exist for all goods simultaneously. That is to say, Say's Law rejects the concept of a general glut, of general overproduction.

This is the way in which Say's Law is normally interpreted, but, as will shortly be seen, statements such as these are essentially ambiguous and open to varying interpretations. Keynes (1936, pp. 21–2), however, summed up the law in the well-defined formula that "supply creates its own demand in the sense that aggregate demand price is equal to the aggregate supply price for all levels of output and employment." Thus, according to the generally acknowledged interpretation of Say's Law, it is stated that an increase in supply gives rise to an increase in demand, but what is not made clear is the time lag of such increase

---

[4] The second of these conditions would, in itself, be *logically* sufficient as a basis for the refutation of Say's Law. But the first creates a social environment that is conducive to recurrent and persistent discrepancies between savings and investment, and hence to the refutation of the law in practice. We are grateful to Professor Richard Musgrave for insisting on this clarification.

(i.e., whether it takes effect instantaneously or eventually). Under Keynes's conception, by contrast, such an increase is assumed to be instantaneous. It is, moreover, assumed that the equating of aggregate supply and aggregate demand under Say's Law holds true not merely at a particular level of production, but for all levels of production. Hence, the aggregate supply function and the aggregate demand function are *identically* equal.

The point of view that understood this law as an identity was endorsed subsequently by Lange (1942) and then by Patinkin (1956) and has, since the war, been widely discussed as the Lange-Patinkin formulation, in the context of the neutrality of money. Schumpeter (1954) and several others have regarded Lange's version as a more exact form of the Keynes version, but this is not our view. Not only are their identities not mutually equivalent, but the conclusions they draw from their respective identities are in each case very different. By this we mean that whereas Keynes believes that under Say's Law there is no obstacle to full employment, the Lange-Patinkin conclusion is that Say's identity implies the indeterminacy of the absolute level of prices.

We must therefore commence by obtaining Keynes's identity in a form comparable to that of Lange. According to Lange, goods and services are divided into primary factors, intermediate products, final products, and direct services. Apart from that, it is assumed that there exist only money and one kind of bond. For the sake of simplicity, it is supposed that the set of direct services is empty, and the subscripts L, I, C, M, B are used to represent primary factors, intermediate and final products, money, and the bond, respectively. If we do this, then according to Walras's Law (the sum of the budget equations of each individual and each enterprise), we get

$$D_L + D_U + D_I + D_C + D_M + D_B \equiv S_L + S_I + S_C + S_M + S_B \quad (1)$$

Here, D_L, for example, represents the total demand for primary factors, and S_I the total supply of intermediate products. The same applies to the other symbols. It is, moreover, possible to divide the total demand for intermediate products into the demand for the replacement of intermediate products used up during the period in question and the demand for a net increase in the stock of intermediate products. These are written D_U and D_I, respectively, the use of the subscript U to represent the first of these two being due to its being equal to Keynes's user cost. Aggregate net output (Keynes's Y) is obtained by subtracting

D_U from the total supply of products $S_I + S_C$; therefore, equation (1) can be written as

$$(D_M - S_M) + (D_B - S_B) \equiv (S_L - D_L) + (Y - D_I - D_C) \qquad (2)$$

It should be obvious from equation (2) that if Keynes's interpretation of Say's Law (the identity of aggregate demand and supply) holds true, then the last term of equation (2) (i.e., the part in the last set of parentheses) will vanish, but because this does not imply that the first term of equation (2) (i.e., the part in the first set of parentheses) will vanish (i.e., that demand and supply of money are identically equal), as Lange (1942) and Patinkin (1956), following Wicksell ([1906] 1935, pp. 159–60), have maintained as the condition for Say's Law, then even if Say's Law is fulfilled in the Keynesian sense, it will not necessarily be fulfilled in the Lange-Patinkin sense, and vice versa.

Later we investigate only Keynes's interpretation of Say's Law. We must first examine the view that Say's Law holds true for a barter economy, but not for a money economy, a view that is still subscribed to by many economists today. If this is correct, it can be taken to mean that along with the gradual historical shift from an economy in which the barter of goods is dominant to one in which they are normally exchanged via the medium of money, Say's Law, which at the beginning is virtually always fulfilled, increasingly ceases to be so, and there is an eventual transition to an Anti–Say's Law economy.

Of course, because in a barter economy money does not exist, Walras's Law, equation (2), does not include $D_M - S_M$, but as long as loans are made, durable goods can serve as a store of value, and a bond that promises to pay as interest at the beginning of each period a denomination of the numéraire [Walras's commodity E and La Volpe's (1936) *finanzamenti*] serves as a standard of deferred payments, the demand and supply of bonds; that is, the second form of equation (2) will exist, as will the demand for and supply of labor [i.e., the third term of equation (2)]. For that reason, just as Lange's Say's Law does not imply the existence of Keynes's Say's Law, so the absence of money does not immediately imply Keynes's Say's Law.

For what kind of circumstances, therefore, does Keynes's definition of Say's Law hold true? (Where it is not specifically stated, any further reference to Say's Law alone will mean the law as defined by Keynes.) If we now write $Y - D_C$ as S, and D_I as I, S represents savings, and I investment. Because the difference between aggregate supply and aggregate demand $Y - (D_C + D_I)$ is equal to $S - I$, it follows that Say's Law holds true when savings are identically equal to investment (i.e., when savings are invested without even momentary leakage). For this to happen, investment plans must be adjusted flexibly and instantaneously to savings; there must not be even the smallest discrepancy between the two.[5] Presumably, if distinct groups specialize in saving and in investment, perfect coordination of decisions must prevail between them. Do these conditions obtain in the economy as viewed by Ricardo?

2.3   Ricardo

Ricardo's society consists of workers, capitalists, and landlords. Depending on the context, capitalists are also frequently referred to as farmers and manufacturers. The produce of society is distributed among these three groups in the form of wages, profits, and rents, respectively. These people are further divided into the productive class (those who reproduce another value) and the unproductive class (those who do not reproduce) (Ricardo, [1817] 1954, p. 151, fn. 1). Leaving aside "the fund for the maintenance of labour," one part of "the actual production" is distributed "under the name of profit to the productive class," and the other part is handed over "under the name rent, to the unproductive class" (Ricardo, [1817] 1954, p. 270).

Ricardo, therefore, regarded capitalists as the bearers of reproduction, whereas the landowners' incoming rents he saw as devoted by them to the purchase of necessities and luxuries, not to the long-term purpose of capital accumulation. Under this interpretation, it is possible to take the view that throughout most of his theory on accumulation, Ricardo assumed capitalists to have a high propensity to save, whereas not only workers but also landlords had a propensity to save that, if not zero, was at most negligible.[6] (Workers could not save

---

[5] This means that, as in Solow's growth model (1956), investment must not be planned and implemented in accordance with some investment function, but must be adjusted to savings without any difficulty or any friction. From this model, Solow drew a conclusion that the difference between his neoclassical model and the Harrod-Domar model rested in the recognition or nonrecognition of substitution between the factors of production (capital and labor), but our view is that the crucial difference between them is really whether or not they accept the existence of an independent investment function. Therefore, the Harrod-Domar instability does not rest on the fixed nature of production coefficients, but is derived from the investment function. Similarly, Solow's stability rests on the nonexistence of an investment function in his system. The concept of assuming this kind of Say's Law in examining the growth process of full employment and full utilization is entirely along classical lines.

[6] This is the interpretation reached by Pasinetti (1974, p. 6). See also Hollander (1979, pp. 324ff.).

because of the low level of their wage rates; for landlords, the rate of rent was high, and their income considerable, but was all squandered on luxuries.) We call the model based on this kind of assumptions the "simple model."

According to Ricardo's simple model, saving is carried out only by capitalists, and it is the capitalists who are at the same time the investors.[7] Where savers and investors are one and the same, there is no difference between aggregate savings and aggregate investment, and for that reason, I is identically equal to S.[8] This does not mean, however, that Ricardo confined himself to this kind of simple model. In a rather broader sense, he did, in fact, believe that all classes of society possessed the capacity to save. Especially landlords were clearly potential savers. Capitalist rentiers, whom he describes as "the monied class," were also regular savers; even workers were accepted, in a footnote appended for the first time in the third edition of the *Principles,* as being able to save (Ricardo, [1817] 1954, pp. 89; 347-9).

Not only in the simple model but also when people other than capitalists have been able to save, they will find no shortage of willing borrowers, because "there is perhaps no manufacturer, however rich, who limits his business to the extent that his own funds alone will

---

[7] In the era of the classical school, when agriculture was an important industry, the production period played an important role in the theory of production. In order to expand production, therefore, it was necessary also to invest in the fund for wages (Marx's variable capital) to be paid out for the support of labor during the production period. In the work of Keynes, production lags are disregarded, and the concepts of the wage fund and variable capital have disappeared. In order to compare Ricardo and Keynes on a common basis, we disregard Ricardo's investment in the wage fund, assuming, as Keynes did, that all investment is undertaken with regard to fixed capital.

[8] In order to reach this conclusion, it is necessary for us to assume that farmers and manufacturers regularly invest exactly the amount that they themselves have saved. As Marx emphasized, however, such a thing is likely to be technically impossible, if gradual accumulation of large sums is required prior to the purchase of a particular kind of machine. Furthermore, an appropriate time for investment will be selected. If it is predicted that a wait of several months will bring a considerable drop in the price of the good in which the investment is being made, then investment is likely to be postponed. For this reason, even in Ricardo's model, in which saver and investor are one and the same, there will be disparity between investment and savings. It must therefore be acknowledged that even in this kind of model, Say's Law will operate only where investment projects are divisible so that savings are immediately invested. This assumption may have some plausibility as long as investment takes mainly the form of a wages fund, but it totally collapses from the moment that fixed capital becomes important. It follows that Ricardo's acceptance of Say's Law reveals the absence, within his own theory, of an effective investment function. More detailed consideration of this point will follow later.

allow: he has always some portion of this floating capital" (Ricardo, [1817] 1954, p. 89). This must be one of the considerations that lead him to conclude, further on in his treatise, that "it follows then from these admissions that there is no limit to demand – no limit to the employment of capital while it yields any profit" (Ricardo, [1817] 1954, p. 296). The importance of profit, on the other hand, is seen as rather crucial.

> The farmer and the manufacturer can no more live without profit than the labourer without wages. Their motive for accumulation will diminish with every diminution of profit, and will cease altogether when their profits are so low as not to afford them an adequate compensation for their trouble, and the risk which they must necessarily encounter in employing their capital productively. (Ricardo, [1817] 1954, p. 122)

This passage can be seen as showing Ricardo's thinking in regard to the investment function. Assuming that the risk that accompanies it is given, investment is an increasing function of the profit rate, and there is no factor that limits investment apart from the profit rate. Ricardo furthermore assumed that the propensity to invest was a highly flourishing one and that the amount of investment would always be at least as great as the amount of savings.[9] Also, he assumed the propensity to consume to be very high; this, too, eliminates possibilities of excess savings.[10] Therefore, Ricardo did not need to deal with the problems of underinvestment and underconsumption that later became the main concerns of Keynes.

2.4   Marx

During the nineteenth century, Ricardo occupied a position in the world of economics analogous to that held by Keynes today. Even sev-

---

[9] In a letter to Malthus, Ricardo wrote: "We agree . . . that effectual demand consists of two elements, the *power* and the *will* to purchase, but I think the will is very seldom wanting when the power exists, – for the desire of accumulation will occasion demand just as effectually as a desire to consume, it will only change the objects on which the demand will exercise itself" (Ricardo, 1952, p. 133; italics in original). If the power to purchase in this sentence is interpreted as Y, and the will to purchase is construed as corresponding to $C + I$, then by the assumption that as long as the power exists the will always exists too, we obtain $Y \equiv C + I$, i.e., $S \equiv I$. On the significance of profits for capital accumulation, see also Hollander (1979, pp. 316ff. and passim).

[10] The letter referred to in footnote 9 also contains the following statement by Ricardo: "I consider the wants and tastes of mankind as unlimited. We all wish to add to our enjoyments. . . . Consumption adds to our enjoyment" (Ricardo, 1952, pp. 134–5).

eral decades after his death a considerable number of economists were still discussing his ideas, and his methods – namely, the eliciting of laws and theorems deductively and purely logically on the basis of strict abstract concepts and definitions – continued to prevail among them. His verbal-logical economics was further refined by Marx and developed into a numerical analysis based on a clearly defined mathematical model, albeit using hypothetical figures. Walras's general equilibrium theory can be seen as the forerunner to today's axiomatic economics, but it is also possible to view it as something that attempted to provide what in modern terminology could be called the microfoundations for Ricardian economics. Marx's commendation of Ricardo's theories as scientific economics is well known; Walras, also despite his critical stance toward Ricardo, respected Ricardo as "the founder of pure economics in England" and devised three Ricardo-like laws as conclusions of his general equilibrium theory (Morishima, 1977, pp. 5–6; Walras, [1874] 1954, p. 398). However, as far as Say's Law was concerned, both Marx and Walras were anti-Ricardian. The fact that the members of the classical school were optimistic regarding the establishment of full employment, despite the categorization of economics as a dismal science, was in part a result of the belief placed in the existence of an automatic regulatory mechanism of the market, stemming from fetishistic faith in Adam Smith's invisible hand, but it was, in part, also due to the view that because of Say's Law, the impossibility of general overproduction was guaranteed. For Marx, with his belief in the collapse of the capitalist system that led him to reject all bourgeois doctrines that failed to comprehend the essence of the capitalist mode of production and disregarded the anarchy (the decentralization) of that machinery of production, the theory of crisis was a highly significant subject. For that reason, Say's Law (which Marx regarded as "an established axiom in English political economy"), with its denial of the possibility of general overproduction, was a clear object of attack for him (Marx, [1905–10] 1968, pp. 165, 400, 468, 493, 502).

His main attack was based on a critical analysis of the formulation of Say's Law by Ricardo, whose statement "no man produces, but with a view to consume or sell, and he never sells, but with a view to purchase some other commodity, which may immediately be useful to him, or which may contribute to *future production*" he quoted in the *Theories of Surplus Value, Part II* (Marx, [1905–10] 1968, p. 493; italics in original). Marx remarked, first, that under conditions of capitalist production, no man produces with a view to consuming his own product. He must sell. The sale, however, is in no sense unconditionally to be followed by a purchase. Paying due regard to his perception that commodity exchange establishes between two producers a relationship mediated but also *interrupted* by money (his well-known formula $C - M \ldots M - C$), he concluded, contrary to Ricardo, that the producer who initiates a sale is under no compulsion and may even be well advised (in times of heightened commercial uncertainty) to abstain from following up the sale with a corresponding purchase. A situation may then arise in which the aggregate supply of all commodities exceeds the aggregate demand for them because "the demand for the *general commodity,* money, exchange-value, is greater than the demand for all particular commodities, in other words, the motive to turn the commodity into money, to realise its exchange-value prevails over the motive to transform the commodity again into use value" (Marx, [1905–10] 1968, Part II, p. 505; italics in original).

If selling (and therefore aggregate supply Y) is cut off from purchase (and therefore aggregate demand $C + I$), then Say's Law, which insists not only on the ex post but also on the ex ante identity of sale and purchase (the whole concept of what James Mill described as "the metaphysical equilibrium of purchase and sales"), will collapse because of this ex ante separation. Y is no longer identically equal to $C + I$; hence a mathematical identity fails to obtain between S and I. Therefore, in the market for all commodities, with the exception of money, it is possible for supply to exceed demand and therefore for the prices of all commodities to fall. It will happen all the more frequently that the aggregate supply of all commodities exceeds the aggregate demand for them. The reason for this is that under the compulsive pursuit of surplus value, which obviously has no limits of physical satiety, and in view of their competing mainly through their products, industrial capitalists, unable in an anarchic market to form anything but a rather vague idea of the total size of output and demand in their respective sectors, tend to overproduce. At the same time, they also tend to restrict aggregate demand by economizing as much as possible on labor and equipment costs, which worsens the effects of overproduction.

Their tendency to overstep the limits of available demand is strengthened by the fact that industrialists do not supply the final consumer, but a wholesaler who is capable, for a certain period, of absorbing excessive output in his stocks. Nor are they dependent on immediate cash sales to cover their needs for short-term working capital, because they can always turn to their bankers for that. They are therefore cushioned against the direct impact of the tailing off of demand at both ends of the circuit of productive capital[11]

$$\left(M - C <^{LP}_{MP} \dots P \dots C' - M' \right)$$

a situation that encourages them to force the pace of production to the breaking point.

Given the foregoing, Marx may be interpreted as seeing in the denial of Say's Law the separation of demand (i.e., investment) from supply (i.e., savings). He also mobilized, in support of his theory of crisis, a very perceptive and thorough dissection of the compound persona of the original capitalist – who combined in one individual the various roles of possessor of means of production, manager, entrepreneur, and investment–decision maker – into its constituent parts and showed how each part was delegated, by a process of historical differentiation, as a special role to a separate section of the bourgeoisie. The rise of distinct rentier, entrepreneurial, and managerial groups, culminating in a complete separation of ownership and control, leads to a social structure ideally suited to the separation of saving and investment.[12]

Marx, therefore, was able to go beyond the mere rejection of Say's Law and isolate at least one of the elements that we consider necessary for an Anti–Say's Law – the rise of separate social groups, one of which specializes in investment. He may even be said, in view of his insis-

---

[11] In Marx's formal representation of the circuit of capital, M stands for money capital advanced, C for commodity capital (inputs), LP for labor power, MP for means of production, P for production process, C' for commodity output (output, gross of surplus value), and M' for the total value of sales, gross of surplus value. The industrialist may borrow M to expand production, before he recovers M' from sales.

[12] It is popularly believed that Marx was examining an economy consisting of two classes, workers and capitalists, but those who read through to the end of Volume 3 of *Capital* will understand that Marx was considering an economy in which two additional personages, the landlord and his capitalist shadow, the farmer, united with the industrial capitalist in the exploitation of the working class. The presence of merchant capitalists and money capitalists was also mentioned. Thus, Marx's world is a multi-social-group economy, and in an economy such as this, those engaging in decision making on investment and those engaging in decision making regarding savings are not necessarily one and the same. In order to harmonise their desires and to render them consistent with each other, either the interest rate must be subject to flexible adjustment or the volume of production Y must be accommodated as a variable to regulate savings, as Keynes believed. It is difficult to imagine Marx accepting such a regulatory role for the rate of interest. In his words, "It is indeed the separation of capitalists into money-capitalists and industrial capitalists that transforms a portion of the profit into interest, that generally creates the category of interest; and it is only

tence on the relatively large degree of independence from the market[13] enjoyed by the industrialist as well as the speculative investor, to have sensed the need for the second Anti–Say's Law element: the presence of an independent investment function. Where he may be said to have failed is in the rigorous specification of such a function.

Within Marx's system, his theory of reproduction is the one that, in terms of mathematical economics, appears as the most advanced and most highly perfected, but the investment function assumed therein by Marx not only is not independent of S (saving) but also is identically equal to S. In making up his tables of the two-class reproduction scheme that yields this conclusion, Marx, contrary to his own much richer exposition in *Capital,* Volume 3, ruled out the problem of the fragmentation of the capitalist class into differentiated strata, while at the same time he hypothesized that the capitalist, who acquires profit, accumulates a part of it and invests it according to the formula described later. Here saving is combined with investment, a combination described as the accumulation of capital.

Marx assumed the following highly singular investment function (Marx, [1885] 1967, p. 514; Morishima, 1973, p. 118). Capitalists in Department I (capital-goods industry) invest $a_1 P_1$, a part of P_1 (profits). Ratio a_1 is referred to as the rate of accumulation, and the size of a_1 is exogenously determined. The rate of accumulation by capitalists in Department II (consumer-goods industry) is given by a_2. But unlike a_1, a_2 is not exogenously determined, being endogenously regulated so as to maintain the balance between the supply and demand for capital goods. As far as expenditure is concerned, Marx assumed that workers did not save, devoting the whole of their wages (W) to consumption,

---

the competition between these two kinds of capitalists which creates the rate of interest" (Marx, [1891] 1971, p. 370).

   This antagonistic determination does not necessarily serve any rational purpose in the allocation of resources. The ultimate regulator, for Marx as well, was the fluctuation in the level of income. This is the meaning of his remark that "crises are always but momentary and forcible solutions of the existing contradictions. They are violent eruptions which for a time restore the disturbed equilibrium" ([1891] 1971, p. 249). On the rate of interest, see also Fan-Hung (1939) and Harris (1976).

[13] The closest Marx came to a literary formulation of the presence of an independent investment function in the capitalist economy was in his well-known dictum "Accumulation for accumulation's sake, production for production's sake: by this formula classical economy expressed the historical mission of the bourgeoisie" ([1867] 1970, p. 595). There are many other passages throughout *Capital* where he returns to the idea of the relative independence of producers and investors ([1867] 1970, p. 595; [1891] 1971, pp. 304, 439–41).

whereas capitalists expended the total amount of their income (profits) remaining after investment. For that reason, the total demand for consumer goods can be expressed as

$$W_1 + W_2 + (1 - a_1)P_1 + (1 - a_2)P_2$$

For simplicity, let us now assume that the economy consists of the capital-goods sector and the consumer-goods sector, producing the necessities of life, while we disregard the sector concerned with the production of luxuries. We also disregard the production period; consequently, there will be no investment in variable capital.[14] After subtracting from the value of output for the capital-goods industry (Department I) and for the consumer-goods industry (Department II) the respective constant capitals C_1 and C_2, corresponding to Keynes's user cost, the net value gained remaining will be shown as Y_1 and Y_2. The balance after subtracting the amount of wages in Department I, W_1, from Y_1 will be the amount of profits in that industry, P_1. Therefore,

$$Y_1 = W_1 + P_1, \qquad Y_2 = W_2 + P_2$$

Because aggregate net output is $Y = Y_1 + Y_2$, aggregate savings are

$$S = Y - [W_1 + W_2 + (1 - a_1)P_1 + (1 - a_2)P_2]$$

However, aggregate investment is

$$I = a_1 P_1 + a_2 P_2$$

Therefore,

$$S - I = Y_1 + Y_2 - (W_1 + W_2 + P_1 + P_2)$$

but given the definition of profit obtained earlier of P_i being the balance obtained after subtracting W_i from Y_i, then $S - I$ will always vanish regardless of the values of Y_1 and Y_2. This means that S is identically equal to I for all values of Y.

Thus, Marx's reproduction scheme fulfills Say's Law in the Keynesian sense, with I not constituting an independent investment function, but coinciding with S itself. Despite his scathing and correct criticism of the regime of Say's Law and his clear intention to extricate himself from its toils, he failed to construct an analytical system founded on Anti–Say's Law. Whereas he made an important step in the transition

---

[14] This is an assumption for the sake of simplicity. As for the case in which there is a production lag, see Morishima (1978, pp. 188ff.).

from Ricardo to Keynes, he went no more than part of the way along the road.

2.5   Walras

Looking at the situation in this way, it is now quite apparent that a separation of the provider of capital (capitalist) from the user of capital (entrepreneur) is imperative if we are to free ourselves from Say's Law. It must be said that it is quite natural that the English school, which "fails to distinguish between the role of the capitalist and the role of the entrepreneur" (Walras, [1874] 1954, p. 423), should not succeed in separating investment from saving, and it is surprising and at the same time somewhat ironic that J. B. Say himself should have devised an extremely pertinent and highly advanced way of comprehending the entrepreneur. At the end of his *Treatise,* Say gave something like a glossary of his main concepts:

Capitalist: He is the one who owns a capital and who earns a *profit* when he uses it himself, or an interest when he lends it to an *entrepreneur* who then uses it, and who, from then on, consumes the services of the capital and draws the profits. . . . Entrepreneur: . . . They are not *capitalists* except when the capital or a portion of the capital which they use belongs to themselves; they are then simultaneously capitalists and entrepreneurs." (Say, 1826, pp. 272–3; italics in original; our translation from the French)

Thus, although there are some people who combine the persons of entrepreneur and capitalist, the two are conceptually independent of each other; moreover, the entrepreneur is the agent who makes the decisions regarding investment, as well as the agent who bears the risk of an enterprise. This means that he is an entrepreneur in the Walras–Schumpeter sense. After distinguishing three activities necessary to production (research, application, and labor), Say adds:

It is rare for one person to undertake all three operations. The most usual is that someone studies the law of nature. He is the scientist. Another person takes advantage of this knowledge in order to create useful products. He is the agriculturist, the manufacturer or the merchant, or, to describe them all by a collective name, the entrepreneur. (Say, 1826, p. 51; our translation)[15]

---

[15] Many of us might consider that there is a substantial difference between Walras's view of the capitalist economy and that of Schumpeter: The former is static, and the latter dynamic. However, it is not unreasonable to think that Schumpeter's view of the development of the capitalist economy might have been suggested by Walras's descriptions: "The continuous market which is perpetually tending towards equilib-

It is therefore clear that Walras is indebted to Say not just for the concept of equilibrium but also for the concept of the entrepreneur, but despite this, Walras had a low opinion of Say. Walras cited a passage in Say's *Treatise* that states that the lending of labor, land, and capital is carried out among the possessors of these three items (i.e., worker, landowner, and capitalist), and wages, interest, and rent are determined as the prices of the various loans (Say, 1826, p. 18). He then adds: "J. B. Say did not fully understand the specific role of the entrepreneur. In fact, this person is absent from his theory" (Walras, [1874] 1954, pp. 425–6). For Walras to evaluate the whole of Say's work in this way would, of course, be unfair, but it is true that as far as Say's model of the market for the factors of production is concerned, the entrepreneur did not exist, except as one of the workers. This was described by Walras as Say following "a certain number of French economists" in regarding "the entrepreneur as a worker charged with the special task of managing a firm" ([1874] 1954, p. 223).

Walras's own model is constructed in the following manner:

Let us call the holder of land a *land-owner,* the holder of personal faculties a *worker* and the holder of capital proper a *capitalist.* In addition, let us designate by the term *entrepreneur* a fourth person . . . whose role it is to lease land from the land-owner, hire personal faculties from the labourer and borrow capital from the capitalist, in order to combine the three productive services in agriculture, industry or trade. ([1874] 1954, p. 222; italics in original)

In the market for consumer goods, the entrepreneur appears as the seller of products, and the landlord, worker, and capitalist appear as the purchasers of products (Walras, [1874] 1954, p. 223). In the capital-goods market, "entrepreneurs who produce new capital goods" ([1874] 1954, p. 42) sell their products to the entrepreneurs who demand them. These entrepreneurs borrow the sums of money needed to purchase new capital goods from a capitalist, who "accumulates his savings in money" ([1874] 1954, p. 270). With regard to this point, it should be observed that Walras noted that "the demand for new capital goods comes from entrepreneurs who manufacture products and not from capitalists who create savings" ([1874] 1954, p. 270). If the volumes of production of consumer goods and capital goods are determined in

rium without ever actually attaining it, because the market has no other way of approaching equilibrium except by groping, and, before the goal is reached, it has to renew its efforts and start over again, all the basic data of the problem [including] the technical production coefficients . . . having changed in the meanwhile" ([1874] 1954, p. 380). "Just as a lake is, at times, stirred to its very depths by a storm, so also the market is sometimes thrown into violent confusion by *crises* which are sudden and general disturbances of equilibrium" ([1874] 1954, p. 381; italics in original).

this manner, then the amounts of labor, land, and capital needed for that production are also determined, and the entrepreneur appears on the services markets in order to satisfy his demand for them. "Here land-owners, workers and capitalists appear as sellers, and entrepreneurs as buyers of the various productive services" ([1874] 1954, pp. 222–3).[16]

Thus, in Walras's system, if investment is decided, this determines the volume of production of capital goods and, as a result, the demand for factors of production in the capital-goods industry, and hence also the wages, interest, and rent to be paid to the relevant individuals by that industry. This being the case, their demand for consumer goods will also be determined and, accordingly, the volume of production of consumer goods. The volume of production thus determined creates the demand for consumer goods arising from wages, interest, and rent paid to individuals connected with the consumer-goods industry, and thus the total demand for consumer goods; that is, the total volume of output of the consumption-goods industry is determined. Because the demand for factors of production is in proportion to the volume of production, the total demand for each factor is determined, and hence its employment, as long as that does not exceed its supply.

Up to this point, the general equilibrium theory of capital formation and credit thus formulated by Walras is in all respects completely Keynesian. Walras's equilibrium formula for the demand and supply of products is a microeconomic version of Keynes's theory of income-determination analysis, and his analysis of the demand for factors of production is a microeconomic version of Keynes's theory of employment. However, because the demand for capital services and the demand for land and labor determined in this way are not necessarily equal to their respective supplies, Walras regards the demand for investment (i.e., for new capital goods) as being adjusted flexibly so as to fulfill the various equations for general equilibrium, including those for factors of production. Hence, full-employment equilibrium is established, but because this version of Walras's system, which assumes flexible investment, of course, lacks an independent aggregate investment function (though Walras himself was not aware of this), it

[16] This is one point of confusion in Walras. Because entrepreneurs borrow from capitalists the money they need to purchase capital goods, the capital goods purchased with this money are owned not by the capitalist but by the enterprise. Consequently, it is not the capitalist who supplies the services of the capital goods; it must be the enterprise itself. Where it is possible for the capital goods to be moved, the entrepreneur is likely to receive an offer of services of the capital goods from another enterprise. This confusion in Walras has been corrected in Morishima (1977, pp. 77–99).

satisfies Say's Law in the Keynesian sense, in contradiction with his emphasis on the independent role of the entrepreneur in decision making.[17] This means that as in an equilibrium regime of perfect competition, prices are flexibly adjusted so as to satisfy the equations for supply and demand at the point of equilibrium. Investment was also dealt with by Walras in much the same manner. Thus, in the Walrasian system there is no place for entrepreneurs who make investment decisions. There are no independent decision makers, but rather instruments of the market who bring into effect whatever investment is determined on at the moment, such that general equilibrium is established. Throughout the volumes of *Eléments,* Walras repeatedly stresses in chapter after chapter the importance of the entrepreneur as an independent entity; yet he accepts the perfect flexibility of investment, turning the entrepreneur quite simply into a *kuroko,* a sceneshifter,[18] and by doing this he just fails to achieve what would have been a remarkable success. The shortcoming lies in the fact that Walras's belief in the existence of general equilibrium whatever the regime (i.e., whether general equilibrium of exchange, of production, of capital formation and credit, or of money and circulation) ultimately makes him accept the idea of the perfect flexibility of investment.[19]

Thus, Walras, too, was unable to escape from Say's Law, and this failure is closely tied to his turning the entrepreneur into a mere stagehand, an entity content to receive no income, just like an auctioneer, who, while adjusting prices, does not receive an income for what he does. In line with this, Walras constructed a mathematical model that

[17] For Walras's system of general equilibrium of capital formation and credit, see Walras ([1874] 1954, pp. 267–312). For this system, the existence of a full-employment equilibrium was rigorously proved under Say's Law by Morishima (1964, pp. 83–92). See also Morishima (1977, pp. 70–122).

[18] In Kabuki, the *kuroko* is an individual dressed in black clothes and wearing a black headdress who appears on the stage to arrange it by such functions as picking up clothes discarded by the actors. His presence is necessary to the play, but he plays no role whatsoever in terms of advancing the sequence of events.

[19] In regard to a general equilibrium of capital formation and credit, there are at least two options for dealing with investment: (1) guaranteeing general equilibrium by assuming the perfect flexibility of investment, or (2) satisfying oneself about a lack of general equilibrium by assuming an independent investment function. Keynes opted for the latter; Walras's choice of the former was undoubtedly a bad choice that stemmed from his prejudice in favor of the existence of general equilibrium. Thus, under Keynes's formulation of Say's Law, equilibrium does exist, whereas under Anti–Say's Law it does not exist. By contrast, under Lange-Patinkin's Say's Law, countless equilibria exist, and under Anti–Say's Law, an equilibrium exists. It should be noted that between Keynes's Say's Law and Lange-Patinkin's Say's Law, the degrees of freedom of the system go down a notch.

he considered equivalent to his literary model ([1874] 1954, p. 270),[20] in which he took the view that capitalists themselves save in the form of capital goods and that the capital goods that they have saved are lent out to each industry. Not just in terms of practical convenience, but also in terms of theoretical significance, there is a considerable difference between this type of mathematical model and his model in which saving is carried out in the form of money, which is then lent to entrepreneurs so that they may satisfy their demand for new capital goods – the kind of model that Morishima has referred to as Walras's literary or first model (Morishima, 1977, p. 73; Walras, [1874] 1954, p. 555). The second, or mathematical, model is essentially no different from the classical model in which the capitalist both saves and invests. Thus, Walras's adherence to his faith in the existence of general equilibrium meant that his drama of capital formation, though conceived in the light of a magnificent plan and vision, became in the end no more than a farce.

Finally, if Walras, with all his emphasis on independent decision making by entrepreneurs, had incorporated an investment function into his system, then, as will be seen later, general equilibrium would no longer be achieved in that system. Seen in this light, we can take the view that Walras's system anticipated Keynes's theory that under Anti–Say's Law, full-employment equilibrium cannot in general be achieved.[21] It would, at the very least, not be surprising to find that someone had, on the basis of Walras's theorem, engaged in direct speculation on this kind of theory as a conjecture. It is ironic that the conjecture was not taken up by Schumpeter, who was well acquainted with Walras and respected him, but by Keynes, who can be regarded as having no great appreciation of Walras's thought.

2.6   Schumpeter

It is generally believed that Schumpeter's hallmarks were the terms "entrepreneur," "innovation," and "new combination." However, as

---

[20] Walras shows no sign of having attempted to prove the equivalence of the two models, but rather rashly immediately concludes their equivalence.

[21] Say's Law was normally discussed with reference to the theory of crisis and the neutrality of money, but Keynes tied it to unemployment. Seen afresh from this kind of perspective, Walras's economics, regarded as providing the microeconomic foundations for classical or Ricardian economics, can also serve to provide the microeconomic foundations for Keynesian economics by incorporating an independent investment function.

has already been explained, these phrases were incorporated in an idea that had already been strongly emphasized by Walras and were, if anything, a direct extension of Walrasian concerns with the importance of the entrepreneur and of technical progress as a change in the coefficients of production due to the entrepreneur's selection of one out of the hitherto impossible new combinations that had become possible as a result of change in the production function (Walras, [1874] 1954, p. 386).[22]

It is our view that Schumpeter's greatest contribution was his assigning to the banker an explicit role as the fifth constituent in the general equilibrium system. This conception can perhaps be regarded not so much as Schumpeter filling in a gap in the theory of Walras, but rather as showing the influence of Marx on Schumpeter. To argue this point in some detail, we take a few paragraphs to give our perspective on Marx's theory of interest.

Marx developed his theory of interest in Part V of Volume 3 of *Capital,* where he also discussed various problems regarding money, capital, and banks, but this part of Marx's work is quite unfinished. The latter half of Part V, which was concerned with the circulation of bank notes and the role of banks or bankers as the largest of capitalist pow-

---

[22] Schumpeter's strict definition of the entrepreneur is as follows: "The carrying out of new combinations we call 'enterprise'; the individuals whose function it is to carry them [new combinations] out we call 'entrepreneurs'" (Schumpeter, [1912] 1934, p. 74). However, by the time the new combinations are established after a certain amount of time, they are no longer new. The entrepreneur who is carrying out this kind of "old" combination ceases to be an entrepreneur in the strict sense of the word if he fails to introduce further new combinations. Thus, Schumpeter's entrepreneur is alternately acting as an entrepreneur, ceasing to be one, then acting as one again. Moreover, what are new combinations? It is said that Japanese technological invention is essentially not something new, but rather only trivial modifications and improvements. Is a combination that has been modified only a little (or in extreme cases not been modified at all) not a new combination? Is the "Japanese" entrepreneur not an entrepreneur at all? Viewed this way, there is little difference between a most generously qualified Schumpeterian entrepreneur and the Walrasian entrepreneur in the sense of an individual who carries out decisions regarding the volume of production and makes decisions regarding investment. Schumpeter states that Walras's entrepreneurs make neither profits nor losses, and whereas they may at best be heads of firms or business managers, they are not entrepreneurs (Schumpeter, [1912] 1934, p. 76). But we interpret Walras in the following manner: What he said was that in an equilibrium situation, enterprises make neither profit nor loss, but because, in fact, the basic data change every moment, their actual position is always out of equilibrium; therefore, entrepreneurs do, in fact, make profits and losses. Interpreted in this manner, his entrepreneur is of the same type as Schumpeter's. See footnote 15. See also Walras ([1874] 1954, pp. 44, 380–1).

ers, was, in Marx's own manuscripts, particularly far from being ready for publication.[23]

In the part on the theory of interest, regarded as relatively complete, found in *Capital,* Volume 3, pages 338–460, Marx first discusses the relationship between active capitalists (Marx's functioning capitalists or entrepreneurs in industry or commerce) and the mere moneylenders, the passive capitalists (Marx's money-capitalists or Ricardo's moneyed classes), who make up the capitalist class. Once a money market has been established and society becomes more prosperous, there are more and more owners of inherited wealth, many of whom retire early from active business and become moneylenders. Apart from these rentiers-by-choice there are also rentiers-by-necessity (i.e., owners of small amounts of capital), who find themselves excluded from independent business activity as a result of the advance of technology and the growth in the minimum size of the firm that accompanies it. Such petty capitalists have no choice but to become either passive capitalists (rentiers-by-necessity) or creditors (nonmanaging shareholders of a joint-stock company). From then on, they strive to maintain and strengthen their positions of capital ownership merely by saving. Being quite numerous, they generate a saving ethos that spreads to almost all individuals in a capitalist society, including workers. The capital accumulated in this decentralized manner is concentrated in banks. "The depositors consist of the industrial capitalists and merchants themselves and also of workers (through savings banks) – as well as ground-rent recipients and other unproductive classes" (Marx, [1891] 1971, p. 484), and bankers become "the representatives of social capital" ([1891] 1971, p. 368).

At the same time, the separation of management from ownership proceeds apace, and capitalists (i.e., potential owner-managers) are forced to become mere rentiers. In this way the economy has reached a stage where it possesses a financial market within which saving is performed by almost all members of society, the vast majority of these savings being concentrated in the hands of the banks, which then supply private operators (entrepreneurs and professional managers) with the funds necessary for their pursuit of private profit. Marx writes as follows:

Since . . . the mere owner of capital, the money-capitalist, has to face the functioning capitalist, while money-capital itself assumes a social character with the advance of credit, being concentrated in banks and loaned out by them

---

[23] See Engels's comments in Marx ([1891] 1971, p. 4).

instead of its original owners, and since, on the other hand, the mere manager who has no title whatsoever to the capital, whether through borrowing it or otherwise, performs all the real functions pertaining to the functioning capitalists as such, only the functionary remains and the capitalist disappears as superfluous from the production process. ([1891] 1971, p. 388).[24]

In this kind of institutional setup it is the banking system that is the link between saving and investment. It would not be an exaggeration to say that whether or not Say's Law holds true (either completely or virtually) will be tied up with the way in which bankers act. Marx, himself, who left his chapter on bankers almost completely unwritten, did not draw such an inference.[25] It is not, on the other hand, surprising that Schumpeter, who was, after all, strongly influenced by Marx, gave considerable emphasis to the role of the banker in his *Theorie der wirtschaftlichen Entwicklung.*

The English-language version of this work by Schumpeter appeared two years before the publication of Keynes's *General Theory,* but the first edition of the original German version came out in 1912 and is a far bulkier volume than its English counterpart. It can be viewed as a work produced in an intermediate period between Walras's *Eléments* and Keynes's *General Theory.*

According to Schumpeter, capital "is a fund of purchasing power" ([1912] 1934, p. 120). *"Capital is nothing but the lever by which the entrepreneur subjects to his control the concrete goods which he needs, nothing but a means of diverting the factors of production to new uses, or dictating a new direction to production"* ([1912] 1934, p. 116; italics in original). "That form of economic organisation in which the goods

---

[24] Compare this passage from Marx with the following from Schumpeter ([1912] 1934, p. 74): " . . . since all reserve funds and savings today usually flow to [the banker], and the total demand for free purchasing power, whether existing or to be created, concentrates on him, he has either replaced private capitalists or become their agent; he has himself become the capitalist par excellence. He stands between those who wish to form new combinations and the possessors of productive means."

[25] But he came very close to it. In *Capital,* Vol. 3 ([1891] 1971, p. 606), Marx wrote: "The banking system possesses indeed the form of universal book-keeping and distribution of means of production on a social scale, but solely the form." Universal bookkeeping and distribution of the means of production is, for Marx, just another way of describing a planned economy, in which a universal balance of supply and demand at a full-employment level everywhere is consciously pursued and achieved; in other words, Say's Law is officially legislated and centrally implemented. Marx did not believe that banks could achieve this in a capitalist regime. He wrote: "There is no doubt that the credit system will serve as a powerful lever during the transition from the capitalist mode of production to the mode of production of associated labour; but only as one element in connection with other great organic revolutions of the mode of production itself" ([1891] 1971, p. 607).

necessary for new production are withdrawn from their settled place in the circular flow by the intervention of purchasing power created *ad hoc* is the capitalist economy" ([1912] 1934, p. 116). It is the bankers who supply the entrepreneurs with purchasing power by furnishing them with credit. Moreover, because they are not able to create credit unlimitedly, they have to select from among the investment plans put forward by entrepreneurs those that they regard as desirable or likely to succeed. The direction that the economy will follow will depend on the investment plans that are chosen, and therefore it is the bankers who constitute the selection committees for investment plans – they are the helmsmen of the capitalist economy.[26]

It goes without saying that the savings accrued by people in society are concentrated in the banks. If the banker were to hand over the money just as it was to the investor, then it would be savings that would regulate investment; although the entrepreneurs will make various investment plans, the investment made must be equal to savings. That is to say, investment adapts to savings (not vice versa), and we always find that $S = I$. This means that in this case, Say's Law will prevail.

However, that is not how bankers act. Bankers are able to create credit on the basis of the money in their possession (i.e., money they have obtained from savers). Although there is a limit to credit creation, as long as they remain inside that limit, bankers may advance the required sums to entrepreneurs with investment plans that they think are desirable. The total of the sums lent out is determined by the quantitative size of the investment plans and by their quality (i.e., by which of the proposed investments bankers think are likely to succeed and on which they are therefore prepared to advance funds). In this way, where credit creation changes flexibly within stipulated limits, the aggregate investment carried out (i.e., effective investment, I) is determined independent of the savings that are available to bankers. Thus, when I is decided, the investment plans backed by bankers will be carried out; capital goods will be purchased, workers hired, and production initiated, with the result that the size of people's savings will change. S will then adjust to I (not vice versa). This is the way in which Schumpeter's model works, but this kind of economy is very much the world of an Anti–Say's Law, and in this Schumpeter has come very close to Keynes. For Schumpeter, the people who severed investment

---

[26] In Schumpeter's words, "He makes possible the carrying out of new combinations, authorises people, in the name of society as it were, to form them. He is the ephor of the exchange economy" ([1912] 1934, p. 74).

from savings and guaranteed the independence of investment were the bankers who served as the intermediaries between savings and investment and intervened between them by carrying out the flexible creation of credit. Savings are made flexible because of the creation of credit and are adjusted to investment. It is thus seen that "banker" and "credit" (rather than, or as well as, "entrepreneur" and "new combination") are inevitably the key words in Schumpeter's economics.

What kind of role will bankers play in this process of adaptation? First, if we assume that labor is supplied only in as far as there is a demand for it, then $S_L = D_L$ in equation (2); furthermore, bearing in mind that $Y - D_C = S$, $D_I = I$, equation (2) can be written[27]

$$S \equiv I + (D_B - S_B) + (D_M - S_M) \tag{3}$$

In order to simplify our discussion, we shall discuss the case in which $D_M = S_M$ prevails initially and assume that individuals do not save in the form of bonds and that the enterprise investment sector holds no money. First, where entrepreneurs carry out investment in excess of the sector's net income after the payment of interest, new bonds have to be issued to the value of the excess. Thus, it is not until they are able to sell that amount of bonds that entrepreneurs are able to carry out their planned investment. Because it is assumed that individuals do not buy bonds, the bond market will be in a state of excess supply.

Let us now assume that the bankers buy up all the excess supply of bonds on the bond market. The equivalent amount of money in the possession of the banking sector thus passes into the hands of the enterprise investment sector through the bond market. The enterprises that have acquired capital in this way will place orders for capital goods, and the capital-goods industry will engage in an expansion of production. At the same time, the money received by the investment sector from the banks will be transferred to enterprises in the capital-goods industry in payment for capital goods, and this money will in turn pass into the hands of those engaged in the capital-goods industry. These individuals will spend a part of it on consumption, and the remainder will either be held in the form of cash or be paid into current accounts. (Note that we have assumed that individuals do not save in

[27] Note that the last two parenthesized parts represent the value of excess demand for bonds and money, respectively. Although these may not initially be zero, they will become zero after adjustment; hence, we get $S = I$, but what changes in this process is not I, but S. That is to say, as a result of adjusting the volume of bonds and money held, S will change and ultimately become equal to a given, independently determined I. In this way, under Anti–Say's Law, we get $S = I$.

the form of bonds.) The money spent on consumption passes into the hands of the consumer-goods industry and ultimately into the hands of the people involved in the consumer-goods industry. They, too, consume a part, and either hold the rest in the form of cash or put it on current account. That part of the cash placed in a current account, of course, passes into the hands of the banking sector, and the remaining cash is held by the private nonbanking sector.

Thus, the amount of money released by the banks to buy the bonds issued by the entrepreneurs is kept by someone in the economy. This means $D_M = S_M$ in equation (3). In short, if bankers act on the bond market so as to achieve $D_B = S_B$, then it follows that $D_M = S_M$, and hence $S = I$ from equation (3). That is to say, as long as there is a balance in the bond market, there will also be a balance in the money market, and at the same time savings will equal investment.

What, then, is the limit to the amount of money that can be released by the banks in order to mop up the excess demand on the bond market?[28] The banks hold cash and current accounts as liabilities. They do not know when current accounts might be withdrawn, but the probability of the total sums being withdrawn all at once is very small; therefore, the rate of cash reserves may perhaps be sufficient if it is low enough, say 10%. It is all right for the banks to have as cash in hand only the amount in accordance with their necessary cash reserve, and all other money apart from that can be advanced to entrepreneurs. The greater the sum advanced by the banks, the greater the number of investment plans that are being given support by the banks, and the lower the marginal quality of the investment plans. Thus, at a time when opportunities for investment are restricted, investment plans regarded by bankers as likely to succeed will soon be completely exhausted, and the cash reserves held by the banks will be far in excess of the necessary amount. The amount of investment undertaken is related to the extent to which entrepreneurs are able to devise attractive investment plans and the magnitude of the investment projects to which bankers are willing to give favorable considerations. When bankers react negatively, even where there remain good-quality investment plans, the aggregate volume of investment that is effective will be small, and when bankers agree to support even a number of poor investment plans, the effective volume of investment will for a time be considerable, but any failure of investment will soon rebound on

---

28 Schumpeter believed that there was the following limitation on the creation of credit: "If the solvency of the banking system . . . is not to be endangered, the banks can only give credit in such a way that the resulting inflation is really temporary and moreover remains moderate" ([1912] 1934, p. 113).

the enterprise and the bank. Because it is the banker, not the entrepreneur, who makes the choice of the investment plans that are to be financed, it is the banker who is the constituent responsible for a decision on investment. So, as long as they remain within the limits of credit creation, even where the level of aggregate investment is high, bankers are able to give financial support to that aggregate investment. Savings then adjust themselves to that level of investment.

This is Schumpeter's theory of banks and credit. As is clear from the foregoing, it can be regarded as constituting an admirable fusion of Marx and Walras. Of course, it is true that it was Wicksell who had developed, before Schumpeter, a dynamic theory that emphasized the role of the banking sector. Moreover, as mentioned earlier, Wicksell, although hesitantly, had renounced Say's Law and was an economist who should be classified as belonging to the Anti–Say's Law camp. Like Lange and Patinkin, however, he was concerned with the Law only in its relation to the determination of the price level. Unlike Keynes, he never associated it with the problem of unemployment of labor. In fact, in the analysis of "the cumulative process," Wicksell assumed full employment of labor. In *Interest and Prices,* he wrote that "all available factors of production will find employment at prices determined by the market situation." (Wicksell, [1898] 1936, p. 132). Also, in the *Lectures:*

As a first approximation we are entitled to assume that all production forces are already fully employed, so that the increased monetary demand principally takes the form of rivalry between employers for labour, raw materials and natural facilities, etc., which consequently leads to an increase in their price. ([1906] 1935, p. 195)

Moreover, concerning Say's Law, Wicksell is a bit confused in the analysis of the cumulative process. In some places he renounces the law and writes, like Schumpeter,

In order to make a clear distinction between the roles of capitalists and entrepreneurs, we may imagine that the latter work entirely on borrowed money and that they derive this money, not directly from the capitalists, but from a special institution, a bank. ([1898] 1936, p. 137)

It lies in the power of the credit institutions, acting in cooperation only with the entrepreneurs, to determine the direction of production and consequently the period of investment of capital, without paying any heed to the actual capitalists, the owners of goods. ([1898] 1936, p. 155)

In other places, however, he seems to support Say's Law: "An increase in the supply of certain groups of commodities means an increase in the real demand for all other groups of commodities" ([1898] 1936, p. 105). Furthermore, his assumption "that all labour and all land, and in its turn all capital, are always seeking employment and are *always* more or less fully employed" ([1898] 1936, p. 131; italics added) can be realized, according to Keynes, where and only where Say's Law prevails. From all these indications we may conclude that, like Marx and Walras, Wicksell was paradoxical between Say's Law and Anti–Say's Law. It is true that he was a predecessor of Keynes in the sense that, before Keynes (and before Schumpeter), he developed a theory that consolidated real-economic and monetary theories into a unity, but he had no substantial theory of unemployment. He was a classical economist in the sense that he remained a full-employment economist, though he revised the classical wage fund theory to a new one of the von Böhm-Bawerk–Wicksell type.

2.7   Keynes revisited

In his *Entwicklung,* Schumpeter attempted to use this kind of theory to explain the development of the economy and business cycles. When this work was written, the economic situation was very different from that prevailing in 1936 when Keynes published his *General Theory.*

The first attempt at an application of Schumpeter's theory to Keynesian circumstances can be seen in his *Capitalism, Socialism and Democracy* (1942). This work is, of course, sociological and does not proceed in terms of economic analysis. In addition, it is more in the nature of science fiction that does not discuss the actual capitalist economy, but the capitalism of the future. However, in this work, Schumpeter does discuss the case where investment opportunity is small and says that the "outstanding facts" that have given rise to this kind of situation – "unemployment, excess reserves, gluts in money markets, unsatisfactory margins of profits, stagnation of private investment" (Schumpeter, 1942, p. 122) – can be explained both by Marx's theory and by Keynesian theory. Although Schumpeter states that "there is surely no such gulf between Marx and Keynes as there was between Marx and Marshall or Wicksell" (1942, p. 119), he does not mention his own theory. Nevertheless, there is clearly little room for doubt that Schumpeter did believe that his old theory of banks and credit could be applied *mutatis mutandis* to this kind of situation. He also points out "that such opportunities for investment as remain are more suited for public than they are for private enterprise" (1942, p. 120), and concludes that "national and municipal investment could thus be expected to expand, absolutely and relatively, even in a thoroughly capitalist society, just as other forms of public planning would" (1942, p. 120).

If we look at things in this way, the distance from Keynes to Schumpeter is very short. Keynes's procedure in the *General Theory* of first declaring his rejection of Say's Law and then undertaking an analysis first of the savings function and then of the investment function so as to establish the separation between saving and investment, and finally making an analysis of money and interest, is, from the reader's point of view, a highly appropriate and logical method of writing.[29]

For economists before Keynes, the problem of Say's Law was the problem whether or not general overproduction was possible or, otherwise, the problem whether money was or was not neutral. Keynes, however, believed that under Anti–Say's Law, inadequate investment would be an obstacle to full employment, so that the final part of *The General Theory* is devoted to discussing unemployment. Keynes thus completed the transition from a Say's Law regime to an Anti–Say's Law regime.

The most basic proposition of Keynes's employment theory is the proposition that under Anti–Say's Law, a general equilibrium in which labor is fully employed and capital fully utilized does not, in general, necessarily exist (and, for that reason, such an equilibrium will not be achieved), and this constitutes a denial of Walras's theory based on Say's Law (i.e., the proposition that general equilibrium must exist). Thus, the transition from Say's Law to Anti–Say's Law is a transition from equilibrium theory to nonequilibrium theory, at least for Keynes.

To establish Anti–Say's Law, Keynes introduces the assumption of diminishing marginal efficiency of capital. Let ξ^* be the amount of real gross investment (i.e., the demand for new capital goods) that will prevail if the rate of interest is set at zero. Then, by virtue of that assumption, the actual amount of investment, I, is necessarily less than ξ, as long as a positive interest rate is established. Let m and n be the labor-input coefficients of the consumption-goods and capital-goods industries, respectively. Then the total employment of labor is given as

$$N = mx + n\xi$$

where x is the output of the consumption-goods industry that corresponds to the output of the capital-goods industry, ξ. Kahn's interin-

---

[29] In Keynes, however, the role that bankers play in establishing the equality between savings and investment remains totally unclear. In Schumpeter, on the other hand, there is no analytical device, such as Keynes's "diminishing marginal efficiency of capital," as discussed later, to explain the low level of investment.

dustrial multiplier theory specifies that x increases according as ξ increases. Therefore, we obtain

$$N < mx^* + n\xi^* = N^*$$

It is now clear that where investment opportunities are scarce, ξ^* and hence x^* are small, so that the total employment N^* corresponding to ξ^* and x^* does not reach the full-employment level, N_F. Therefore, $N < N_F$ for all feasible values of N. Of course, one may say that the labor-input coefficients m and n are flexible, depending on the real wage rate, and so forth, but the possibilities of technical substitution between labor and capital are rather limited, so that the flexibility of m and n is not large enough to fill up the gap between N and N_F. It is thus shown that where investment opportunities are poor, full employment will not be achieved.[30]

Attention must now be drawn to the fact that Walras's system of general equilibrium of capital accumulation and credit does not accommodate the assumption of diminishing marginal efficiency of capital. Therefore, in his model, investment (i.e., the demand for new capital goods, in his terminology) can be expanded without limit, so that the industrial demand for labor can be as large as the labor supply at the full-employment level. This fact, that investment is perfectly flexible, has been described before as a lack of an independent investment function, which is nothing else but a lack of the assumption of diminishing marginal efficiency of capital in Walras's model. A form of the marginalist idea is thus used by Keynes in order to deny Say's Law.

2.8   Conclusion

Within economics there exist two schools of thought that rest on two different "axioms of parallel lines." One is the so-called orthodox school, which assumes the validity of Say's Law and supports economic analysis based on this assumption, especially on the existence of full-employment equilibrium; whereas the other supports Anti–Say's Law and consequently rejects the concept of the existence, in general, of full-employment equilibrium. In the transition from the former to the latter, Marx, Walras, and especially Schumpeter made substantial contributions to the shift, but the first two remained, to

---

[30] The foregoing proof of the nonexistence proposition is a revised version of the proof of the overdeterminancy of general equilibrium conditions under Anti–Say's Law that has been proposed by Morishima (1977, pp. 100–2).

varying degrees, in a somewhat paradoxical position between the two laws, so that the transition was not completed until the advent of Keynes. Closest to Keynes among the pre-Keynes critics of Say's Law is Schumpeter. His pre-Keynesian work ([1912] 1934) clarified the role of bankers in adjusting savings to investment in an Anti–Say's Law economy, while his post-Keynesian work (1942) examined the same situation Keynes was concerned with. Although the positions of Walras and Marx were unclear, it would probably be fair to say that the former belonged to the first, the full-employment-equilibrium school, and the latter to the second, the antiequilibrium school. As far as Say's Law is concerned, however, heterodoxy has now become orthodoxy, and non-Euclidean economics is the economics to which support must, in general, be given. This is true regardless of whether or not Keynesian economic policies are supported.

References

Baumol, W. J. (1977). "Say's (At Least) Eight Laws or What Say and James Mill May Have Really Meant." *Economica*, 40(May):146–61.

Baumol, W. J., and Becker, B. S. (1952). "The Classical Monetary Theory." *Economica*, 19(November):355–96.

Fan-Hung (1939). "Keynes and Marx on the Theory of Capital Accumulation, Money and Interest." *Review of Economic Studies*, 6:28–41.

Harris, L. (1976). "On Interest, Credit and Capital." *Economy and Society*, 5(2):145–77.

Hicks, J. (1983). *Classics and Moderns*. Oxford: Basil Blackwell.

Hollander, S. (1979). *The Economics of David Ricardo*. London: Heinemann.

Keynes, J. M. (1936). *The General Theory of Employment, Interest and Money*. London: Macmillan.

Lange, O. (1942). "Say's Law: A Restatement and Criticism," in Lange, O., et al. (eds.), *Studies in Mathematical Economics and Econometrics*. University of Chicago Press.

La Volpe, G. (1936). *Studi sulla teoria dell'equilibrio economico dinamico generale*. Napoli: Casa Editrice dot. Eugenio Jovene.

Leijonhufvud, A. (1968). *On Keynesian Economics and the Economics of Keynes*. Oxford University Press.

Marx, K. [1867] (1970). *Capital*, Vol. 1. Moscow: Progress Publishers.

   [1905–10] (1968). *Theories of Surplus Value, Part II*. Moscow: Progress Publishers.

   [1885] (1967). *Capital*, Vol. 2. Moscow: Progress Publishers.

   [1891] (1971). *Capital*, Vol. 3. Moscow: Progress Publishers.

Morishima, M. (1964). *Equilibrium, Stability and Growth*. Oxford: Clarendon Press.

(1973). *Marx's Economics. A Dual Theory of Value and Growth.* Cambridge University Press.

(1977). *Walras' Economics: A Pure Theory of Capital and Money.* Cambridge University Press.

Pasinetti, L. (1974). *Growth and Income Distribution – Essays in Economic Theory.* Cambridge University Press.

Patinkin, D. (1956). *Money, Interest and Prices.* New York: Row, Peterson & Co.

Ricardo, D. [1817] (1954). *On the Principles of Political Economy and Taxation,* in Sraffa, P. (ed.), *The Works and Correspondence of David Ricardo.* Cambridge University Press.

(1952). "Letters," in Sraffa, P. (ed.), *The Works and Correspondence of David Ricardo,* Vol. 6. Cambridge University Press.

Say, J. B. (1826). *Traité d'économie politique* (3 vols.). Paris.

Schumpeter, J. A. [1912] (1934). *The Theory of Economic Development.* Oxford University Press (originally published in German as *Theorie der wirtschaftlichen Entwicklung*).

(1942). *Capitalism, Socialism and Democracy.* London: George Allen & Unwin.

(1954). *History of Economic Analysis.* Oxford University Press.

Solow, R. (1956). "A Contribution to the Theory of Economic Growth." *Quarterly Journal of Economics,* 70:64–94.

Sowell, T. (1972). *Say's Law: An Historical Analysis.* Princeton University Press.

Walras, L. [1874] (1954). *Elements of Pure Economics, or The Theory of Social Wealth.* London: George Allen & Unwin (originally published in French as *Eléments d'économie politique pure,* translated by William Jaffé, published for the American Economic Association and the Royal Economics Society).

Wicksell, K. [1898] (1936). *Interest and Prices.* London: Macmillan (originally published in Swedish as *Geldzins und Guterpreise*).

[1906] (1935). *Lectures on Political Economy,* Vol. 2. London: Routledge (originally published in Swedish as *Föreläsningar I Nationalekonomi: Teoretisk Nationalekonomi,* Haft 2).

Discussion

EDUARD MÄRZ

In these comments on the excellent chapter by Morishima and Catephores on the century-long transition from a Pro–Say's Law position to an Anti-Say's Law position, epitomized by such outstanding figures of our economic discipline as David Ricardo, on the one hand, and

John Maynard Keynes, on the other hand, I shall focus attention primarily on a theorist of the intermediate period, namely, Joseph Alois Schumpeter. I propose to do this on two grounds: first, because Schumpeter is, so to speak, the *persona dramatis* of this founding session of the International Schumpeter Society; second, because I think that Schumpeter's contribution to a nonorthodox or antiorthodox view in regard to Say's Law of Markets is in need of further clarification. I also want to remark that for the purpose of this discussion, the Law of Markets will be interpreted in its most widely accepted meaning, namely, that although sectional disequilibria may occasionally arise, no *general* glut of the market is likely to develop.

Morishima and Catephores suggest that Schumpeter's most noteworthy achievement in the long march toward a "non-Euclidean" economic theory is his introduction of the *banker* as the strategic constituent of the equilibrium system. "It would not be an exaggeration to say," so these two authors maintain in Section 2.6, "that whether or not Say's Law holds true (either completely or virtually) will be tied up with the way in which bankers act." This is so, we are later told, because "credit creation changes flexibly within stipulated limits." Morishima and Catephores thus conclude: "When bankers react negatively, even where there remain good-quality investment plans, the aggregate volume of investment that is effective will be small, and when bankers agree to support even a number of poor investment plans, the effective volume of investment will for a time be considerable." In this view, the bankers become the "helmsmen of the capitalist economy," whose prime function lies in the adjustment of savings to investment.

Morishima and Catephores believe that the other constituent elements of the Schumpeterian system (the entrepreneur, his innovative endeavors, and the disequilibrating shocks resulting from these activities) are largely derived from ideas formulated by Léon Walras almost a generation before the publication of Schumpeter's *Theory of Economic Development*. On the other hand, the banker as the main strategist within the capitalist system, so these authors claim, has been foreshadowed in certain passages of Volume 3 of *Das Kapital* by Karl Marx, a work that considerably predates *Les Éléments* by Walras. Although there can be little doubt that both Karl Marx and Walras exercised considerable influence on the writings of Schumpeter, I should hesitate to subscribe fully and wholeheartedly to the dictum of these authors that Schumpeter's theory of banks and credit "can be regarded as constituting an admirable fusion of Marx and Walras." As I shall try to show, both contemporary ideas and strong institutional peculiarities of the Austrian economic landscape with which the young Schumpeter was perfectly familiar had a strong if not decisive impact on the genesis of the Schumpeterian system. Let me first turn to some of the contemporary sources that nourished the nascent ideas of the young Schumpeter.

Schumpeter's teacher and benefactor was, as is generally known, the great Austrian economist Eugen von Böhm-Bawerk, who repeatedly served as finance minister under Emperor Francis Joseph and was instrumental, in that capacity, in devising a major tax reform. As a theorist, Böhm-Bawerk ranked together with Carl Menger and Friedrich von Wieser as a founder of the Austrian school of economics – men who, in the distinguished company of Jevons, Walras, and Wicksell, effected a decisive break with the hitherto dominant classical tradition concerning the theory of value. Schumpeter's admiration for and devotion to his teacher are well documented, especially in his moving tribute to Böhm-Bawerk, who died quite unexpectedly in 1914, shortly before the outbreak of World War I.[1]

I do not intend to dwell on that very learned and persuasively written memorial article except to say that Schumpeter put the performance of Böhm-Bawerk on equal footing with the classics and Karl Marx. Only the latter, so Schumpeter thought, had recognized the *central* significance of the phenomenon of interest and profit. After Marx, so Schumpeter argued, Böhm-Bawerk was one of the few to appreciate the quintessential nature of these economic categories, which, once fully grasped, put a decisive imprint on the remaining theoretical structure. In this way, Schumpeter acknowledged another of the vital intellectual influences that went into the construction of his own theoretical edifice. And, just as in the case of Böhm-Bawerk, Schumpeter gave ample credit in that article, as well as on later occasions, to what he believed were the lasting achievements of the theorizing revolutionary from Trier.[2]

In the manner of the neoclassical school, Böhm-Bawerk had established a static system that, one must add, was subject to exogenous impulses such as population growth, technological advances, and

---

[1] Schumpeter's article "Das wissenschaftliche Lebenswerk Eugen von Böhm-Bawerks" was first published in *Zeitschrift für Volkswirtschaft, Sozialpolitik und Verwaltung* (1914b). A shorter version of this article, edited by Professor Gottfried Haberler, is contained in a posthumously published book: J. A. Schumpeter, *Ten Great Economists, From Marx to Keynes* (1952).

[2] References to Marx, all of them respectful, albeit not always uncritical, can be found in all major works of Schumpeter. A case in point is the article cited earlier in *Ten Great Economists;* see especially page 147.

changes in consumers' preferences. Soon after he had absorbed the neoclassical gospel in its Böhm-Bawerkian version, Schumpeter was to discover that Walras, rather than Böhm-Bawerk, had given it its most rigorous and elegant expression. From then on, he never ceased to extol the virtues of the Walrasian system and made it his life work to "dynamize" what he thought was the best theoretical model of a stationary economy. His monumental work *Business Cycles* is of course his most ambitious, if not entirely successful, attempt at combining economic statics and dynamics. But I must reiterate that the initial stimuli that prompted Schumpeter to undertake his arduous theoretical life work came from Böhm-Bawerk and Marx rather than from Walras.

I do not want to create the impression that Schumpeter was an uncritical admirer of the Böhm-Bawerkian system. In point of fact, his first major theoretical work, *The Theory of Economic Development*, published in 1912, can hardly be considered as conceived in the spirit of the Austrian neoclassical school, and it came under immediate and rather merciless attack from his revered teacher. It was precisely the Schumpeterian theory of interest – the quintessential element of an economic theory, if we are to heed Schumpeter's view – that provoked the sternest and (I believe) not entirely undeserved rebuke from the pen of his admired teacher.[3] Schumpeter made a long-winded but rather weak attempt to refute Böhm-Bawerk's critical review. However, I am not concerned here with the merits or demerits of Schumpeter's case, but rather with the fact that his *Theory of Economic Development* contains all the elements that since have become known under the trademark of the Schumpeterian system: the stationary state that is devoid of both enterprising men and profits; the sudden emergence of *homines novi,* who, through their will to lead and conquer, introduce destabilizing new combinations; the readiness of banks to support such endeavors by financing them by newly created purchasing power; the resulting disequilibrating shocks as resources and men are shifted from old fields of industrial application to new ones.

Morishima and Catephores argue that Schumpeter's hallmarks, such as entrepreneur, innovation, and new combinations, were ideas emphasized by Walras and thus cannot be regarded as constituting novel or original contributions by Schumpeter. This statement contradicts somewhat (I believe) the statement of Morishima and Catephores

---

[3] Eugen von Böhm-Bawerk's criticism appeared in 1914 in *Zeitschrift für Volkswirtschaft, Sozialpolitik und Verwaltung* (22:1–62). Schumpeter's reply appeared in the same volume (22:599–639). It was followed by Böhm-Bawerk's concluding remarks (22:640–56).

that "in the Walrasian system there is no place for entrepreneurs who make investment decisions. There are no independent decision makers, but rather instruments of the market" (Section 2.5). I cannot help but deduce from this observation that the Walrasian entrepreneur and the Schumpeterian entrepreneur are two very different animals. But even if one concedes that the Walrasian entrepreneur was a sort of forerunner of the later species, albeit a very distant relative, it remains doubtful that the early opus of Schumpeter (i.e., his *Theory of Economic Development*) was decisively influenced by Walras. I propose that there existed more immediate and more powerful influences. One of them stemmed from another teacher of the young Schumpeter, the third of the Austrian triumvirate, Friedrich von Wieser.

In his very suggestive paper "Schumpeter's Vienna and the Role of Credit in Innovation" (1981), Professor Erich Streissler draws attention to a passage in a textbook on economics published by Wieser in 1914, two years after Schumpeter's early theoretical contribution. Schumpeter, who, as he himself emphasized, had the closest intellectual affinity to Wieser (Schumpeter, 1908), had no doubt familiarized himself with Wieser's theoretical framework during the latter's lectures in the first decade of this century. The passage mentioned earlier runs as follows: "It is not capital which brings success, for capital itself is largely formed out of accrued profits. It is its role as market leader which has brought success to an enterprise. The men who pioneered new ways had to be supremely gifted men who combined technical abilities, a sense for the market and organizational power and in addition the audacity of the innovator" (Wieser, 1914, p. 375). The "audacity of the innovator" became one of Schumpeter's favorite phrases in many of his later publications. It may be added that Wieser's elitist strain of thought was later carried to its logical conclusion when the celebrated economist, shortly before his death in 1927, began to espouse antidemocratic and even racial theories. As Professor Streissler observed in another paper, "it was Friedrich von Wieser . . . who was one of the first social scientists constantly using the term Führer in the early 20th century" (Streissler, 1986, p. 89).

His early acquaintance with and undisguised attraction to the elitist ideas of Friedrich von Wieser may also explain Schumpeter's affinity with writers like Vilfredo Pareto, Gabriel Tarde, and Lévy-Bruhl. Pareto, especially, must be seen as an important source of inspiration for Schumpeter's theory of social classes. Both men considered differences in individual abilities as the basis for the evolution of social classes. The remarkable persistence and resistance of these differences to change Schumpeter attributed to a biological law, the heritability of mental faculties. No doubt, the early influence of Wieser proved a powerful factor in the formation of Schumpeter's *Weltanschauung,* even at a much later stage of his scientific career. The mature Schumpeter may have been confirmed in his early opinions by two authors who rose to prominence before and after World War I: Sir Francis Galton and Karl Pearson. From the latter, Schumpeter borrowed a phrase he was particularly fond of quoting: "Ability runs in stocks."

In the view of Morishima and Catephores, Schumpeter's greatest contribution to a non-Euclidean theoretical position "was his assigning to the banker an explicit role as the fifth constituent in the general equilibrium system. This conception," so these authors emphasize, "can perhaps be regarded not so much as Schumpeter filling in a gap in the theory of Walras, but rather as showing the influence of Marx on Schumpeter" (Section 4.6). In what follows I shall argue that Marx's influence on Schumpeter was more complex than Morishima and Catephores assume and went far beyond the introduction of the banker as a strategic decision-making social entity in the equilibrium system. From Professor Haberler (1951, p. 26) we have learned that Schumpeter made the acquaintance of three renowned Marxist writers, Rudolf Hilferding, Emil Lederer, and Otto Bauer, at a seminar held by Böhm-Bawerk in the academic year 1905–6 and that the four young men engaged in many interesting and heated discussions. This early occupation (perhaps preoccupation) with the Marxist theory is, I think, clearly discernible in Schumpeter's *Theory of Economic Development.* In a well-known passage in that work he refers to J. B. Clark's conception of the dynamic character of the economic process and cites five causes of disturbance enumerated by Clark. Among these causes, so Schumpeter argues, two must be considered of special significance: changes in technology and in the organization of production. Disturbances caused by these two entrepreneurial measures take us, so Schumpeter emphasizes, beyond the stationary state.

That statement is followed by this passage:

The fact that this was overlooked constitutes the most important single reason for all that appears unsatisfactory about economic theory. From this humble source flows, as will be seen, a novel conception of the economic process which is capable of overcoming a number of fundamental difficulties which justifies the new formulation of the problem in the text. This new formulation of the problem runs rather *parallel to that of Marx.* For he recognizes an endogenous economic development and not simply an adjustment to certain changing parameters. (Schumpeter, [1912] 1926, p. 92, fn. 2; my translation)

Schumpeter concludes this observation with a compliment to the genius of Karl Marx: "But my edifice covers only a small part of the ground occupied by him." A similar passage can be found in the Preface to the Japanese edition of Schumpeter's *Theory of Economic Development*.

Schumpeter does not seem to have been aware of the fact that the similarity between his system and that of Marx goes beyond the rather general observation that both theories consider economic change as primarily caused by endogenous impulses. There are numerous passages in the first and third volumes of *Das Kapital* and in a smaller essay, "Wage Labour and Capital," in which the Schumpeterian concept of the innovator who succeeds in securing for himself a temporary advantage by the introduction of new and less costly methods of production seems to have been largely anticipated. After describing in his "Wage Labour and Capital" how the innovating capitalist can reap an extra profit through improvement of old equipment or application of new equipment, Marx proceeds to show the forces that combine to undermine the temporary monopoly position thus created. Marx then states the following:

> The privileged position of our capitalist is not, however, of very long duration. Other competing capitalists introduce the same machines, the same division of labour on the same or even larger scale, so that the new methods will become generally known and the price of linen ware will fall to the level of its new cost of production. . . . We thus see how the forces of production will be continually transformed and revolutionized and how the division of labour will procreate an even higher degree of the division of labour. . . . This is the law which continues to dislodge well established routines of production and which compels the capitalist class to mobilize all available forces of labour, as a response to a previous stage in the mobilization of labour; it is the law, which keeps capital on the run by constantly exhorting it: March! March! It is the same law that brings about within the fluctuations of the trade cycle the inevitable levelling of the prices of commodities to their cost of production. (1953, pp. 86–8; my translation)

It seems clear that almost all the dynamic forces so persuasively exhibited by Schumpeter in both his early and more mature works are contained *in ovo* in the foregoing passage from "Wage Labour and Capital." Similar quotations could be cited from Volume 1 and Volume 3 of *Das Kapital*. But Marx, it must be emphasized, did not draw from these and similar observations the conclusion that gives the Schumpeterian system its unique position, namely, that the category of profit must be understood solely as a dynamic phenomenon. In considering entrepreneurial gain, no matter how small or large, as a steady concomitant of the capitalist system, Marx was, of course, in full accord with classical tradition and with the more modern neoclassical school. Perhaps another vital difference between Marx and Schumpeter should be noted in this context. Whereas Marx sees the main motivation of the entrepreneur's quest for profit in the latter's acquisitive instincts, Schumpeter, in accordance with Friedrich von Wieser and other elitist theorists, stresses noneconomic motives such as the desire to lead and conquer and the founding of a dynasty as the *primum movens* of the entrepreneurial class.

Morishima and Catephores remind us of Marx's scathing attack on David Ricardo, an author he otherwise held in high esteem, because of the latter's full endorsement of J. B. Say's Law of Markets. Contrary to Ricardo, Marx believed, as we are told by Morishima and Catephores, that "the producer who initiates a sale is under no compulsion and may even be well advised (in times of heightened commercial uncertainty) to abstain from following up the sale with a corresponding purchase" (Section 2.4). Taking this statement in conjunction with the dynamic conception of the Marxist theoretical system outlined earlier, one is forced to conclude that the transition from a pro-Say position to an anti-Say position was fully effected by Marx in his *Theories of Surplus Value,* if not at an even earlier date.

This is, however, not the opinion of Morishima and Catephores. They point, with some justification, to Marx's famous reproduction scheme, contained in Volume 2 of *Das Kapital,* that indeed presupposes the complete identity of saving and investment. We are thus confronted with an apparent contradiction in the Marxian system. Whereas in many of his verbal statements Marx presented a dynamic model wherein he negated an ex ante identity between saving and investment, his mathematical exposition of a dynamic economy is predicated on the validity of Say's Law of Markets. The contradiction resolves itself, however, if we take cognizance of the fact that Marx originally, in 1857, designed a far more ambitious outline of his chief theoretical work than that which he actually left behind. His 1857 plan consisted of six, rather than three, volumes; the sixth of the projected parts was to deal with the world market and trade cycles. One of the best students of the evolution of the Marxian system, Roman Rosdolsky, reminds us that Marx, while working on the third volume of *Das Kapital,* decided to put aside the analysis of "competition on the world market" and of the related problem of "industrial trade cycles," intending to reserve them for separate treatment (Rosdolsky, 1968, pp. 27, 29). The elegant, though inadequate, formulation of Marx's famous reproduction scheme in Volume 2 of *Das Kapital* may thus be considered as a stepping-stone toward a more elaborate model, very much in the same way as the value theory of Volume 1 is a preparatory stage for the more complex production price theory of Volume 3. The work on trade cycles, like so much else in Marx's plan of study, unfortunately never came to fruition.

As I pointed out at the beginning of this discussion, Morishima and Catephores assign to the banker a strategic role in the equilibrium system as conceived by Schumpeter, and they further maintain that this concept was derived from a rather incompletely sketched chapter in Volume 3 of *Das Kapital*. I suggest that it was Rudolf Hilferding, rather than Marx, who introduced the banker as the linchpin of the *modern* capitalist system and that he derived this novel institutional category not so much from his study of *Das Kapital* as from his acute observation of the central European economic environment in the last decades before World War I. Rudolf Hilferding's main theoretical contribution was his book *Das Finanzkapital* ([1910] 1927), which was published two years before Schumpeter's *Theory of Economic Development*. Marx had shown, before Hilferding, the central role of the banking system in the process of concentration. Hilferding took that observation as his point of departure for his analysis.

The commercial banks, in the opinion of Hilferding, promote the process of concentration primarily through three stratagems: the incorporation of hitherto nonincorporated firms and the infusion of new capital; the interpenetration and fusion of the business and banking communities through the setting up of executive boards and supervisory boards composed of bankers and industrial entrepreneurs in both communities; and the introduction of the concept of "orderly competition," whereby established leading positions in both industry and commerce are further cemented through the formation of cartels and other business associations.

Hilferding conceives this stage of development of the capitalist system as characterized by a position of hegemony of the commercial banking system. "The dependence of industry on the banks," he writes, "is also the consequence of the existing property relationships. A steadily growing part of the industrial capital does not belong to the entrepreneurs who invest it. . . . More and more the capital applied in industry is finance capital, i.e. capital available to industry, but disposed of by the banks" ([1910] 1927, p. 238). Thus, Hilferding formulated with greater precision an idea that had already been advanced by Marx.

This brings us back to Schumpeter's analysis. Capital, we remember, "is a fund of purchasing power" provided by the banks. Thus, the ultimate responsibility for choosing among competitive investment plans passes, so Morishima and Catephores argue, from the hands of the entrepreneur to the hands of the banker. Schumpeter, in close companionship with Hilferding, introduces a new dominating social group that, through its command over the money hoards of the nation and guided by its hopes and hunches about the future, may or may not bring about the matching of savings and investment. Thus, it comes hardly as a surprise when Morishima and Catephores conclude that "closest to Keynes among the pre-Keynes critics of Say's Law is Schumpeter" (Section 2.8).

Logical as this conclusion may seem, it does not necessarily reflect the real state of affairs, neither in pre–World War I days nor in the more recent past. The Schumpeter-Hilferding thesis does seem to have been of special relevance for the economic development of the Habsburg Empire during the last decades of its existence. Eugen Lopuszanski, a high official of the Austrian finance ministry and a writer on current economic affairs, observed a few years before the outbreak of World War I that the connection between the banking community and industry had turned into a power relationship in which power was located predominantly on the side of banking. But I think that Lopuszanski would have conceded that the truly outstanding Austrian industrial entrepreneurs of that period, the Wittgensteins, Skodas, Schoellers, and Krupps (the latter being an Austrian descendant of the famous German industrial family), were the equals of the Austrian financial tycoons and thus determined their investment programs relatively independently, knowing quite well that they were in a position of tapping the financial resources of any of the major commercial banks without outside interference.

The Schumpeter-Hilferding thesis in regard to the predominance of "finance capital" seems less applicable to imperial Germany than to the Austro-Hungarian Empire. Soon after the publication of Hilferding's book, a number of German social scientists, among them the well-known German economist Jacob Reisser (1912),[4] pointed out that German banking capital had never succeeded in arrogating to itself in some of the major industries that preeminent influence attributed to it by Rudolf Hilferding. In France, and especially in England, I may add, the influence of the financial community over the process of decision making in industry seems to have been even less pronounced than in Germany.

In examining trends in the more recent periods of history, the Schumpeter-Hilferding thesis may be even less relevant than in the more distant past. In the United States and Japan, most of the leading industrial corporations, which control a major part of the national

---

[4] The author argues that the big commercial banks exercised little control over one of the major German industries, the chemical enterprises. For a fuller discussion of this problem, compare Wilfried Gottschalch (1962, p. 101).

product, have been capable of financing a fair share of their investment plans out of their own previous earnings. The bankers in these countries, so it seems to me, can hardly be considered to be the "helmsmen" of their respective economies. The situation in Western Europe appears to be more complex than that in the United States or in Japan. Here, the banks seem to have retained a certain share of their former influence over industrial decision making, but, in addition, a new financial power has arisen, namely, the modern mercantilist state, which finds its most visible outward expression in the various nationalized banking sectors. Despite the recent efforts to turn back this development, I know of few Western European countries to which the Schumpeter-Hilferding thesis would fully apply today.

Let me summarize the main points of my discussion: The shift toward a non- or Anti-Say's Law position seems to have been fully effected by Marx, although his mathematically formulated reproduction scheme seems to contradict this assertion. But, as I have pointed out before, it is most likely that the equations presented in Volume 2 of *Das Kapital* were meant as a preparatory step toward a fuller treatment of the problem at some later date. With Schumpeter, I believe, the transition toward a non-Euclidean viewpoint appears well-nigh complete. The latter's break with the classical and neoclassical traditions does not rest, I propose, on his introduction of the banker as the *deus ex machina* of the process of decision making, but rather on his novel conception of the mechanism of economic growth that, as a consequence of the periodic clustering of innovations, proceeds in wave-like motions. Every theory of cyclical growth presupposes, of course, periodic divergence between saving and investment. Schumpeter, it must be admitted, muddled his position somewhat by asserting in his *Business Cycles* that situations marked by a dearth of profitable investment opportunities were conceivable in certain isolated industries, but not in the system as a whole ([1939] 1961, p. 162). But this remark, so I think, was prompted less by his insight into the mechanics of economic growth than by his age-old rivalry with Keynes and his critical reception of the slowly evolving Keynesian system.

References

Böhm-Bawerk, Eugen von (1914). "Eine 'dynamische' Theorie das Kapitalzinses." *Zeitschrift für Volkswirtschaft, Sozialpolitik und Verwaltung,* 22:1–62, 640–56.

Gottschalch, Wilfried (1962). *Strukturveränderungen der Gesellschaft und politisches Handeln in der Lehre von Hilferding.* Berlin.

Haberler, Gottfried (1951). "Joseph Alois Schumpeter, 1883–1950," in Seymour E. Harris (ed.), *Schumpeter: Social Scientist.* Freeport, N.Y.: Books for Libraries Press.

Hilferding, Rudolf [1910] (1927). *Das Finanzkapital.* Vienna: Brand.

Marx, Karl (1953). "Lohnarbeit und Kapital." *Ausgewählte Schriften,* Vol. 1. Berlin.

Reisser, Jacob (1912). *Die deutschen Grossbanken und ihre Konzentration.* Jena.

Rosdolsky, Roman (1968). *Zur Entstehungsgeschichte des Marxschen "Kapital,"* Vol. 1. Frankfurt/Main: Europaische Verlagsanstalt.

Schumpeter, J. A. (1908). *Das Wesen und der Hauptinhalt der theoretischen Nationalökonomie,* Vol. 9.

[1912] (1926). *Theorie der wirtschaftlichen Entwicklung.* Leipzig: Duncker & Humblot.

(1914a). "Eine 'dynamische' Theorie des Kapitalzinses." *Zeitschrift für Volkswirtschaft, Sozialpolitik und Verwaltung,* 22:599–639.

(1914b). "Das wissenschaftliche Lebenswerk Eugen von Böhm-Bawerks," in *Zeitschrift für Volkswirtschaft, Sozialpolitik und Verwaltung,* 23:454–528.

[1939] (1961). *Business Cycles: A Theoretical, Historical, and Statistical Analysis of the Capitalist Process.* New York: McGraw-Hill (German edition, 1961, Göttingen).

(1951). *Ten Great Economists, from Marx to Keynes.* Oxford University Press.

Streissler, Erich (1981). "Schumpeter's Vienna and the Role of Credit in Innovation," in Helmut Frisch (ed.), *Schumpeterian Economics* (pp. 60–83). Vienna.

(1986). "Arma virumque cano, Friedrich von Wieser – the Bard as Economist," in Norbert Leser (ed.), *Die Wiener Schule der Nationalökonomie.* Vienna.

Wieser, Friedrich von (1914). "Theorie der gesellschaftlichen Wirtschaft," in *Grundiss der Sozialökonomik 1/1, Grundlagen der Wirtschaft.* Tübingen.

Discussion

YUICHI SHIONOYA

Let me begin with a general remark on method. The Morishima-Catephores (hereafter M-C) chapter is an application to Schumpeter of Morishima's method developed in his *Walras' Economics* (1977). In that book he paid attention to those views of Walras that were expressed in verbal terms but were not necessarily consistent with Walras's major mathematical model, because he found them important as a basis for Anti–Say's Law. Morishima's method is to revise

Walras's model so as to make it consistent with those views and derive their economic implications. This ingenious method in the history of economic thought, which I would call a "counterfactual method," may be compared to that of "new economic history," according to which one can reconstruct economic history by hypothetical theorizing: It is shown what past history would have been if the conditions and behaviors involved in the history had been different from those that actually obtained. One will never regard the counterfactual history as the actual one. Similarly, in the case of the history of economic thought, it is important to identify the major vision of an economist in question. Economists' visions of society are such a prescientific activity that these can include many views that are in conflict with each other. Even if it is possible, with hindsight, to reconstruct new models that are based on some of their visions, we should be careful in presenting these models as an interpretation and reconstruction of the authors' original models.

Specifically, M-C call Walras's "literary model" the verbal description that was not incorporated into his "mathematical model" and was concerned with, among other matters, a separation of the capitalist and the entrepreneur and a distinction between lending of money and physical capital. But it seems to me that his "literary model" is merely an institutional description of reality that ordinary people cannot fail to observe. Only his "mathematical model" was a theoretical construction. Relevant here will be his distinction between the usages "in reality," on the one hand, and "from the theoretical point of view," on the other, when he shifted from the former to the latter (Walras, [1874] 1954, p. 270).

Second, I have a doubt about M-C's conception of an independent investment function as the second presumption of Anti–Say's Law. It is my understanding that both Say's Law and Anti–Say's Law are consistent with the existence of an independent investment function. We can legitimately assume the same investment function (a Keynesian schedule of marginal efficiency of capital or fixed investment) in the neoclassical economy and in the Keynesian economy. Whether or not Say's Law holds true depends not on the absence or existence of an independent investment function but on the nature of adjustment between saving and investment. In the neoclassical economy, both investment and full-employment saving are equated by changes in the rate of interest; in the Keynesian economy, the rate of interest, determined by demand and supply of money, in turn determines investment, and saving is equated to investment by changes in the level of income.

In his 1937 article "The Theory of the Rate of Interest," Keynes clarified the difference between the classical theory and his own theory, starting from the commonly accepted proposition on the equality of supply price and demand price of a capital asset, which implies the equality of the marginal efficiency of capital and the rate of interest. It will be useful to quote his summary of the classical theory:

> To each possible value of the rate of interest there corresponds a given volume of saving; and to each possible value of the marginal efficiency of capital there corresponds a given volume of investment. Now the rate of interest and the marginal efficiency of capital must be equal. Thus the position of equilibrium is given by that common value of the rate of interest and of the marginal efficiency of capital at which the saving determined by the former is equal to the investment determined by the latter. (Keynes, [1937] 1973, p. 104)

I cannot find a reason why Keynes's formulation of the classical theory of interest should fail.

Third, when we discuss the relevance of Schumpeter to the school of Anti–Say's Law, we should notice the fact that the final establishment of Anti–Say's Law in Keynes required the formulation of a consumption (or saving) function in addition to the denial of the classical theory of interest that explains the equality of saving and investment. As I explained earlier, the mere existence of an independent investment function does not constitute Anti–Say's Law. Schumpeter's innovation of entrepreneurs as the cause of business cycles is nothing but an upward shift of the marginal efficiency of capital. Whereas M-C are right in emphasizing Schumpeter's proposition that investment is financed by bankers independent of saving, explicit formulation of a saving function that is not fixed at full-employment income is rather crucial for Anti–Say's Law.

Even after the publication of Keynes's *General Theory,* Schumpeter did not recognize the importance of the Keynesian saving–investment relation. In *Business Cycles* (1939), he explicitly wrote: "It is desirable ... to make quite sure that the saving–investment mechanism, as such, does not produce anything that could qualify for the role of an explanation of crises or depressions" (1939, Vol. 1, p. 78). "Most writers unduly stress the mere mechanics of the saving–investment process" (1939, Vol. 2, p. 1,034). In Chapter 28 of *Capitalism, Socialism and Democracy,* a new chapter added in the second edition in 1947, Schumpeter maintained this view even more clearly, referring to the Keynesian theory of stagnation in terms of the excess of saving over investment: "The salesman mentality of the country coupled with the experience of the twenty years preceding the war is all the explanation

I can offer for the astounding fact that the theory in question is not simply laughed out of court" (Schumpeter, 1947, p. 394).

Schumpeter's positive theory of saving and investment is rather that "decisions to save depend upon and presuppose decisions to invest" (1947, p. 396). This is Schumpeter's genuine alternative to both Say's Law and Anti–Say's Law and might be called an "inverted Say's Law." In spite of the crucial importance of a saving function, Schumpeter was so obstinate as to maintain that "our proposition shows that the stagnation thesis cannot be based upon the element of saving" (1947, p. 396).

In Schumpeter's own view, Anti–Say's Law was not his central problem. Although he was seriously concerned with business cycles, this does not mean in itself a departure from Say's Law or an access to Anti–Say's Law. Keynes aptly remarked in the 1937 article: "If I am right, the orthodox theory is wholly inapplicable to such problems as those of unemployment and the trade cycle, or, indeed, to any of the day-to-day problems of ordinary life. Nevertheless it is often in fact applied to such problems" (Keynes, [1937] 1973, p. 106). Thus, he pointed out the inconsistencies involved in the attempts of the contemporary economists. It is certain that Schumpeter departed from their camp. But whereas in his criticism of the orthodox theory Keynes was directly concerned with a change from Say's Law to Anti–Say's Law, Schumpeter was concerned with a change from statics to dynamics. Moreover, his view of the phases of business cycles as an inseparable, holistic process, which made it beside the point to worry about depression and unemployment, was tied up with his Walrasian or Saysian belief in the automatic adjustment mechanism of the capitalist economy.

Reference

Keynes, J. M. [1937] (1973). "The Theory of the Rate of Interest," in A. D. Gayer (ed.), *The Lessons of Monetary Experience: Essays in Honour of Irving Fisher;* reprinted 1973 in *Collected Writings of Keynes,* Vol. 14. London: Macmillan.

Morishima, M. (1977). *Walras' Economics.* Cambridge University Press.

Schumpeter, J. A. (1939). *Business Cycles* (2 vols.). New York: McGraw-Hill.
    (1942). *Capitalism, Socialism and Democracy.* New York: Harper & Brothers.
    (1947). *Capitalism, Socialism and Democracy* (2nd ed.). New York: Harper & Brothers.

Walras, L. [1874] (1954). *Elements of Pure Economics* (translated by W. Jaffé). London: Allen & Unwin.

Reply

MICHIO MORISHIMA AND GEORGE CATEPHORES

In the first part of his discussion, Professor Shionoya criticizes not our joint chapter in this book but a book written by one of us, *Walras' Economics* (Morishima, 1977), where the author of the book distinguishes two models, the "literary model" and the "mathematical model," as he calls them, respectively. Morishima observes them in Walras's analysis of general equilibrium of capital formation and credit. In the former, capitalists have money, which they lend to entrepreneurs, who buy the new capital goods they want and repay the money at the expiration of the loan; in the latter, the role of entrepreneurs is minimal, because this model delegates their role of deciding on investments to the savers by assuming that new capital goods are chosen and bought by capitalists and then lent to entrepreneurs in kind. Of course, the reality is nearer to the former than to the latter. But Walras himself, though acknowledging this fact, claims that it is immaterial, from the theoretical point of view, whether one adopts one or the other of the two.

Morishima questions this claim and has developed a mathematical model on the basis of Walras's description of the "literary model." In this new mathematical model, the deviation from Walras's own mathematical model is kept as small as possible. Then Morishima concludes that the distance between the newly constructed mathematical model and the Keynesian model is very small, because entrepreneurs (investors) and capitalists (savers) are independent in both of these models, so that Keynes's problems concerning effective demand, unemployment, and so forth, could have been dealt with by using this "Walrasian" model.

These points are all clear if one reads Walras's *Elements,* in particular pages 211–36 and 267–70, and Morishima's book, in particular Part II; also see Morishima (1980, pp. 554–7). However, Shionoya criticizes this treatment of Walras as a "counterfactual method." He says: "One will never regard the counterfactual history as the actual one." But all that Morishima has said is based on facts, and the careful reader will clearly see that he has presented the newly constructed model as his own model based on Walras's literary model. Where is a counterfactual element?

Mathematical analysis, such as that offered by Morishima concerning Walras's work, will become more and more important in the field of the history of economic thought, because in the future the historians will have to deal with works by great mathematical economists. A conventional historical method is certainly powerless for the purpose of clarifying their economic thought.

Second, on the basis of Keynes's 1937 article, Shionoya argues that Keynes describes the classical theory of interest as a theory that determines the rate of interest at a point where investment equals full-employment savings. But this is a view that very much distorts what Keynes is concerned with in that article.

Keynes, in fact, shows the opposite: The classical theory of interest described earlier is *not* valid unless the following very special assumptions are satisfied (Keynes, 1937, pp. 147–8):

1. "The marginal efficiency of money in terms of itself ... is independent of its quantity." (This means that the quantity theory of money does hold.)
2. "The scale of investment will not reach its equilibrium level until the point is reached at which the elasticity of supply of output as a whole has fallen to zero."

Keynes then argues that full-employment equilibrium may not be realized if these peculiarities are removed and replaced by more realistic, general assumptions (Keynes, 1937, p. 148):

1. "The marginal efficiency of money in terms of itself is, in general, a function of its quantity."
2. "Aggregate investment may reach its equilibrium rate ... before the elasticity of supply of output as a whole has fallen to zero."

He thus concludes that classical economics assumes "a state of affairs very different from that in which we live" (Keynes, 1937, p. 152) that collapses when faced with a general investment function decided by entrepreneurs independent from savings.

Finally, referring to Schumpeter's general proposition that "decisions to save depend upon and presuppose decisions to invest" (Schumpeter, [1942] 1976, p. 396), Shionoya concludes that "this is Schumpeter's genuine alternative to both Say's Law and Anti–Say's Law and might be called an 'inverted Say's law.'" But what does he mean by an inverted Say's Law? If he means that demand creates its own supply in the sense that savings are adjusted and equalized to any given level of investment, then the law is nothing else but Keynes's principle of effective demand. Alternatively, if he means by it the absence of the savings function, the Schumpeter thus interpreted would, as will be seen later, be far and remote from Schumpeter himself.

It is clear from what Schumpeter writes in that part of his book that he does not subscribe to the simple savings function as is proposed by Keynes as a psychological law. In fact, he says:

Normally people save with a view to some return, in money or in services of some "investment good." It is not only that the bulk of individual savings – and, of course, practically all business savings which, in turn, constitute the greater part of total saving – is done with a specific investment purpose in view. The decision to invest precedes as a rule, and the act of investing precedes very often, the decision to save. (Schumpeter, [1942] 1976, p. 395)

This passage simply means that savings are decided by examining opportunities for investment and calculating and comparing returns from them, rather than by a psychological law. It also obviously implies that savings are not identically equal to investment at every point in time. Schumpeter allows for possibilities of excess savings and excess investment. Where savings are not equal to investment, the bond market or other financial markets will be in a state of disequilibrium. Then the prices of bonds, stocks, and shares and the rates of interest will be adjusted so as to clear all the financial markets. Then investment and savings will be stimulated or discouraged and eventually will be equalized with each other, when all financial markets are settled in a state of equilibrium. Corresponding to the level of investment finally reached, an aggregate equilibrium output is obtained, but it may not necessarily be great enough to secure full employment.

We have now to conclude, regrettably, by saying that in spite of the existence of the passage Shionoya quotes in the exact place he mentions, the conclusion he derives from it is far different from, and contrary to, what Schumpeter actually maintains in the relevant part of his book. The same is unfortunately true for Shionoya's discussion of Keynes's article. He thus completely fails to see what Keynes and Schumpeter say.

References

Keynes, J. M. (1937). "The Theory of the Rate of Interest," in A. D. Gayer (ed.), *The Lessons of Monetary Experience*. London: George Allen & Unwin.

Morishima, M. (1977). *Walras' Economics*. Cambridge University Press.

(1980). "W. Jaffé on Leon Walras: A Comment." *Journal of Economic Literature,* 18:550–8.

Schumpeter, J. A. [1942] (1976). *Capitalism, Socialism and Democracy*. London: George Allen & Unwin.

CHAPTER 3

Schumpeter and technical change

ARNOLD HEERTJE

But is it really untrue to life or artificial to keep separate the phenomena incidental to running a firm and the phenomena incidental to creating a new one?

J. Schumpeter (1961, p. xi)

3.1 Introduction

Schumpeter's emphasis on the significance of innovations for dynamic competition, business cycles, long waves, and the evolution of capitalism has given rise to the opinion that he made a major contribution to the economic theory of technical change.[1] This chapter examines the question whether or not and to what extent this view is justified. To this end I describe in Section 3.2 not only the evolution of Schumpeter's view on the concept of innovation but also his views on such concepts as the entrepreneur, economic development, and business cycles, which are closely linked to his theory of innovation. It is noteworthy how the actual contents of these very essential concepts and the analysis of the connections between them gradually change in his publications from 1908 until his death in 1950.

Sections 3.3 and 3.4 are devoted to a more detailed discussion of innovation and its relation to technical change and the production function. In Section 3.3, I discuss my view that Schumpeter's interpretation of innovation is both broader and narrower than his interpretation of technical change. I argue that Schumpeter did not present us with an economic theory of the process of technical change, although the stimulus he provided for empirical research and analysis of technical change is beyond dispute. As Schumpeter also identified innovations with the setting up of a new production function, I consider it appropriate to confront Schumpeter's view on innovations with pos-

The author wishes to thank Professor P. Hennipman for his helpful critical notes.

[1] Useful general guidelines to Schumpeter's thinking are provided by Perroux (1965), Wolff (1982, pp. 65–163), and Clemence and Doody (1951).

sible interpretations of the production function. The argument underlines the conclusion drawn in the preceding paragraph.

In Schumpeter's vision, enormous importance is assigned to the behavior of the elite in society, in particular the entrepreneurs, whose drive for innovation is based on a rough and partly impulsive comparison of uncertain benefits and accountable costs, and who, in the process, are changing the economy from within. Profits should not be regarded solely as the financial outcome of economic activities; they also reflect the entrepreneur's social prestige. Since the 1970s, these basic ideas have led to what may be called a body of Schumpeterian economics, although Schumpeter himself did not produce a school, and even was opposed to the idea.[2] The questions he raised have opened a field of research that may be called Schumpeterian economics, even if the analytical methods used are not always similar to his, and the answers given are in contradiction to the conclusions he reached and the predictions he made.

Section 3.5 provides a brief sketch of the main topics of Schumpeterian economics.

3.2   Innovation, the entrepreneur, and economic development in Schumpeter's writings

In his first book (1908), Schumpeter hinted more than once at new combinations; at a later date he called these changes in production and the market system "innovation." These activities are essential for the explanation of interest, which has to be paid on loans to create new industries, new forms of organization, new technologies, and new products.[3] Interest and profit exist only in a dynamic setting, where development and change are taking place.[4] According to Schumpeter, economic theory prior to the beginning of this century *implied a purely static analysis in which development did not take place,* so that neither interest nor profit could be explained within the system.[5] In the last

---

[2] "Wenn ich eine Funktion habe, dann die Türen nicht zusondern aufzumachen, und niemals habe ich das Bestreben gehabt, so etwas zustande zu bringen wie eine Schumpeterschule" (Schumpeter, 1952, p. 600). The quotation is from his valedictory speech at the University of Bonn in June 1932.

[3] "Für die Erklärung des Zinses sind also jene Neuschöpfungen entscheidend" (Schumpeter, 1908, pp. 417, 425).

[4] "Wieviel wurde die Statik und die Nationalökonomie überhaupt gewinnen, wenn man auch für Zins und Gewinn dauernde Quellen wie Arbeit und Boden, also z.B. Abstinenz und ein besonderen 'Unternehmerdienst' annehmen könnte" (Schumpeter, 1908, p. 440).

[5] "... alle Krisentheorien, was immer ihre Natur und ihr Wert sein mag, sind essentiell dynamisch" (Schumpeter, 1908, pp. 587–8).

chapter of that book on possible developments in economic theory, Schumpeter refers rather vaguely to "new combinations of elements of our system."[6] Applied technology and economics do influence one another, whereas technology and economics as theoretical subjects are independent of each other.[7] Schumpeter asks whether or not we can have economic development. Of course, we can. The question is, however, whether or not economic development can be explained by economic causes. To that end, an "energetic" economic theory is needed.[8]

A few years later, Schumpeter published his book on the theory of economic development, in which much attention is paid to the psychological characteristics of the happy few in society who take initiative and who can be described as men of action.[9] These individuals determine economic development because they bring about a fundamental and discontinuous endogenous change in the economy. All other changes in the economy are due to exogenous causes, coming from outside. Within an economic context, creative individuals[10] are the initiators of different allocations of resources.[11] A first example of such a new combination is the production of an entirely new product. Schumpeter also considers the introduction of a new quality or a new application of an existing product as a new combination. The same applies to a new method of production of an existing product. The opening up of a new market, a change in the economic organization, such as the creation of a trust or the introduction of large-scale production, are other examples of new combinations. The most typical case, however, which encompasses all possibilities and represents the

6 " . . . neue Kombinationen der elemente unseres Systemes" (Schumpeter, 1908, p. 602).
7 " . . . Wir glauben dass die Einfürung und der Methoden und Theoremen der Ökonomie in das Gebiet der Technik zu praktisch wie theoretisch wertvollen Resultaten führen wird und im Prinzipe ohne Weiteres möglich ist" (Schumpeter, 1908, p. 61).
8 "Noch mehr liesse sich anderes, wie z.B. das Moment des 'effort' vielleicht zu einer 'energetischen' Theorie der Ökonomie verwerten, die etwas über eine ökonomische Entwichlung sagen könnte" (Schumpeter, 1908, p. 621).
9 "die Bedeutung unseres Typus für unsre Zweck liegt darin das wir in ihm das Gesuchte agens der Entwicklung finden." They belong to the category of dynamic or energetic individuals, to be distinguished from the category of static or hedonistic individuals (Schumpeter, 1912, p. 147).
10 "Das schöpferischen Gestalten verandert, wie wir sehen werden, die Daten auch der statischen Wirtschaften" (Schumpeter, 1912, p. 154); " . . . die stärksten Individualitäten werden anders handeln, als man nach den Sätzen der Statik annehmen sollte. Aber wie? Sie werden Neues schaffen und Altes zerstoren . . . " (Schumpeter, 1912, p. 157).
11 "Das ist es, was wir unter der Durchsetzung neuer Kombinationen verstehen" (Schumpeter, 1912, p. 158).

new organizational, commercial, and technical aspects, is the formation of a new enterprise. In that book, Schumpeter has, in general, the creation of a new firm in mind when writing about new combinations, and he regards the previously mentioned fundamental changes that start within existing firms as partially new combinations.[12] The question is how a new combination will be implemented. Schumpeter points out that the new combinations exist in the minds of a small group of economic subjects.[13]

Most people do not recognize the new possibilities.[14] Apart from the perception of the economic potential of new combinations, individuals have to make good use of the possibilities in order to realize a new combination. In a modern economy, the individual known as an entrepreneur is a man of action, with energy and willpower, who implements the new combinations, although they are not necessarily discovered by him.

It is essential to distinguish between the stock of technical knowledge in general and the knowledge actually applied in production. The role of the entrepreneur differs fundamentally from that of the inventor.[15] In Schumpeter's vision, the entrepreneur needs the bank to create the money with which to finance the implementation of new combinations, which are expected to be more profitable than the old ones. Risk is undertaken not by the entrepreneur but by those who provide the money. Profits are directly related to the entrepreneur in his role as the man of action who organizes the new combinations. But profits disappear as followers or imitators enter the market and copy the new combination, an undertaking for which no entrepreneurial capacity is needed. This view is particularly relevant when there is a question of a newly established firm that markets a new product. Then, to a large extent, the entrepreneurial profit means a monopoly of profit.

Economic development starts endogenously with entrepreneurs who destroy the static economic circular flow by introducing new combinations.[16] The entrepreneurs are followed by others, who are less pioneering, but who nevertheless contribute to the upswing. After

---

[12] " . . . eine partielle Neugründung" (Schumpeter, 1912, p. 160).

[13] "In der Psyche einer kleinen Gruppe der Wirtschafts-subjekte" (Schumpeter, 1912, p. 162).

[14] "Eine Minorität von Leuten mit einer schärfern Intelligenz und einer beweglichern Phantasie sehen zahllose neue Kombinationen" (Schumpeter, 1912, p. 143).

[15] " . . . für die Vorgänge der Wirtschaft kommt nur der Unternehmer in Betracht, Erfindungen haben dafür enie ganz sekundäre Rolle – sie vermehren nur die ohnehin schon unbegrenste Zahl der vorhandenen Möglichkeiten" (Schumpeter, 1912, p. 179).

[16] "Es wächst die Wirtschaft nicht von selbst in höheren Formen herein" (Schumpeter, 1912, p. 487).

some time, profits decline, banks are less prepared to continue their financing, and restructuring is needed to cope with the effects of the disruption during the upswing. Schumpeter's two-period scheme is simple, but it integrates growth and cyclical elements.[17] The second edition of Schumpeter's book on economic development was published in 1926. The analysis is shorter, more precise, and, in Schumpeter's own words (1926, p. xii), more correct. The second chapter on the basic issues of economic development has been completely rewritten. Schumpeter now introduces the concept of innovation, although not as a reaction to new wants of consumers. The new wants are provoked by the supply side, so that demand and supply are no longer independent of each other, as is still the usual assumption in static neoclassical theory. If innovations take place that through the supply side influence the demand side of the economy, it is no longer possible to describe the economic phenomena in terms of a traditional equilibrium of demand and supply (Schumpeter, 1926, p. 100). This important idea of the dependence of consumer preferences on innovations on the supply side was not further elaborated in later publications by Schumpeter, nor, as far as I know, by any other economist.

From Schumpeter's point of view, economic development refers to the implementation of new combinations in a discontinuous manner. To the list of new combinations mentioned in the first edition of his book, he adds the conquest of a new source of supply of raw material or semimanufactured goods, irrespective of whether this source already exists or must be created. On the other hand, Schumpeter now omits his emphasis on the establishment of new firms as the typical form of implementation of new combinations. He now points out that the new combination may be introduced by those who already control the old combination, or by individuals who enter the entrepreneurial scene for the first time, so that both economic and social changes take place in a discontinuous manner.[18] The said individuals are then called entrepreneurs. The new combination makes use of idle capacity, in particular of labor, but as a rule a reallocation of resources takes place.

The chapter on business cycles raises the question why economic development does not follow a regular path, but is characterized by periods of prosperity and depression. Schumpeter's answer to this question is very straightforward and precise. Because the innovations

[17] "Die Entwickelung ist ihrem innersten Wesen nach eine Störung der bestehenden statischen Gleichgewichts ohne jede Tendenz diesem oder überhaupt irgendeinem andern Gleichgewichtszustande wieder zu zustreben" (Schumpeter, 1912, p. 489).

[18] " . . . es waren, im allgemeinen nicht die Postmeister, welche die Eisenbahnen gründeten" (Schumpeter, 1926, p. 101).

take place in bursts, new firms do not emerge independent of each other. Where one leads, another follows, facilitating and compelling others to take part in the upswing. In most cases, the new combinations do not drive out the old ones, but compete with them. The new firms exercise an investment demand, and the process of innovation inevitably entails mistakes, which are to be corrected in the depression. The innovators are followed by imitators, who pave the way for the depression, insofar as profits decline. The fact that innovations appear in bursts explains both the phase of prosperity and the subsequent period of depression, which must be regarded as the economy striving for a new equilibrium.[19]

In the preface of the new English edition of that book, published in 1934, Schumpeter observes that he no longer takes it for granted that there is only a single wave-like movement (Schumpeter, 1961, p. ix). In his opinion there are at least three such movements, a viewpoint that is worked out in detail in his 1939 book on business cycles. Starting from the idea that on the time scale there are neighborhoods of equilibrium, in which the system approaches equilibrium, innovations are introduced as the disturbing factors that move the system out of these neighborhoods. The standard case is now the introduction of new commodities, nowadays called product innovations. However, innovation also covers technological change in the production of commodities already in use, the opening up of new markets or of new sources of supply, Taylorization of work, improved handling of material, and the setting up of new forms of business organization, such as department stores. Innovation and invention are clearly distinguished. Schumpeter acknowledges that most innovations can be traced to theoretical or practical knowledge in the immediate or remote past. But innovation is also possible without inventions, and inventions do not necessarily induce innovation. In Schumpeter's view, as expressed here, invention is of no importance to economic analysis and therefore must be considered an exogenous factor. Innovation, on the contrary, is an endogenous phenomenon because it is entirely a matter of business behavior. He describes the changes in the economic process brought about by innovation, all their effects, and the responses to them by the economic system as "economic evolution."

Schumpeter goes on to define innovation as the setting up of a new production function.[20] In his view, this definition covers the different

---

[19] " . . . Das Ringen der Volkswirtschaft um einen neuen, den durch die 'Störung' des Aufschwungs veränderten Daten angepasten Gleichgewichtszustand" (Schumpeter, 1926, p. 342).

[20] "If we vary the form of the function we have an innovation" (Schumpeter, 1939, p. 87).

cases of new combinations put forward in his earlier books. He also observes that innovation entails construction of new plant and equipment and assumes that they require much time and investment. Schumpeter restricts innovations to these important cases. Furthermore, he argues as though every innovation is embodied in a new firm (Schumpeter, 1939, pp. 94, 96) and is always associated with the rise to leadership of new men. This last assumption explains why new production functions do not typically grow out of old businesses. However, Schumpeter adds that in the case of big concerns, the innovations may take place within the company, so that new men, but no new firms, are associated with it. The concept of "trustified capitalism" is introduced to take care of this phenomenon. This world of a few established giant concerns differs from that of competitive capitalism, in which many new firms compete with one another, and, in particular, new firms enter permanently.

Innovations tend to cluster and to be concentrated in certain sectors of the economy (Schumpeter, 1939, pp. 100–1). Furthermore, they disrupt the system, whether the innovating firms are large or small. The individuals who carry out the innovations are still called the entrepreneurs. Risk bearing is no part of the entrepreneurial function; it is the capitalist who eventually may lose the money involved. Entrepreneurial profit in a competitive society is the premium put on successful innovation. It is temporary by nature and will vanish in the subsequent process of competition, adoption, and imitation. Schumpeter generalizes this case of the emergence of profits to other innovations and other market conditions.[21]

Entrepreneurial activity moves the system away from the neighborhood of equilibrium to the upside, but with the release of new products, it becomes more difficult to calculate costs and benefits, and the difficulty of planning and the risk of failure increase (Schumpeter, 1939, p. 135). In the end, the innovative activity ceases completely. The system shows adaptation to the new things created, including the elimination of what is incapable of adaptation and resorption of the results of innovation, and it leads to a new neighborhood of equilibrium, with new production functions and zero profits, in which enterprise will occur again (Schumpeter, 1939, p. 107).

Economic evolution is characterized by upward-moving neighborhoods of equilibrium that are separated from one another by two dis-

[21] Compare his remark in the preface to the Japanese edition of *The Theory of Economic Development,* published in 1937: "Practically every innovation, especially if it consists in the introduction of a new combination, at first creates that kind of situation which is designated by the term Monopolistic Competition" (Schumpeter, 1951, p. 162).

tinct phases. During the first, the system draws away from equilibrium under the impulse of innovations, and during the second, it moves to another equilibrium (Schumpeter, 1939, p. 138). This process of internal change can be regarded as a cyclical movement. This simple scheme consists of two phases only, namely, prosperity and recession; the more complicated scheme, due to traditional factors of the business cycle, consists of prosperity, recession, depression, and recovery. During the phases of depression and recovery, the neighborhood of equilibrium is below the level it reaches in the simple scheme (Schumpeter, 1939, p. 148). Schumpeter now argues that there is no reason why the cyclical process of evolution should give rise to only one wavelike movement. Innovations, being at the root of cyclical movements, differ in periods of gestation and in absorption of effects. In the 1939 book, therefore, Schumpeter concludes that there are three classes of cycles: Kondratieff, Juglar, and Kitchin. The first Kondratieff cycle extends from 1789 until 1842, the second from 1842 until 1897, and the third from 1898 on.

The influence of the longer waves on the short waves makes it possible that the process of innovation not only may start from a neighborhood of equilibrium but also may start when the long wave is in full swing. In Schumpeter's view, there is no distinction between trend and cycle; the trend, being understood as successive neighborhoods of equilibrium, is simply the result of the cyclical process or a property of it. In order to express this, Schumpeter calls it the "result trend" (1939, p. 206).

We now turn to Schumpeter's book on the development of capitalism, probably his best-known work: *Capitalism, Socialism and Democracy* (1942). In the books mentioned earlier, he discusses growth, development, economic development, economic evolution, and business cycles primarily as a result of innovations, but in the 1942 book he also deals with the effects of innovation on the evolution of capitalism. However, as the following quotation shows, his characteristic approach, in which he combines analysis with the definition of concepts, is still very much in evidence:

Capitalism, then, is by nature a form or method of economic change and not only is but never can be stationary. And this evolutionary character of the capitalist process is not merely due to the fact that economic life goes on in a social and natural environment which changes and by its change alters the data of economic actions; this fact is important and these changes (wars, revolutions and so on) often condition industrial change, but they are not its prime movers. Nor is this evolutionary character due to a quasi-automatic increase in population and capital or to the vagaries of monetary systems of which exactly the same thing holds true. The fundamental impulse that sets and keeps the capitalist engine in motion comes from the new consumers' goods, the new methods of production or transportation, the new markets, the new forms of industrial organization that capitalist enterprise creates. (Schumpeter, 1942, pp. 82–3)

The main characterizing feature of capitalism is the introduction of new combinations. This endogenous process, which Schumpeter calls creative destruction, incessantly revolutionizes the economic structure from within, and this is the essential fact about capitalism. The large monopolistic enterprises bring the innovations into effect in their hunt for profits, and they are the special modus operandi of capitalism, manifested in the expansion of production. Schumpeter admits that the productive capacity of capitalism could also be explained by factors that are independent of capitalism. After rejecting several external factors, however, he wonders if the special features of capitalism are due to that stream of inventions that revolutionized the techniques of production rather than to the businessman's hunt for profits (1942, p. 110). The answer is no, because the essence of that hunt is to bring about these changes, and invention itself is a function of the capitalistic process, so that it no longer has the exogenous character it had in his previous publications. The rate of growth of production is not reduced because the technical possibilities are exhausted, but the outlook for capitalism becomes gloomy because a change in the function of entrepreneurs takes place. The function of the entrepreneur is to innovate, and it consists in getting things done, but this social function he sees as losing its importance. On the other hand, it is now easier than before to do things that lie outside familiar routine – innovation itself being reduced to routine. Technical process is increasingly becoming the business of teams of trained specialists who turn out what is required and make it work in predictable ways. On the other hand, characteristics such as personality and willpower count for less in environments that have become accustomed to technical change (1942, p. 132). Economic development acquires an impersonal and mechanical character.

Because capitalist enterprise, by its very achievements, tends to automatize progress, we conclude that it tends to make itself superfluous – to break to pieces under the pressure of its own success. The perfectly bureaucratized giant industrial unit not only ousts the small or medium-size firm and "expropriates" its owners but also, in the end, ousts the entrepreneur and expropriates the bourgeoisie as a class, which in the process stands to lose not only its income but also what is infinitely more important, its function. The true pacemakers of socialism were not the intellectuals or agitators who preached it, but the Vanderbilts, Carnegies, and Rockefellers (Schumpeter, 1942, p. 134).

It is of the utmost importance to note that Schumpeter no longer refers to the establishment of new firms or to the entry of new entrepreneurs; innovative activity, if it exists at all, is concentrated in large monopolistic firms that block potential competition.[22]

Finally, I refer to Schumpeter's observation – more or less in passing – on the character of technical change. Whereas technical change is generally seen as purely labor-saving, Schumpeter states that new technological methods tend to become increasingly capital-saving and that in fact almost any new process that is economically workable economizes on both labor and capital (1942, p. 119–20).

In his monumental work on the history of economic analysis, Schumpeter's interpretation of the production function comes more to the fore than in any of his other works (Schumpeter, 1954). In this work, the production function comprises "the given technological possibilities *within the horizons* of producers" (1954, p. 1,026). A change in the technical horizon, by the discovery of a new method of production or making a known process financially feasible, leads to a new production function. Later, Schumpeter, seemingly without realizing it, gives a wider definition by placing the production function "in a world of blueprints, where every element that is technologically variable at all can be changed at will, without any loss of time, and without any expense" (1954, p. 1,031). Furthermore, he recognizes explicitly a third interpretation of the production function that concerns enterprises that actually exist: a "realistic" production function, which can be constructed on the basis of factual observations of production and factors of production, and which should be clearly distinguished from the "logically pure" production function (1954, p. 1,031).

This brief overview of Schumpeter's publications in German and English, from which I singled out in particular his discussion of the importance and the effects of innovations, illustrates that some important changes have occurred. Although I stuck to the main body of his dynamic framework, which constitutes in particular his evolutionary view of capitalism, the fact that he seems to have lost sight of the relative importance of the establishment of new, often small firms as the carriers of major innovations does fundamentally influence his per-

---

[22] The importance of the shift from the initial emphasis on entrepreneurs who are outsiders to entrepreneurs working within a big firm has also been mentioned (Winter, 1984, pp. 294–5); see also Herbert and Link (1982, p. 80).

spective on the decay of capitalism. To identify innovation with the setting up of a new production function is, on one hand, a refinement, but at the same time it is a restriction of this analysis.

3.3   Innovation and technical change

Let us therefore confront Schumpeter's concept of innovation with technical change. The process of technical change consists of the development of new technical possibilities, the application of new technical possibilities, and the diffusion of these applications. Principally, Schumpeter's innovations belong to the category of applications, but not all of them have the character of a technical innovation. For example, the opening up of a new market may, but need not, imply a product innovation. An existing product may be introduced in another market, so that a commercial but not a technical innovation is at stake. As he wrote himself, not only technical but also commercial and organizational innovations in Schumpeter's writings encompass more than just technology.

Part of the technical innovations summed up by Schumpeter are nowadays called process innovations, and others are known as product innovations. In Schumpeter's scheme, the process innovations, which are fundamental, belong to the category of technical change embodied in capital. New capital goods are needed to implement new technology. It is interesting to note that Schumpeter draws the attention to capital-saving technical change not only because in most literature the emphasis is on the labor-saving aspect but also in the light of the striking capital-saving character of the recent boom in new technology.

Of course, even in the technical sense, innovation is only one aspect of the process of technical change. Originally, Schumpeter conceived of innovations as independent of invention, and he treated invention as an exogenous factor without any economic implications. In his later work on trustified capitalism, he presented a slightly more integrated view of invention and innovation, both being products of giant firms with strong market positions, and invention, moreover, being the product of investment in research and development. This change in emphasis goes along, more or less, with a change in view about the entrepreneurial function. In Schumpeter's earlier work, the entrepreneur is an outsider who sets up a new firm with a new product and new capital equipment. On a small scale, new combinations, not invented by him but chosen out of a set of technical possibilities, are carried out. In his later work, the entrepreneur may also be a manager of an already existing and established firm, usually large, with a department for research and development, so that invention and innovation are linked to one another. Within this context, the innovative role of the entrepreneur is less prominent.

There is no theory of the diffusion of technical change in Schumpeter's writings. However, the role of imitators of the original innovations in the cyclical process of economic evolutions may be considered a vehicle for diffusion of applications of new methods of production and of product innovations. The imitations are governed by the profit motive, just like the innovations, but there is no theoretical analysis of the speed of diffusion or of the time pattern. In this respect, Schumpeter discusses the length of the waves emerging from the burst of innovation. However, he restricts himself to a few general remarks on the influence of the importance, character, and speed of adjustment to the innovation.

Schumpeter's discussion of innovations and the role innovation plays in the processes of economic development, economic evolution, the business cycle, and capitalism explains why Schumpeter's name is often mentioned in connection with economic analysis of technical change. In particular, his treatment of innovation as an endogenous process, triggered by entrepreneurs who implement new combinations in order to make profits, justifies this impression.

On the other hand, technical change, in the strict sense of the development of new technical knowledge and possibilities, and the diffusion of knowledge are almost wholly absent from his exposition. So it seems fair to conclude that Schumpeter dealt only incidentally with technology and that he did not present us with a systematic economic analysis of technical change.

3.4   Innovation and the production function

In the course of his discussion of innovation, Schumpeter identifies innovation with the setting up of a new production function. I would therefore like to discuss more thoroughly the possible interpretations of the production function in view of Schumpeter's description of innovations.

Empirical production functions, which link the actual recorded output at the microeconomic level with the actual factor inputs, should be sharply distinguished from theoretical production functions, which describe the relationship of production and the factors of production ex ante. In the latter, the production function tells us which technical possibilities are available to the firm. In a simple model, the combination of the factors of production chosen is determined by the objectives of the firm and the prices of the factors. In principle, such equilibrium combinations are reflected in the empirical data. In empirical investigations, however, by studying the behavior ex post of output and input over time, one examines a whole set of relationships, of which the theoretical production function is only one element.

We can divide theoretical production functions into subjective and objective types. The subjective variant comprises the technical possibilities known to the firm, so that the production function expresses the technical knowledge that the firm possesses. The production function then does not reflect the general state of technology, because this may be more advanced. The objective function, on the other hand, reflects technology in general. If a complete and instantaneous diffusion of technical knowledge is assumed, there is no difference between the two interpretations of the production function. In practice, however, this assumption is not justified, partly because the diffusion of technical knowledge is inevitably slow and partly because it is deliberately opposed by enterprises that have incurred financial costs to acquire the new technical knowledge. By applying for a patent, the firm abandons secrecy, but this does not promote the diffusion of knowledge needed for application of the new methods and products in society.

As a rule, new empirical production functions are brought about by innovations, and new theoretical production functions by inventions. The relevance of the distinction between objective and subjective production functions, in both the empirical and theoretical senses, is determined by the process of diffusion of new insights and new applications in the sphere of technology. The diffusion process transfers subjective knowledge within the horizon of a firm into general information about the new methods of production and new products.

According to Schumpeter's interpretation, innovations are taken broadly, so that commercial and organizational changes of a discontinuous character are also implied. The production function, being, by definition a description of the technological aspect of production, is not suitable to describe those nontechnical innovations. For example, the opening up of a new market as such can hardly be seen as the setting up of a new method of production. These examples indicate that Schumpeter had the empirical production function in mind.

However, a critical assessment of his ideas is difficult, because he does not explicitly state to which of the possible interpretations of the production function he is referring. According to his subjective interpretation, the production function expresses the technical possibilities that lie within the horizon of the entrepreneur. This means that a new theoretical function is created whenever the entrepreneur increases his technical knowledge. Practical application of the techniques known to him does not shift the production function, so that according to this subjective interpretation, an innovation does not give rise to a new production function. Schumpeter's second interpretation implies that the production function fully reflects the state of technology. Here again, the application of an available technique does not lead to a new production function. In his terminology, only an invention (not an innovation) will give rise to a new theoretical production function. Only his third interpretation of the production function, according to which the production function describes how production and the factors of production are related in practice, is compatible with product or process innovations. Then the actual application of a new combination means that a new production function emerges.

The objection to this last version is that the empirical production function no longer provides a survey of the technical alternatives; it reflects the entrepreneur's decision, based on technical and economic considerations. Furthermore, because even in the case of constant technology, a change in relative factor prices leads to a new empirical production function, the emergence of a new empirical production function can no longer be identified with a technical innovation.

If Schumpeter's second interpretation is accepted, an innovation does not cause a shift in the production function, because it does not involve a change in the technical knowledge available. Because this second interpretation is the dominant one in economic thought, it is surprising that the view that Schumpeter dealt in depth with technical development is rather popular. If one adopts the notion that practical application of a known technique leads to greater technical knowledge, then innovation can give rise to a new production function, again according to Schumpeter's second interpretation. In that case, however, his distinction between inventions and innovations is less sharp.

This confirms the conclusion that Schumpeter did not really analyze the development of technical possibilities and their effects on economic life, despite his often fascinating account of what he calls the dynamics of capitalism. The central features in his theory are the emergence of entrepreneurs with certain psychological characteristics and the effects of their innovations, rather than the more objective aspects of the technology of production.

The conclusion that Schumpeter was only incidentally concerned with technical change as such does not detract from the special position accorded to him in this field. Schumpeter's sharp distinction between innovations and inventions has triggered several reactions, and both theoretical analysis and empirical research have been directed to the question whether or not innovations are really as independent of inventions as Schumpeter, on the whole, supposed. A critical evaluation of Schumpeter's theory has led to a discussion on the nature of technical change, the length of the period between an invention and its application, and the diffusion of new techniques. Mansfield, who has made some important contributions in this field, remarks that, quite apart from the question whether or not an invention and its application should be so sharply separated, "innovation is a key stage in the process leading to the full evaluation and utilization of an invention" (1968, p. 83).

3.5   Innovation and Schumpeterian economics after Schumpeter

Schumpeter's concern with the fundamental changes in economic life showed the limited value of static equilibrium theory. Even today, his vision is a stimulus to economic theory and research, as may be seen from the following list of topics inspired by his work. First of all, I am inclined to regard the recent neo-Austrian literature – in which the market is viewed as a dynamic process of creative discovery, instead of merely as a mechanism for the static allocation of scarce resources – as a direct elaboration of Schumpeter's vision on the innovative character of monopolistic market structures. The idea that entrepreneurs operate in a world of partly unknown preferences of consumers, partly unknown technical possibilities, and uncertain prospects of their activities and that they therefore try to gather information about profitable new methods of production and new products and in doing so discover marketable projects that keep the capitalistic machinery going has Schumpeter's process of creative destruction as its background.[23]

Other Schumpeterian approaches include studies in which changes within and between firms, changes in the market structure within and between industries, and changes in competitive performance within and between nations are related to the diversity of technical change at the level of development, diffusion, and application of new methods and products. These approaches build on Schumpeter's concepts of invention, innovation, and imitation. The well-known book by Nelson and Winter (1982), in which concepts like natural trajectories and technological regimes describe the purely technical developments in a

---

[23] Hayek (1948, pp. 77–91); see also Machlup (1977, pp. 13–59) and Kirzner (1973, 1979, 1985). A short introduction to neo-Austrian thinking is presented by Littlechild (1986).

more precise and general way than is the case with Schumpeter's concept of innovation, is a notable example. Their evolutionary theory of economic growth is basically microeconomic, as it centers around non-maximizing firms, for which innovations involve a change in routine. In this sense it has much in common with Schumpeter's thinking. Nelson and Winter also share his descriptive and institutional approach. But their writing, as well as that of others, introduces formal model building into the evolutionary approach.[24] A promising new development is the application of catastrophe theory to the innovative behavior of Schumpeterian entrepreneurs (Ursprung, 1984).

A particular feature of these evolutionary models is the possible emergence of new firms and new industries, an aspect that goes back to Schumpeter's earlier writings, but that is omitted in his later publications. One of the reasons for Schumpeter's prediction of the decay of capitalism lies in his overlooking the fact, which we are experiencing again, that, notwithstanding the existence of large, monopolistic firms, the process of technical change also appears to be accompanied by the establishment of many new firms operating on a small scale.

To a certain extent, the modern formal theory of macroeconomic disequilibrium goes back to Schumpeter, insofar as markets are not cleared by price adjustments. If product innovation, rather than price competition, is characteristic of the competitive struggle, markets are permanently out of equilibrium, so that stocks of goods and of factors of production pile up and finally find their way into the informal sector of the economy. Although the analysis of this situation is farfetched, an element of Schumpeterian flavor cannot be denied.

The recent literature on the long wave in economic life is more directly related to Schumpeter. There is an important discussion, on a theoretical and empirical level, of the questions whether or not basic innovations appear in clusters and whether or not they are able to explain a long wave.[25] Not all participants in the debate are convinced that a long cycle really exists. There is also a serious discussion about the selection of innovations that are responsible for the upswing in the cycle. However, time and again, the literature on long waves refers back to Schumpeter, sometimes confirming his views, sometimes criticizing them, but always using them as a major source of inspiration.[26]

---

[24] See, for example, Sato and Tsutsui (1984, pp. 1–38).

[25] "The analytical framework is too narrow, too fragile, to carry the weight of explaining business cycles" (Goodwin, 1983, p. 610).

[26] Examples are van Duijn (1983), Freeman (1984), Rosenberg and Frischtak (1984, pp. 7–24), and Solomon (1986, pp. 101–12).

I may add that this literature restricts itself to technical change in the applied sense of process innovations and product innovations and to the diffusion of those applications, leaving aside the development and diffusion of new technical possibilities, in short, inventions.

Lastly, Schumpeter's thoughts on the effects of the size and monopoly power of firms on technical change have given a strong impetus to the study of perhaps the most important question in economics, namely, the relationship between technical change and the market structure.[27] The attempts to determine market structure and inventive activity simultaneously appear to be very promising.[28]

3.6   Conclusion

We could dispute for a long time the question whether or not Schumpeter's emphasis on the entrepreneur as the individual who carries out innovations should be considered a theory of technical development.[29] In my opinion, this would go too far. As far as major innovations are concerned, Schumpeter pays far more attention to their effects and consequences than to analysis of the innovation process itself. The main reason for entrepreneurs to innovate is their hunt for profits.

Schumpeter's insight is indispensable for a better understanding of the dynamics of capitalism, but many questions are left open, such as the time pattern and nature of applications of new technology. When will the new technology be implemented? What is the role of demand factors, in particular, in the case of new products? What kind of equipment will be introduced?

In Schumpeter's conception of innovation, the continuous stream of minor improvements in equipment and products, sometimes called continuous technical development (Heertje, 1977, p. 70), is completely lacking. Even more striking is the absence of theories of invention and diffusion. If invention crops up in his writings, it is treated as an exogenous phenomenon. A notable exception is found in his book on the development of capitalism, in which Schumpeter recognizes the possibility that invention may be the outcome of the capitalist process. The imitators who follow the innovators are driven by expected profits, but the mechanism itself is not dealt with.

The relationship between invention of new methods of production

[27] See, for example, Sylos Labini (1984).
[28] This approach has been opened up by Dasgupta and Stiglitz (1980, pp. 266–93; 1981, pp. 137–58).
[29] See, for example, Rosenberg (1976, pp. 66–8).

and products and diffusion of the new knowledge, and the relationship between application of the new technical possibilities and diffusion of these technical innovations, are not discussed at all. From the preceding discussion it may be inferred that Schumpeter's distinction between invention and innovation has been very fruitful. It has stimulated both the development of an economic theory of technical change and empirical research in this fast-growing field. Economic analysis and empirical studies have taught us that, on the one hand, invention, diffusion, and innovation depend at least partly endogenously on allocation of scarce resources and that, on the other hand, technical change decisively determines the growth rate of the economy in a quantitative and qualitative sense. This circular character of technical change and economic growth is also an aspect of the set invention, diffusion, and innovation, so that, in fact, complex interrelationships exist.

Finally, I can only express regret that Schumpeter did not stick to his original idea of considering the setting up of new firms as an important vehicle for innovations. The revival of Schumpeterian economics in the eighties seems to go hand in hand with the establishment of many new firms in the formal and informal sectors of the economy. Most of them are reacting to the commercial potential of both process and product innovations and are driven by a Schumpeterian spirit.

References

Clemence, R. V., and Doody, F. S. (1951). *The Schumpeterian System.* Cambridge, Mass.: Addison-Wesley.

Dasgupta, P., and Stiglitz, J. (1980). "Industrial Structure and the Nature of Innovative Activity." *The Economic Journal,* 90:266–93.

(1981). "Entry, Innovation, Exit." *European Economic Review,* 137–58.

Freeman, C. (ed.) (1984). *Long Waves in the World Economy.* London: Butterworth.

Goodwin, R. M. (1983). "Schumpeter: The Man I Knew." *Richerche Economique.*

Hayek, F. A. (1948). *Individualism and Economic Order.* Chicago University Press.

Heertje, A. (1977). *Economics and Technical Change.* New York: Wiley.

(ed.) (1981a). *Schumpeter's Vision: Capitalism, Socialism, and Democracy after Forty Years.* New York: Praeger.

(1981b). "Schumpeter's Model of the Decay of Capitalism," in H. Frisch (ed.), *Schumpeterian Economics.* New York: Praeger.

Herbert, R. F., and Link, A. N. (1982). *The Entrepreneur.* New York: Praeger.
Kirzner, I. M. (1973). *Competition and Entrepreneurship.* University of Chicago Press.
(1979). *Perception, Opportunity, and Profit.* University of Chicago Press.
(1985). *Discovery and the Capitalist Process.* University of Chicago Press.
Littlechild, S. C. (1986). *The Fallacy of the Mixed Economy.* London.
Machlup, F. (ed.) (1976). *Essays on Hayek.* New York University Press.
Mansfield, E. (1968). *Industrial Research and Technological Innovation, An Economic Analysis.* New York: Norton.
Nelson, R. R., and Winter, S. G. (1982). *An Evolutionary Theory of Economic Change.* Cambridge, Mass.: Harvard University Press.
Perroux, F. (1965). *La Pensée Economique de Joseph Schumpeter.* Paris: Libraire Drox.
Rosenberg, N. (1976). *Perspectives on Technology.* Cambridge University Press.
Rosenberg, N., and Frischtak, C. (1984). "Technological Innovation and Long Waves." *Cambridge Journal of Economics.*
✓ Sato, R., and Tsutsui, S. (1984). "Technical Progress, the Schumpeterian Hypothesis and Market Structure." *Zeitschrift für Nationalökonomie.*
Schumpeter, J. A. (1908). *Das Wesen und der Hauptinhalt der theoretischen Nationalökonomie.* Leipzig.
(1912). *Theorie der wirtschaftlichen Entwicklung.* Leipzig: Duncker & Humblot.
(1926). *Theorie der wirtschaftlichen Entwicklung* (2nd ed.). Leipzig: Duncker & Humblot.
(1939). *Business Cycles,* Vols. I and II. New York: McGraw-Hill.
(1942). *Capitalism, Socialism and Democracy.* New York: Harper.
(1951). *Essays* (edited by R. V. Clemence). Cambridge, Mass.: Addison-Wesley.
(1952). *Aufsätze zur ökonomischen Theorie.* Tübingen: J. C. Mohr.
(1954). *History of Economic Analysis.* Oxford University Press.
(1961). *The Theory of Economic Development* (translation of 2nd German edition by Redvers Opie). Oxford University Press.
Solomon, S. (1986). "Innovation Clusters and Kondratieff Long Waves," *Cambridge Journal of Economics.*
Sylos Labini, P. (1984). *The Forces of Economic Growth and Decline.* Cambridge, Mass.: MIT Press.
Ursprung, H. W. (1984). "Schumpeterian Entrepreneurs and Catastrophe Theory or a New Chapter to the Foundations of Economic Analysis." *Zeitschrift für Nationalökonomie, Suppl.,* 39–70.
van Duijn, J. J. (1983). *The Long Wave in Economic Life.* London.
Winter, S. G. (1984). "Schumpeterian Competition in Alternative Technological Regimes." *Journal of Economic Behaviour and Organizations.*
Wolff, J. (1982). *Les Grandes Oeuvres Economiques* (Vol. 4). Paris.

Discussion

KURT W. ROTHSCHILD

To be a discussant of Arnold Heertje's chapter is not an easy task. He has managed to condense into a very small space an excellent, fair, and yet critical survey of the evolution of Schumpeter's ideas and their significance for present-day research. When the first reaction to a presentation is full agreement with the author, it is difficult to find a suitable entry for a discussion. So what I am going to do is simply to offer a few remarks and impressions that are meant to underline and supplement Heertje's arguments and then add some observations on two minor points.

I think that considering all the subjects treated in this conference, Professor Heertje has been given the most difficult, if not to say impossible, assignment. The blunt fact is that Schumpeter did not deal with and did not develop a theory of the big white area on the economist's map that is called "technical progress." This fact is clearly seen by Heertje when he says at the end of his Section 3.3 that "technical change, in the strict sense of the development of new technical knowledge and possibilities, and the diffusion of knowledge are almost wholly absent from his [Schumpeter's] exposition. So it seems fair to conclude that Schumpeter dealt only incidentally with technology and that he did not present us with a systematic economic analysis of technical change."

True enough. And yet, strangely enough, few of us will have felt discomfort when reading the title "Schumpeter and Technical Change" in the program; on the contrary, it seems to point to one of the main reasons why we experience a Schumpeterian renaissance in these days of huge and accelerated technical change. How is this apparent contradiction to be explained?

I think the key to an answer has to be found in a sharp distinction between evolution and technical change. Schumpeter's enormous achievement and significance in his own day and up to our times have been due to his consistent vision of economic phenomena as evolutionary processes. This sets him apart from the dominant thinking in static theories, with their stress on unique equilibria and their neglect of institutional and historical influences. This vision and Schumpeter's desire to investigate the dynamic and historical process explain the paradox of why this man, who probably more than anyone else had absorbed and mastered economic theory in its full breadth, hardly wished to join the rewarding game of sophisticated formalization to which his ideas could not (yet?) be subjected. This indifference to current fashions means that Schumpeter and his tradition probably will have to remain for some time in the double role of outsider and challenger.

Schumpeter was drawn to the problem of evolution *not* because of a primary interest in technical change. One reason probably was his keen realistic observation of the rapid economic changes taking place in the Habsburg monarchy in his formative years.[1] Another reason was endogenous to the theoretical debate, namely, the problem of explaining the existence of positive profits and interest. Both these factors, together with the experience of cyclical phenomena, pointed to change and evolution as an important category. Such change can have many origins, all of which were clearly in Schumpeter's mind: population growth, capital accumulation, political and institutional changes, and, last but not least, technical progress and innovation. Of these, technical progress has, both because of its obvious importance for over 200 years and because of its affinity to basic economic factors, always attracted the special attention of economists. But because of the preponderance of static theories or comparative statics, at best, technical *change* tended to be a nuisance, and so technical conditions were largely reduced to existing technical knowledge and relegated to an exogenous framework.

Schumpeter's vision of an evolutionary theory opened the way for making technical *change,* not just technical knowledge, an integrative element of economic theorizing. Therefore, it is obvious and correct to associate the theme of "technical change" with the name of Schumpeter; as compared with mainstream economics, his approach at least permitted a proper treatment of technical progress. But more than that, Schumpeter had borrowed his vision, to some extent, from Marx, with whom he shared some views *in this respect;* and in Marx's vision of the evolutionary process, technical change certainly plays *the* decisive role. So this intellectual affinity to Marx's dynamic approach brought Schumpeter into close contact with technical change.

But here the story ends, because when it comes to concrete and detailed discussion of the driving forces of economic evolution, Schumpeter tends to neglect population growth, technical progress, and other factors to concentrate on one element, the innovating pioneering entrepreneur. Now, there is no doubt that this category is an important element in any descriptive and theoretical treatment of

[1] On this and some later remarks, see März (1964, pp. 363–88).

economic evolution. It was also an important feat of Schumpeter to try to personify the evolutionary process, to show that economic events are not just the outcome of a mechanical process, as some theories seem to suggest. But by putting excessive weight on the pioneer entrepreneur, Schumpeter cut himself off from searching for a fuller theory of evolution in which several factors of equal importance would be closely interwoven. This applies even to the question of entrepreneurship itself. As Redlich and others have shown, Schumpeter's sharp division between innovators and imitators is hardly tenable, with regard both to definitions and to their role in economic development.

But the really sharp neglect occurs with technical change. Here the contrast with Marx is striking. Whereas in the first volume of *Das Kapital* (Marx, 1961, pp. 352–532) the two chapters on division of labor and on machinery cover almost one-quarter of the book and are full of concrete material regarding technology, technical facts and the process of technical invention play only a minor part in Schumpeter's writings. Apart from his ideas on long waves, we find few attempts to lay bare the causes and circumstances that favor technical progress, inventory activity, diffusion and so forth. There is also no sign that Schumpeter was interested in the admittedly sparse and unsatisfactory literature on technical progress. He also seemed to deny inventors the admiration that he so richly bestowed on his special entrepreneurs.

So we see that the door that Schumpeter opened to analyze technical change and its role in economic development was more or less locked for him by the lopsided view of the total process. It could be an interesting question why he leaned so heavily on this single element, the Schumpeterian entrepreneur. Here I only want to hint at possible answers. They all are somehow connected with the personal and historical background in which Schumpeter grew up. First, Schumpeter, who was perhaps the last great economist with truly all-round erudition, was specially suited to an interdisciplinary approach. However, he was, because of his personal leanings and a predominantly humanistic-classical education, deeply interested in history, sociology, and psychology, but knew little (and probably cared little) about the nature of progress in the natural sciences and about engineering problems. These aspects of knowledge counted little in the still semifeudal atmosphere of imperial Austria's society. There is also another specific Austrian factor in the stress on the role of the daring entrepreneur: Schumpeter could not but recognize that this species was relatively scarce in Austria, as compared with the more advanced Western European industrial states, and that this fact may have been one (but not the only) reason for Austria's backwardness.

In addition to the environmental influences, Schumpeter's personality traits have to be mentioned. From all biographical accounts and from his educational background, Schumpeter clearly emerges as a very romantic personality. We also know that in his young days he was interested in and attracted by the then fashionable elite theories of Pareto and others. These romantic and elitist views clearly influenced his evolutionary ideas. We must not forget what the Schumpeterian entrepreneur really looks like.[2] He is ideally a man without means who has new ideas and a creative urge that drives him to passionate action, where costs and risks are not counted; he obtains the necessary credits for these actions; he dreams of creating a dynasty; and all this will lead him to success, though only for a limited period. Although this picture of the entrepreneur may be valuable as a counterbalancing view to the bloodless profit-maximizing calculating machine that appears as entrepreneur in traditional economics, it is certainly equally unrealistic. But, in particular, it adds nothing to a proper understanding of technical change or of the role to be played by scientists, imitating capitalists, learning workers, social and political innovations, and so forth. So we come to the conclusion, obviously shared by Heertje, that somebody who wants to study technical change will not find it very rewarding to turn to Schumpeter, but that for the *economist* who feels that change, including technical change, needs more attention, Schumpeter's approach, vision, and writings remain a continuing source of inspiration.

In conclusion, let me take up two specific points in Heertje's presentation. In discussing the relationship between Schumpeter's innovative activities and the concept of the (objective) production function, Heertje points out that innovation frequently is only a change in the *subjective* production function (i.e., increased knowledge of *existing* possibilities) and that this has nothing to do with technological development. I am unsure whether or not this is too strict a judgment. If we acknowledge the existence of x inefficiency and the difficulties of information gathering as important, then the picture looks a bit different. Innovation activities *within* the production frontier may then have two positive effects on technical progress: (1) They present large-scale experiments with regard to improved blueprints and will thus foster new insights. (2) More lively innovation to overcome x inefficiency might in itself act as a stimulus to new technological research and invention.

The second point is really very minor. In Section 3.5, on post-

[2] On this, see also Albach (1984, pp. 126–8).

Schumpeterian developments, Heertje tentatively remarks that to some extent the modern formal theory of macroeconomic disequilibrium goes back to Schumpeter, insofar as markets are not cleared by price adjustments. He admits that this may be a bit farfetched, but thinks that "an element of Schumpeterian flavor cannot be denied." This is probably the only point on which I disagree with Heertje. The modern disequilibrium theory is mainly concerned with introducing *rigidities* into neoclassical equilibrium thinking in order to come to terms with the Keynesian challenge of underemployment equilibrium. Schumpeterian *dynamics* make no appearance. But as I said before, this is a minor point and should not distract from Heertje's other observations about the value and stimulus that Schumpeterian thinking has provided to some recent developments in economic research.

References

Albach, H. (1984). "Die Rolle des Schumpeter-Unternehmers heute," in D. Bös and H. D. Stolper (eds.), *Schumpeter oder Keynes? Zur Wirtschaftspolitik der neunziger Jahre* (pp. 125–46). Berlin: Springer.

März, E. (1964). "Zur Genesis der Schumpeterschen Theorie der wirtschaftlichen Entwicklung," in T. Kowalik (ed.), *On Political Economy and Econometrics. Essays in Honour of Oskar Lange* (pp. 363–88). Warsaw: PWN.

Marx, K. (1961). *Das Kapital. Kritik der politischen Ökonomie,* Vol. 1. Berlin: Dietz.

CHAPTER 4

Luck, necessity, and dynamic flexibility

BURTON H. KLEIN

When economists think of economic models, they generally have in mind either deterministic or stochastic models. The Walras general equilibrium model is an example of the former, and the Nelson-Winter model is an example of the latter.

However, observation should teach us that often in real life any two forces do not work independently. Suppose that competitive necessity is pushing firms in, say, the computer industry to bring about innovations. To be sure, if they were equally lucky in bringing about innovations, only necessity would be at work. But with both good and bad luck involved, the two forces will be working jointly, and because they are unwilling to trust their destinies to luck alone, they will try to find ways to put good luck on their side while minimizing the consequences of bad luck.

In the past, biologists debated whether evolution began by chance events or as a result of deterministic forces. But over the past 20 years or so, biologists have concluded that the forces work jointly. As Sewall Wright, a pioneer in the field of population genetics has written, "The Darwinian process of continued interplay of a random and a selective process is not intermediate between pure chance and pure determinism, but in its consequences qualitatively utterly different from either."[1]

Consider, for example, biologists' experiments on the behavior of ants when progressively denied a food supply. If the process were completely deterministic, they obviously would be programmed to proceed directly to the nourishment. On the other hand, if search were completely random, the ants' search patterns would not depend on the degree of necessity involved. These experiments have shown that the forces indeed work jointly. When first denied food, their immediate reaction was to search in the vicinity of the former supply, but, over time, the search process became highly random. It is the randomness of their search combined with necessity that has enabled the ants to be among the 0.01 percent of species that have survived.

[1] Quoted by Mayr (1978, p. 8).

95

Not all ants that go out into the wilderness to find a new food supply survive; most do not. Biologists describe them as "altruistic" ants, because whereas their genetic diversity does not enable individual ants to survive, it does enable an entire population to survive.

Among the general similarities and important differences between the economics to be discussed in this chapter and biology are the following: First, the theories are nondeterministic; that is, both ants and firms have some, though by no means perfect, control over their destinies. Second, what biologists describe as "evolutionary progress" (the adaptation of species to new circumstances), Schumpeter understood as the "process of creative destruction." Third, what biologists describe as altruistic behavior, economists describe as risk taking. A firm unlucky in bringing about a particular innovation is widening the industry's search process no less than an ant that is unsuccessful in locating a new food supply. Fourth, by "adaptation," biologists mean "that the external world sets certain 'problems' that organisms need to 'solve,' and that evolution by means of natural selection is the mechanism for creating these solutions" (Lewontin, 1978, p. 115). Adaptation, in other words, brings necessity and good luck into a supportive relationship. In this chapter it will be argued that "dynamic flexibility" – the capability of firms to make rapid adjustments to new circumstances *in both R&D and production activities* – plays more or less the same role. Dynamic flexibility is so described to distinguish it from static flexibility, which is the ability to produce several products on a single preprogrammed production line. By contrast, dynamic flexibility provides the means to make changes in a production process and a product mix *not programmed beforehand*. Fifth, biologists describe as the driving force in evolutionary progress "a highly opportunistic kind of competition" (Mayr, 1978, p. 7) within particular species and between various species that causes them to make good use of their genetic inheritance. So, in modern evolutionary economics, the driving force is opportunistic risk taking, in which hints from previous innovations are used as a springboard to generate new innovations. When opportunistic risk taking (whose outcome cannot be calculated beforehand) is successful, pressure is imposed on other firms to take risks and to be dynamically flexible if they hope to survive. Such competition, in turn, drives both the various species and business organizations away from a static equilibrium.

There are two principal differences between modern evolutionary economics and biology: First, physical necessity – mainly in the form of a scarce food supply – is the underlying driving force in biological evolution. Indeed, the science of biology began when Darwin asked himself whether or not, in Malthus's world, all species would necessarily have the same reproduction rates. On the other hand, in economics, the driving force is the competitive games firms play. Economic and technological progress will be most rapid when they are positive-sum games – games characterized by a high degree of opportunistic risk taking. Second, the inputs for biological evolution in the form of genetic diversity are entirely different from the inputs for economic and technological progress in the form of a diversity of hints that can be utilized by means of a cross-fertilization process to bring about further innovations. This means that whereas, according to biologists, the supply of genetic diversity has remained more or less constant, the diversity of hints has been increasing ever since *Homo sapiens* began constructing elementary tools. As a consequence, technological progress can and has occurred at a far faster rate than biological evolution. Moreover, whenever the rate of evolution declines, whether in biological or economic terms, this cannot be blamed on a shortage of the needed inputs. To starve to death in the midst of a constant supply of riches is one thing; to starve in the midst of an increasing supply is quite another.

4.1 Nature of the innovation process

An economic innovation consists of an improved product or production process that is better than previous alternatives on cost-effectiveness grounds, with buyers being the final judges of cost-effectiveness, and its significance depending on the degree of opportunistic risk taking involved. Cost-effectiveness is defined as providing a greater degree of effectiveness at the same cost or the same degree of effectiveness at lower cost. Synthetic fibers, for example, represent a true economic innovation on both grounds: Initially, before the cotton-fiber industry rose to the challenge, synthetic-fiber garments cost less and required less ironing than cotton fabrics. Robots employed in production processes not only result in impressive cost savings but also, when employed to relieve workers in the most monotonous tasks, achieve equally impressive results in terms of improving reliability.

In fact, much, if not most, economic progress results from innovations relating to the production process, as distinct from product innovations. Suppose that the top leadership in a firm wants to assure that its products will remain competitive in either or both of the dimensions just described. When others also are attempting to bring about product innovations, firms simply cannot hope to compete only in similar terms. In addition, ways must be found to produce their products on the basis of fewer capital and labor inputs. Indeed, it is the quest to remain competitive that is the fundamental reason why productivity gains come about. Like other innovations, those associated with improving productive efficiency are part and parcel of the economic process: the process of changing production functions.

Schumpeter once made the same point:

Capitalism is essentially a process of (endogenous) economic change. Without that change, or, more precisely, that kind of change we have called evolution, capitalist society cannot exist. . . . Hence the capitalist organism cannot, in case opportunities for innovations give out, settle down into a stationary stage without being vitally affected, as it could if "changes in production functions" were an incident to its life process and not the essence of it. (1939, p. 1033)

To provide an example: During the 1960s, the leadership of Black and Decker tool company found that the ability of the firm to compete in international markets was declining. An analysis of various competitor products was made, with the objective of finding ways to provide Black and Decker tools with the same advantages of the more competitive Japanese tools, but at a lower cost. This was done by employing automation in a highly ingenious and flexible manner that resulted in production of electric motors for tools at a base rate of 600 per hour using 4, instead of 27, operators.[2] That, indeed, was a change in production function that was endogenous to the capitalistic process.

The role of luck? According to Alvin P. Lehnerd, the president of Black and Decker:

It was determined that double insulation and the threat of its legislation was of [sufficient] importance to us that we decided to turn this "cloud of gloom" into an "opportunity." This was an opportunity to study the entire product line in the short time period. (personal communication)

Innovations, as already described, result in economic evolution because they change the probability distributions of the world: After an innovation has been added to the number of available substitutes, the probability of finding an acceptable substitute is greater than it was before. Moreover, inasmuch as additional substitutes increase the elasticity of demand, the ability of firms to control their prices is weakened.

How, then, are innovations born? Do they come out of thin air? Or, as Schumpeter suggested, are they to be regarded as heroic acts? Rather, I suggest that the process of discovering the concepts of innovation has a logic all its own. It is my conviction that all innovations,

---

[2] This discussion is based on materials supplied by Alvin P. Lehnerd in 1986.

minor or major, result from a cross-fertilization (i.e., synergetic) process in which hints from consumers, from the same or other technologies, or, occasionally, from science are utilized to develop new concepts.

For example, a chemist at the Minnesota Mining & Manufacturing Company (3M), who also sang in a choir, was very annoyed when the paper clips used to mark particular songs kept falling off the pages. Another chemist, who was working on adhesives, happened, quite by accident, to discover an adhesive that could be removed from a page without any damage to the print. The result of their interaction was a paper substitute for the paper clip – one of the 50,000 products produced by 3M, many of which have resulted from similar intellectual processes. But, as this example shows, it is not luck alone that leads to a new product. The first chemist's necessity was the second chemist's luck. Or, considering the strong internal drive within 3M to generate new products in order to stay ahead of the competition, it can be said that the second chemist's necessity was the first chemist's luck.

When Whittle was engaged in developing the jet engine, devising a satisfactory combustion scheme proved to be a far more serious obstacle than he had imagined. His luck consisted in finding an oil-burner manufacturer at the British Trade Industries Fair whose engineers were willing, on the basis of the hints supplied by Whittle and their information obtained in the course of making oil burners, to try to develop a satisfactory combustion scheme. So a new combustion system was developed by this oil-burner manufacturer based on a cross-fertilization of hints. Or, to take another example, for many years solid-state physicists had been working on a device to replace vacuum tubes. But the crucial hint for the development of transistors arose in the course of a Bell Laboratories project not directly related to the development of transistors. Or, as I pointed out in my book *Dynamic Economics,* Henry Ford's dream of an inexpensive and rugged car was spoiled by the fact that the first Model T cost more than a Buick. Therefore, a frantic search began for ways to reduce costs, during which one of his employees, Clarence Avery, who had observed automatic production lines in meat-packing plants, asked why the process might not be reversed for making automobiles.

What, then, is an entrepreneur – and what is the difference between an entrepreneur and a profit maximizer? As is generally known, the left and right sides of the human brain perform quite different functions, with the left side being the analytic side, and the right being, among other things, the imaginative side. A true entrepreneur uses both sides of the brain, but a profit maximizer, figuratively speaking, uses only the left side.

Finally, is it not conceivable that imagination and hints play roles not only in ordinary innovations but also in "hard" sciences such as physics? Consider the following quotation from *The Feynman Lectures on Physics:*

Experiment is the *sole judge* of scientific "truth." But what is the source of knowledge? Where do the laws that are to be tested come from? Experiment, itself, helps to produce these laws, in the sense that it gives us hints. But also needed is *imagination* to create from these hints the great generalizations – to guess at the wonderful, simple, but very strange patterns beneath them all, and then to experiment to check again whether we have made the right guess. (Feynman et al., 1966, p. 1)

Apparently, scientific "entrepreneurs" do not behave completely differently from other entrepreneurs; only profit maximizers ensconced in a static equilibrium live in a world of their own.

It may be noted that this fact of life was long ago recognized by Adam Smith, writing in the *Wealth of Nations:* "The progressive state is in reality the chearful and the hearty state to all the different orders of the society. The stationary is dull; the declining, melancholy" ([1776] 1938, vol. 2, p. 249). In present-day terms, the "hearty" state occurs when competition within a firm or within an industry must be described in terms of a positive-sum game.

Furthermore, Adam Smith also recognized that innovations require the presence of necessity:

The man whose whole life is spent in performing a few simple operations of which the effects are perhaps always the same, or very nearly the same, has no occasion to exert his understanding or to exercise his invention in finding out expedients for removing difficulties which never occur. He naturally loses, therefore, the habit of such exertion, and generally becomes as stupid and ignorant as it is possible for a human creature to become. ([1776] 1938, p. 264)

4.2   How necessity and luck can be made to go hand in hand: the example of 3M

Although earlier innovation was supplied by the 3M top leaders, the people in corporate planning said that over the past 20 years or so (when 3M's growth greatly accelerated), the innovational factor has been "competition," as described earlier.[3] For example, one of their fiercest competitors, they said, was Sony. Instead of purchasing mag-

---

[3] Based on interviews with 3M executives for a forthcoming book, *Opportunistic Competition: Making Luck and Necessity Go Hand in Hand,* financed by a grant from the Carnegie Corporation.

netic tapes from 3M, Sony, for reasons of its own, developed its own production capacity, including the machinery, and later sold the machinery to computer firms who had been some of 3M's best customers, including IBM, so that they could produce their own magnetic tapes.

A few words, first, about the history of 3M. The company started with the purchase of a mine in northern Minnesota that was supposed to furnish grit for making sandpaper. However, because no other firm was willing to buy the grit, 3M set up a manufacturing facility to attempt to show them how it could be profitably used – which led to the conclusion that their mine was worthless. Though expensive, this experience of having to respond to necessity certainly was not worthless.

The evolution of 3M toward the company that it is today began when, during the 1930s, its sales manager insisted that whereas previously their salesmen had called only on wholesalers, they should begin calling on the furniture and auto manufacturers actually engaged in using the sandpaper, in order to obtain firsthand information on the real problems that the users experienced. This activity had two effects on the firm's methods of operations that continue to this day. First, 3M continues to develop new products in close association with final users. Second, this experience put 3M in the "hints" business. The customers could discuss problems encountered when using various brands of sandpaper, but they did not have the knowledge to rectify them; hence, the users' problems were regarded as "hints" for improving the quality of the product. To translate those hints into improved products, the firm hired several chemists from the University of Minnesota, who were told to see what they could do by way of dealing with these problems.

The company today has more than 50 R&D laboratories that employ some 5,000 people. The second phase of the firm's evolution began when it recognized that cross-fertilization of hints between various laboratories could play a major role in the development of profitable new products. The 3M operating philosophy is that whereas the products belong to the some 40 operating divisions within the firm, the technology belongs to the company, because the company may want to utilize the technology as a springboard to develop new products via a cross-fertilization process. Furthermore, the people in 3M headquarters are aware that a genuine trade-off is involved. The firm does not aim for perfection, for the highest possible degree of refinement that might be obtainable in any product line; if it did that, the central R&D laboratories would be supporting the various divisions, and the technology would belong not to the company but to the operating divisions. True, about 75 percent for the firm's R&D effort is concentrated in divisional laboratories that directly support the operating divisions. But allocating as much as 25 percent for especially risky projects undertaken in the central R&D laboratories, whose principal aim is the generation of new products, certainly involves an emphasis on long-term, as distinct from short-term, profits. This is not to say, of course, that competition does not occur in older product lines. It does. Risk taking in support of the older product lines mainly takes the form of bringing about improvements in productivity, which, as already indicated, are needed if the firm's products are to remain competitive.

As far as the principal R&D laboratories are concerned, some of the measures employed to make luck and necessity go hand in hand are the following. First, like other entrepreneurial firms, promotion within 3M does not require the assumption of more and more managerial responsibilities. A creative chemist who wants to devote all of his or her time to research can become a senior chemist and receive a salary equivalent to that of a company vice-president. Quite obviously, utilizing chemists in this manner multiplies opportunities for good luck. Second, if they have a germ of an idea for a cross-fertilization process, research people in one or another central laboratory can apply for a grant from a headquarters group whose main aim is to encourage this and related activities. Third, there are those who, rather than remain creative chemists, would prefer to start their own companies. They can do this within 3M, because all of the many plants are operated as individual profit centers in which the plant managers have a far greater degree of autonomy than is provided in the typical conglomerate. Fourth, 3M encourages a great deal of internal competition, and I gather that internal competition is particularly keen for "setting up new firms" within 3M. There are, of course, winners and losers in every round of the internal game, but inasmuch as over time there are more winners than losers, this game may be described as a positive-sum game. Moreover, no one jeopardizes a career by making a mistake – providing, of course, the same mistake is not made twice.

Fifth, 3M sponsors an annual "technology fair" of emerging technologies and new products. Because its main aim is to encourage interchange of ideas, the atmosphere, as in any other such fair, is highly informal. Technology fairs always have played an important role in providing hints for new innovations. As was pointed out earlier, Whittle was able to obtain an idea for solving his combustion problem when he attended a British Trade Industries Fair. A Swedish manufacturer of drilling equipment obtained an idea for utilizing the basic technology for making oil-drilling equipment while attending an oil-drilling equipment fair in Texas, and as a consequence he later became a highly successful exporter of such equipment. What 3M has done is to institutionalize this practice within the company.

Sixth, a variety of measures are employed to make the boundaries between the various laboratories very thin. These include in-house symposia, lecture series, meetings between company experts and academic research people, and the use of technical forum chapters, ranging in size from 50 to 500 people, to bring about an interchange of ideas. In short, the major aim of all of 3M's policies is to make necessity and good luck go hand in hand.

How, then, does 3M go about generating a new product line? As already stated, its policy always has been to develop new products in close association with consumers. Consequently, whereas those in research can engage in a variety of exploratory projects aimed at new products, before an entire series of innovations is initiated the customer is brought into the act, beginning with a simple innovation. For example, about five years ago, 3M initiated its drive into the medical field by developing, in association with the surgeons at a local hospital, a plastic surgical gown as a replacement for the customary cotton surgical gown. This association with surgeons has resulted in a variety of medical products, including artificial hip bones and knee sockets, as well as lenses to be used after cataract operations. Today, these medical products account for 17 percent of the firm's sales, and a somewhat greater proportion of its profits.

The central aim of the company's policies is to repeat this kind of process once every five years. But there is no master plan for doing this. Moreover, not all attempts to develop new product lines have been successful. These mainly have included cases in which particular lead innovations, though mostly successful in their own right, did not result in a succession of further innovations because the various laboratories were not able to support a continuing process. However, it is difficult to know beforehand just how far people can go in stretching their luck.

Because bad as well as good luck is inevitable in such undertakings, the firm employs procedures for minimizing the consequences of bad luck. Specifically, a group of people from a variety of laboratories perform an audit function, whose aim is to ensure, before products reach an advanced state of development, that the "new" innovation will be successful from a commercial point of view as well as from a technical point of view.

Of course, 3M is not unique in undertaking to make necessity and good luck go hand in hand, while at the same time minimizing the consequences of bad luck. To be sure, the particular measures employed vary a great deal from company to company, but all must do this to survive.[4]

For example, consider the Sony Television Corporation of America, which is located in San Diego.[5] According to the people in charge, the company must generate productivity gains of 5 to 10 percent annually just to stay even with the competition. Furthermore, on the basis of information shown to me, there is no significant difference between Sony productivity performance in Japan and that in San Diego (on the basis of similar TVs made on similar production lines). Whether Sony competes in quality or price terms, it should be apparent that the basis for such competition is the reduction of real costs.

How, then, is this remarkable productivity performance explained? In brief, it involves the use of a variety of measures to make good luck and necessity go hand in hand. Whenever the competitive position of the firm weakens, meetings are held between management and workers to discuss the situation. Invariably, these are followed by meetings soliciting ideas with respect to improving productivity performance. Recently, this was done on an eight-year-old production line. A diversity of internal interactions is encouraged by having managers and workers eat in the same cafeteria, and informal "quality circles" are employed to analyze performance and generate new ideas. As in other industrial firms, industrial engineers are responsible for prescribing the order in which various tasks are to be completed. But workers are asked to take these only as guidelines and to introduce a variety of small-scale innovations that will enable them to do better. Finally, although the newer, more automated production lines are developed by Sony in Japan, where feedback from workers plays an indispensable role in the development of more advanced equipment, when visiting the Sony plant in San Diego I observed workers engaged in revamping a production line to produce a new TV model. "Why do workers and not technicians do that?" I asked. "The Sony way," I was told, "consists of making workers think for themselves" – which, of course, is the most basic way of making necessity and good luck go hand in hand.

---

[4] Recently, I have had discussions with people at Corning Glass and Hewlett-Packard regarding their approaches to making luck and necessity go hand in hand. They are different, but no less ingenious.

[5] Based on interviews with people at Sony Television Corporation of America.

4.3   Dynamic flexibility and positive-sum games

A system – any system, economic or other – that at *every* given point in time fully utilizes its possibilities to the best advantage may yet in the longer run be inferior to a system that does so at *no* given point of time, because the latter's failure to do so may be a condition for the level or speed of long-run performance. (Schumpeter, 1942, p. 83)

The purpose of this section is to show that the condition under which Schumpeter's famous statement holds true is the practice of dynamic flexibility in the context of a positive-sum game. The concept of specialization implies nearly perfect adaptation to an existing environment. Its central concern, therefore, is to make best use of existing possibilities at every moment. By contrast, dynamic flexibility is defined as the ability to make speedy adaptations in the face of new circumstances. In short, because the first is concerned with operating in a highly predictable environment, and the second, in a highly unpredictable environment, they are opposed characteristics.

Suppose that someone believes that it is possible to do a good job predicting changes in the stock market, and for a while expectations are confirmed – so much so that the speculator operates with a zero cash balance. That person is taking best advantage of existing possibilities. However, as Keynes, who successfully managed a private investment company, suggested many years ago, there are circumstances in which it may be prudent to keep some assets in a relatively liquid form, even if it means a sacrifice in current earnings. In particular, in this context, dynamic flexibility consists in keeping both mental and other assets in a relatively liquid form; so even though a sacrifice in current earnings might be involved, the investor is better insured against unpredictable changes in the market. If an unanticipated bargain appears, the investor is in a position to exploit it; if an unanticipated decline in the market occurs, and if the decline seems to be temporary, the investor is not forced to sell on a particular day.

The investor cannot, of course, do anything to change the likelihood of good or bad luck in the market. Rather, the name of the game is to reduce the market uncertainties in a manner so as to make the investor's assets grow as rapidly as possible. And it is dynamic flexibility – the ability to make speedy adaptations to new circumstances – that makes good luck and necessity go hand in hand, while at the same time minimizing the consequences of bad luck.

Consider, again, 3M's strategy. To take best advantage of existing possibilities, it would have to put all of its effort into making current products better or less expensive. But if it operated, so to speak, on the left side of a bifurcation diagram, 3M would never be able to climb the higher hill on the right side of the diagram. By contrast, the ability to expand into profitable new areas, when disclosed by internal research and market possibilities, permits the firm to climb far steeper hills than otherwise would be possible.

To return briefly to the Sony example: To take best advantage of existing possibilities, it would have to build plants in a manner so as to minimize production costs at a given point in time, but Sony does not do that. Despite the fact that under especially intense competitive pressures during the last five years Sony managed to double its productivity rate, only one of three production lines is, in terms of current standards, "fully automated." "Why not go to full automation?" I asked. The essential reason is that whereas automation can improve productivity – no doubt of that – taking full advantage of present possibilities will reduce the scope for further innovations. Conversely, according to newspaper accounts, Ford and General Motors are in deep trouble for having tried to automate in a manner so as to minimize production costs at a point in time.

There are actually two kinds of dynamic flexibility, one for bringing about particular innovations and the other for setting up an ongoing production process to facilitate dealing with new circumstances. However, whereas in principle a firm might be dynamically flexible in the first respect, but not in the second, I doubt if there ever was such a firm. Typically, innovative firms compete with other innovative companies, which means that they must be able to respond quickly to a good deal of unpredictability in their external environments. To do that, they must be able to move fast in generating and introducing innovations.

Flexibility in bringing about innovations

Suppose that an artist were to paint a picture by first forming a mental image of the final product (in order to take full advantage of his possibilities). This might be done by copying another picture, but what cannot be done is to bring about an innovation. Indeed, for this reason artists typically start with rough sketches and work from the general to the particular.

Something like half of the battle to bring about a technological innovation consists in generating an appropriate concept. However, just as paintings evolve after the first rough sketches, so do technological innovations. To make this evolution as rapidly and inexpensively as possible, all of the innovative organizations that I know about employ a remarkably similar logic. They begin with a very definite idea of the acceptable costs of the products (and, in this sense, their objective is unchanging). There is no way to predict beforehand whether or not they can implement the innovation within a particular cost constraint. Nevertheless, often, but not always, they do have a fair idea of the technological uncertainties that first must be reduced to ascertain whether or not there is something like a 50/50 chance of bringing about the innovation in question. For example, a demonstrator model aircraft engine, which costs about one-quarter as much as a full-scale engine, can be developed to ascertain how well a variety of novel components will perform together, other than in bench tests. A new TV picture tube (e.g., the Sony Triniton tube) based on several highly novel ideas will be tested in very rudimentary form to discover how well it works. A new telephone microwave system predicated on obtaining substantial cost savings by using traveling-wave tubes will go through an exploratory development phase before a commitment to full-scale development is made.

Such a procedure has two definite advantages. First, something like three out of four attempts to implement significant innovations fail. Consequently, there is a definite incentive to learn as quickly and inexpensively as possible whether or not a particular innovation is likely to succeed – and, if not, to allocate scarce risk-capital funds to other seemingly worthy projects. Second, in every case I have examined, several new hypotheses have had to be generated before an innovation has succeeded in overcoming the crucially important uncertainties. However, good luck is more likely to occur in generating a new hypotheses if the developer fully understands why the original hypothesis did not work as expected. Ordinarily, the uncertainties are not like those of tossing a fair coin; although the initial hypothesis may have worked in some respects, commonly it does not in others. Consequently, by concentrating on difficult problems early, rather than postponing them by working on a detailed configuration of the final product, developers have far better ability to put good luck on their side.

A diagrammatic picture of the argument is shown in Figure 4.1. Panel A of the diagram, a highly idealized case, shows how the uncertainties might be reduced from the viewpoint of Bayesian probability theory, which assumes that no matter what particular prior probability distribution is employed to initiate the process, no new hypotheses will have to be formulated. Under this assumption, relatively few experi-

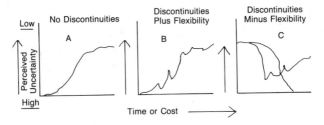

Figure 4.1. Strategies for bringing about innovations.

ments would be required to determine whether or not the prior was in the right region. So, initially, the curve will rise rapidly, flattening when further experiments result in relatively insignificant changes in a prior. However, because Bayesian probability theory assumes no genuine discontinuities (in the form of generating new hypotheses), it provides an unrealistic picture.

A more realistic picture of the process is shown by panel B of the diagram: Though the overall trend is toward reduced uncertainty, the curve falls from time to time – more when the curve rapidly rises than when it flattens. This picture occurs when innovators start with the hard problems, but not only that: Innovative designers typically start with a design that is easy to change even when a bad surprise occurs early in a program. For example, Donald Douglas, Sr., promulgated a significant law stating that the Douglas Company could not optimize an airplane to the engine initially programmed for it, although that meant an inevitable loss in performance. In the case of the DC-3, it is fortunate that the Douglas Company had such a rule, because the initially programmed engine turned out to be a "dud." Consequently, the curve not only would have turned downward, it might never have recovered. To provide another example, Pratt & Whitney, a highly innovative aircraft-engine developer, typically constructs heavier engines than its competitors to leave a margin for error.

Finally, suppose that the developer tries to proceed directly to the final product, as in panel C. The consequence, then, will be for the curve to dip so steeply that it never recovers, or, if it does, recovery will be exceedingly difficult and expensive. The unsuccessful attempt of the Ford Motor Company during the 1970s to develop a stratified-charge engine for automobiles (as is used in the Honda), so that it could be directly competitive with the 6- and 8-cylinder diesels then being developed by General Motors, provides a good example, just as does General Motors' attempt to develop a diesel quickly merely by converting a gasoline engine – leaving all the difficult problems, notably the development of stronger components, until the end. In short, highly specialized firms lack the dynamic flexibility to bring about significant innovations.

A dynamically flexible production process

A production process can be designed to manufacture a product at the lowest possible cost at a particular time, and if it is, it will be designed to take best advantage of its current possibilities. Or it may be designed to evolve rapidly over time, in which case costs cannot be minimized at any point in time. For example, Japanese auto plants are only about one-third or one-quarter the size of American auto plants producing similar cars. But their automobile executives insist that if they were to build larger plants than they have today, it would be virtually impossible to preserve the characteristics that have enabled their plants to evolve rapidly.

A description of the manner in which Japanese auto plants operate should serve to make clear why they cannot simultaneously pursue both goals. Honda has a machine tools division composed of several hundred people under the head of engineering that is responsible for developing tools likely to provide special advantage for the company. If my understanding is correct, so do most, if not all, Japanese auto firms. From where does the feedback come for developing those tools? In good part it comes from workers and managers whose environment is highly interactive. They eat in the same cafeteria, they play baseball together on Saturdays, and often they engage in joint studies. For example, Honda's decision to develop highly specialized robots to replace workers in their most monotonous tasks was undertaken as a result of a joint manager-worker study. This is a highly informal environment in which plants operate as communities, and it would be virtually impossible to build larger plants and still preserve this spirit, Japanese automobile executives say.

Why, then, is the rate at which productivity is increased in the Japanese auto industry about three times that in the American auto industry? A good part of the reason, no doubt, is that inasmuch as new machines are introduced into the production process one at a time, the Japanese can afford to take greater risks than would be possible if they

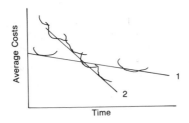

Figure 4.2. Cost-minimization strategies (1, at points in time; 2, over time).

were engaged in making lumpier production decisions. Furthermore, because good luck thrives in a highly informal environment with a great deal of emphasis on self-responsibility, the Japanese are in a far better position to make necessity and good luck work hand in hand. On the other hand, they are also in a good position to minimize the consequences of bad luck. Not only are machines tested in their laboratories before being introduced into the production process, but anyone visiting a Japanese auto plant can see an older portion of a production line still being operated while a newer portion is being debugged. Moreover, just as 3M's activities are highly *unspecialized,* so are those in Japanese auto firms: Workers are shifted to entirely different jobs about every 6 months, and managers are shifted once every several years.

From where does the element of necessity come for producing highly reliable cars? On the basis of what I have been told, Japanese consumers simply would not accept the contrast between the earlier, rather shoddy Japanese cars and the highly meticulous character of their home lives. So an enormous effort was made to improve reliability as a means of "saving face."

But a high degree of reliability is not a free good. Consequently, to improve reliability, while at the same time making highly competitive products, a Japanese firm wanting to stay in business has to generate rapid productivity gains, and to do that it has to acquire a high degree of dynamic flexibility.

What dynamic flexibility buys in terms of productivity gains is indicated in Figure 4.2. The average cost curves are drawn close together because, according to Japanese auto executives, with a continuously changing production process, costs can be pinned down for only about six months. On the other hand, the less steeply sloping curve results from a more traditional philosophy of building plants to minimize costs at a particular point in time.

The relationship with positive-sum games

Suppose that firms in an industry operate on the expectation that as a result of their combined efforts to rapidly improve cost-effectiveness by engaging in opportunistic risk taking, a more than proportional sales increase will take place. In such an industry there will be winners and losers during every round of the game, but it is a positive-sum game in the sense that, owing to the increase in demand, the gains will exceed the losses. True, there is no way of knowing beforehand whether or not a particular game will become positive-sum. All that can be said is that, as in the case of gold mining, if a few firms strike it rich, many others will enter the contest, as happened in the cases of semiconductors and computers and, of course, the Japanese auto industry.

The competition associated with such a game I describe as "cooperative dynamic competition." True, we often think of "competition" and "cooperation" as polar opposites. But what other type of "cooperation" would have succeeded better in making Japanese auto firms the world's leading producers? I describe positive-sum-game competition as "dynamic" because innovations added to the menu of substitutes change the probability distributions of the world. Moreover, it should be kept in mind that the very essence of such entrepreneurial risk taking is that it is highly opportunistic. By using existing technologies as a springboard to create entirely new products, the people at 3M surely are engaged in opportunistic risk taking, just as are Japanese auto makers by changing production functions as rapidly as they do.

It obviously is impossible to fully internalize the benefits from cooperative dynamic competition, because if gains were captured in the form of higher prices, the increase in total output would not be forthcoming. Therefore, genuine social gains are involved – gains that increase per capita real income and the discounted value of a country's wealth. If the playing of positive-sum games is associated with Adam Smith's "hearty state," then the wealth of any nation will depend on the weighted average of that country's industries that are involved in positive-sum games.

On the other hand, zero-sum games, in which gains and losses precisely offset each other, are not likely to feature a significant degree of risk taking. On the assumption that firms do take their strategic interactions into account, why should several firms take large gambles when the impact is unlikely to increase total sales of the industry?

What, then, determines the extent to which firms actually engage in risk taking? If my argument is correct, the differences in average propensities to engage in risk taking (i.e., PERK) within industries are much smaller than the differences between industries. Think of investing in R&D as investing in a stock market portfolio. A firm might not take any risk, or it might insist on engaging in R&D projects expected to pay off in a year or less, or it might buy a mixed portfolio of projects that might be completed with only a little good luck and others that would require a great deal. In an industry such as computers, where a firm's average PERK is large, a firm easily can go out of business betting on minor short-term payoff possibilities while its competitors are taking major gambles likely to mature only in several years' time. But so can a firm go out of business betting on possibilities not likely to bear fruit within, say, 10 years. Entrepreneurship does not consist of living on hope.

To be sure, firms have no way of knowing beforehand the value of the PERK for their rivals; they can judge that only on the basis of the products that emerge. Hence, the value of the PERK for the entire industry is kept reasonably stable by a mutual-adjustment process. This process, in turn, provides a high degree of discipline for the members of every industry, with one important exception: If firms in an industry take almost no risk, then there is not very much risk in betting on just a little luck.

What is the relationship between dynamic flexibility and positive-sum games? If firms are to survive, dynamic flexibility is a requirement in a positive-sum game, because given the nature of the game, they will have to cope with a great deal of uncertainty in their external environments. Only in the case of a completely specialized world in which the PERK equals zero is there no requirement for dynamic flexibility.

We see, therefore, that Schumpeter's famous statement (quoted at the beginning of this section) concerning a static–dynamic trade-off holds true under the assumption of dynamic flexibility coupled with positive-sum games – games in which the value of the PERK is well above zero. To be sure, this is not the same position Schumpeter took when he wrote *Capitalism, Socialism and Democracy,* where he argued that monopolies were in an advantageous financial position to bring about innovations, and because the process of bringing about innovations was becoming automatic, no special competitive pressures were likely to be required in the future. Consequently, economists must decide for themselves which of Schumpeter's arguments is more descriptive of the real world.

4.4 Decline in the competitiveness of the U.S. economy

Why has the productivity rate in the U.S. economy declined relative to other economies, despite the decline in the value of the dollar? My hypothesis is relatively simple. In the era before the U.S. economy was challenged by foreign competition, firms in many uncompetitive industries, including automobiles, tended to become overly specialized and routinized – and, as such, became highly adapted to a very slowly changing environment. Hence, a lack of dynamic flexibility prevented both the realization of larger productivity gains and better results in international competition.

Is this a reasonable proposition? No doubt, the most cost-effective products enter international competition. Americans have bought more and more Japanese cars, presumably because they have realized that their money is buying more effectiveness. A principal way to generate more cost-effective products is to improve productivity rates. Consequently, explaining the productivity decline relative to other countries also can explain why there has been a loss in the competitiveness of American products. Indeed, if the U.S. manufacturing economy cannot shift to a less specialized and routinized method of operations (e.g., as in the case of the Japanese auto industry), American living standards will continue to erode. How else can they ensure that their products will remain competitive?

To make this argument, I first briefly describe a model that implicitly assumes that necessity and luck (bad as well as good) do go hand in hand *at the level of the firm*. The following are the three principal assumptions:

First, recall the argument made in the preceding section with respect to differences in the value of the PERK – the differences are smaller within industries than between industries. If this argument is correct, it is tantamount to assuming that as long as any particular firm in an industry does not change its strategic policies with respect to risk taking, other firms will have no incentive to change theirs. It is tantamount, in other words, to assuming a dynamic equilibrium that can be thought of as a moving average brought about by a more or less constant readjustment process on the part of firms striving to maintain their competitive positions. Therefore, the problem is to predict the rate of productivity change – the average annual value of this moving average – as a function of the value of the PERK.

Second, although it is certainly conceivable that in some industries a high value of the PERK might be reflected in productivity rates, and in others in the development of new products, in fact, a high degree of risk taking in developing new products goes hand in hand with splendid productivity performance. For example, no one will question that in terms of developing new products, the computer and semiconductor industries can be described as high-PERK industries. They also are the best productivity performers in the U.S. economy, for good reason: When the management of a firm cannot be sure if it will win a particular round of the game and cannot know how rapidly a successful new product will be imitated, it must pursue a mixed strategy.

The most important condition for the continuance of a dynamic equilibrium is the following: Either there must be new entry in the form of newly established firms in an industry willing to take greater risks than well-established firms or there must be entry in the form of foreign competition. Otherwise, one or another firm will begin to shade its degree of risk taking, and when it is successful, other firms will follow suit.

Third, it is assumed that when the value of the PERK is fairly high and luck and necessity go hand in hand, productivity gains at the levels of both the firm and the industry will come about in the form of highly irregular cycles having no relation to the business cycle. Why will the gains come about at the level of the firm? Part of the reason is that those firms hard-pressed for productivity gains will not be equally lucky. Even more important is the fact that the incentives of winners and losers differ: The losers in a particular round have an obvious incentive to improve their productivity rates and to produce better or less expensive alternatives; the winners, on the other hand, do not have the same incentive to work at white heat. Productivity gains come about in the form of irregular cycles at the industry level, because there is a lag between the time the losers receive bad news and the time they respond.

Is this a reasonable assumption? It would not appear so on the basis of highly aggregated productivity data. But an examination of the data for all of the four-digit industries compiled by the Bureau of Labor Statistics (which, although not published, can be obtained by requesting the computer tapes) discloses that in the higher-productivity industries, *all* of the series move in the form of irregular cycles.[6]

On the basis of these assumptions, the average value of the PERK will be reflected in the spread of cost outcomes. Moreover, it also will

---

[6] It may be noted that many industries whose productivity performance is low receive negative feedback mainly during economic downturns. Hence, their productivity performance is highly related to the business cycle.

be reflected in the spread in profit rates, because the less fortunate firms will find that to prevent inventories from accumulating, they must reduce their prices. Therefore, the PERK is measured in terms of the spread of the cost distribution. As will be shown, the wider the spread, the more rapid will be the rate of productivity gain. More fundamentally, the problem is to explain in mathematical terms the difference between a zero-sum world and more and more hearty positive-sum worlds. For reasons already given, when expectations are based on a zero-sum game, in which firms can gain only at the expense of rivals, they will aim for only slight improvements, and when they do, the spread of outcomes, with respect to the best expected reduction in costs, will be relatively narrow and will result in a minimal productivity rate. On the other hand, if expectations based on more and more robust positive-sum games materialize (if buyers continue to respond to significant improvements in quality and/or reductions in costs), the best expected reduction in costs will become greater and greater, and the spread of cost outcomes larger and larger, with corresponding differences in productivity performances.[7]

In an entire industry of n firms (n is on the order of a dozen, but the exact number is unimportant), what is the mean corresponding to the *best* outcome and the spread around the outcome, assuming that every firm in the industry is keeping its own value of the PERK close to the industry average? This is important to know because it and associated differences in profit rates provide a measure of the degree of pressure brought against less successful rivals. They might respond by trying to bring about more significant cost-reducing innovations, by intensifying a search outside of their industry for more promising technologies, or, if a rival has found such a technology, by trying to catch up as rapidly as possible. It is this constant readjustment process that keeps the industry value of the PERK steady. Thus, the rate of productivity advance of the industry will be more rapid if the mean of the *maximum* outcome for the n firms is higher. This will occur in spite of the fact that in a high-PERK industry, relatively bad luck for more than half of the companies will give them a sticky time catching up with the luckier firms, those whose cost outcomes will be found on the far right side of Figure 4.3. This is, of course, the kind of distribution associated with expectations of a positive-sum game. Although it should be intuitively obvious that it would be highly irrational for firms whose expec-

[7] I am very grateful to Edward Posner, an applied mathematician at the California Institute of Technology, for having worked out the following mathematics.

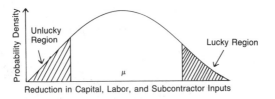

Figure 4.3. Cost outcomes.

tations are based on a zero-sum game to pursue the same policy, the mathematics enable us to pin down the reasons more precisely.

In mathematical terms, here are the equations for the mean $\mu_{max}^{(n)}$ and spread $\sigma_{max}^{(n)}$ of the best normally distributed outcomes among n firms with a common expected value (i.e., mean) μ and common spread (standard deviation) σ, if n is not too small:

$$\mu_{max}^{(n)} \doteq \sigma\{2 \log_e[n/2\sqrt{\pi}]\}^{1/2} + \mu$$
$$\sigma_{max}^{(n)} \doteq [\sigma\pi/(2\sqrt{3})]/\sqrt{n}$$

Thus, $\mu_{max}^{(n)}$ increases slowly with n (assuming more than just a few firms in the industry), but increases rapidly with σ, whereas $\sigma_{max}^{(n)}$ – the spread around the best outcome – actually decreases with n. Also note that with a low-risk (small σ) policy, there is great likelihood that the best outcome in the industry will be close to the mean value μ, with a trivial chance of large gains. Therefore, while having $\sigma_{max}^{(n)}$ small reduces the short-term uncertainty in an industry, it also results in small and highly uncertain productivity gains. As is shown in Figure 4.4, it should be clear that expectations with respect to whether a game will turn out to be zero-sum or positive-sum really do matter. If firms engaged in playing close to a zero-sum game behave as if the distribution is broad, their behavior will be eminently irrational; if they behave in a manner to make the rewards commensurate with the risks, the distribution will be narrow, with very slim possibilities for exciting improvements in their ability to compete in price or quantity terms.

Also note that for small μ (firm mean), the ratio $\mu_{max}^{(n)}/\sigma_{max}^{(n)}$ of mean of the best outcome to the standard deviation is approximately independent of σ if σ is not too small. Thus, as in Figure 4.5, with a large σ and so also a large $\mu_{max}^{(n)}$, significant advances can add up to a large and steady rate of productivity gain.

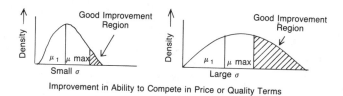

Figure 4.4. Probability of good outcome, moderate number of firms.

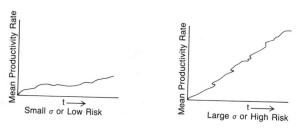

Figure 4.5. Productivity rate versus time (t).

To illustrate the arguments contained in Figures 4.4 and 4.5, consider two widely different industries: the cosmetics and computer industries. It seems safe to assume that unless some radical improvements should occur in cosmetic products, such as might make them a good substitute for plastic surgery, the prospects for growth in the total market are rather dim. In such a static market, therefore, a firm can increase its share of the market only at the expense of one or another rival. In such an industry, a firm will have to be very lucky, indeed, to make up for the frequent years in which results are poor and its market share drops. All firms in such an industry can make the same calculation and recognize that there is no serious threat from competitors. Indeed, for this reason, advertising is employed as the principal means of wooing customers to change their product affiliations. Hence, under such conditions, the expected value $\mu_{max}^{(n)}$ will be small – and an actual productivity rate of 1 to 2 percent annually hardly should be regarded as surprising.

By contrast, in a positive-sum world, such as computers, the leaders of firms have no way of knowing whether they will be lucky or unlucky during a particular play of the game. What they are in a position to know is that growth in the total size of the market is likely to be highly responsive to significant improvements in cost-effectiveness. There-fore, they are in a position to know that when they win, they will win big. In terms of the logic of the mathematical argument, it should not be surprising that in the computer industry, productivity gains have averaged about 10 percent annually.

Is winning "big" necessarily better than winning "small" when one possible outcome of being involved in such a game is losing "big"? Not necessarily. People are not alike. Some prefer games in which the stakes are very high; some do not. But playing in a game in terms of a small σ when other players are playing for big stakes is inviting disaster.

How, then, is it possible to test this model?[8] Assume that in some group of industries the value of the PERK, as measured by the vari-ance of the cost distribution, has been relatively high for two decades. What price behavior should be exhibited by the industry as a whole? Firms typically compete by lowering prices of their less expensive products and improving the quality of their more expensive products. However, even in the latter case, such competition occurs in the con-text of tight price constraints. Moreover, there is no reason to suppose that over a series of games there will be a significant change in the relative emphasis placed on quality and price competition. Therefore, by dividing all industries into four groups, depending on their relative price performance, we should be able to infer their values of the PERK and make predictions about their relative rates of productivity advance.

Some economists, of course, might question which is cause and which is effect: the reduction in relative prices or the associated high productivity performance. However, it should be a matter of common knowledge that firms acting in their own self-interest will charge the highest prices the market will tolerate. But trying to get away with higher prices for relatively equivalent products in a positive-sum game is a prescription for going out of business.

If we can thus obtain a direct measure of the PERK, why attempt to infer the value of the PERK on the basis of assumed cost distribution? For one thing, our interest is not only in making predictions. The rea-soning is equally important. For another, once a higher rate of pro-ductivity increase is demanded by a fairly abrupt reduction in an

---

[8] For a more detailed discussion of the statistical results in this chapter, see my book *Prices, Wages, and Business Cycles* (Chapters VI, VII, and VIII).

industry's relative prices, we have no way of knowing beforehand how rapidly the adjustment toward lower costs will occur. To be sure, even in a dynamic equilibrium, not all industries will be equally lucky in being able to maintain or exceed a particular productivity rate. But if a reasonably large number of industries is considered, such differences can wash out. On the other hand, a number of industries pressed for a higher rate of productivity gain may fail to respond simply because they lack the needed dynamic flexibility. If some industries could not widen their cost spreads in the face of adversity, how else could we explain their lack of response?

Moreover, we cannot hope to know on the basis of a priori reasoning the general relationship between price behavior and dynamic flexibility. Is there a linear relationship between the price behavior of industries in a preceding period and their ability to respond to a greater degree of competitive necessity in a given period? Or is there some threshold of better average price performance below which industries are at a marked disadvantage when responding to increased pressures to restrain price increases? Only the data can enable us to answer that question.

The data analysis involved dividing all 387 four-digit industries into four groups, based on their price performance during the 1960s and again during the 1970s. The A group was composed of industries that during either or both periods raised their prices one standard deviation or more *less* than the average, which means that there was a marked decline in their relative prices. The D group was composed of industries that during either or both periods raised their prices one standard deviation or more *above* the average. The B and C groups were obtained by splitting the middle of the distribution (which provided better statistical results). Of the 387 industries, 145 remained in the same rankings during both periods. The model predicts, therefore, that when going from A to D industries, classified in terms of their price performance, we can expect to observe increasingly less impressive productivity performance. This is not to say, however, that when moving toward the D group we can expect to observe the same rate of productivity gain during both decades. Quite obviously, if firms can raise their prices by more than one standard deviation for an entire decade, without encountering equally serious output penalties, their incentives to generate steady improvements in productivity will not remain unchanged.

On the other hand, 136 industries moved up in price performance during the 1970s – a few from D to B, although none from D to A. The main reason for this, as revealed by matching the BLS data and the foreign-trade statistics, was increased pressure from foreign competition. These were the industries that operated under increasing degrees of necessity. Although, statistically speaking, we can predict that the ability to respond will be highly related to previous price performance, as already pointed out, there is no way of knowing beforehand whether the relationship will turn out to be linear or highly nonlinear.

There were 106 industries that declined in price performance, some all the way from A during the 1960s to D during the 1970s, because most were either directly or indirectly protected from foreign competition (e.g., protecting steel also means protecting the substitutes for steel). All of these industries operated under declining degrees of necessity. Hence, we can predict declining productivity performance depending on how far they fell in price performance.

The statistical results for all three groups were as follows. Consider, first, the industries that remained in the same price performance group during both periods. The average rate of productivity gain for the A group during both periods was almost 50 percent higher than that for the B group (more than 7 percent, as compared with less than 4 percent annually), and it dropped to about 2.5 percent for the C and D groups.

On the other hand, it is also apparent that stochastic elements were involved that affected the fortunes of entire industries. Thus, during the 1970s, about half of the industries in the A group exceeded their 1960s rates of productivity growth, and half fell below. Those industries that experienced somewhat disappointing productivity gains, as compared with the 1960s, experienced 15 percent losses in their productivity performance; those whose productivity performance rose during the 1970s experienced more than 50 percent improvements in their productivity performance.

On the other hand, whereas about 45 percent of the industries in the B group exceeded their previous rates of productivity gain by about 25 percent, the losers experienced a similar drop in productivity performance. By comparison, in the C group, about 35 percent of the industries exceeded their previous productivity rates, and the losers experienced sharper changes in productivity performance than the winners. Finally, only one-tenth of the D industries exceeded their previous productivity performance during the 1970s, and the losers experienced even sharper changes in productivity performance than the winners.

How are these results to be interpreted? The fact that loser industries in the A price performance group experienced relatively modest productivity rate losses, and the winners relatively handsome gains, strongly suggests that firms in those industries were acting to put good luck on their side while minimizing the consequences of bad luck. According to the basic model, after the width of the distribution reaches some threshold value, we should expect to find that productivity performance is highly sensitive to the value of the PERK. This is the apparent reason why the A group generated average productivity gains of 7 percent annually, as compared with 4 percent for the B group.

For reasons already discussed, the high-performance industries, in terms of generating new products, were also the high-performance productivity performers: The electronic computing industry's rate of productivity gain accelerated to 9 percent annually during the 1970s; that for the semiconductor industry was 10 percent, for the organic-fiber industry 10 percent, for the television industry 10 percent, and for the scientific instruments industry 8 percent.

As might be predicted, all of the high-PERK industries were engaged in playing positive-sum games. Although in manufacturing as a whole, output declined during the 1970s, in the computer industry it increased by about 15 percent annually, in the semiconductor industry by 13 percent, and in the television industry by 7 percent.

All of the industries in the B group increased their output rates during the 1970s, though by less than they did during the 1960s. The auto industry, which was the single most important industry in the B price performance group, experienced an output gain that fell 33 percent below that of the 1960s, and it was the industries in that category whose productivity gains worsened during the 1970s. Consequently, it may seem that the auto industry could have done a better job of stemming foreign imports if it had reduced its relative prices more than it did during the 1970s. But because productivity gains during the 1960s occurred largely as a result of shifting the product mix toward larger cars (whose price differences were much larger than their cost differences), achieving more significant productivity gains while emphasizing smaller cars would not have been easy. It also must be remembered that import quotas on Japanese cars imposed during the 1970s provided an incentive for Japanese automakers to upgrade their products, thereby stimulating a contest in gadgetry rather than in price terms.

Finally, it will be recalled that both the C and D industries generated productivity gains of about 2.5 percent annually during the two decades and that during both periods these industries experienced above-average price increases. Part of the reason that there was no real difference in productivity performance is simply that when the value of the PERK declines below the threshold, productivity gains are not highly sensitive to its value. Furthermore, when incentives for productivity performance are, on the whole, poor, differences in their negative values are probably of little consequence.

Thus, it should be apparent that there is an important asymmetry in the statistical results: Whereas going above the B threshold makes for a real difference in productivity performance, going below the threshold does not.

Next, consider those industries that were obliged to exercise a greater degree of price restraint during the 1970s. Those that moved up two steps in price performance increased their average rate of productivity performance by about 40 percent (from 2.4 percent annually during the 1960s to 3.4 percent annually during the 1970s), and those that moved up one step increased by about 30 percent (from 2.5 to 3.3 percent annually). Moreover, only about one-fifth of the industries in both groups experienced lower productivity rates during the 1970s, whereas four-fifths experienced higher rates.

Nevertheless, closer inspection of the data indicates a highly bimodal distribution with respect to the responses. On the one hand, those industries in the B price performance group during the 1960s and the A group during the 1970s exhibited the same productivity performance during the 1970s as those in the A price performance group during both periods, with productivity gains exceeding losses to an even greater degree. On the other hand, those in the C and D groups displayed far lesser ability to deal with adversity, for the apparent reason that they simply lacked dynamic flexibility.

Thus, a number of industries, including buttons, fluid milk, phonograph records, paint, power hand tools, sporting goods, and women's suits and coats, were able to double or more than double their rates of productivity gain during the 1970s. All these industries had been in the B price performance category during the 1960s, but had moved to the A category during the 1970s.

At the other end of the distribution were those industries in which dynamic flexibility apparently was lacking: They suffered declines of 50 percent or more in their productivity rates. These included prefabricated wooden buildings, newspapers, copper rolling and drawing, canned fruits and vegetables, and cutlery industries. All of these industries were in the C or D price performance category during the 1960s and were forced to move up one or two notches during the 1970s. As was already suggested, poorer than average price performance clearly implies an inability to deal with new circumstances.

Nevertheless, the data also strongly suggest that when industries are forced to operate under a higher degree of necessity to restrain price increases, firms in those industries are affected by changes in their incentives. All three groups of industries that moved up one or two grades in price performance during the 1970s improved their productivity rates by more than those that remained in the same price category. If we consider those industries in the D group during both decades, only 1 of 10 achieved improvement in its productivity rate. On the other hand, if we consider those industries that were in the D price performance group during the 1960s, but were forced to come up to B or C ranking during the 1970s, 4 of 10 increased their productivity rates. In short, if we liken the results to baseball, it is apparent that although a B pitcher has a distinct advantage over C and D pitchers, when it comes to playing tougher teams, even C and D pitchers can be expected to perform better in the major leagues than they did in the minor leagues.

Furthermore, the data clearly indicate that the probability of a positive-sum game developing is a function of productivity performance. Thus, of the 38 industries that boosted their productivity rates, most (out of 136 subject to increasing competitive pressures) experienced very substantial output gains during the 1970s (in 10, the output growth rate was up 100 percent as compared with the 1960s). But the probability of becoming involved in a positive-sum game was strongly related to an industry's previous price performance. Thus, whereas only one of five industries in the D price performance category and only one of four in the C category during the 1960s made the grade, three of five industries in the B category did. As common sense should suggest, the closer an industry's performance approximates a zero-sum game, the smaller the probability of turning it into a positive-sum game.

Finally, consider those industries whose relative prices went up more than the average. On the average, their productivity rate declined by about 40 percent between the two decades. Of the 25 largest industries in this category, three managed to boost their productivity rates, and two of them were in the A price performance category during the 1960s. On the other hand, of those experiencing productivity losses, there was no relation between previous price performance and a drop in the productivity rate, nor was there any clear relation between the degree prices zoomed in a particular industry and the output penalties it paid. On the other hand, the common thread that ran through nearly all the industries involved was this: Negative rewards in the form of output penalties were exceeded by positive rewards in the form of higher prices.

In other words, whereas the industries operating under diminishing price pressures were playing positive-sum games as far as the participants were concerned, they were playing negative-sum games as far as society was concerned, for the principal reason that they became more and more protected from foreign competition. The steel industry, which became increasingly protected in the late 1960s, raised input costs in manufacturing by as much as OPEC. By protecting steel, the government also was involved in protecting substitutes, such as lumber, cement, and aluminum – whose prices went up by almost as much as those of steel. A negative-sum game for other manufacturing industries was involved because of resulting losses in the competitiveness of their products.

Moreover, the press notwithstanding, it certainly can be said that during the 1970s, at least, the role of foreign competition was very positive: Whereas the output rate in all the industries subject to increasing price pressures (mainly from foreign competition) was down only 10 percent as compared with the 1960s, the output rate for those industries directly or indirectly protected from foreign competition was down by 40 percent!

Finally, it may be noted that although all the foregoing results measured productivity only in terms of labor inputs, I also had data on purchases of machinery and material inputs from other industries. The data clearly show that firms were quite indifferent whether to save in terms of capital, labor, or material inputs. Thus, the industries most pressed by foreign competition actually experienced larger declines in equipment purchases than those that were directly or indirectly protected, despite differences in their output rates.

The statistical test employed was Wilcoxon's Signed Rank Test at the 5 percent confidence level – and in all but nine industries the test could not falsify the hypothesis that when analyzing *entire collections of industries,* luck and necessity went hand in hand. But splendid statistical results do not imply splendid economic performance. In particular, luck and necessity may appear to go hand in hand at the industry level only because firms do not possess the dynamic flexibility to respond. Indeed, if the hypothesis that necessity and luck go hand in hand at the industry level could not have been falsified at the 10 percent rather than the 5 percent confidence level, the productivity performance in manufacturing would have been better.

For example, suppose that a greater proportion of industries in the

A price performance category had been as lucky as the computer and semiconductor industries in being able to boost their rates of productivity gain during the 1970s. If that had happened, the performance of the American economy would have been better, and at the same time, fewer of the A industries would have fallen into the acceptance region demanded by the statistical test.

More to the point, when an entire collection of less competitive industries behaves as if within them luck and necessity are working hand in hand, we can be quite certain that the same is not happening at the level of the firm. Of course, these industries cannot benefit equally from various technological advances, but surely that is not the only factor involved in explaining such results. It was not bad luck alone that prevented the U.S. auto industry from doubling its productivity performance during the 1970s; the same opportunities available to the Japanese auto industry were available to it. Nor can it be said that the Japanese auto industry was merely engaged in catching up with the U.S. auto industry in productivity performance: In several industries, Japan and other countries have surpassed the United States in productivity performance. So whereas the productivity performance of auto firms contributed to making the statistical distinction between the A and B industries as sharp as it was, it did not contribute as much as it might have to improving the performance of the American economy.

As we have already seen, those in the B price performance category were provided with a very distinct advantage from the point of view of being able to boost productivity gains when demanded by foreign competition and from the vantage of turning adversity into opportunity.

What, then, do these statistical results imply for improving the United States' balance-of-payments position? Inasmuch as productivity performance and innovative performance in generating improved products are highly correlated, it should be apparent that productivity performance can be employed as a predictor of a country's balance-of-payments position: If, after taking into account wage differentials, a country has more or less the same productivity performance as other industrialized countries, it should have neither a significant balance-of-payments surplus nor a deficit. If its productivity performance is better than the average, its balance-of-payments position should improve; if not, it should worsen.

As it happens, the United States' productivity performance has been averaging only about half of the Swedish rate (which is close to the average for all industrialized countries), and this is reflected in its balance-of-payments position. If we actually had comparable productivity and price data for Sweden, what would they show? My guess is that Swedish industries, like U.S. industries, are highly disparate in their productivity gains – with gains ranging from 1 or 2 percent annually to 10 percent or better. Something like half of Sweden's industrial output is not exported, and there is no reason to suppose that unchallenged Swedish industries do any better than unchallenged U.S. industries. On the other hand, there is no reason to suppose that those Swedish industries that do well in international competition have any worse productivity performance than those U.S. industries that do well. But it also seems very likely that the proportion of Swedish industry engaged in generating productivity gains at a better than 5 percent rate is decidedly higher than it is for the United States, and the proportion of those generating productivity gains at a lower rate is decidedly smaller.

On the basis of these considerations, it would appear that the challenge facing the U.S. economy, if its balance-of-payments position is not to continue to worsen, is to bring average productivity performance in manufacturing up to the rate now enjoyed by the B industries – not an easy task, but certainly not impossible.

To return to Schumpeter's concept, those industries not engaged in making the best possible use of resources at every moment, because they are dynamically flexible, can enjoy a more rapid rate of performance. The task is to get a greater number of industries into that category.

4.5   Socialism versus capitalism

As was pointed out in the preceding section, Schumpeter's famous proposition about the level of long-run performance simply does not stand up in an uncompetitive world. Moreover, if he were alive today, Schumpeter surely would recognize that the financial position of a firm does not in itself make the firm innovative. If the financial positions of firms were all that mattered, the United States still would be the undisputed technological leader of the world. And if socialist economies operated with the same pressures for risk taking, the Soviet economy would be in far better shape than it is today. The fundamental difference between socialism and capitalism is not a price system; rather, it is that, because of the lack of risk taking, socialistic economies tend to be zero-sum economies.

But as Edward Mason (1982) pointed out several years ago, Schumpeter himself never favored the establishment of a "Schumpeterian school." In fact, he was rather contemptuous of all so-called schools of economics. For example, in his lectures, Schumpeter described the attempts to reduce Keynes's arguments to simple ISLM diagrams as "Keynes for the kiddies." Moreover, as a teacher, there was nothing Schumpeter wanted more than to make his students think for themselves. Thus, his grading system, which he always announced at the beginning of each of his classes, consisted in the grade of A for exceptionally brilliant students, Radcliffe girls, and Jesuit fathers – everyone else received B. An "exceptionally brilliant student" need not even answer the questions in an exam directly; as long as an answer was tangentially related to the question, one could write on anything that demonstrated an ability to think for oneself. And, of students who merely repeated his own arguments, Schumpeter had been known to say: "That fellow is so stupid he will be a full professor before he is thirty!"

It is my belief that Schumpeter's wish that no school be named for him and his desire that students think for themselves were premised on the belief that economics itself should evolve in the direction of a better understanding of economic reality.

References

Feynman, Richard P., Leighton, Robert B., and Sands, Matthew (1966). *The Feynman Lectures on Physics.* New York: Addison-Wesley.

Klein, Burton H. (1977). *Dynamic Economics.* Cambridge, Mass.: Harvard University Press.

(1984). *Prices, Wages, and Business Cycles.* Elmsford, N.Y.: Pergamon.

Lewontin, Richard C. (1978). "Adaptation." *Scientific American,* 117(September).

Mason, Edward S. (1982). "The Harvard Department of Economics from the Beginning to World War II." *Quarterly Journal of Economics,* 97(3):383–433.

Mayr, Ernst (1978). "Evolution." *Scientific American,* 117(September).

Schumpeter, Joseph A. (1939). *Business Cycles.* New York: McGraw-Hill.

(1942). *Capitalism, Socialism and Democracy.* New York: Harper & Brothers.

Smith, Adam [1776] (1938). *An Inquiry into the Nature and the Causes of the Wealth of Nations.* London: J. M. Dent & Sons Ltd.

Discussion

HENRI J. VARTIAINEN

Professor Klein's stimulating and voluminous chapter discusses the nature of economic phenomena in relation to biology and other worlds, bringing out the similarities and differences between evolutionary economics and biology. According to him, there is a long-run trade-off between specialization and flexibility. This is borne out in the Scandinavian context as well; in times of turbulence, too rigid a commitment to basic technologies has caused difficulties among Swedish construction companies.

Chance plays a role in a great part of our economic activities: We happen to see somebody, hear or read a piece of interesting news; we happen to be in the right place at the right time. An active person, no doubt, can multiply his chances in this respect. Chance is like the fellow we meet on the road: Grab at his bushy hair on the forehead! If you don't do it at once, you will find him bald at the back of the head.

Professor Klein discusses zero-sum and non-zero-sum games. Distinction between these two worlds may often be less clear. In our experience, there may be companies that, in their own field and *inter pares,* face a zero-sum competition, but that engage in a joint effort to make the market grow. This can be done through their central association, distributing the costs of development evenly among the participants.

Professor Klein notes that output in those industries that were protected declined more than in those that were subject to the pressure of imports. This is a classic example of how a declining industry seldom, or never, can be saved, or turned to a new upward trend, by protection. But the question may be raised about the strategies of the import-competing firms. Were not they also obliged to save labor in order to counter the competition from countries with cheap labor?

A factor I would like to single out for discussion is the significance of *cooperation* as an economic resource. In our textbooks it is mostly ignored, as all our atomistic competitors are assumed to work in a social vacuum independent of each other. Coalitions are frowned on as an abuse of market power. Nevertheless, as long as the entrepreneurs are working on market conditions, cooperation between entrepreneurs (1) helps the companies find the optimal trade-off between their own production and purchases from other companies, (2) gives more information about the market, (3) helps in achieving cost reductions and economies of scale, (4) brings together market-oriented and product-oriented persons, the inventor and the financier, or a development company with resources and a company with assets but not enough vitality, (5) helps to find new markets, new products, or new applications and opens new development avenues for recent inventions or basic research, and (6) brings about cross-fertilization of new ideas, given that the crucial test lies in exposing the ideas to discussion.

Cooperation may take place not only among companies but also between the company and the society at large. Legal, technical, or other expertise may be underutilized if employed by one company only. A proper division of labor may achieve optimal use of this expertise in the society.

Professor Klein's reference to positive responses to increasing degrees of necessity, in the vein of stimuli to cultures, as described by the famous English historian Arnold Toynbee, brings to mind interesting connotations. I recall, in this connection, the war indemnities that the Soviet Union imposed on Finland in 1944 as the victor's right: 300 million dollars in goods at 1938 prices (600 million in current dollars), in products not easily created by the then existing industrial structure based on forest industries, and with exorbitant penalty-rate clauses to assure prompt delivery. For a country exhausted of its resources and a part of its territory, the task was really at the outermost edge of any possibility frontier. However, the debt was duly paid off with an unprecedented national effort that made it possible; the effort can be understood only if one considers the grim political alternative! The social capability brought out by Professor Abramovitz was undoubtedly there. The necessity experienced at that time gave birth to the modern and competitive engineering industry of today.

Discussion

ALFRED MAUSSNER

Professor Klein's chapter shows brilliantly how ideas from biological evolutionary theory, imaginatively mixed with economic concepts, result in a rich theory of economic progress. The chapter is full of ideas, propositions, and explanations. In my view, its most fundamental contributions are in applying biological evolutionary theory to the study of economic progress and in uncovering the role competition plays in stimulating innovative effort. Hence, in the following, I shall limit my attention to the evolutionary concept underlying Professor

Klein's theory and to the proposed relation between the degree of competition and the average propensity to engage in risk taking (PERK).

I start with the differences between biological evolution and economic progress or, more generally, the evolution of human societies. Two principal differences are mentioned by Professor Klein. These are different driving forces (physical necessity versus survival in competitive markets) and different kinds of inputs (a roughly constant genetic diversity versus an ever increasing diversity of hints for successful innovations). I think there is a third major difference: Only human beings are able to discover what governs both biological evolution and socioeconomic evolution, and the knowledge we have obtained about the world's laws of motion gives us the power to take our own destiny in hand. This is certainly a philosophical argument, but, in as far as it is accepted, it changes the role of competition in socioeconomic evolution. Let me elaborate this point.

From the viewpoint of methodological individualism, competition is a social institution established by agreement of a sufficient number of individuals as a means to deal with scarcity. Individual agreement to this institution hinges on the benefits accruing from it. As Professor Klein has pointed out, in the long run, competition is a positive-sum game, but in the short run, there are winners and losers. Now suppose that people are more concerned with today's gains and losses than with future gains. In this case, competition is less favorable, and there will be efforts to reduce it.[1] Think, for example, of increasing protectionism. As a consequence, the pressure for technological improvement and thus economic progress decreases. At the same time, it is profitable to exhaust the given technological potential to a higher degree. Therefore, dynamic flexibility, as defined by Professor Klein, declines. Hence, the economic system will be more vulnerable to exogenous shocks. Furthermore, if we accept the hypothesis of Uzawa (1968) that increasing prosperity shifts people's attention toward today's events, it will be possible to explain the productivity slowdown during the past decade in most Western industrialized countries as a consequence of the rapid growth after World War II.[2]

What I have just tried to explain is that there is a connection between the outcomes of given market structures (and thus given degrees of competitiveness and the PERK) and the forces determining

---

[1] I have elaborated this point more precisely elsewhere (Maussner, 1986).
[2] Neumann (1985) develops a theory of long swings in economic evolution based on the interplay between growing prosperity and the favorableness of competition.

these structures. I think that evolutionary economics should take into ✓
account the mechanism based on this connection.

Let me now turn to the propositions concerning the relation between
necessity brought about by dynamic competition and the PERK, as
measured by the innovative performance of a firm. Professor Klein
argues that increasing competitive pressure tends to raise a firm's
PERK and that without the threat of foreign competition or the entry
of more competitive rivals, the PERK will decline.

Both propositions seem strange from the perspective of traditional
economic theory. A firm has command over a variety of instruments
to protect profits from erosion by competitors. This variety ranges
from product prices to advertising to lobbying for protection from
competition. Thus, there cannot be a single road from more competition to more innovative effort. Furthermore, in a Nash equilibrium,
by its very definition, a firm does not change its strategy as long as its ✓
competitors do not do so.

In order to prove these claims, I set up a simple model that includes
the main ingredients of Professor Klein's model, namely, competitive
pressure, product and process innovation, long-run profit maximization that implies that profits per period fall short of the profits a one-
period profit maximizer could acquire, and the concept of a Nash equilibrium; that is, the firm takes (implicitly) the actions of its rivals as
given when choosing its optimal strategy.

I consider a firm that seeks to maximize its present value (i.e., the
discounted value of its net cash flow).[3] In order to do so, the firm has
two instruments: the price of its product p and the degree to which it
tries to bring about innovations π, which is a measure of the PERK.
The model is entirely deterministic and contains no imaginative entrepreneur. Thus, it cannot compete in richness with Professor Klein's
model, but even in this simple model it is by no means clear that an
increase in competitive pressure raises the PERK. There are values of
the elasticity of demand with respect to product quality $\epsilon_{q,x}$ conceivable
for which an increase in competitive pressure will result in lowering
the target level of the PERK.

This model may also help to explain changes in the interindustry
pattern of the PERK, for its predicts that rising real interest rates (such
as we have experienced in the more recent past) will induce firms operating in markets with a high $\epsilon_{q,x}$ to increase the PERK, while firms
operating in quality-insensitive markets may find it profitable to
reduce the PERK.

---

[3] The model is described and analyzed in the Appendix that follows.

Finally, I should point out that the firm faces no incentives to change the PERK as long as its rivals do not change their strategy, that is, $\bar{x}$ (competitive pressure) remains unchanged. Thus, only if the number of firms in a market is small, so that collusion is highly possible, is it conceivable that they commonly will agree to lower the PERK.

In concluding, I must stress that these results are derived from a simple model and thus have to be taken with care. Nevertheless, I hope they will stimulate the discussion of Professor Klein's ingenious chapter.

Appendix: Price and product policy of a profit-maximizing firm – a simple example

Consider a firm facing a linear, downward-sloping demand curve for its output q. If the firm does not try to improve the quality of its product via R&D effort, it will lose customers to its more innovative rivals. This is formally captured by shifting the demand curve toward the origin. Denote the firm's product price by p, and the shift parameter by x. Then the demand function can be written as[4]

$$q = q(p, x), \qquad q_p, q_x < 0, \qquad q_{pp}, q_{xx}, q_{px} = 0 \tag{1}$$

The change in x is given by the differential equation

$$\dot{x} = \bar{x} - \pi x, \qquad \bar{x} > 0 \tag{2}$$

where $\bar{x}$ measures the competitive pressure on the firm to improve the quality of its product, and π is a measure of successful innovations per unit of time t. If $\pi = 0$, $x(t) = \bar{x}t$, and the demand curve shifts smoothly toward the origin.

In addition to preventing the firm from losing customers, innovative activity decreases unit production costs c in successive periods of time according to

$$\dot{\tilde{c}} = -\pi\tilde{c} \tag{3}$$

Unit costs at a given time t are assumed to be independent of total production and are given by

$$c = a + \tilde{c}, \qquad a > 0 \tag{4}$$

Finally, assume that bringing about innovations costs $R(\pi)$, $R(0) = 0$,

---

[4] I denote partial derivatives of the function $f(y, z)$ by f_y, f_z, f_{yy}, f_{zz}, and f_{yz}. Derivatives of a function in one variable are denoted by prime. Derivatives with respect to time are denoted by a dot. All variables depend on time. For notational convenience, this is not made explicit.

0, R', $R'' > 0$. Hence, profit at time t is

$$(p - c)q(p, x) - R(\pi) \tag{5}$$

The firm seeks a price and product policy that will maximize the discounted value of its profits. Assuming a constant discount rate $r > 0$, this policy is found as the solution of the following optimal-control problem:

$$\max_{\{p, x\}} \int_0^\infty [(p - c)q(p, x) - R(\pi)]e^{-rt}\, dt$$

where

$$\dot{x} = \bar{x} - \pi x, \qquad \dot{\tilde{c}} = -\pi\tilde{c}, \qquad x(0) = x_0, \qquad \tilde{c}(0) = \tilde{c}_0$$

This solution[5] satisfies the following conditions:

$$q(p, x) + (p - c)q_p = 0 \tag{6a}$$
$$R'(\pi) = -\psi_1\tilde{c} - \psi_2 x \tag{6b}$$
$$\dot{\psi}_1 = \psi_1(r + \pi) + q(p, x) \tag{7a}$$
$$\dot{\psi}_2 = \psi_2(r + \pi) - q_x(p - c) \tag{7b}$$
$$\dot{x} = \bar{x} - \pi x \tag{7c}$$
$$\dot{\tilde{c}} = -\pi\tilde{c} \tag{7d}$$

The equations (6) determine at every $t \in [0, \infty]$ for given values of the state variables x and $\tilde{c}$ and the costate variables ψ_1 and ψ_2 the optimal values of the control variables p and π. These determine, in turn, via the equations of motion (7), the state and costate variables of the next period.

Obviously, equation (6b) implies that intertemporal profit maximization requires $\pi > 0$, and hence profits per period are lower than they were under short-run profit maximizing ($\pi = 0$).

A rest point of the system described by equations (6) and (7) is an equilibrium where $\dot{\psi}_1 = \dot{\psi}_2 = \dot{x} = \dot{\tilde{c}} = 0$. The values for the optimal instruments p and π in this equilibrium are the solutions of[6]

$$q\left(p, \frac{x}{\pi}\right) + (p - a)q_p = 0 \tag{8a}$$

$$-R''(\pi) - \frac{\bar{x}q_x(p - a)}{\pi(r + \pi)} = 0 \tag{8b}$$

---

[5] Because $(p - c)q(p, x) - R(\pi)$ is strictly concave in (p, π), and $\dot{x} = \bar{x} - \pi x$ and $\dot{\tilde{c}} = -\pi\tilde{c}$ are linear in π, a solution exists if $(p - c)q(p, x) - R(\pi)$ and the two equations of motion (7c) and (7d) are continuous and bounded with bounded derivatives. (Kamien and Schwartz, 1981, p. 203).

[6] For my linear demand curve, this solution is unique and satisfies $0 < \pi < 1$, $p > a$.

It can be shown that a sufficiently low elasticity of demand with respect to product quality $\epsilon_{q,x}$ implies that there is only one path converging to this equilibrium.[7]

From the equations (6) it can be inferred that along that path, successful innovations may have opposite effects on the product's price: In as much as they lower unit costs, they induce a price decrease, but in as much as they lower competitive pressure, they induce a price increase. The innovative effort decreases with decreasing costs and decreasing competitive pressure.[8]

Now, consider a sudden change in the firm's environment brought about by either a rise of the discount rate r or competitive pressure $\bar{x}$.

---

[7] The Jacobian of (7) evaluated at the rest point is

$$
J = \begin{bmatrix}
\dfrac{\psi_2 x}{R''} - \pi & \dfrac{\psi_1 x}{R''} & 0 & \dfrac{x^2}{R''} \\[2ex]
0 & -\pi & 0 & 0 \\[2ex]
\dfrac{q_x}{2} - \dfrac{\psi_1 \psi_2}{R''} & \dfrac{q_p}{2} - \dfrac{\psi_1^2}{R''} & \pi & -\dfrac{\psi_1 x}{R''} \\[2ex]
\dfrac{q_x^2}{2q_p} - \dfrac{\psi_2^2}{R''} & q_x - \dfrac{\psi_1 \psi_2}{R''} & 0 & \pi - \dfrac{\psi_2 x}{R''}
\end{bmatrix}
$$

with tr $J = 0$ and

$$
\det J = -\pi^2 \left(-\pi^2 + \frac{\psi_2 x}{R''}\pi - \frac{q_x^2 x}{2q_p R''} \right)
$$

Sufficient for $\det J > 0$ is

$$
\frac{\psi_2 x}{R''}\pi - \frac{q_x^2 x}{2q_p R''} < 0
$$

Because the stationary value of ψ_2 from equation (7b) is $\psi_2 = q_x(p - a)/(r + \pi)$, some manipulations of the foregoing inequality yield [notice that, from (8a), $(1 - a/p) = 1/\epsilon_{q,p}$]

$$
\epsilon_{q,p} < \frac{4\pi}{r + \pi}
$$

where $\epsilon_{q,p} := -q_p p/q$ ($\epsilon_{q,x} := -q_x x/q$) is the elasticity of demand with respect to the price (product quality).

If $\det J > 0$, J must have two positive and two negative eigenvalues, because tr $J = 0$. Thus, the stationary equilibrium is a saddlepoint.

[8] The analytical expressions derived from equations (6) are

$$
\frac{\partial p}{\partial x} = \frac{-q_x}{(2q_p)} < 0, \qquad \frac{\partial p}{\partial \tilde{c}} = \frac{1}{2} > 0, \qquad \frac{\partial \pi}{\partial x} = \frac{-\psi_2}{R''} > 0, \qquad \frac{\partial \pi}{\partial \tilde{c}} = \frac{-\psi_1}{R''} > 0
$$

From equation (8), the following formulas for the direction of change of the target levels of p and π can be derived:

$$\frac{\partial \pi}{\partial r} = -2\Delta^{-1} \frac{q_p q_x x(p - a)}{(\pi + r)^2} \tag{9a}$$

$$\frac{\partial \pi}{\partial \bar{x}} = \Delta^{-1} \frac{q_x q(\epsilon_{q,x} - 2)}{\pi(\pi + r)} \tag{9b}$$

$$\frac{\partial p}{\partial r} = -\Delta^{-1} \frac{q_x^2 x^2(p - q)}{\pi(\pi + r)} \tag{9c}$$

$$\frac{\partial p}{\partial \bar{x}} = \Delta^{-1} \left(\frac{q_x R''}{\pi} + \frac{q_x^2 x(p - a)(1 - 2 - r)}{\pi^2(\pi + r)} \right) \tag{9d}$$

$$\Delta := -2q_p R'' + \frac{q_x q x}{\pi(\pi + r)} [\epsilon_{q,x} - 2(r + 2\pi)], \qquad \epsilon_{q,x} := -q_x x/q$$

Hence, the target level of π declines when r rises, if the demand is not too sensitive with respect to changes in the quality of the product ($\epsilon_{q,x} < 2r + 4\pi$). In this instance it is better to increase the target price level. For a sufficiently large $\epsilon_{q,x}$ (so that Δ becomes negative), it may be optimal to increase innovative efforts and to lower the price. An increase in competitive pressure increases π, if $\epsilon_{q,x} < 2 < 2r + 4\pi$. This also holds true if $\epsilon_{q,x}$ is sufficiently large, so that both Δ and $q_x q(\epsilon_{q,x} - 2)$ become negative. But there are constellations of $\epsilon_{q,x}$, r, and π conceivable that will result in a decline in π when $\bar{x}$ rises. No clear-cut answers can be given with respect to price changes as a result of increased competitive pressure.

Because, in this example, the firm disregards possible reactions of its competitors, the solution concept implicitly employed assumes a Nash equilibrium.

If one firm reduces its innovative effort as a result of a higher interest rate, and so do its competitors, the necessity to bring about innovations $\bar{x}$ will decline, reducing π even more.

In conclusion, this example aims to demonstrate (1) that in a Nash equilibrium there is no incentive for a profit-maximizing firm to reduce π (and thus the PERK) as long as its environment remains unchanged, (2) that increasing necessity might not result in more innovative effort, and (3) that given a certain environment, the degree of using prices or product quality as competitive instruments depends on the relative effectiveness of the two instruments.

References

Kamien, Morton I., and Schwartz, Nancy L. (1981). *Dynamic Optimization.* Amsterdam: North Holland.

Maussner, Alfred (1986). *Market versus Political Decision Making.* Unpublished manuscript, Nurnberg.

Neumann, Manfred (1985). "Long Swings in Economic Development, Social Time Preference and Institutional Change." *Zeitschrift für die gesamte Staatwissenschaft,* 141:21–35.

Uzawa, H. (1968). "Time Preference, the Consumption Function, and Optimum Asset Holdings," in J. N. Wolfe (ed.), *Value, Capital and Growth* (pp. 485–504). Edinburgh University Press.

CHAPTER 5

Enterprise ownership and managerial behavior

FREDERIC M. SCHERER

Who owns the modern business enterprise, and what difference does ownership make behaviorally? On this, as on so many fundamental questions of capitalist organization, Schumpeter had strong views. He believed that the process of enterprise-building and rationalization eliminated "a host of small and medium-sized firms," whose owner-managers comprise "the very foundation of private property and free contracting" (Schumpeter, 1942, p. 140). And that change mattered greatly, he asserted:

The capitalist process, by substituting a mere parcel of shares for the walls of and the machines in a factory, takes the life out of the idea of property. It loosens the grip that once was so strong – the grip in the sense of the legal right and the actual ability to do as one pleases with one's own; the grip also in the sense that the holder of the title loses the will to fight, economically, physically, politically for "his" factory and his control over it, and to die if necessary on its steps.... Dematerialized, defunctionalized and absentee ownership does not impress and call forth moral allegiance as the vital form of property did. (Schumpeter, 1942, p. 142)

In this chapter I summarize the evidence on U.S. enterprise ownership and behavior from a much longer paper presented at the Schumpeter Society conference, but whose publication had been promised for another medium.[1] My insights are limited by available statistical and historical materials, which unfortunately do not enumerate the entrepreneurs who gave their last full measure of devotion at the factory barricades. Nevertheless, some progress can be achieved toward illuminating Schumpeter's economic (as distinguished from his sociological and political) concerns.

[1] See Scherer (1988). I am indebted to the American Academy of Arts and Sciences for their financial support for the underlying research.

5.1   The increasing dominance of the corporate form

In present-day America, as in other Western industrialized nations, the corporation is the dominant form of business organization. The current structure reflects an evolution that had its most dynamic phase during the nineteenth century. In 1801, the United States was home to fewer than 350 business corporations (Handlin and Handlin, 1945, p. 4). By 1900, the Census Bureau found that corporations were operating 37,161 establishments in the manufacturing sector alone. Still, the process had not reached its limit. In 1900, 65 percent of the value of output in manufacturing originated in plants owned by corporations. The corporate share of manufacturing output rose to 87.7 percent in 1919, 91.9 percent in 1947, and 98.0 percent in 1982.

Manufacturing is not completely typical. In other industrial sectors, the trend toward corporate organization has gone less far. In agriculture, only 27.1 percent of 1978 sales were made by corporations, in construction, 76.3 percent, in retail trade, 79.9 percent, and in the large and diverse services sector, 63.5 percent. The analogous figure for manufacturing (not precisely comparable with the Census Bureau data of the preceding paragraph) was 98.8 percent.

During the early 1980s, nearly 3 million business corporations filed U.S. income tax returns annually. Most were small, but the roughly 50,000 enterprises with sales of $10 million or more accounted for three-fourths of total corporate sales. Even among the larger corporations, the vast majority were privately held, that is, without securities traded openly on the stock exchanges. Only about 6,000 corporations share the distinction of having their shares "publicly" traded.

Most privately held corporations conform more or less closely to the classic business-enterprise model, with common stockholders (usually confined to one or a few family groups) playing an active role in the company's direction and management. Corporations with publicly traded shares are quite different. For them, ownership interests tend to be widely dispersed. It is rare now that a single family holds a majority stock-ownership position in a "public" corporation. In 1985, IBM had 798,152 common stockholders, and retailer Sears Roebuck had 318,686. The median industrial corporation on the *Fortune* 500 industrials list for 1956 (the last year for which comprehensive data were reported) had 9,117 shareholders. A New York Stock Exchange survey for 1985 shows that 47 million Americans held some shares of stock in public corporations. Despite this, stock ownership continues to be preponderantly the province of the wealthy. A 1972 survey – the latest available – shows that 56.5 percent of the personally held corporate stock by value belonged to the wealthiest 1 percent of all adult wealth-holders.[2]

Although in one sense corporate ownership is concentrated among a relatively small capitalist class, in another sense "people's capitalism" has made impressive strides. A large and growing fraction of all corporate stock resides in the portfolios of financial intermediaries, among which pension funds and insurance companies are particularly prominent. A Securities and Exchange Commission (1981, p. 117) survey for 1979 showed that institutional holdings comprised nearly 35 percent of the market value of outstanding common and preferred stock. Although comparable data are not yet available for more recent years, there is reason to believe that institutional positions, and especially those of the pension funds, have grown disproportionately rapidly. Among the 1,000 largest U.S. public corporations in 1985, ranked by *Business Week* according to the market value of their outstanding stock, the median top-500 member reported half of its shares to be in the hands of financial institutions, while for companies 501 to 1,000, institutions held 37 percent of the median firm's shares.[3]

At least in principle, the vast portfolio holdings managed by financial institutions confer power to shape operating enterprise decision making. Thomas Dye (1983, pp. 865–6) attempted, for the *Fortune* 500 industrials of 1981, to identify "strategic ownership positions," defined as persons or organizations numbered among the top five listed shareholders of a company, and with 1 percent or more of the company's outstanding common shares. Of the 2,156 positions so identified, 486 were held by banks, 860 by financial holding firms (such as trust companies, mutual funds, and employee stock trust managers), 101 by insurance companies, and 122 by pension funds. Altogether, 72 percent of the strategic ownership positions were occupied by financial intermediaries.

The implications of a "people's capitalism" intermediated by pension, mutual, and other fund managers are poorly understood. One channel for control is voting in periodic proxy solicitations. Most fund managers exercise that prerogative directly, rather than passing it back to the ultimate beneficiaries, and at least on occasion they vote against the recommendations of management.[4] A more visible channel is

---

[2] U.S. Department of Commerce, *Statistical Abstract of the United States: 1979*, p. 470 (from research by James D. Smith and Stephen D. Franklin).

[3] Tabulated by the author from "The 1,000 Largest U.S. Companies Ranked by Stock Market Valuation." *Business Week*, April 18, 1986, pp. 62–119.

[4] See Kotz (1978, pp. 68, 137–8), drawing on a Securities and Exchange Commission survey.

membership on a corporation's board of directors. Edward Herman (1981, pp. 130–1) found that in 1975, 162 of the 200 largest U.S. non-financial corporations had at least one financial-intermediary official on their boards. How such positions influence decision making is less clear. Herman believes that financial-intermediary representatives play a largely passive role except during crises; Kotz, on the other hand, believes that they exercise more pervasive and powerful control.[5]

In one sense, the 1980s have witnessed a significant reversion of corporate ownership structures to more traditional forms. This has occurred through "going private" transactions, in which parts of larger corporations are spun off and established as free-standing enterprises whose stock is held by only a small circle of investors, including the new entity's top managers. Or, in other cases, entire corporations have "gone private" when a group, usually including management, has bought out public shareholder interests. In 1985, such "management buyout" transactions transferred shares valued at $29.1 billion from old to new shareholder groups (Grimm, 1986, pp. 105, 117). To let managers become substantial common-stock investors, the new companies are usually highly "leveraged," with debt financing exceeding common-stock equity capital by four to six times – more like the financial structure of the typical Japanese corporation than U.S. enterprises. Following such transformations, invigorated efforts to cut costs and eliminate organizational "fat" are often observed (Ravenscraft and Scherer, 1987a, chap. 5). Insufficient evidence exists to determine how much these behavioral changes are attributable to the strengthened ownership interest of managers, how much to the cost consciousness necessitated by risky debt financing, and how much to the accompanying organizational simplifications (e.g., from complex multidivisional form to unitary structures). Empirical research on such transformations is severely hampered because organizations that have "gone private" no longer publish annual financial reports.

5.2   Ownership structure and behavior: theory

The central question raised by the changes in business-enterprise ownership structures is how differing structures affect corporations' operating decisions and performance. A seminal contribution to the debate came from Berle and Means (1932). They argued that large "public" corporations were becoming increasingly dominant in the economy, that the stock ownership in public corporations was becoming increas-

---

[5] Compare Kotz (1978, pp. 60–71, 119–30) with Herman (1981, pp. 121–61).

ingly dispersed and divorced from managerial control functions, and that this "separation of ownership and control" could lead to behavior advancing management interests while sacrificing the fulfillment of owner goals.

The Berle and Means book precipitated a lively debate over how one identifies the point at which ownership becomes so dispersed that managers are by default the sole or principal controllers of corporations' destinies. Berle and Means believed that management control was likely when there was no "compact" stockholder group with 20 percent or more of outstanding shares. By this standard, 88 of the largest 200 U.S. nonfinancial corporations were management-controlled in 1929, and 161 were management-controlled by 1963 (Larner, 1970, p. 22). Other investigators, such as Burch (1972, pp. 68, 96), argued that effective owner control could be exercised by groups with ownership shares as small as 4 to 5 percent. By this criterion, Burch found, only 41 percent of the leading 300 U.S. industrial corporations were management-controlled in 1965.

How managerial behavior might change when ownership and control are separated has been the subject of equally intense debate. Berle and Means believed that managers might profit at stockholders' expense from sham transactions and market manipulation, reinvest too much of the enterprise's profits to expand their personal empires, offer excessively generous wages and working conditions, or improve product quality beyond the point of maximum profitability. Scholars observing the more recent business scene have added other possibilities, such as overspending on luxurious offices, bloated staffs, corporate jets, and similar amenities. Or nonowner managers might fail the critical Schumpeterian test: shunning risk, letting innovation fall victim to bureaucratic inertia, or opting for "the quiet life."

As always, the thesis that markets fail, in this instance as a result of problems involving internal organizational structure, has evoked strong antitheses. Among the most original of the answers to Berle and Means has been the contribution of Jensen and Meckling (1976). They argue, inter alia, that to expect a perfect solution to the problem of controlling and motivating the modern corporation is to engage in the "Nirvana fallacy." Rather, a trade-off must be struck between the costs incurred to ensure that managers properly serve owner interests and the costs generated by deviations from that norm. Helping ensure an optimal (even if imperfect) solution to this "principal-agent" problem is competition among would-be managers to accept performance contracts correlating their rewards with the advancement of owner interests. Also, as Jensen and Meckling proposed, a "bonding" mechanism can help induce good performance when operating corporations borrow from banks and other intermediaries sufficiently well organized to monitor closely what goes on in the borrowing entity.

Another possible constraint on managers' ability to stray from the advancement of owner interests is the threat of takeover. If managers fail to maximize profits, they may attract the attention of outsiders who, offering a stock price premium justified by the expectation of increased future profits, gain a majority control position, displace the delinquent executives, and implement new business policies. Because takeover activity in the United States and the United Kingdom mounted to record-setting levels during the 1980s, and perhaps also because some observers see takeovers as a corrective to palpably disappointing productivity growth and other shortcomings, the takeover theory of managerial discipline has captured the imagination of economists, politicians, and the public alike.

However, takeovers can create problems as well as solve them. For one thing, fear of takeover induces managers not only to hew more closely to the profit-maximization norm but also to avoid risk and take defensive measures inconsistent with any plausible definition of profit maximization. This is a particular danger when selection as a takeover target entails substantial chance elements (e.g., when "raiders" err in their judgments that profits are not being maximized, or when a takeover can be set in motion by stock-market valuation errors as well as incumbent management lassitude). Second, it is far from clear what "profit maximization" means, and especially how stock markets trade off short-run profit increases against ensuing strategic position losses when higher prices or reduced investment encourage rival-firm expansion. The danger is particularly great when stockholdings are concentrated increasingly in the hands of institutional fund managers under heavy pressure to show good portfolio returns in the short run of a single calendar quarter or year. Finally, the theory assumes that the groups effecting corporate takeovers will manage the organizations they seize more profitably than the executives they displace. However, evidence on a substantial number of U.S. takeovers consummated during the 1960s and early 1970s reveals neither an increase nor a decrease in basic operating profitability nine years on average after the takeovers occurred (Ravenscraft and Scherer, 1987b).

5.3   Statistical evidence on ownership structure: performance links

There are severe limits to what one can learn from one's armchair about the links between the ownership structure of modern corporations and their ultimate economic performance. There are disagreements as to how much autonomous control nonowner managers have, how widely they exploit their position to serve their own (as distinguished from owners') goals, and what mechanisms are effective in reconciling owner and manager objectives. Confronted with these ambiguities, economists have turned to statistical analysis in an attempt to understand more fully the links between ownership structure and performance.

One line of research has shown that even in large corporations whose stock ownership is widely dispersed, managers may nevertheless have equity interests sufficient to motivate behavior consistent with profit maximization. A small fraction of a large corporation's equity capital may be a sizable fortune to the individual top executive. Thus, Kevin Murphy (1985) examined the stockholdings and compensation of 461 U.S. corporate executives, 41 percent occupying the office of chairman or president, and the remainder at lower levels. He found that the average executive's 1983 stockholdings amounted to $4.7 million – 13 times his annual salary and bonus compensation. If such an executive could, by heroic efforts, move his company from the lowest decile in terms of 1964–81 common-stock investor annual returns to the top quintile, the value of his own stockholdings would increase by roughly $5 million. Although a transformation of this magnitude may be impossible owing to forces beyond the manager's control, executives certainly must recognize that their own wealth depends significantly on the quality of their stewardship for other shareholders.

To the extent that appropriate incentive provisions are adopted, top executives' salaries and bonuses should also be correlated with profitability. Numerous statistical studies have tested this hypothesis. The weight of evidence supports it, albeit weakly. In one of the most recent studies, Murphy (1985, p. 26) found that managers of companies with stock-price declines exceeding 30 percent suffered, on average, pay decreases of 1.2 percent per year, while those whose stock increased in value by 30 percent or more received compensation gains averaging 8.7 percent per year. Probing beyond the broad averages, some have hypothesized that more powerful executive incentive contracts are designed when a company's board of directors includes strong outside ownership interest representation than when the board is controlled by internal management. The tests to date of this hypothesis have yielded equivocal results.[6]

A third line of approach is to determine if there are discernible statistical links directly from ownership structure to profitability or the

---

[6] See, for example, McEachern (1975, pp. 77–84), Stigler and Friedland (1983, pp. 248–54), and Santerre and Neun (1986, pp. 685–7).

growth of common-stock values. The numerous studies of this genre provide no clear or consistent picture. Some show no correlation between structure and performance, whereas others find a relationship, but disagree concerning its sign. One of the most recent contributions (Morck et al., 1986) obtains a nonlinear relationship, with common stockholders benefiting as the proportion of shares held by board-of-directors members rises into the 5–20 percent range, but suffering value losses at higher owner-representation fractions. The implication drawn is that manager-directors with strong ownership positions can indulge their personal whims without fearing displacement by take-over or the revolt of minority shareholders. This result, it must be noted, seems inconsistent with the evidence that performance improvements follow when corporations "go private" and substitute concentrated manager ownership for diffused stockholdings. A possible reconciliation suggested by Morck et al. is that concentrated manager ownership is conducive to profit maximization in the early stages of a corporation's life cycle, but that as time goes on, the perpetuation of control by an inside owner group leads to increasing divergence between owner-manager and outside-owner interests.

5.4   Conclusion

The process of creative destruction has brought the corporation to the forefront of business organizational forms. Much remains to be learned about which ownership structures are best suited to the challenges of the contemporary economy or, more likely, how the rich diversity of existing structures adapts to the varying demands of the marketplace and how, within any given structure, performance outcomes vary with differing owner–manager principal–agent relationships.

References

Berle, Adolf A., Jr., and Means, Gardiner C. (1932). *The Modern Corporation and Private Property.* Chicago: Commerce Clearing House.

Burch, Phillip H., Jr. (1972). *The Managerial Revolution Reassessed.* Lexington, Mass.: Heath.

Dye, Thomas R. (1983). "Who Owns America: Strategic Ownership Positions in Industrial Corporations." *Social Science Quarterly,* 64(December):862–70.

Grimm, W. T., & Co. (1986). *Mergerstat Review: 1985.* Chicago: Grimm & Co.

Handlin, Oscar, and Handlin, Mary F. (1945). "Origins of the American Business Corporation." *Journal of Economic History,* 5(May):1–23.

Herman, Edward S. (1981). *Corporate Control, Corporate Power.* Cambridge University Press.

Jensen, Michael C., and Meckling, William H. (1976). "Theory of the Firm: Managerial Behavior, Agency Costs, and Ownership Structure." *Journal of Financial Economics,* 3(October):305–60.

Kotz, David M. (1978). *Bank Control of Large Corporations in the United States.* Berkeley: University of California Press.

Larner, Robert J. (1970). *Management Control and the Large Corporation.* Cambridge, Mass.: Dunellen.

McEachern, William A. (1975). *Managerial Control and Performance.* Lexington, Mass.: Heath.

Morck, Randall, Shleifer, Andrei, and Vishny, Robert (1986). "Management Ownership and Corporate Performance: An Empirical Analysis." Cambridge, Mass.: National Bureau of Economic Research Working Paper No. 2055.

Murphy, Kevin J. (1985). "Corporate Performance and Managerial Remuneration: An Empirical Analysis." *Journal of Accounting and Economics,* 7(April):11–42.

Ravenscraft, David J., and Scherer, F. M. (1987a). *Mergers, Sell-offs, and Economic Efficiency.* Washington, D.C.: Brookings Institution.

(1987b). "Life After Takeover." *Journal of Industrial Economics,* 36(September).

Santerre, Rexford E., and Neun, Stephen P. (1986). "Stock Dispersion and Executive Compensation." *Review of Economics and Statistics,* 68(November):685–7.

Scherer, F. M. (1988). "The Ownership of U.S. Corporations," in American Academy of Arts and Sciences symposium on the U.S. business corporation.

Schumpeter, Joseph A. (1942). *Capitalism, Socialism and Democracy.* New York: Harper.

Securities and Exchange Commission (1981). *Annual Report: 1980.* Washington, D.C.: U.S. Government Printing Office.

Stigler, George J., and Friedland, Claire (1983). "The Literature of Economics: The Case of Berle and Means." *Journal of Law and Economics,* 26(June):237–68.

Discussion

REINHARD BLUM

Entrepreneur without ownership

I agree with the starting point of Scherer's chapter that in capitalism, according to traditional theorizing, entrepreneurial behavior follows from ownership of capital. The relation of ownership and behavior in reality, however, is a different question, and that is the topic the chapter deals with. But our symposium is concerned with the Schumpeterian spirit. As for this spirit, I would like to depart slighty from Scherer's chapter to set up the proposition that this spirit points in just the opposite direction to an entrepreneurial behavior that is not necessarily the result of ownership of capital. In this sense, Schumpeter establishes a new paradigm of capitalism.

First, I shall justify my argument by characterizing the two ways of traditional economic thinking according to the theory of comparative economic systems and its consequences, in order to demonstrate where Schumpeter's new paradigm on entrepreneurial behavior and evolution originates. Second, I shall use the approach of modern industrial-organization theory to elucidate Schumpeter's view and its consequences.

Comparative-economic-systems approach

The traditional theory of comparative economic systems follows either "individual rationality," bottom-up from the sovereign consumer to a welfare maximum, or runs top-down, guided by "collective rationality" according to political goals. The coordination mechanism is either market (market economy) or plan (planned economy). Both ideal economic systems start from antagonistic philosophies, namely, economic liberalism and socialism (Williams and Findlay, 1981). Consequently, following the "laws of logic," the one philosophy denies what the other one declares to be a central institution for freedom and efficient economic behavior. Thus, there is either private ownership of capital or state ownership. But common to both ideal systems is an ideal man: Economic man, in one case, or socialist man, in the other, secures harmony within the system.

Logical confusion arises if (as we observe in reality) the central elements (especially market and plan) are mixed, and we arrive at the so-called mixed economies of our textbooks. Socialist theorizing derives a class struggle between capital and labor, leading to a collapse of capitalism, according to the "founding father," Karl Marx, or, according to his successors, to "monopoly capitalism." Traditional theorizing following economic liberalism forecasts "the road to serfdom" (Hayek, [1944] 1976) or "the march into socialism" (Schumpeter, [1950] 1972). But "Schumpeterian socialism" loses one of socialism's central evils, as Schumpeter concludes in his book *Capitalism, Socialism and Democracy*. Here socialism appears to be compatible with democracy. Taking into consideration Schumpeter's idea of extending competition as a coordination mechanism from the economic to the political sphere, modern welfare states may be mixed economies and free societies at the same time.

One of the adherents to "Schumpeterian institutionalism," J. K. Galbraith, approached the issue from a different angle: First, he developed the idea of a "new invisible hand" to explain the American economic and political system as a system of countervailing power. Later he moved closer to the approach of "state-monopoly capitalism" by describing the United States as a coalition of military and economic managers. Fortunately, the Federal Republic of Germany (FRG) has experienced, contrary to traditional economic theorizing, the "social market economy," a third way between capitalism and socialism. This new economic philosophy created the well-known "German economic miracle" and the new word *Wirtschaftswunder*. This contrasts with modern predictions of senescence in other industrialized countries (now also put forward for U.S. industry in the chapter by M. Perlman).

I would like to suggest that these forecasts arise from the logical dilemma in traditional economic theorizing, which tells us that there are only two ways for mankind to go: a good way and a bad way. "Third ways" cause collapses of the system. Trying to solve this dilemma by internalizing policy in economic thinking as the "economic theory of policy, democracy, and property rights" leads again to dead ends indicated by solutions labeled "theorem," special "theory," or "paradox" (e.g., impossibility theorem, second-best theory, Arrow paradox, or voting paradox, in our textbooks). Applied to economic policy or policy in general, the "economic theory of policy" justifies policy by "market deficiency." But this avowal challenges traditional economic theorizing. That "state deficiency" hurts welfare more seriously than "market deficiency" can be derived from the same theory. Economic policy can only arrive at "second-best solutions." This also happens, unfortunately, to the social market economy in the FRG, which, fortunately enough, in reality represents a *Wirtschaftswunder*. Perhaps it is worthwhile for traditional theorists to quarrel about the ranking of "miracle" and "welfare maximum."

Industrial-organization-theory approach

Schumpeter's new paradigm offers another solution to the problem of "third ways." It takes into consideration that welfare in a free society also originates in democracy and that entrepreneurial behavior is not necessarily tied to an entrepreneur's ownership of capital. To elaborate on this point in more detail, I consider modern industrial-organization theory a better approach than traditional economic theorizing, which argues bottom-up from single markets to the market economy and market society and disregards the admonitions of A. Marshall to restrict economic theory to partial analysis.

The industrial-organization approach looks at the performance of an economic system in relation to organizational culture, structure, and behavior. Traditional economic theory is concerned with structure only. Perfect competition is implied by perfect markets. This market structure is characterized by Schumpeter's host of small and medium-size firms cited in Scherer's chapter. But theorizing on the basis of "owner-entrepreneurs" or "owner-managers" is not exactly based on Schumpeter's ideas. His "dynamic entrepreneur" brings into being a vision of an entrepreneur independent of ownership of capital. The capital requirements of modern industry are so high that no single capitalist can meet them. What the new "dynamic entrepreneur" needs are "capitalists without entrepreneurship" and an "organizational culture" of society encouraging free enterprise. Free enterprise of this kind is, according to a Civil War amendment to the U.S. Constitution, not a natural but a legal person. A "social climate," conflicting with free enterprise, is what Schumpeter recognized as responsible for the "march into socialism."

The necessary "organizational culture" corresponds to institutional changes that accompanied industrialization: capitalists without entrepreneurship looking for corporations with limited liability. This type of organization encourages investment in risky innovations without making investors fully liable to loss of their entire private property in case of failure. Like "dynamic entrepreneurs," these capitalists need a banking system and financial intermediaries. These institutional provisions enable the "dynamic entrepreneur" without private ownership of capital to become an economic and cultural giant, managing huge corporations toward permanent innovation and escaping from imitators through new innovations. An entrepreneur of this kind may be highly motivated to take risks instead of looking only for guaranteed profits, because he is not an "owner-manager" or "owner-entrepreneur" who is afraid of losing his property.

This new paradigm for capitalism and ownership raises new issues for the control of business, but at the same time creates the opportunity for "worker-capitalists" (workers' or people's capitalism) to receive a share of the profits without being liable in case of losses – a crucial problem, especially in discussions about German worker co-determination within firms. In modern organization theory, labor in a firm also changes from being merely a "factor of production" into holding a kind of "entrepreneurship within the firm," accompanied by the application of "market principles within the firm," as German managers and the members of the German "Board of Economic Experts" *(Sachverständigenrat)* like to mention. "Buy-outs" of managers then result from following the strategy of profit centers within the firm. The new paradigm of Schumpeter, therefore, changes the traditional relationships in capitalism among ownership, market structure, and behavior.

The host of small and medium-size firms is no longer a necessary condition of economic development and evolution along market principles and their inherent rationality. Structure follows from behavior, not behavior from structure. It arises from comparative advantage in "size competition" – a well-known catchword in the FRG's policy toward small- and medium-scale enterprise. But the conditions for survival in "size competition" differ. Small- and medium-scale firms die (as Schumpeter is correctly quoted in Scherer's chapter) if they run the once-chosen way of owner self-determination or "call forth moral allegiance." In the struggle for economic survival, only the most fit firms, as measured by profits, are selected. But big firms are capable of surviving because of better organization, as well as organization that follows market principles, if necessary, to avoid inefficiencies due to "organizational deficiency," as Williamson demonstrates.

This leads – by economic rationality – to big corporations becoming the spearhead of economic development and the basis for a kind of new "Schumpeter hypothesis" in industrial-organization theory. "Dynamic entrepreneurs" replace consumer sovereignty by "producer sovereignty," as Schumpeter stated in his *Theory of Economic Development* in 1912. Here, again, J. K. Galbraith ([1967] 1972) turns out to be a true scholar of Schumpeter, rediscovering old Schumpeterian wisdom that brings into being a new problem of control in capitalism. Antitrust policy and the welfare state are democratic solutions, representing a "march into socialism," according to conventional wisdom in the theory of comparative economic systems.

Last, but not least, the Schumpeterian spirit as a new paradigm changes (pure) economic theory of policy, democracy, property rights, and management back to the original political economy, eliminating the concept of pure rationality that starts from individual utility and profit maximization and arrives at a welfare maximum for society. These ends of individual freedom of economic man replace freedom by rationality. This is in contradiction to the starting point of capitalism, which is individual freedom. Thus, the Schumpeterian spirit may also help us to interpret the "impossibility theorem" of our textbooks in the logically correct way: The crucial issue is not the impossibility of the social-welfare function in a free society, but the impossibility of the concept of a welfare maximum.

References

Galbraith, J. K. (Norbert Wölfl, trans.) [1967] (1972). *Die moderne Industriegesellschaft* (4th ed.). München: Knaur.

Hayek, F. A. [1944] (1976). *The Road to Serfdom*. London: Routledge & Kegan Paul.

Schumpeter, J. A. [1912] (1964). *Theorie der wirtschaftlichen Entwicklung* (6th ed.). Berlin: Duncker & Humblot.

(Dr. Susanne Preiserk, trans.) [1950] (1972). *Kapitalismus, Sozialismus und Demokratie* (3rd ed.). München: UTB/Francke.

Williams, E. E., and Findlay, M. C. (1981). "A Reconsideration of the Rationality Postulate: Right Hemisphere Thinking in Economics." *American Journal of Economics and Sociology*, 40(2):17–36.

CHAPTER 6

Schumpeterian innovation, market structure, and the stability of industrial development

GUNNAR ELIASSON

6.1   The experimental nature of the capitalist market process

The name Joseph Schumpeter is intimately associated with the concepts of entrepreneurial activity, technological development, technical change, and "creative destruction" of economic structures,[1] in short, the dynamics of structural change. From the mid-1930s on, economists grew increasingly uninterested in the problems of structural change as Keynesian economics took root in neoclassical microeconomic theory. The macroeconomic version of Schumpeter's theoretical structure is the growth cycle, but it has become associated too much with technological innovation in Schumpeterian literature. It is the inner dynamics of aggregates (market allocation processes) and the institutional organization of the market that move the growth cycle. Market processes and institutional dynamics are lacking in classical and modern received theory and are not explicit at the microeconomic level in Schumpeterian theory. Yet both are needed to formulate an acceptable growth theory. The concern of this chapter is to take a few steps toward remedying this situation by bringing behavioral economics to bear explicitly and quantitatively on macroeconomic development. Institutional dynamics, broadly defined, are concerned with the selection processes in the market, notably the entry and exit processes, meaning that a market-regime analysis must pay special attention to the *deregulation* issue. This integrated theory of economic growth can be illustrated through the Swedish micro-to-macro (M-M) model. The new intellectual structures that emerge have clear policy implications, especially for optimal design of (market) decision processes in society.

Bo Carlsson, Erik Dahmén, Lars Jagrén, Kenneth Hanson, Rolf Henriksson, Pavel Pelikan, and Stephen Turner have been very helpful in suggesting improvements in this draft. Any remaining errors are, however, of my making.

[1] I shall try to be consistent in my use of the term "technology" as the knowledge of techniques, and "technical change" as the result of the application of new technology.

151

6.1.1   Dynamic market coordination

This chapter explores the M-M link between innovative activity and macroeconomic dynamics. I emphasize the following:

1. The transformation of manufacturing firms from predominantly factory-oriented producers to *information processors,* with their competitive bases in product technologies, and
2. The organization of economic intermediation, linking entrepreneurial activity and technological change, at the micro level, and economic growth, at the macro level. This is often referred to as the transmission or diffusion of technology. I prefer to discuss it more broadly in terms of the organization of market competition and pricing in an economic regime characterized by innovative technological change, or dynamic coordination across agents and over time in the market economy – the Smithian invisible hand at work, if you will.

Information processing occurs (1) *between firms* in the market and (2) *within firms* in the form of administrative coordination. Innovative activity is carried out by (Schumpeterian) entrepreneurs, who, as a rule, change the internal structures and outer forms of firms. Traders of all sorts play a dominant role in coordinating all agents' activities in the market. We observe (Eliasson, 1985b) that information processing makes up the bulk of total resource use in a modern firm. This means that productivity growth – as it is measured at the macro level – is market-determined, rather than technically determined.

Economies of scale move the growth process: The Schumpeterian notion of technological change is that creative entrepreneurs see and implement "new business combinations" and force "creative destruction" on old, inefficient activities through competition. Such new combinations take place at all levels and constitute the transformation process of firms, as mentioned earlier. At some level it can always be regarded as an instance of Smithian division of labor, allowing new combinations (joint production) to be formed, thus generating economies of scale within firms and joint rents to be distributed. But to be credible, the Schumpeterian model needs two additional features. It needs clear process representations of the ways in which micro decisions influence macro behavior and how macro behavior feeds back into micro decisions. It needs a mechanism that keeps economies of scale from generating unlimited concentration.

6.1.2 Diffusion of innovations

This formulation of our modeling problem introduces what I have previously called the *experimental* nature of the capitalist market process. Even though careful reading of Schumpeter's works does not support the simplistic view I now restate, it is "the common view" of him in the literature. The "young" Schumpeter (1912) saw innovations and entrepreneurial activity as predominantly unpredictable, something that arose in the economy via a deus ex machina. The "old" Schumpeter (1942), having observed the emergence of giant corporations, began to believe that innovative activity could occur in a routine fashion through planned research and development (R&D). This simplistic distinction between unpredictable and planned innovative activities carries a strong didactic content. The implications in the two cases are far-reaching and fundamentally different, and they can be empirically evaluated against each other.

The ideas of the young Schumpeter correspond to my notion of an experimental economy. The ideas of the old Schumpeter are closer to the auctioneer-based, static, general equilibrium theories that have provided the theoretical or ideological bases for the centrally policed, socialistic economy and that still provide the basis for the mainstream economic theory taught at Western universities. Arrow's study (1962b) implying that socialization of innovation may be efficient argues a related theme. On the basis of a set of postulates supported by empirical observations, I argue that the young Schumpeter was fundamentally right. He captured the basics of the economics of very long run growth, whereas the old Schumpeter departed from that understanding. In arguing that point, the following three concepts provide the cornerstone of my reasoning.

Knowledge: The first concept is that of an experimental economy that is intrinsically unpredictable as to micro outcomes.[2] I develop that notion by introducing, in the same fashion as Pelikan (1986), Simon's concept (1955) of "bounded rationality" and Polanyi's concept (1967) of "tacit" knowledge. People and organizations form simplified decision models in order to cope with environmental complexity and to be able to draw conclusions. This ability to create intellectual order out of a complex environment is part of their local competence. However, this competence is, in an industrial context, so complex and involved

---

[2] This, however, does not necessarily preclude predictability at aggregate levels.

that it cannot be easily communicated. It is "tacit." Bounded rationality, furthermore, means that various decision makers' perceptions
of a given reality are different, often are incorrect, and are ad hoc in
the sense of being only temporarily relevant. Taken together, the two
concepts remove the convexity and market-clearing properties necessary to derive "optimal policies" in the way characteristic of the literature based on general equilibrium theory. [That critical knowledge is,
in fact, tacit and that decision making is "rational," but typically
bounded, are things that I have frequently been confronted with in my
own research (Eliasson, 1976a).]

Stability: The second concept is Darwinian (Winter, 1964) in spirit. It
postulates (Eliasson, 1984a, 1986c) that stability of long-term macroeconomic growth requires a steady turnover of quasi rents in the economy, generated through innovative entry at all levels.[3] New entrants
compete old rent receivers out of business, thus preventing concentration and preserving a healthy, but variable, diversity of structure in the
economy. To achieve this, free competitive entry must be allowed, and
barriers to entry must be kept low.[4] One implication is that the capital
market can never be in equilibrium[5] in a growth economy. Hence, the
notion of equilibrium in other markets becomes undefined in the inter-
dependent-process economy we are discussing. (In fact, the implication is that if we force the economy closer to equilibrium in the capital
market, the macroeconomy becomes increasingly unstable.) I have
developed this argument in previous work (Eliasson, 1984a, 1985a),
and we are carrying on further research in that direction at the Industriens Utrednings Institut (IUI).

Market coordination and intermediation: The third concept brings in
institutions as intermediators in the economic process. They facilitate
the economic process, and they make its output and its consequences
desired and accepted in the market. Institutions are endogenously self-
organizing (Pelikan, 1986). This takes us somewhat beyond Schum-

---

[3] In this presentation I use the very broad definition of entry needed to capture innovative activities that sometimes occur through the entry of parameterized firms (as in
the Swedish M-M model), sometimes through the development and launching of new
products (Granstrand, 1986) and sometimes through improvements of products and
processes at even lower levels.

[4] This has long been the theoretical foundation of U.S. antitrust policy.

[5] Dynamic market coordination means that agents may be chasing a moving *ex ante*
equilibrium position that they never reach because the chase itself affects its position.
This is how we interpret equilibrium in the Swedish M-M model in Section 6.4. Also
see Eliasson (1983).

peter. To make my point clear, I use what I have frequently referred to as Åkerman's four fundamentals of economic theory. Åkerman (1950) argued that these are the four fundamental elements of any useful economic theory:

1. Interdependence
2. Welfare
3. Process
4. Institutions

I use the term "institution" in Åkerman's dictionary sense as covering the set of rules that monitors the economy and its organizations.[6]

The first concept of the experimental economy can be introduced analytically. The second concept can be quantified, as it has been within the M-M modeling framework. This, however, takes parameterized institutions as given, including entry and exit (Hanson, 1986). When we now introduce the concept of endogenized institutional change, we leave the domain of quantitative analysis, but in systematic fashion, I prefer, and must resort to, language as the tool of analysis. The third concept is that institutions are paramount in facilitating the innovation process and in making its consequences acceptable in society.

The first aspect of the institutions concept is the incentive problem. If the market economy is fundamentally experimental, the innovative problem amounts to organizing the rules of the economic system in such a fashion that enough broad-based experimental, innovative activity will occur to filter out a sufficient number of winners (Dahmén and Eliasson, 1980) and to contain the concentration that will follow from economies of scale; this concentration is the result of the efficient routinized R&D in large companies that the old Schumpeter worried about. I conclude later that with vast business opportunities and local competence, Schumpeterian competition will check such tendencies,

---

[6] The broad concepts discussed in this chapter unavoidably make for terminological problems when we get down to an operational level. This we have to do when the quantitative aspects associated with the Swedish M-M model are integrated into the broader conceptual framework of institutional change. I am departing from the definition of an institution used in modern economic literature and staying with the common dictionary meaning of an "institution." To avoid confusion when context does not clarify the meaning, I use Pelikan's distinction (1985) between "institutional rules" and "organizational structure." Sometimes I refer to an institutional "regime" instead of "rules." The "institutions" of the dictionary, however, cover all these concepts, and I am not throwing out that general term, because it is apt to confuse the reader who is not familiar with the fine distinctions of literature, and these fine distinctions are needed only at times.

provided competitive entry is not restricted by the political system or barriers to trade. This is really what Schumpeter (1942) worried about. Entrepreneurship, on the other hand, as he saw it, does not have to be restricted to small firms or individuals. The tendency toward unlimited growth at IBM because of the competence developed through routine innovative activities is checked both by small competitive entrants and by innovative activities of other large firms, but this process generates a lot of change at the micro level.

The second aspect corresponds to the argument (Day, 1984) that institutions make it possible for the economy to operate out of equilibrium. To operate out of equilibrium means, if the reader will excuse my use of the term, that Pareto-incompatible income and capital transfers become acceptable and can occur without any detrimental effects on dynamic production efficiency. Through evidence of the long-term beneficial effects, and through indoctrination, people are willing to accept the short-term sacrifices. To make this happen was the idea of the "old Swedish policy model," to which we shall return at the end of this chapter. Before starting the analysis, I illustrate my theoretical notions with some historical statistics.

6.2   Three theories of economic growth seen through a long historical perspective

6.2.1   Questions asked

Beginning in the second half of the eighteenth century in England, and appearing in some other countries during the nineteenth century, the industrial revolution created an economic elite of nations that currently make up the world of the Organisation for Economic Co-operation and Development (OECD). Roughly speaking, those countries that did not make it from the beginning have not really made it later. The standard explanation for this is technical innovation. Questions that arise in economic historical analysis include whether or not initiation of the industrialization phase was due to sudden emergence and diffusion of new techniques of production that started the industrial revolution and whether or not a burst of exogenous innovative activity in some nations was related to some country-specific factors.

Recently, many of the elite industrial nations, notably the first industrial nation, have been subjected to severe economic problems of stagnation, unemployment, and inflation. Terms like deindustrialization, or some sort of reversal of the industrialization process, have been used to describe what is happening.

A more disturbing possibility is that perhaps the industrial revolution was initiated by a unique constellation of factors (local competence) at different places that made it possible to exploit a technological potential that had existed for a long time. North and Thomas (1973) have emphasized different systems of institutional rules to explain the different levels of innovative activity in the initiation of the industrial revolution in Holland and England, on the one hand, and in France and Spain, on the other. This suggests that local human-capital and institutional factors determine the potential of a nation or a region to seize upon new, internationally available technologies. The implication is that a new wave of growth may occur very selectively and according to the distribution of these specific factors of local competence. Thus, there is no guarantee that growth must continue to occur among the already wealthy industrial countries.

More precisely, if we can demonstrate that specific human-capital factors were at play in the middle of the nineteenth century to move the currently wealthy industrial nations to where they now are, this argument gains in credibility. We shall look more closely at that possibility in what follows.

Figure 6.1, showing Sweden's manufacturing growth, is the result of heroic statistical work. Despite the doubtful quality of statistical observations over this 450-year time span, the kink observed at some time just before the middle of the nineteenth century is a more or less accepted empirical fact. Something dramatic happened about that time in the Swedish economy. The little "kink" at the upper-right-hand corner reflects the current "crisis" in a 450-year perspective. This figure is useful because it demonstrates the impact of the industrial revolution in terms of its effects on output. The nations that missed the revolution followed the old trend. Whereas it took 300 years (1549–1850) for Swedish manufacturing to reach 50 times its initial production volume, it took less than half that time to increase output volume about 250 times above its middle-nineteenth-century level. Had Sweden missed the technological opportunities and followed the old trend, the Swedes would currently be enjoying significantly less than one-fiftieth of their current per capita national income, or roughly the difference currently recorded between Sweden and India (Figures 6.2 and 6.3).

6.2.2   Three different stories

At the time represented by the "kink," three fundamental changes occurred, each corresponding to a particular and frequently voiced theory of economic development:

1.   For several nations, including Sweden, import demand from the first industrial nation was growing very rapidly.

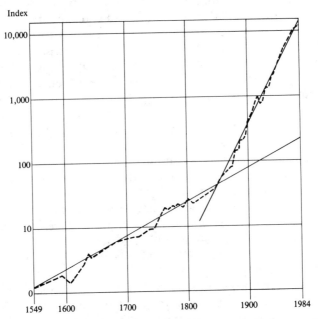

Figure 6.1. Indices of industrial production in Sweden, 1549–1984 (1870 = 100). Thin solid lines are trends. *Source:* Lars Jagrén has been very helpful in collecting the data needed to construct this diagram.

2. The level of technical and organizational innovation increased sharply during the late eighteenth century.
3. Regulation of economic activities was generally removed.

For purposes of exposition, I am going to associate John Maynard Keynes – or Karl Marx – with the first observation, Joseph Schumpeter with the second, and Adam Smith with the third explanation. We have three respective explanations: a demand pull, an innovation supply push, and a deregulation release of incentives. There is a rich literature advocating each of these, and simple statistical analysis could be used to support each story individually: a demand pull that generated incentives for innovators, a Schumpeterian type of exogenous innovative process, and a release of fettered economic forces. These stories carry widely different implications for the role of government in economic development.

My argument is that parts of all three processes have to be at work simultaneously to generate sustainable macroeconomic growth. This

GNP/Capita

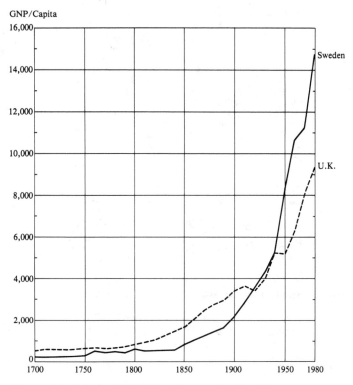

Figure 6.2. Relative GNP development in Sweden and the United Kingdom, 1700–1980 (1980 U.S. dollars). *Source:* Same as for Figure 6.1.

takes any simplicity out of economic policy-making. It provides a rationale for less policy-making and much caution in arguing for centralist manipulation of the economy. This revelation probably will be the main thrust of the "Schumpeterian revolution" that currently appears to be replacing the "Keynesian revolution" in economics. Let us go through the three "theories" in turn, beginning with the deficient-demand story.

Deficient demand: The deficient-demand story originated with Marx, who argued, as I do, that the productivity potential of an industrial economy, for all practical purposes, is unlimited, but that demand may be insufficient. Depressions and stagnation will occur regularly, and capitalists will aggressively look for new markets in which to unload

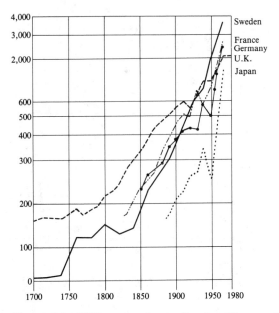

Figure 6.3. GNP per capita in Sweden, France, Germany, United Kingdom, and Japan, 1700–1980 (1967 U.S. dollars). *Sources:* Rostow (1980), Maddison (1962, 1977), and OECD national accounts statistics.

their surplus products. Keynes borrowed that notion. His deficiency of "effective demand" became a rationale for government to boost demand through taxation and public-sector growth. It was analytically presented as a difference between *ex ante* investment and *ex ante* savings, or a nonclearing capital market. As Morishima and Catephores elaborate in their chapter in this volume, this is synonymous with saying that Say's law does not hold and that failure of market clearing has to be a typical characteristic of Schumpeterian thinking. However, that is also the backbone of the Wicksellian cumulative process (Wicksell, [1898] 1965). Hence, instead of the Keynesian investment and savings gap, the gap between the *ex ante* rate of return that drives investment decisions and the rate of interest that controls the amount of savings in the economy is used to represent the capital-market disequilibrium.

There are, however, two important aspects to the deficient-demand argument in our context. First, when it is transformed into an issue of capital-market imperfections, we are confronted with a micro problem of relative prices. A nonclearing capital market, or a deficient-demand situation, can quite well exist, even though the average expected marginal return to capital equals the average loan rate in the market (Figures 6.4A and 6.4B). Second, as Schumpeter emphasized, capital-market imperfections, or depressions, are needed to clear markets of inefficient producers (creative destruction). Taken together, we have an extensive type of game (Shubik, 1985), with a variable number of players, that provides the basis for the "growth cycle" to be described later.

As a consequence, the macroeconomic demand-pull explanation can be ruled out from the beginning as a general explanation of the industrial revolution, or of macroeconomic growth. Demand is preceded by innovative activity, by the entry of superior technology that forces bad performers to exit. However, at all aggregation levels below the national level, demand-pull effects are key elements in any growth process. Without demand feedback, no growth process can be sustained. Part of this takes the form of domestic demand through income generation. Part of it comes through foreign trade, which depends on relative prices. In the latter case it becomes apparent that the demand explanation can never be separated from price and cost considerations, or the ways in which relative prices are set in the market.[7]

Innovative activity and entry of new technologies: What sustains innovative activity and entrepreneurship that is needed to maintain the capital-market disequilibrium and fuel a fast growth cycle? Empirical evidence on the origin of innovative activity is scant. What can be observed are later successful outcomes of the innovative process, but we miss most of the failures, especially those that do not survive long after their conception. Figure 6.5 gives some hint of the extremely differentiated performance picture at the micro level. As Jagrén (1986) demonstrates, the aggregate growth in output for a random sample of

---

[7] It is nevertheless interesting to ask to what extent a rapidly growing demand from the first industrial nation pulled a growth process along in other nations (Figure 6.2). Basic raw-material exports from Sweden (iron ore, forest products), and even agricultural products to the British industrial machine, certainly helped to finance industrialization (Carlsson, 1980). This happened in Sweden. Why has it not happened at all other places, notably in the developing countries? Under what circumstances can we then talk about industrialization? What differences are there among Norwegian oil-fueled growth, South Korean profit-generated export growth (Chen, 1979), and Japanese growth said to be dependent on U.S. demand? Norway has been attempting to transform oil wealth into industrial-knowledge capital with limited success and now has to cope with the opposite situation: a blown-up political demand for consumption, while resources are disappearing. South Korea is developing industrially, and Japan has developed industrially without any raw material resources to finance the transformation process.

A. *Years 1974-79*

Percent rate of return
over industrial loan rate

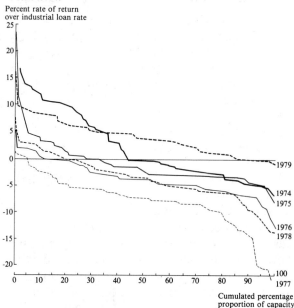

Cumulated percentage
proportion of capacity
that earns a return
above rate on vertical
axis

B. *Years 1979-1984*

Percent rate of return
over industrial loan rate

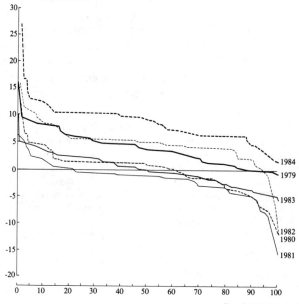

Cumulated percentage
proportion of capacity
that earns a return
above rate on vertical
axis.

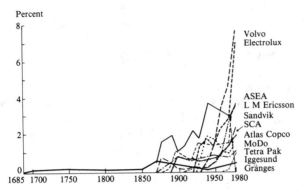

Figure 6.5. Share of value added in Swedish manufacturing generated by selected large business groups, 1685–1980. The firm value added is the group (global) value added. *Source:* Jagrén (1986).

115 firms from a population of firms in the 1920s for a 60-year period was pulled along by only two winners, Electrolux and Bofors (see Figure 6.5 for Electrolux). Other survivors led a stagnant life, and the majority of the initial cohort has been eliminated. If this is the normal picture, one is inclined to believe that very broad-based and intense innovative activity will have to be going on all the time to keep the economy growing steadily 50 years from now. The nature of this innovative activity must have a lot to do with societal incentives and the way society at large is organized. If we leave culture, attitudes, and values of society outside our explanation, then we perhaps have to be satisfied with the young Schumpeter's notion of an exogenous innovative activity. If we want to explain such activity, we should not look primarily at the way R&D is organized within large firms, but at the institutional organization of society at large.[8]

[8] We must remember that outside of the refined context of their textbooks, the great economists often agreed on the basic economic mechanisms. Thus, an optimistic Keynes (1930) argued that people would solve the problem of economic growth if they organized the economic system accordingly.

←————————

Figure 6.4. Rate of return over loan-rate. Distributions over the firm population, 1974–1984 – part of the initial state description of the Swedish M-M model. The vertical axis measures ϵ/K for divisions and firms in terms of equation (3). *Source:* MOSES database. Thomas Lindberg at IUI has organized and compiled the data for this diagram.

Market deregulation or technology: The question now is how technology and the organization of an economy affect each other over time. Should we take economic organization as the exogenous datum and make changes in the institutional rules of the market system the policy issue?

Thus, for instance, some would argue, contrary to Heckscher (1953), that deregulation of the Swedish economy (item 3) in the middle of the nineteenth century did not really release innovative forces in society (item 2). It was the other way around: Innovative forces were breaking down regulatory barriers insofar as they mattered. This, if true, is a clear example of endogenous institutional change (the last item in Åkerman's earlier listing), but to understand economic growth requires that one explain how technological advance arises in the first round.

The deregulation hypothesis is nevertheless compelling. In the first half of the nineteenth century, the straightjacket of industrial regulations was gradually taken off. Earlier, in Sweden, every form of innovative commercial activity had required a permit – from the establishment of a new firm to the introduction of a new product or even a better product. The name for that permit – a "privilege" – reveals its monopoly-based nature. The king of Sweden was the supreme industrial policymaker. At least in those days, exogenous technology was not strong enough to break down his rule. Hence, institutional rules can be interpreted as one form of technology. As to its effects, it cannot be distinguished from other forms of technology. From a scientific point of view, efficient procedure is to so define our concepts that whatever has to be left exogenous is allocated to the institutional rules category. This includes policy-making as well, if it is going to be treated as an exogenous factor. We achieve this taxonomy of our theory through introducing the concept of the international opportunity set and through linking it up with a stylized M-M theory.

M-M theory captures the market regime: The M-M model described in the Appendix allows us to illustrate the theory of growth we are seeking in a way that integrates all three theories. For a given state of internationally available technology (the opportunity set) and a given parameterization of the market processes (the market regime) that can be manipulated through policies, the M-M model integrates all three theories by closing the economy through income-generation–demand feedback that constrains the price- and quantity-setting behavior of individual agents. One illustration of the use of the model as an explanation for growth is that it has been possible to generate macro growth paths describing manufacturing output for 50-year periods that differ almost as much as do the "new" and the "old" trends in Figure 6.1. The only difference between simulation experiments has been a resetting of the "market regime" that determines the parameters that regulate the speed of price and quantity adjustments of agents in response to the same price and quantity adjustments of all other agents. The only qualification needed is that the technology potential (or, in our jargon, the international opportunity set) be sufficiently large (Eliasson, 1983). Deregulation is a change in market regime, releasing the technology potential. We shall return to this later. The important thing to note here is that the typical convexity assumptions of traditional theory have been removed and replaced by the extent and speed of the exploitation of the opportunity set. This sets the upper boundaries on economic growth and controls the market processes. Having said this, we also have to define the international opportunity set more clearly.

6.3 The economic nature of technological change – the opportunity set

Joseph Schumpeter's name has long been associated with the concept of an exogenous stream (wave) of innovations that is diffused through the production system and gives rise to a delayed long wave of production growth. This theory of economic growth, when applied in empirical research, often becomes quite mechanistic and closely related to the macro-production-function approach. It reduces technology to discrete measurable (e.g., by patents) factor inputs. It makes international technology feed right into the shift factor of the local macro production function, and I do not think Joseph Schumpeter would at all like being associated with this idea of a growth process. The problem with this approach is that it disregards the fact that technology is a necessary but not sufficient factor behind growth. Local competence, among other factors, is needed to transform technical opportunities into economic (commercial) action.

6.3.1 The international opportunity set defined

Marx introduced deficient demand as the limiting factor to the exploitation of what he believed was an unlimited set of technical opportunities. We add technical and commercial competence as a local factor that bounds the economic process from above. Competence is acquired through education, and hence, like other forms of capacity expansion, is an endogenous investment process. I prefer to emphasize the experimental (boundedly rational) participation in the market process, not formal schooling or institutionalized research, as the important competence-expanding process.[9] By assuming that at any point in time there exists a virtually unlimited set of combinatorial possibilities to search, test, and learn from, we have both defined and introduced the international opportunity set. Economic historical studies support this idea, and later we shall provide both further evidence and argument.

Technology plays an important role in the Schumpeterian growth process. But Schumpeter's notion of technology was broader than is represented in many econometric applications, and the diffusion process is accordingly broad. It is better seen in terms of an experimental learning process, where technology is internationally available and competence is local, bounded, tacit, and difficult to communicate.

Erik Dahmén's (1950) concept of *development blocks* is particularly useful here. It emphasizes the productivity potential, or the synergistic effects of technical and commercial complementarities that the entrepreneur seizes on. Dahmén's development blocks do not have to be far-reaching and revolutionary like the steam engine and electricity. We can think of them at all levels. They represent synergistic effects around a new technology that generates a wave of investment and growth. Thus, for instance, the gasoline engine made the automobile possible, and that in turn made road building and investment in gasoline production and distribution profitable, and so on. In the long run, the automobile has significantly changed our ways of living and traveling. Quite often a firm is formed around a development block. And Schumpeter ([1912] 1934) himself saw "a new combination" as the setting up of a firm. Tetra Pak (Figure 6.5) and Pharmacia are good examples for Sweden. This broadened notion of technical change is capable of explaining the differential impact of technology on various nations in historical perspective.

6.3.2 Technologies with universal applications may create giant expansions of the opportunity set, but also expose firms and nations to increased competition

With this broad notion of technical advance, the degree of universality of technologies begins to matter. The opportunity set was introduced earlier as the union of all possible combinations of technologies and

---

[9] In fact, this argument has been built on the basis of extensive observations and argument (Eliasson et al., 1986).

organizational structures into development blocks. Only small fractions of these possible combinations are being exploited commercially, and each exploitation (an innovation, a new combination, a new firm) is probably adding to the opportunity set.[10] However, certain technologies are more nearly universal in their applications than others and therefore contribute more forcefully to the infrastructure pool of possible combinations.

The waves of innovation commonly referred to as generators of long-term economic growth are innovations of wide applicability and of an infrastructure type. The steam engine, the railroad, electricity, and the automobile are the standard examples. These all dramatically widened the international opportunity set, allowing for a great range of new commercial combinations to develop. But the economic outcome of this expansion of opportunity depends on the local competence.

Bring Western high technology into the midst of Africa – very little will happen, because local competence is lacking. England is an example of a country that, despite a high level of formal education, lacks the competence to exploit commercial and technological opportunities at the level at which the economy is currently operating. Sweden, perhaps, provides the opposite example of relative excellence (Pavitt and Soete, 1981), but many would argue that Japan is the best illustration of a nation organized for efficient economic exploitation, not imitation, of the commercial and technological opportunity set available internationally. This illustrates the complementary relationship between international technological opportunities and the local competence to exploit their economic potential,[11] but it also epitomizes the danger indicated early in this essay for a firm or a nation that lacks the necessary competence. If the assumption of the vast opportunity set is accepted, it also provides for the strong local argument in favor of the "young" and against the "old" Schumpeter. With free competitive access to the opportunity set and locally bounded competence, there is

[10] The turbocharged engine is an example. The turbo had been installed in Diesel truck engines for many years. The Scania engine people in the truck division came up with the solution for the Saab-Scania automobile engine. It partly had to do with the availability of heat-resistant materials and more demanding requirements in automobile engines than in truck engines. After some time, Volvo came up with a turbo engine complemented by an "intercooler." Now a large number of automobile manufacturers offer different "turbo" solutions.

[11] I have developed this point at length in a separate paper (Eliasson, 1986c) and refer to it for further elaboration.

no way for centralized, routine R&D in large corporations to beat the multitude of competing entrepreneurs in the long term, except in three arenas: (1) by breaking through the assumption of bounded rationality (assumed not to be possible); (2) where scale effects in financing are enormous; (3) by teaming up with the political system to close down free competitive entry. The last was really what Schumpeter (1942) worried about.

6.3.3   Limited local knowledge of the organization of production – a shop-floor illustration

That this exploitation process is piecemeal and bounded can be amply illustrated from the shop floor. Robotization, it is agreed, has a tremendous rationalizing, labor-saving potential. In fact, however, this new technique appears to shift technical change in a relatively more capital-saving direction (Eliasson, 1985b). This is understood as soon as one looks at the context in which automation devices are introduced. However, the introduction of robotics and automation always requires complementary knowledge (a code or explicit program to run the process) at central levels that did not exist in the old factory organizations. What has held back the rate at which extensive factory automation has been introduced has to some extent been deficient measurement and sensor techniques. Surprisingly enough, however, the real obstacle to the introduction of robotics has not been robot technology per se, but the lack of local competence in the form of precise, centralized knowledge of the production process itself. This knowledge has traditionally been diffused (decentralized) to individuals throughout the factory and been linked together through an organizational structure (Eliasson, 1980). The communication of that knowledge to a central production monitor has been very costly and time-consuming. The "language" has been the limiting factor (Pelikan, 1969). In most Swedish engineering factories, operations knowledge is still decentralized and "tacit." The potential that is currently beginning to be exploited is, however, not to automate an existing production process, but to change the entire factory organization in conjunction with a change in product design. New materials in combination with new machines and centralized process control are currently breaking industrial society loose from a 150-year-old machine and materials technology and the associated worker culture. This is only the beginning of the exploitation potential of the new information technology, but the availability of local competence will set the pace of exploitation.

6.3.4   The universality of communications technology – the case of the printed word

It is interesting to observe in this context that an earlier innovation of even broader applicability than the common examples has not attracted the attention it deserves, namely, the "technology" of the printed word, dramatically upgraded some 50 years before the beginning of the historical curve in Figure 6.1. In many treatises on economic growth, this "technology" is not even referred to; in some (Braudel, 1981; North, 1981; Parker, 1984; Rosenberg and Birdzell, 1986), it is referred to only in passing, or in a special context. In a few studies, its importance has been placed in focus (Eisenstein, 1979). There is a great similarity in broadness of application to the new electronically based information technologies, and there should be ample opportunities to learn about the possible impacts of electronics from historical studies.

Effective economic use of the printed word could not be achieved faster than the corresponding development of local competence to read and write. The lags have been so long that it is impossible to ascertain quantitative relationships. However, if the printed word had significant economic effects through its potential for organizing, coordinating, and communicating technical and commercial knowledge, the new information technology associated with the "electronics revolution" appears to offer a potential of much greater magnitude, as well as of a strong differential impact on economic growth. But it will take such a long time that it should rather be called the "electronics evolution" (Eliasson, 1981). My conclusion that the effects will be large and differentiated is based on two observations: The electronics-based information technology is spreading much faster than did the printed word, and nations are much more integrated economically today than they were 500 years ago. Hence, great opportunities are certainly opening up, but the differential, competitive impact of the introduction of this technology on long-term economic growth among firms, regions, and nations may be very large indeed.

6.3.5   The nontechnical side of economic growth

This takes me back to the title of this section: the economic content of technical change. Even with normal rates of pure technical change at the firm level, reallocation of resources between firms appears to account for more than 50 percent of macro productivity growth (e.g.,

Carlsson, 1981). Furthermore, as emphasized by many economic historians, there would not have been much of an industrial revolution were it not for a matching institutional and organizational development that provided the incentives for competitive exploitation of technical and commercial opportunities. Ashton (1948) even suggests that the development of new financial institutions was what made the industrial revolution possible. It made possible the pooling and redistribution of large volumes of savings at reasonable loan rates to innovative and growing industries. In short, venture capital became available. This exemplifies the fourth and last of Akerman's four fundamentals. "Institutional technology" may be what really matters, and I shall come back to it in the final section.

6.4   The economic dynamics of general monopolistic competition

This section explains why the market economy needs a steady innovative input to generate long-term, stable macroeconomic growth. The next section explains why the capitalist market organization with free competitive entry and exit may be the only viable institutional superstructure capable of delivering the needed innovative input – in short, *the experimental economy*. It also explains why a matching social superstructure is needed to handle the social consequences of the experimental economy. It demonstrates how the consequences of unpredictable change at the micro levels can be made politically and socially acceptable. The point of this section can be condensed into one question: *What happens when we make general equilibrium theory dynamic, or into a process model?*

6.4.1   Making market theory dynamic

Once competition is introduced as an experimental, profit-driven search activity, questions arise: Can this dynamic process be formalized so that we can quantify the interaction of agents in markets that together generate macro behavior? Will differences in the organization of market processes make any difference for macroeconomic growth? The Swedish M-M model developed at IUI makes such formalization possible. In this model, the way market interaction is organized and timed makes a significant difference for long-term macroeconomic production in the model. The reason is the dynamic effects on resource allocation of profit-driven investment and labor allocation at the micro market levels. This makes it possible to quantify some of the market interactions we introduced earlier and relate the results of this quantitative analysis verbally to the broader picture of economic progress in which we are interested.

The M-M model includes core parts of the three theories introduced in the preceding historical analysis: the demand-pull story, the innovation supply-push story, and the deregulation story. Technology is "internationally available" and enters firms through their local investment behavior. This means that the economy will always be operating below the upper limits set by the introduction throughout the economic system of the most efficient technologies at each point in time.[12] The model captures, I argue, the dynamics of general monopolistic competition of Schumpeter and of Clark (1961). It combines innovative competitive activity à la Schumpeter ([1912] 1934), a Wicksellian ([1898] 1965) micro disequilibrium in the capital market that drives the investment process,[13] and dynamic market coordination à la Smith. The welfare implications of this economy are also those of the invisible hand of Adam Smith, not those of Pareto. The aim of the social technology of the capitalistic market system has always been to find efficient and accepted ways of – if I again may use that term – "overcoming Pareto." This is why institutions enter and why institutional action is such a resource-using activity in modern society – so resource-using that the costs associated with it and its efficiency have to be considered when analyzing the performance and equilibrium characteristics of the entire economy. To this we shall return in the concluding section.

6.4.2   *Why stable macroeconomic growth requires microeconomic instability*

Constant experimentation keeps pushing the upper limits (the opportunity set) of the M-M model economy outward and actual production ahead. This experimental process is exogenously fueled through entry of new competitors, through the upgrading of old investment, and

---

[12] Hence, a narrow version of the "international opportunity set" is explicit and exogenous in the model in the form of labor and capital productivity assumptions associated with new investment. The unexploited part of this narrow opportunity set is represented by the difference between a macroeconomic development, with all firms continuously using best-practice methods, and actual economic development. (This is the difference between the straight max line and the simulations in Figure 5A, p. 317, in Eliasson, 1983.) Local competence is represented by the ability to introduce these productivities profitably through the investment decision. That this process takes time and that economics plays a role have been demonstrated inter alia in Eliasson (1981).

[13] For details and specifications, see the Appendix.

through forced exit of low performers. This activity of agents is reflected in a constant turnover of rents from temporary monopoly positions that also drives the investment process at the firm level. Agents respond to prices and profit targets, and there is a demand feedback in the dynamic coordination of the economy. Hence, self-regulation occurs through the endogenization of price setting at the micro level – not through a central auctioneer or policymaker.

The welfare problem associated with free dynamic coordination through the price system, in a process model, is the stability over time of quantitative activity. The dynamic market processes controlling the development of quantities over time have to be reined in so that the economy stays in a preset, bounded region, an *n*-dimensional tunnel (see the discussion in Eliasson, 1983). Classical macro theory associates that task with macro policymakers. However, once M-M dynamics have been introduced, such notions are no longer convincing. To make the Smithian invisible hand operational in a dynamic M-M model, something that corresponds to the convexity assumption in static theory has to be introduced.

In any dynamic M-M system, each period is characterized by a final-state description of distributions that are carried onward in time through the economic action in the model. These distributions matter for the properties of the model. In a macro model, these states will include, for instance, the cyclical position of the economy (e.g., capacity utilization). In an M-M model there is a tremendous wealth of information on which the economy operates. We have distributions over firms of capacity utilization, actual and potential productivity, size by various definitions, profitability (Figure 6.4), wages, prices, financial ratios, and so forth. These factors all influence decisions at the micro level and hence the macro behavior of the model. For an economy not operating in equilibrium, prices for a given product, wages for the same labor input, and returns to capital vary across the population of firms. The shapes of these states, as they are carried forward in time, control the period-to-period stability of the behavior of quantities like output, employment, and so forth.

Simulation analysis with the Swedish M-M model suggests that a significant variation over time, and diversity over time in regard to performance and price structures of individual agents, must be present for the model to generate stable macroeconomic performance. If not, small disturbances can be very disruptive. For instance, if all financial decision units (firms and divisions) are operating at the same rate of return equal to or close to the market loan rate ("capital-market equilibrium"), a small increase in the interest rate can force a large proportion of the firms to drastically reduce investment simultaneously. [In mathematical terms, this notion can be likened to optimization on a horizontal plane. It is difficult to find a stable position that is better than all other positions. The economy begins to behave in a disorganized manner, and price signals lose their information content (Eliasson, 1985a, pp. 333ff.).]

The problem of stable economic growth in the Swedish M-M economy is to keep a significant spread of performance characteristics alive in the economy. Because competition makes low performers exit, this can be achieved only through vigorous innovative entry.[14] The relationship of micro variability to the macro stability problem that we have discussed is, in principle, the same as that of cyclical diffusion among sectors in an economy, and between nations in a world economy, as has been observed and quantified in a number of NBER studies (e.g., Hickman, 1959; Moore, 1961).

Because the adjustment of quantities is not immediate, some of the immediate adjustment has to be carried by flexible prices. A dynamic growth process will always be a mixture of the two processes of quantity and price adjustments. Because markets are not cleared and prices not fully adjusted, the information carried by market prices will not provide reliable indicators of scarcity. This is not solely a result of the exogenous innovative process that moves the growth process; it also depends on the interdependence of price and quantity adjustments throughout the entire economy.

As a consequence, policymakers are confronted with the choice of accepting the unpredictability that comes with viable innovative activity or imposing an institutional superstructure that restores order and predictability and, presumably, reduces innovative activity. That is the topic of the next section. It is, however, interesting to observe that top executives of large business groups experience exactly the same problem, and for the same reasons (Eliasson, 1976a).

6.5 The way institutional rules matter

When seen through the eyes of the conventional economist, the problem of economic growth is seen to be how "capitalism administers existing structures, whereas the relevant problem is how it creates and

---

[14] The more vigorous the entry, the more forceful is competitive exit, and the greater is stable long-term growth in macro output. However, if innovative entry is not keeping up with exit, performance distributions may flatten, as they did (see Figure 6.4) in the second half of the 1970s, and macro instabilities develop. This was my argument elsewhere (Eliasson, 1984a).

destroys them" (Schumpeter, 1942, p. 84). He continues: "As long as this is not recognized, the investigator does a meaningless job."

6.5.1   Endogenous institutional change

The point of this section can be condensed into a question: What happens when institutional change is made endogenous, and Åkerman's fourth fundamental falls into place in theory? The problem is that with the recognition of endogenous self-reorganization, immense complexity enters economic analysis. We have managed, in the previous section, to get entry and exit of given, parameterized agents into our quantified M-M model. This endogenizes part of the change in the structural composition of macro aggregates. Now much more is demanded.

The two critical properties arising out of the earlier discussion are, briefly speaking, the ability of the economic system to perform and the willingness to adjust. Within the intellectual framework of this chapter, these properties depend on how institutions are organized. Can the production organization of the economy generate *sufficient innovative activity and competitive entry at the levels needed to maintain a stable long-term growth process,* and are individuals and organized interests willing and able to endure the exit process that follows?

The first aspect concerns primarily the allocation of resources (capital and labor) over the production system. The second concerns the political part of the economy and all the vested interests that are disrupted in the process. Because the second "function" draws by far the largest share of resources in the economy, analysis of institutions as intermediators of information and interests cannot be neglected any longer. The technology of this intermediation, including shifts in this technology, causes difficult problems, both theoretical and empirical. It is obvious that the intermediation carried out by institutions, if badly organized, can have a strongly negative effect on overall economic performance. This is a general problem of economic analysis that is increasingly becoming associated with the problems of the modern welfare state (Eliasson, 1986a, 1986b; Meyerson, 1985).

6.5.2   Efficiency of the filter

When introduced in this way, the market process is presented as a filter, and the institutions constitute the organizational design of that filter. One property of the filter has to do with the rules regulating participation in the game of exploiting and updating the international opportunity set. The more limited the access to the game, the smaller the number of losers and the more orderly the game, but also the larger the probability that the scarce winners will be rejected. With a hierarchical design of the economy, as in a firm or in a planned economy, the central filter will limit the entry process in the name of stability. The more broad-based the access to the game (free entry), the more bad players in the game that will later be forced to exit (welfare is affected), but also the higher the probability that the few good players will be let in. We now have a free market economy. Stated in this way, a market economy is characterized by the degree of *free entry* (on this argument, also see Pelikan, 1985). The market lets in more players, good or bad. Because the bad players are forced to exit, the free market system will outperform the centrally filtered economic system, because it has more good players, but it will also have to find ways to cope with the welfare side of the exit process. North and Thomas (1973) had a similar notion in mind when they concluded that without the right configurations of institutional rules, innovative activity will be on the low side.

6.5.3   Inertia of institutions

To complete the introduction of institutions as the technology of efficient filter (market process) design, we make two additional observations. First, institutions (filter designs) change more slowly than the rate at which other forms of technology change the economic environment and the commercial opportunities. This is a Marxian view of industrial action. Hence, the political system will often be in defensive conflict with the capitalistic economic organization fueled by technological (in a broad sense) change. Coming back to North and Thomas (1973), we can reinterpret their argument by saying that because institutional rules are slow to change, institutional rules will actively control innovative activity. If they depress innovative activity, innovative activity will not be potent in breaking up rules. Hence, the interaction of institutional rules and technology must be a matter of centuries, not years and decades. The models capable of representing this development have to be path-dependent, each initial state determining the future course of the economy (see Section 6.6.8). Historians have to be brought into economics, a conclusion Joseph Schumpeter would have been happy to acknowledge.

Second, the political system is normally designed to reduce the unpredictability associated with the experimental economy.[15] If not checked by market forces – for instance, individuals breaking the rules or the laws by creating an underground economy (Feige, 1986), or technology simply eliminating the effects of controls – control will eventually be imposed to the extent that predictability prevails, allowing reasonably straightforward and transparent policies to be carried out. This is the rationale for the existence and the size of the political system. If uncontrollable market forces reduce the powers of controllability of the central authority, its existence, measured by its present size, is threatened. Arguments, on similar gounds, for a significantly reduced scope of action and authority on the part of "big government" are currently taking root in a large part of the Western world. The rationale behind such argument is partly that big government impairs democracy – an old Schumpeterian (1942) argument – but also, and perhaps more forcefully, that overall economic performance is impaired. The reason for lowered economic performance is the same as for the policies enacted to increase "order and predictability," namely, restrictions on entry and/or reductions in the number of independent players. As we have shown, such policy also reduces macroeconomic performance. To achieve such paradoxical policies, simplified abstractions ("theories") of the economic system that conform with policymakers' desires have been developed. They reflect the economy more or less well, and they give different advice about how to run it. The organization of the economy cannot be seen as independent of the "theory" by which it is run.

Hence, the political system in a broad sense sometimes can gain control of the economic system in the sense of being able to impose control on the economy by legal force or by indoctrination. If beliefs or ideologies are forced on the economy, its organization will change. This is one instance of the endogenization of institutions within Åkerman's framework (1950). However, the experimental economy that I am proposing in this chapter can never be modeled in such a fashion that simple central policy-making will replace the Smithian invisible hand in a way that will improve economic efficiency. Policy regimes that want to interfere extensively with their economies need much better theories to intellectually support argument and policy than mainstream economics can provide. Whether such analysis will support or reject centralistic policy is still beyond theoretical evaluation (Axell,

---

[15] The liberals should be the exception, but if we look at liberal political configurations in the Western world, they often are as keen on restricting the experimental economy as are their socialist or social democratic opponents.

1985). However, the more central interference that is desired, the more simplistic and hierarchical the representation of the economy, and the more unlikely it is, it appears to me, that the immense complexity of adjustment needed for the observed acceptable performance of a capitalistically organized market economy can be reproduced in an alternative, centrally planned design. I have argued that the particular formulation of an equilibrium developed in economic theory based on Walrasian postulates means imposing a monolithic hierarchy on the policy model and bringing the entire master decision together at one point in time.[16] The more such notions are imposed, the more the innovative process is thwarted and economic growth stalled, something that eventually undermines the power structure of the centralist political system itself.

My conclusion on policy can now be summarized as (1) the need for micro instability as a source of macro stability and growth in output and (2) the willingness of vested interests to accept painful adjustments. The political problem boils down to designing institutional rules that inhibit forces that would impede the adjustment process from gaining political control. Some would call this undemocratic, and others would say that this is a form of coercion needed to make democratic practice workable. And whatever the moral, we can observe how each national state has found its own practical solution to the dynamic balance of these forces. I shall conclude with a brief discussion of how this policy problem was solved, and then inadvertently "dissolved," in Sweden through what has come to be called the Swedish policy model.

6.5.4 The old Swedish model

The Swedish policy model is a particularly interesting example of intellectual policy control of an economy because it has features of both the planned economy and the market economy, because it was extremely efficient in its earlier use, and finally because its successful use changed the institutional foundations for its continued successful use in a way that Olson (1982) has touched on.

The old Swedish model can be said to epitomize the capitalistic market regime in the production organization and, in its earlier days, a soft

---

[16] Technically, in this model, the general equilibrium model transformed into a centralist planning model by, for example, Malinvaud (1967), the sequence by which the planning solution is arrived at does not matter. In such a conceptual framework, dynamics are effectively removed.

version of a planned regime on the distribution side. The old Swedish model has the following four characteristics:

1. Noninterference with the production decision
2. Free innovative entry (free trade, free technical change, and forced exit through unified wage policies)
3. Active labor-market policy (move people to the jobs)
4. Redistribution through taxes and public-sector growth (equity)

These four items correspond to *decentralization* of production and ownership, *efficiency* through free trade and competitive entry and exit, *full employment* through labor-market mobility, and *equity* through redistribution via the public sector. These four items were more or less explicitly formulated as an understanding among the unions, the employers, and the (social democratic) government. The understanding was mostly implicit, but it was partly coded in agreements and in other forms of documentation.[17] Items 1 and 2 very much represent a recognition of the Schumpeterian notion of economic dynamics that we outlined earlier. Items 3 and 4 are the institutional setting – call it the indoctrination part – that made the adjustment consequences of the Schumpeterian economy acceptable to people at large. One can safely say that the model was a success in terms of facilitating superb economic performance through the depression and until the end of the 1960s. What happened can be formulated in economic terms.

Success in phase I: The entry policies and active labor-market policies (items 2 and 3) forced people to adjust. It simply was not part of the socioeconomic mode not to adjust to the market. At the time, given noninterference (item 1), there was no place to ask for help except help to move to jobs (item 3). This was especially the case for firms. Public ownership in manufacturing was very low. Until the beginning of the 1970s there was not even a Department of Industry (Eliasson and Ysander, 1983). If people did not adjust, they took the consequences, and because most people were not capable of making deliberate adjustment decisions ahead of time, the consequences of market-induced structural changes were quite unevenly distributed. To buy insurance against these risks is a luxury good, and as the level of economic well-

[17] The Swedish policy model has a much broader focus than is usually assumed. It definitely goes much beyond the narrow focus on the labor market (item 3), with which it is usually associated (Lundberg, 1985). All four items can be extensively documented in the context of what has come to be called the Swedish policy model (Eliasson and Ysander, 1983).

being rose, protection from the vagaries of the market economy were demanded.

Phase II. Excessive public-sector growth: It could, perhaps, be called a market failure that a private insurance system did not develop rapidly enough to take care of the demands for such insurance. As a consequence, insurance to a large extent became part of the political system. To make a long story short, the rapid growth of the public sector financed through rapid growth of the private sector gradually undermined the institutional regime that had facilitated the successful noninterventionist, free-trade Swedish production system (Eliasson, 1986a). At the beginning, this was a form of gradual addictive public consumption, and as everybody knows, one cannot change consumption habits easily when public income unexpectedly stagnates. The worst part, however, probably was the departure from the noninterventionist open-economy conceptualization of a working economy (item 1). It occurred in two ways. First, the relatively faster growth of the public economy meant that the noninterventionist, open, free-entry economy was diminishing in relative size. The latter sector absorbed the bulk of adjustment and became relatively smaller, forcing an inequitable distribution of the adjustment burden and creating instabilities in the economy. The second phase began in the late 1960s as part of the rather aggressive egalitarian policies that required, it was argued, increased centralization and standardization of production in both public and private domains.

However, once attempts are made to control the micro outcomes of innovative change on equity grounds, the individualistic picture of economic action of the young Schumpeter ([1912] 1934) gives way to the worries about concentration and threats to democracy of the old Schumpeter (1942). The Schumpeter of 1942 believed that this changed picture would occur because of the emergence of new and efficient organizational techniques for planned innovative activity. The empirical evidence, however, still supports the young Schumpeter. Political institutions[18] trying to control the economy by limiting access

---

[18] In this respect, there is no principal difference between political control and the control of the market exercised by a private monopoly. An enormous literature exists on bad private (monopolistic) behavior and the need for antitrust policies. However, no corresponding literature exists on similar bad policy practice on the part of governments, because we somehow think that is has been sanctioned by a democratic political process, and thereby has been made "good." Government economic action is controlled neither by the market (except through illicit or wrongful activities) nor by external legal forces, only by "itself" (Ysander, 1986).

to the international pool of opportunities appear to reduce commercially successful innovative activity (Eliasson, 1984b). Thus, after having recognized a possible failure of the growth machinery of the economy as a consequence of ambitious welfare policies for a couple of decades or so, the Swedes are currently trying to find ways and excuses for getting back to the old Swedish policy model. It at least seemed to generate economic growth. But the political process is not easy to reverse, because it requires that the nonmarket sector be significantly reduced, against the will of well-entrenched vested interests, and the reversal process itself is essentially tacit (Eliasson, 1986a, 1986b). The task of developing the kind of theory presented at the beginning of this chapter still remains to be accomplished.

6.6   Appendix: Dynamic-disequilibrium adjustment modeling – a brief presentation of the Swedish M-M model economy

6.6.1   The M-M economics of information

Information and knowledge are obvious elements in economic theory. This fact, however, has mostly been ignored. Information has been assumed to be freely available, and everybody has been assumed to be fully informed, or at least fully knowledgeable about the costs of being fully informed. In deriving aggregate dynamics from micro behavior, theory must be explicit about the ways in which information is gathered, analyzed, and used for market transactions. Consequently, a market should be treated as a process rather than as an equilibrium condition. Following Stigler (1961), I call this intelligence gathering in the Swedish M-M model a "search" activity, even though "search" in the M-M model is more broadly defined to include both the gathering and use of information and the actual implementation and later evaluation of decisions.

This appendix introduces the Swedish M-M model from the point of view of its use of information related to the information activities discussed earlier. The dominant intelligence gathering and interpretation activities of a manufacturing firm concern technical information used for product development and marketing. Information activity in the market is a major investment and resource-using activity in large manufacturing firms (Table 6.1). If this activity is not somehow explicitly accounted for, the firm is grossly misrepresented, and – I claim – aggregate dynamics are misspecified. Lack of data and lack of academic insight regarding the nature of information use in business

Table 6.1. *Investments by the 5 largest and the 37 largest Swedish manufacturing groups, 1978*[a]

	The 5 largest groups		The 37 largest groups	
Investments	All groups (%)	Foreign subsidiaries only (%)	All groups (%)	Foreign subsidiaries only (%)
R&D	25	10	21	6
Machinery and buildings	45	41	52	42
Marketing	30	49	27	52
Total	100	100	100	100

[a]Investments in marketing and R&D have been estimated from cost data. Firms have been ranked by foreign employment.
Source: Eliasson (1985b).

organizations thus far means that we have had to be crude in modeling this search phenomenon.

The ultimate problem associated with introducing information processing explicitly in economic modeling – and hence with economics – arises when technical change in information processing is allowed. If such technical change has to be assumed to be unpredictable, on empirical grounds, as to micro outcomes, the results of mainstream economics will have to be revised fundamentally.

6.6.2 Aggregation through dynamic markets

M-M theory is concerned with aggregation through markets. There are two dimensions to this: (1) the sequence that goes from micro decisions to macro and (2) modifying micro theory to make it respond to macro feedback through demand and prices. The latter is "missing in general equilibrium micro models" (Diamond, 1984).

The first observation to make is that transactions take place between agents in the market, not between each agent and "the market" – or the auctioneer – as in general equilibrium theory. This defines the market as the combined actions of all agents, which is the only meaningful definition of a market. The agents spend time and other resources attempting to upgrade their positions in the market. We have observed (Table 6.1) that resources spent on "search" within the firm may be larger than other factory production costs. If we introduce costs for all institutions engaged in intermediation between individuals and firms (as discussed in Section 6.5), factory-goods production costs may even become a minor part of the total.

The discussion in this Appendix departs from classical Walrasian analysis, or classical search theory, in two additional respects (Diamond, 1984, p. 2): First, agents (firms) do not explicitly apply maximizing routines in their search behavior; they strive for *ex ante improved positions*. I have called this MIP targeting.[19] Second, I remove the additional role of the auctioneer in Walrasian economics, namely, achieving consistency and making correct forecasts possible. Agents in M-M theory normally misperceive their environment and make forecasting mistakes. This means that trade will not take place at market-clearing prices or price distributions. Hence, the most interesting part of M-M economics is how the markets sort out *ex ante* inconsistencies in the *realization process* that eventually is registered as *ex post* behavior (Eliasson, 1969; Modigliani and Cohen, 1963). Thus, analysis in M-M theory deals with dynamic market coordination out of equilibrium, not only (as in search theory) with information costs associated with costly coordination toward an equilibrium. The two departures from Walrasian economics – upgrading behavior and incorrect forecasting – can probably be seen as two sides of the same thing. This means that the notion of equilibrium has to be redefined and that perfect information is not normally an achievable state, even with the application of unlimited costs. To my mind, this is the dividing line between classical, Walrasian-based theory and the new theory – let us call it Schumpeter-inspired M-M theory. We have a dynamic extended economic game, implied by the experimental economy, to play. I shall return to this briefly at the end.

6.6.3   Introducing technology, intelligence gathering, and bounded rationality

How do we model the firm as an information processor in dynamic markets, and in a long-term perspective? The earlier text has introduced innovative activity by way of three concepts: (1) the international opportunity set, (2) local "tacit" knowledge, and (3) "bounded rationality." The opportunity set is available to all players in the market to a degree determined by their ability (knowledge), which is limited ("bounded") and "tacit" and hence cannot be treated as infor-

---

[19] MIP, for maintain or improve profits (Eliasson, 1976a, pp. 175, 236ff., 291ff.).

mation communicable and tradable in markets. This makes industrial knowledge local and assures that only a fraction of the opportunity set is exploited at each point in time, and not in a foreseeable way. Bounded rationality is enough to ensure frequent forecasting mistakes. Kenneth Arrow (1982, p. 7), acceding that standard notions of rationality may not stand up to empirical evidence, gives a bizarre illustration from the medical field of how the content (the "interpretation") of the same information may change "with the frame of reference." The micro consequences of knowledge application become unpredictable under tacit knowledge (i.e., when the choice of frame of references is left unexplained).

Profit incentives keep firms searching for ways to exploit opportunities through imitation and piecemeal innovative improvements, generating innovative activity and updating the opportunity set such that it constantly keeps well abreast of its exploiters. It is an empirically unsettled issue whether or not any additional "basic" technological development of the kind associated with collective subsidized government activity (Arrow, 1962b; Dasgupta and Stiglitz, 1981) is needed to make this come true. I enter a negative conclusion at this point, until we know more. (Unpredictable micro activity causes painful social adjustments. Willingness to put up with these ajustments was discussed in the text, but is not part of the model, and hence is left out here.)

Information processes in the Swedish M-M model occur in two dimensions: through *analysis and interpretation* (prediction), and through *search and risk taking*. Some form of intelligence (interpretation) precedes all decisions. This activity enters through *expectations functions* related to product prices, wages, and sales (market development) and *targeting* and is most elaborate in the short-term production decision, as described later. However, expectations often are wrong, and in an economic environment where critical knowledge is "tacit," one cannot choose until one has tried and observed the outcome. In fact, much of intelligence gathering in real life is experimental "learning by doing." All business organizations are designed to cope with such experimental learning (Eliasson, 1976a), and I call the whole sequence – analyze, try, evaluate, learn, and analyze again – *search*.

It is important to understand that whereas expectations are concerned with predicting the external environment of the firm, targeting focuses on bringing interior information up to the corporate level with the sole purpose of setting reasonable performance criteria, neither too high nor below what is feasible. This is a typical instance of bounded rationality (Eliasson, 1976a, pp. 39ff.), highlighting the fact that top management in a large firm may be as uninformed about the interior of their firm as they are about their external environment.

Because rationality is bounded and past experiences differ, correct predictions at the micro level are rare and randomly distributed. Search, therefore, is followed by more or less success, including failure, and the experience feeds back in the form of learning, updating, and improving one's interpretation methods. (Expectations functions in the M-M model are to some extent updated and improved through learning from experience.)

In the particular context of this chapter, the information side is rather crudely modeled. The international opportunity set is represented by new and better exogenous technology embodied in new investment vintages. What distinguishes this from a traditional vintage-production-function approach is the endogenous investment decision of each individual firm that, first, represents its ability (local technical competence) and, second – together with the endogenous production decision underneath the production frontier – ensures that no "classical" production function can exist over time.

The past business success of the firm determines the financial resources available for investment through the profit flow and through "credibility" with external sources of finance. Long-term "expectations" determine the forecasts that guide the willingness of the firm to take on risks. What we do not have, but are working on (Eliasson, 1985a, pp. 280ff.), is explicit intelligence gathering as to the nature of the international opportunity set, beyond "search," or the learning experience of actually trying through investing.

6.6.4   The M-M model economy[20]

When seen "from above," the macro mapping of the Swedish M-M model is a Keynesian-Leontief 11-sector model with a nonlinear Stone-type consumption system, wealth creation being treated as a separate consumption category ("savings"), with complete feedback through demand and investment capacity growth. Underneath the macro level, exogenous Schumpeterian innovative activity upgrades the characteristics of new investment of individual firms, à la the

---

[20] Also called the MOSES model. Both the M-M model used and the experimental designs are too complex to be fully described in this chapter. For more detail, we refer the reader to other publications (Eliasson, 1976b, 1978, 1985a); likewise for a short presentation of the labor-market process (Albrecht and Lindberg, 1982; Bergholm, 1983; Eliasson, 1986c).

young Schumpeter.[21] New technology is brought into firms through their individual investment decisions determined by a Wicksellian disequilibrium in the capital market, related to the return of the firm over the market loan rate (Figure 6.4) (Eliasson, 1986c). Hence, rate-of-return criteria imposed through the capital market dominate long-term dynamics in the model. A Smithian invisible hand coordinates the whole economy dynamically through monopolistic competition in the product, labor, and capital markets. Foreign prices, the foreign interest rate, and the labor force are exogenous.

Referring back to the main text, the "three theories" discussed in the context of the long historical diagram are represented: *Schumpeterian innovative activities* (exogenous) and the efficiency of the *Smithian invisible hand* (more or less regulation) through the *Wicksellian disequilibrium* adjustment process. Together, these mechanisms determine the dynamics of *resource allocation*. The *Keynesian demand feedback* needed to keep the economy growing enters in three ways: through endogenous income formation and demand feedback (the system is complete), through exogenous government, fiscal, and monetary policies, and through foreign trade. The M-M economy is regulated by the interaction of domestic endogenous and foreign (exogenous) prices. Hence, Marxian demand-deficiency (or excess demand) situations of varying length occur all the time in the model through failure of demand plans to meet supply plans. Markets do not clear, and stocks and later prices adjust. Experience from model work tells us that cycles of different lengths occur as a consequence, and occasionally they develop into severe depressions of long duration.

One should also note that M-M theory, as represented by the MOSES model, can be regarded as an extended game of infinite duration with a variable number of players, forming and enacting decisions on the basis of "intermediated information" from the markets. In retrospect, the latter is particularly interesting, but crudely represented in the model. Because each firm cannot be in touch with all other firms individually, *it interprets various items of aggregate information generated by the market process,* provided with a delay by traders, intermediators, and institutions that are not explicit in the model. On this point, an interesting theoretical development should be possible considering the two facts that this intermediation is the dominant resource-using activity in an economy and that practically nothing seems to have been done in this area of research.

---

[21] Work is in progress to endogenize it partly, at the individual-firm level (Eliasson, 1985a, pp. 280ff.).

Model overview: The M-M model is oriented mainly toward analyzing industrial growth. Therefore, the manufacturing sector is the most detailed sector in the model. Manufacturing is divided into four industries (raw-material processing, semimanufactures, durable-goods manufacturing, and manufacture of consumer nondurables). Each industry consists of a number of firms, some of which are real (with data supplied mainly through an annual survey), and some of which are synthetic. Together, the synthetic firms in each industry make up the differences between the real firms and the industry totals in the national accounts. The 250 real firms, or divisions, in the model cover 70–75 percent of industrial employment and production in the base year, currently 1982. The model is based on a quarterly time specification.

6.6.5 Markets as a process

The fact that all firms together take inconsistent decisions on the basis of limited knowledge (bounded rationality) means (1) that expectations rarely come true and (2) that the firms always operate well below what is feasible. Hence, neither the firm nor the economy ever comes to rest on a steady growth path.

Endogenous pricing decisions: In contrast to most econometric macro models, domestic prices and wages are determined endogenously and by individual agents in MOSES. These, in turn, influence the firms' profits and therefore their production plans, the allocation of sales to the domestic and export markets, their investments, and therefore their productivity. This is the main mechanism through which resource allocation is determined. These features make the model especially well suited for analyzing the effects of policy measures, which can be expected to influence the expectations and plans of firms and the development of prices and wages. The advantage of a micro-based simulation model is that one can introduce various policy measures affecting individual firms, rather than industries, and analyze the effects. In a more traditional macro model, one usually is forced to make assumptions regarding the resource-allocation effects; that is, one must *assume* "structure" (i.e., a large part of the results).

The labor market: Firms in the model constitute short- and long-run planning systems for production and investment. Each quarter they decide on their desired production, employment, and investment. Armed with these plans, they go into the labor market, where their employment plans confront those of other firms, as well as labor supply.[22] The labor force is treated as homogeneous in the model (i.e., labor is recruited from a common "pool"). However, labor can also be recruited from other firms. Hence, even though labor is homogeneous in the sense that the productivity of one unit of L is completely determined by the job on which it is allocated, each unit of L has a different wage experience that affects its willingness to move in the market. Hence, labor is heterogeneous in MOSES in the sense of having different reservation wages that are constantly updated and significantly affect labor supply. This process determines the wage level, which is thus endogenous in the model. Wages vary significantly among both firms and industries, and tendencies of wages to converge depend on the way the labor-market regime is parameterized. Because the labor market is subdivided only into industries, not regions, mobility in the labor market probably is overestimated. This is important in interpreting the results.

The M-M model features an endogenous exit device for firms. It is activated when the net worth of a firm goes below a certain minimum level in percentage of total assets (bankruptcy) and/or when the firm runs out of cash (liquidity crisis). The firm, of course, gradually fades away through lack of investment if its cash flow diminishes and if it cannot borrow in the capital market at the going interest rate.

Domestic-product prices and the production volume in the four product markets are determined through similar processes.

Anti–Say's law: Rather than coming to rest on a growth trajectory (q) with market-clearing prices (p) that accurately reflect equilibrium, the M-M process model is characterized by a sequence of states in the form of *distributions* of (p, q), carried forward in time, quarter by quarter. When we discussed the need for diversity of structures to maintain long-term macro stability, we meant sufficient diversity of these state descriptions to keep the macroeconomic process reasonably bounded. Because boundedness is a form of welfare criterion (Eliasson, 1983), diversity of structure corresponds to the requirement of convexity in static analysis to obtain equilibrium properties. Another difference in the MOSES case is that diversity is maintained through endogenous adjustment processes in the model economy, notably investment, entry (Hanson, 1986), and exit.

The state distributions that we talk about include wages, productivity, and rates of return, as illustrated in Figure 6.4. The model is started

---

[22] Chapter II in Eliasson (1985a) includes a rather detailed account of the labor-market pricing process.

on such an initially measured state, not on a construed equilibrium state. Over any foreseeable future, the model exhibits initial state-dependent behavior, suggesting that equilibrium and welfare analysis on such models cannot use conventional concepts. A market that cannot clear without causing disruptions at the macro level is represented (Figure 6.4) by the price distributions $(R - r)$ in the capital market, measuring the rate of return of a firm or division (R) over its loan rate (r). Following Morishima and Catephores (see Chapter 4), this means that Say's law does not hold up. Investment and savings plans do not clear the market, resulting in a deficit, or an excess-demand situation of the kind discussed both by Marx and by Keynes, but most succinctly by Wicksell ([1898] 1965) – the cumulative process. This situation must also be characteristic of a Schumpeterian-type model.

6.6.6 Profits and allocation of capital – the investment decision

To outline the capital-market dynamics of the M-M economy, we derive the profit-targeting and profit-monitoring formulas used for both production and investment decisions. These guide the firm in its gradient search for a rate of return in excess of the market loan rate. To derive these formulas, we decompose the total costs (TC) of a business firm, over a one-year planning horizon, into

$$TC = wL + p^l \cdot I + \left(r + \rho - \frac{\Delta p^k}{p^k} \right) p^k \cdot \overline{K} \tag{1}$$

where w is the wage cost per unit of L, L equals units of labor input, p^l is input price (other than w and p^k) per unit of I, I equals units of input, r is the interest rate, ρ is the depreciation factor on $K = p^k \cdot \overline{K}$, p^k is the capital-goods price (market or cost), and $\overline{K}$ equals units of capital installed. In principle, the various factors $(L, I, \overline{K})$ *within* a firm can be organized differently and still achieve the same total output. Depending on the nature of this allocation, the firm experiences higher or lower capital and labor productivity (as defined and measured later). In what follows, we investigate the capital/labor mix as it is achieved through dynamic market allocation of resources *among* firms.

The firm is selling a volume of product $(\overline{S})$ at a price p^* $(S = p^* \cdot \overline{S}$, such that there is a surplus revenue, ϵ, over costs, or profit):

$$\epsilon = p^* \cdot \overline{S} - TC \tag{2}$$

The profit per unit of capital R^N is the rate of return[23] on capital in excess of the loan rate:

$$\frac{\epsilon}{K} = R^N - r \tag{3}$$

In this formal exercise, K has been valued at current reproduction costs, meaning that ϵ/K expresses a real excess return over the loan rate, but that r is a nominal interest rate.

In the MOSES M-M model, firm owners and top management control the firm by applying targets on R^{EN}, the return on equity capital. This is the same as to say that they apply profit targets in terms of ϵ. Hence, we have established a direct connection between the goal (target) structure of the firm and its operating characteristics in terms of its various cost items.

The control function: Using equations (1), (2), and (3), the fundamental control function of a MOSES firm can be derived as[24]

$$R^{EN} - M \cdot \alpha - \rho + \frac{\Delta p^k}{p^k} + \epsilon \cdot \phi = R^N + \epsilon \cdot \phi \tag{4}$$

$$M = 1 - \frac{w}{p^*} \cdot \frac{1}{\beta} \tag{5}$$

where M is the gross profit margin (i.e., value added less wage costs in percentage of S), $R^{EN} = (p^*\overline{S} - TC)/E$, the nominal return to net worth ($E = K -$ debt), $\alpha = \overline{S}/\overline{K}$, $\beta = \overline{S}/L$, $\phi = $ debt$/E = (K - E)/E$, and $\epsilon = (R^N - r)K$.

Management of the firm delegates responsibility over the operating departments through equation (4) and appropriate short-term targets on M (production control) and long-term targets on ϵ that control the investment decision; $\epsilon \cdot \phi$ defines the contribution to overall firm profit performance from the financing department.

At any given set of expectations on (w, p^x) in equation (4) determined through individual-firm adaptive error learning functions, a target on M means a labor productivity target on $\overline{S}/L$. Hence, the profit

---

[23] The rate of return is then defined as $R^N = (p^* \cdot \overline{S} - TC + r \cdot K)/K$. Also observe that $\ldots p^k$ in equation (1) is the standard, neoclassical definition of the cost for a unit of capital service $\overline{K}$ as valued in the external markets for credit. Observe that when the capital market is in equilibrium (the standard assumption in general equilibrium theory), then all $\epsilon = 0$ and TC completely exhaust the total value produced. $TC \equiv p^* \cdot \overline{S}$ in equation (2). Say's law holds. There is no investment–savings gap.

[24] For proof of equations (4) and (5), see Eliasson (1976a, 1985a, pp. 110ff.).

margin can be viewed as a price-weighted and "inverted" labor productivity measure.

Long-term objective function: The objective function guiding long-term investment behavior is to select investment projects that satisfy *(ex ante)*

$$\epsilon/K = R^N - r > 0$$

where r is the local loan rate of the firm. The local loan rate depends on the firm's financial-risk exposure, measured by its debt–equity position.

The ϵ of an individual firm is generated through innovative technical improvements at the firm level (Schumpeterian innovative rents) that constitute Wicksellian-type capital-market disequilibria defined at the micro level. The ϵ drives the rate of investment spending of the individual firm. The standard notion of a Wicksellian capital-market equilibrium is that of "average" $\epsilon_i = 0$ for the market. As a rule, this state is not achieved. Unused capacity may prevent the firm from expanding capacity even though investment in the long term is expected to yield $\epsilon > 0$. More important, however, is the fact that realized investment comes much later than the current quarter and that firms continue to make mistakes.

Technology: A new investment vintage can be regarded as a "new firm" with exogenous capital-productivity ($\alpha = \overline{S}/\overline{K}$) and labor-productivity ($\beta = \overline{S}/L$) characteristics. A new investment can be seen as a new vintage of capital with these particular technology (α, β, ρ) characteristics in the profit-control function (4) that mix with capital installations in existing firms.[25] Technology is exogenous and is embodied in new investment vintages. Hence, the *international opportunity set* introduced earlier is represented by current (α, β, ρ) specifications of new investment vintages, and *local competence* is defined by the local investment process (and, of course, the short-term production decision) that upgrades the technical specifications (the "frontier") of the firm, under which quarterly production decisions are taken.

6.6.7   The quarterly production decision

This decision determines where production occurs underneath the production frontier, moved by the investment decision. Each quarter,

---

[25] In a fashion described in Eliasson (1978, pp. 63ff.).

the firm determines its production volume in two steps. First, it determines its desired production volume, taking into account desired changes in its inventories of finished goods, based on its expected total sales (including exports), which are in turn based on the firm's historical experience.

MIP targeting: The production decision is typically boundedly rational in the sense of Simon (1955). Top-level management does not know enough to impose the flow structure that would maximize ϵ in equation (2) through the components of M in equation (4), given capital installations.[26] It resorts to MIP targeting. Expected (p, w) are applied to historical data on β and suggested to lower-level management, thus initiating an internal negotiation, called *production search,* eventually resulting in a preliminary agreement (a plan). The negotiation process continues as long as management believes that M will stay above targets *without resulting in a lowering of ex ante profits.* Concavity is thus preserved, and decisions correspond to a gradient approach to maximum *ex ante* profits, which will be reached if other environmental conditions remain unaltered. However, normally it is not possible to impose the latter conditions on a dynamic micro-based model of this kind.

This first production plan is revised by the firms with regard to profit targets, capacity utilization, and the expected labor-market situation. After this revision, the production plan is executed.

Interaction with other markets (interdependence): The production volume is distributed to the export and domestic markets according to an export share, which is dependent on that from the previous quarter, but which also depends on the difference during the previous quarter between the export price and the domestic price. If this export price (which is exogenous) was higher than the domestic price, the firms try to increase their export shares during the current quarter. However, the adjustment takes place over several quarters, not instantly. If the export price is lower than the domestic price, the firms do not try to lower their export shares, but rather maintain them at constant levels. In spite of this asymmetry concerning the effects of positive or negative price differences between exports and the domestic market, it turns out that the export shares in the various markets can both increase and decrease. This depends on whether firms with high export shares fare better or worse than other firms in the market. The import shares in

---

[26] Observe that β represents the structure of the entire production organization.

the four markets are also determined by the difference between export and domestic prices, with a certain time delay. High domestic prices relative to foreign prices lead to increasing import shares.

There is also a capital market in the model where firms compete for investment resources and where the rate of interest is determined. At this given interest rate, firms invest as much as they find it profitable to invest, given their profit targets.

Public-sector employment is determined exogenously, and the rate of wage increase in the public sector has been set equal to the average wage change in manufacturing, preserving the relative average salary and wage differential between the two sectors.

6.6.8   *Economic growth in M-M theory and its policy implications*

The complex disequilibrium market adjustment that regulates the growth process of an economy can now be presented more succinctly. It is apparent that the ways market processes are organized and interact also control the adjustment processes and hence influence the efficiency of resource use. This is so because the adjustment process determines how efficiently information can be put to use in the economy. Technological know-how, residing in the exogenous opportunity set, limits the real operating domain of the economy from above at each point in time. This is the Schumpeterian, innovative supply-push part of the story.

How far below what is technologically feasible the economy will operate depends on a delicate balance between the *speed of adjustment of resource use, given perceived prices,* on the one hand, and on how the direction and speed of all micro adjustments affect prices, on the other (i.e., on the information content of realized market prices and hence on predictability). If prices are persistently biased predictors of future prices (e.g., because of the way markets are organized, inertia, regulations, and tax wedges), then resources can be constantly misallocated, and/or demand can be insufficient to sustain stable and rapid growth in output. This is how the Keynesian demand-pull part of the story enters. It takes us beyond macroeconomics.

Dynamic coordination occurs through multimarket price interaction in general, but through the investment decision and the capital market in particular. This is the reinterpretation of Wicksell ([1898] 1965) that I have ventured. Through this market process, the output generated through the innovative process is distributed over factor inputs, including labor and capitalists, and hence forms the incentive system for future innovative activities (Eliasson, 1986c). Several important new methodological and policy questions emerge from this. What makes all the difference is (1) the realistic and unavoidable introduction of explicit, endogenous price and quantity adjustment processes in an overall "general equilibrium" framework and (2) the acceptance of the fact that because of imperfect information, the economy is persistently operating below the upper limits set by technology.

Against this background I have three final observations to make on economic analysis, and the theory of economic growth in particular.

First, the complete, multimarket setting of the M-M model gives perspective to partial analysis. In the M-M setting, the "experimental design" imposed on economic behavior makes partial analysis no longer viable. Variables held constant and exogenous in partial analysis are endogenous and cannot be made exogenous and often cannot be regarded as insignificant. Small modifications of assumptions often can be shown to completely reverse the predictions of the simple partial model that are in turn reversed as a result of further modifications. Phillips-curve analysis of wage setting is one example. The conclusions are entirely different, depending on whether labor behavior or firm behavior is studied in isolation or the behaviors of both agents are studied simultaneously (Eliasson and Lindberg, 1986). The partial-analysis tradition of economics is a particular form of ad hocery that is not very scientific and is especially disturbing in policy analysis, because economists often do not even bother to discuss the relevance of their little ad hoc model in a more general theoretical framework. In a dynamic, multimarket M-M framework, the whole Walras-Arrow-Debreu model becomes partial and ad hoc and is not a very reliable tool for policy analysis. This is certainly a case for computable equilibrium-model exercises.

Second, a dynamic micro-based process model has to substitute something for the traditional convexity assumptions of general equilibrium analysis to keep the economic process bounded. Because economies of scale of various sorts exist, something has to prevent concentration of all production in one single firm. The dynamics of Schumpeterian competition, through unpredictable new entries, are what keep this from happening. We have not yet explored all the implications of this for dynamic systems behavior. However, this analysis has forced us to look carefully at the concepts of equilibrium and stability in a process setting (Eliasson, 1983, 1984a) and the conflict that exists between stability and predictability of behavior at the macro level and at various lower levels. We do know that concentration tends to create macro instabilities (Eliasson, 1983, 1984a) and that concentration is prevented by free, unpredictable entry. The tentative conclusion we have is that "chaotic" behavior at various lower levels of dis-aggregation is a necessary requirement for stable macroeconomic growth. We have also related the existence of a large part of the societal institutional framework to a need to smooth the social side of chaotic behavior at the micro level.

Third, and most important of all, the initial state of the model at each point in time critically determines its future trajectory underneath the upper limit set by technology and the speed of adjustment that is socially acceptable. This means that for all future time spans that are interesting in a policy perspective, *the analysis becomes path-dependent.* A historical method must be resorted to for anything meaningful to be said about the future. A theoretically interesting question that I have, so far, not been able to answer is under what organizational forms a dynamic M-M economy will become path-independent in the limit (Eliasson, 1985a, chap. VII), that is, under what conditions all trajectories will converge to the same ultimate state, irrespective of the initial state. This question definitely is not only academic. If such limiting state independence can be shown to exist, or assumed to be a reasonable property of dynamic economic theory, that makes it possible to derive more powerful conclusions than would otherwise be possible regarding the nature of adjustment processes and regarding policy in a dynamic-process economy. For instance, if state independence prevails, the error-correction, "learning-expectations" functions that each agent in the M-M model uses in each market will have to be designed so that they will mimic rational-expectations behavior in a limiting sense. Thus, policy controllability and equilibrium properties come together. This suggests extreme caution in imposing narrow equilibrium conditions on models used for policy analysis, especially static equilibrium properties and the simplistic rational-expectation assumptions commonly imposed.

References

Åkerman, J. (1950). "Institutionalism." *Ekonomisk Tidskrift.*
    (1952). "Innovativa och kumulativa förlopp." *Ekonomisk Tidskrift,* 54(4):185–202.
Albrecht, J., and Lindberg, T. (1982). *The Micro Initialization of MOSES.* IUI Working Paper No. 72. Stockholm: IUI.
Alexander, S. S. (1958). "Rate of Change Approaches to Forecasting – Diffusion Indexes and First Differences." *Economic Journal,* 68(June):288–301.
Arrow, K. J. (1959). "Toward a Theory of Price Adjustment," in M. Abra-

movitz et al. (eds.), *The Allocation of Economic Resources.* Stanford University Press.

(1962a). "The Economic Implications of Learning by Doing." *Review of Economic Studies,* 29(June)(80):155–73.

(1962b). "Economic Welfare and the Allocation of Resources for Invention," in *The Rate and Direction of Inventive Activity: Economic and Social Factors.* Princeton University Press, for NBER.

(1982). "Risk Perception in Psychology and Economics." *Economic Inquiry,* 20(January)(1):1–9.

Ashton, T. S. (1948). *The Industrial Revolution 1760–1830.* London: Oxford University Press.

Axell, B. (1985). *Kan Inflation förbjudas?* (Can Inflation be Prohibited?) Stockholm: IUI.

Bergholm, F. (1983). *The MOSES Manual – The Initialization Process.* IUI Working Paper No. 118. Stockholm: IUI.

Braudel, F. (1981). *The Structure of Every Day Life, Civilization and Capitalism 15th–18th Century.* New York: Harper & Row.

Carlsson, B. (1980). "Jordbrukets roll vid Sveriges industrialisering," in E. Dahmén and G. Eliasson (eds.), *Industriell utveckling i Sverige. Teori och verklighet under ett sekel* (Industrial Development in Sweden. Theory and Practice during a Century). Stockholm: IUI.

(1981). "The Content of Productivity Growth in Swedish Manufacturing," in *IUI 40 Years 1939–1979 – The Firms in the Market Economy.* Stockholm: IUI.

(1983). "Industrial Subsidies in Sweden: Simulations on a Micro-to-Macro Model," in *Microeconometries, IUI Yearbook 1982–83.* Stockholm: IUI.

Chen, E. K. Y. (1979). *Hyper-Growth in Asian Economies.* New York: Holmes & Meier.

Clark, J. M. (1961). *Competition as a Dynamic Force.* Washington, D.C.: Brookings Institution.

Dahmén, E. (1950). *Svensk industriell företagarverksamhet 1919–1939* (Entrepreneurial Activity in Swedish Industry, 1919–1939). Stockholm: IUI.

(1984). "Schumpeterian Dynamics: Some Methodological Notes." *Journal of Economic Behavior & Organization,* 5(March)(1):25–34; also published in R. Day and G. Eliasson (eds.), *The Dynamics of Market Economies.* Stockholm: IUI. Amsterdam: North Holland.

Dahmén, E., and Eliasson, G. (1980). "Företagaren i det ekonomiska skeendet" (The entrepreneur in the market environment), in E. Dahmén and G. Eliasson (eds.), *Industriell utveckling i Sverige. Teori och verklighet under ett sekel* (Industrial Development in Sweden. Theory and Practice during a Century). Stockholm: IUI.

Dahmén, E., and Eliasson, G. (eds.) (1980). *Industriell utveckling i Sverige. Teori och verklighet under ett sekel* (Industrial Development in Sweden. Theory and Practice during a Century). Stockholm: IUI.

Dasgupta, P., and Stiglitz, J. E. (1980). "Industrial Structure and the Nature of Innovative Activity." *Economic Journal,* 90(June)(358):266–293.

(1981). "Entry, Innovation, Exit: Towards a Dynamic Theory of Oligopolistic Industrial Structure." *European Economic Review,* 15:137–158.

Day, R. H. (1984). "Disequilibrium Economic Dynamics: A Post-Schumpeterian Contribution." *Journal of Economic Behavior & Organization,* 5(March)(1):57–76; also published in R. Day and G. Eliasson (eds.), *The Dynamics of Market Economies.* Stockholm: IUI. Amsterdam: North Holland.

Day, R. H., and Eliasson, G. (eds.) (1986). *The Dynamics of Market Economies.* Stockholm: IUI. Amsterdam: North Holland.

Diamond, P. (1984). *A Search-Equilibrium Approach to the Micro Foundations of Macroeconomics.* Cambridge, Mass: M.I.T. Press.

Eisenstein, E. L. (1979). *The Printing Press as an Agent of Change* (2 vols.). Cambridge University Press.

Eliasson, G. (1969). *The Credit Market, Investment, Planning and Monetary Policy – An Econometric Study of Manufacturing Industries.* Stockholm: IUI.

(1976a). *Business Economic Planning – Theory, Practice and Comparison.* New York: Wiley.

(1976b). *A Micro Macro Interactive Simulation Model of the Swedish Economy.* Preliminary documentation, Economic Research Report No. B15. Stockholm: Federation of Swedish Industries (with the assistance of Gösta Olavi and Mats Heiman).

(1978). *A Micro-to-Macro Model of the Swedish Economy.* Stockholm: IUI.

(1980). "Elektronik, teknisk förändring och ekonomisk utveckling" (Electronics, Technical Change and Economic Development), in *Datatenik, ekonomisk tillväxt och sysselsättning* (DEK). IUI booklet No. 110. Stockholm: IUI.

(1981). "Electronics, Economic Growth and Employment – Revolution or Evolution?" in H. Giersch (ed.), *Emerging Technologies, Consequences for Economic Growth, Structural Change and Employment.* Kiel: Institut für Weltwirtschaft.

(1983). "On the Optimal Rate of Structural Adjustment," in M. Sharefkin, G. Eliasson, and B.-C. Ysander (eds.), *Policy Making in a Disorderly World Economy.* IUI Conference Reports 1983:1. Stockholm: IUI.

(1984a). "Micro Heterogeneity of Firms and the Stability of Industrial Growth." *Journal of Economic Behavior & Organization,* 5(September–December)(3–4); also published in R. Day and G. Eliasson (eds.), *The Dynamics of Market Economies.* Stockholm: IUI. Amsterdam: North Holland.

(1984b). "The Micro-Foundations of Industrial Policies," in A. Jacquemin (ed.), *European Industry: Public Policy and Corporate Strategy.* Oxford University Press.

(1985a). *The Firm and Financial Markets in the Swedish Micro-to-Macro Model – Theory, Model and Verification.* Stockholm: IUI.

(1985b). *Information Technology, Capital Structure and the Nature of Technical Change.* IUI Working Paper No. 138. Stockholm: IUI.

(1986a). "Is the Swedish Welfare State in Trouble? – A New Policy Model." *Scandinavian-Canadian Studies*, 2(May):167–89; also IUI Booklet No. 218.

(1986b). "The Stability of Economic Organizational Forms and the Importance of Human Capital," in R. Day and G. Eliasson (eds.), *The Dynamics of Market Economies*. Stockholm: IUI. Amsterdam: North Holland.

(1986c). *Innovative Change, Dynamic Market Allocation and Long-Term Stability of Economic Growth*. IUI Working Paper No. 156. Stockholm: IUI.

Eliasson, G., et al. (1986). *Kunskap, information och tjänster. En studie av svenska industriföretag* (The Manufacturing Firm as an Information Processor and Service Producer – a Study of the Industrial Knowledge Base of a Country and the Transformation of Manufacturing Firms into Service Producers). Stockholm: IUI.

Eliasson, G., and Lindberg, T. (1986). *Industrial Targeting – Defensive or Offensive Strategies in a Neo-Schumpeterian Perspective*. IUI Working Paper No. 171. Stockholm: IUI.

Eliasson, G., and Ysander, B.-C. (1983). "Sweden: Problems of Maintaining Efficiency Under Political Pressure," in B. Hindley (ed.), *State Investment Companies in Western Europe*. IUI Booklet No. 154. London: Trade Policy Research Centre.

Feige, E. (1986). *Sweden's Underground Economy*. IUI Working Paper No. 161. Stockholm: IUI.

Granstrand, O. (1986). "On Measuring and Modeling Innovative New Entry in Swedish Industry," in R. Day and G. Eliasson (eds.), *The Dynamics of Market Economies*. Stockholm: IUI. Amsterdam: North Holland.

Hanson, K. (1986). "On New Firm Entry and Macro Stability," in *The Economics of Institutions and Markets. IUI Yearbook 1986–1987*. Stockholm: IUI.

Heckscher, E. (1953). *Industrialism – den ekonomiska utvecklingen sedan 1750*. Stockholm IUI; translated into English as *Industrialism – Economic Development since 1750*.

Hickman, B. (1959). "Diffusion, Acceleration and Business Cycles." *American Economic Review*, 49:535–565.

Jagrén, L. (1986). "Concentration, Exit, Entry and Reconstruction of Swedish Manufacturing." in *The Economics of Institutions and Markets. IUI Yearbook 1986–1987*. Stockholm: IUI.

Keynes, J. M. (1930). "Economic Possibilities for Our Grandchildren. *Nation and Athenaeum* (October); also published 1932 in *Essays in Persuasion*. London: Macmillan.

Krugman, P. R. (1984). "Import Protection as Export Promotion: International Competition in the Presence of Oligopoly and Economies of Scale," in H. Kierzkowski (eds.), *Monopolistic Competition in International Trade*. Oxford: Clarendon Press.

Lundberg, E. (1985). "The Rise and Fall of the Swedish Model." *Journal of Economic Literature*, 23(March)(1):1–36.

Maddison, A. (1962). "Growth and Fluctuation in the World Economy 1870–1960." *Banco National del Lavoro Quarterly Review,* 15(June):127–195.

(1977). Phases of Capitalist Development, *Banco National del Lavoro Quarterly Review.*

Malinvaud, E. (1967). "Decentralized Procedures for Planning," in E. Malinvaud and O. Bacharach (eds.), *Activity Analysis in the Theory of Growth and Planning.* New York: Macmillan.

Meyerson, P.-M. (1985). *Eurosclerosis – The Case of Sweden.* Stockholm: Federation of Swedish Industries.

Modigliani, F., and Cohen, K. (1963). *The Role of Anticipation and Plans in Economic Behavior.* Urbana: University of Illinois Press.

Moore, G. H. (ed.) (1961). *Business Cycle Indicators* (2 vols.). Princeton University Press, for NBER.

MOSES Database [General reference to the complete micro-to-macro data base organized and compiled for the MOSES; a full documentation, is in progress; until it is ready, see Chapter 8 in Eliasson (1985a)].

North, D. C. (1981). *Structure and Change in Economic History.* New York: Norton.

North, D. C., and Thomas, R. (1973). *The Rise of the Western World. A New Economic History.* Cambridge University Press.

Olson, M. (1982). *The Rise and Decline of Nations.* New Haven: Yale University Press.

Parker, W. N. (1984). *Europe, America and the Wider World – Essays on the Economic History of Western Capitalism.* Cambridge University Press.

Pavitt, K., and Soete, L. (1981). "International Differences in Economic Growth and the International Location of Innovations (mimeograph). Science Policy Research Unit, University of Sussex.

Pelikan, P. (1969). "Language as a Limiting Factor for Centralization." *American Economic Review,* 59(4):625–31.

(1985). *Private Enterprise vs. Government Control: An Organizationally Dynamic Comparison.* IUI Working Paper No. 137. Stockholm: IUI.

(1986). *The Formation of Incentive Mechanisms in Different Economic Systems.* IUI Working Paper No. 155. Stockholm: IUI.

Polanyi, M. (1967). *The Tacit Dimension.* Garden City, N.Y.: Doubleday.

Rosenberg, W., and Birdzell, L. E. (1986). *How the West Grew Rich.* New York: Basic Books.

Rostow, W. W. (1980). *Why the Poor Get Richer and the Rich Slow Down.* Austin: University of Texas Press.

Schumpeter, J. [1912] (1934). *The Theory of Economic Development.* Cambridge University Press.

(1939). *Business Cycles – A Theoretical, Historical and Statistical Analysis of the Capitalist Process* (2 vols.). New York: McGraw-Hill.

(1942). *Capitalism, Socialism and Democracy.* New York: Harper.

(1954). *History of Economic Analysis.* Oxford University Press.

Shubik, M. (1985). "The Many Approaches to the Study of Monopolistic Competition." *European Economic Review,* 27(1):97–114.

Simon, H. A. (1955). "A Behavioral Model of Rational Choice." *Quarterly Journal of Economics,* 69(February):99–118.

Stigler, G. J. (1961). "The Economics of Information." *Journal of Political Economy,* 69(3):213–25.

Wicksell, K. [1898] (1965). *Geldzins und Güterpreise* (Interest and Prices). New York: AMK.

Winter, S. G. (1964). "Economic 'Natural Selection' and the Theory of the Firm." *Yale Economic Essays,* 4(Spring):225–272.

——— (1986). "Schumpeterian Competition in Alternative Technological Regimes," in R. Day and G. Eliasson (eds.), *The Dynamics of Market Economies.* Stockholm: IUI. Amsterdam: North Holland.

Ysander, B.-C. (1986). "Public Policy Evaluation in Sweden," in *The Economics of Institutions and Markets. IUI Yearbook 1986–1987.* Stockholm: IUI.

Discussion

DIRK IPSEN

Questions

Evolutionary economics tends to widen the field of traditional economics enormously. Eliasson's chapter is a good example of this tendency: It covers history as well as present policy, modeling, and empirical study, the eternal essentials of capitalist development and the changing institutions of our society. No doubt, many questions arise from this discussion: How is an understanding of evolutionary economics promoted in this chapter? How do the central theses of the chapter relate to empirical research on, for example, innovation and market structure? What is the concept of stability in the Eliasson approach of disequilibrium? How do we define stable macroeconomic growth without a concept of equilibrium? How are institutions and institutional changes introduced, and what is the result of this approach?

My questions will follow the three main theses in the Eliasson chapter:

1. The capitalist market process is essentially of an experimental nature; only this structure secures a steady stream of innovations.

2. This experimental nature is a sufficient basis for Schumpeter's "Prozess der schöpferischen Zerstörung," and this process results in stable macroeconomic growth in the long run.

3. People do not like this type of growth process because they are
    obliged to make permanent adjustments. This is the role of the
    (political) institutions of a society: These institutions have to
    make the results of the growth process acceptable to the
    people.

The character of the innovation process

Gunnar Eliasson favors the young Schumpeter's ideas of innovations
as strongly linked with decentralized (i.e., unplanned) entrepreneurial
activity. This starting point is the basis for all further steps of the argument. Macro stability is built up by this specific type of innovation
process, and the function of the institutions is, according to Eliasson,
to keep this type of innovation-generating process running. Hence, this
concept should be carefully established. If I understand correctly, the
choice for the young Schumpeter's concept of innovation is substan-
tiated by the relevance of the nontechnical side of an innovation.
Technology is more or less internationally available, but "local competence" and commercial and institutional activity are necessary to
exploit the given technology. The role of the entrepreneur is to perform
this type of activity. Market competition and short-term monopoly
rents are the driving forces behind the search process for exploitable
technology and adequate organizational forms.

I wonder if we can take over this picture of the innovation process
from Marx and Schumpeter without examination. In particular, an
evolutionary theory has to deal with institutional changes, and the
innovation process may be one example of this. There are two points
that seem to be suggestive of changing patterns in the innovation-generating process:

1. The first deals with the different roles of small and large firms
    in the process of innovation. The small firms play the role of
    troublemakers in a market by introducing product or process
    innovations (Nathusius, 1979); the large firms utilize merger
    policies to integrate the innovational results in the framework
    of giant firms. The outcome is an intrafirm planning process
    for the type and timing of innovations (McGowan, 1971).
    Innovation planning becomes one element of entry deterrence.
    So far, we have to link the innovation process to the market
    structure. Schumpeter was optimistic about the role of oligo-
    polistic rivalry, but that is by no means a valid empirical
    notion for our times. Cowling (1982) argues that rivalry and
    collusion can be seen as two sides of a coin.

2. The second point introduces the role of the state. I agree with Eliasson's emphasis on the nontechnical side of innovation; local competence is a necessary condition for adaptation and improvement of technology. But we can observe, historically and in the present, political activity by the state to create and protect this necessary local competence.

This direct influence of the state in our times is, of course, not a Japanese innovation, but the typical Japanese way of organizing innovation policy enforces a tendency to centralize R&D planning on a national level in order to compete with other nations. There are obviously counteracting tendencies in the process of innovation, and I am not so sure about the overall result of these changes.

In the last instance, it is a question of the aims of an evolutionary theory. In my understanding, evolutionary theory has to explain the empirically observable evolution; this means to endogenize the changing rules of the game. It is not clear whether Eliasson wants to say that, in reality, no changes have occurred in the innovation process, or that we should avoid these changes.

The concept of macro-stability

Eliasson refers to simulation analyses on the Swedish M-M model that suggest a positive influence of the variation of individual-performance indicators on macro stability: "If not, small disturbances can be very disruptive" (Section 6.4.2). I suppose the empirical representation of stable macroeconomic performance is formulated in terms of quantitative indicators of macroeconomic activity (i.e., the variance of the GDP or employment). If I understand corrrectly, the underlying hypothesis can be expressed in the following way: The variance of macroeconomic output is negatively correlated with the microeconomic variance of adequate performance indicators. In this form, the hypothesis could be tested in time series analyses as well as in cross-country studies.

My own research on the process of destabilizing growth in the Federal Republic of Germany showed that there was by no means a reduction of variation in economic performance criteria at the industrial level in the period before 1975. On the contrary, I observed increased variation in profitability; one group of industries showed a significant decrease in profitability, and the other group was able to stabilize profit rates. The former group was characterized by stronger innovative activity; the latter showed certain monopolistic tendencies: slower rates of growth, lower investment ratios, lower productivity. Hence my question: Is it the variation in the level of economic performance that matters here? As far as I can see from Figures 6.4A and 6.4B, the level of the incentive indicator changed, but not the variation.

Another field of research that combines the aspects of level and structure deals with the inflation problem. There is no doubt that the rising level of inflation in the sixties and seventies was positively correlated with price variability (Blejer and Leiderman, 1980; Foster, 1978; Gahlen, 1983; Vining and Elwertowski, 1976). The path into crisis is characterized by growing variability.

It may be that here we are considering problems of comparability between our data and the data that feed the Swedish M-M model, but I think the key problem of understanding is linked with the concept of "stable macroeconomic growth." In conventional analysis, the concept of stability is related to equilibrium. This concept can be broadened to include the institutions of the economic system (Müller et al., 1978). Macroeconomic stability is thus defined by the ability of economic institutions to reproduce the conditions of equilibrium. Systematic deviations from equilibrium are indicators of instability or cyclical crisis or, in the long term, "structural or growth crisis." In particular, the long-term economic crisis seems to have no endogenous mechanism of correction. Unsolved social problems seem to exist, and normally this situation is one of conflict between alternative ways of further development.

These points of view are dependent on a concept of equilibrium that works as a theoretical landmark. But that cannot hold in our context. Instability is a key factor in the explanation of dynamic growth, according to Eliasson. Hence my question: What is the concept of stability in evolutionary economics? I suppose that the concept of stability of evolutionary processes cannot be linked to quantitative output criteria. "Stable evolution" of capitalism can be understood as a situation where the rules of behavior change, but not the rules of investment behavior. It seems to be paradoxical. I presume Eliasson solved the paradox by taking over the young Schumpeter's view of the innovation process; that seems to be the fixed point in a changing world.

The role of institutions

A main topic of evolutionary theories is to endogenize institutions. Hence, the process of generating and changing institutions has to be explained, as well as the feedback of social institutions on economic processes. That is a very high level of aspiration indeed. One of the important questions is the relation between institutions and the economic system: Can the institutions be treated as functional substitutes for unsolved economic problems? So, for example, if we have unemployment as a result of economic processes, can it be expected that political institutions will solve this problem? The answer of Eliasson is a little ambiguous. On the one hand, we are told that institutional changes occur more slowly than economic changes, with the consequence of defensive conflicts between the political system and the economic environment. The political system is, in this respect, relatively independent of the economic system. On the other hand, we have learned from Eliasson that the role of institutions is to make the unplanned results of the economic process acceptable to the people. That is what I describe as the position of functional substitution. If institutions really act in this way, if they are self-organizing in this sense, there will be no problem of stability at all.

But in the last instance, Eliasson hesitates to believe this and switches to another aspect of the problem. He argues that "the political problem boils down to designing institutional rules that inhibit forces that would impede the adjustment process from gaining political control" (Section 6.5.3). However, this seems to be a normative solution of a theoretical problem. How can such political trends be prevented in a democratic system? Neoclassical theory expresses a vision in which individual preferences govern all other parts of the economy. Individual preference is the one and only authority that is accepted. Here we find a reversal: The only accepted authority is the innovative investor, and all other parts of society have to adjust to his activities. I wonder if either of these positions is a realistic or desirable model of society. There seem to exist more than one predominant authority: the family influencing the generative behavior and the supply of labor, the workers with their changing values toward working conditions and security, and last, but not least, the political system acting in its own way.

If we accept the existence of more than one authority, we have another perspective on society: Conflicts may arise, and hence the pressure to solve problems. In this way, institutional changes could be introduced into our theoretical approaches. As I have stated elsewhere, "social learning processes" could be a key in analyzing evolution (Künzel, Ipsen, and Rohwer, 1985).

References

Blejer, M. I., and Leiderman, L. (1980). "On the Real Effects of Inflation and Relative Price-Variability. Some Empirical Evidence." *Review of Economics and Statistics,* 62:539–44.

Cowling, K. (1982). *Monopoly Capitalism.* New York: Macmillan.

Foster, E. (1978). "The Variability of Inflation." *Review of Economics and Statistics,* 60:346–50.

Gahlen, B. (1983). *Der Einfluss der relativen Preise auf die Faktorallokation in der BRD.* Berlin: Mimeo Wissenschaftszentrum.

Ipsen, D. (1983). *Die Stabilität des Wachstums – theoretische Kontroversen und empirische Untersuchungen zur Destabilisierung der Nachkriegsentwicklung.* Frankfurt/M.: Campus-Verlag.

Künzel, R., Ipsen, D., and Rohwer, G. (1985). "Wachstumskrise, soziale Probleme und Theoriebildung," in R. Künzel and Ipsen, D. (eds.), *Die gegenwärtige Wachstumskrise* (pp. 1–23). Regensburg: Transfer-Verlag.

McGowan, J. I. (1971). "International Comparisons of Merger Activity." *Journal of Law and Economics,* 14:233–50.

Müller, G., Roedel, U., Sabel, Ch., Stille, F., and Vogt, W. (1978). *Ökonomische Krisentendenzen im gegenwärtigen Kapitalismus.* Frankfurt/M.: Campus-Verlag.

Nathusius, K. (1979). *Venture Management; ein Instrument zur innovativen Unternehmensentwicklung.* Berlin: Duncker und Homblot Verlag.

Vining, R. D., and Elwertowski, T. C. (1976). "The Relationship Between Relative Prices and the General Price Level." *American Economic Review,* 66:699–708.

CHAPTER 7

An evolutionary approach to inflation: prices, productivity, and innovation

FRITZ RAHMEYER

7.1 Introduction

Economic development in the Federal Republic of Germany and the United States during the 1970s was characterized by an acceleration of price growth (inflation) and a slowdown of output and productivity growth. Neither the Keynesian mainline model nor the post-Keynesian neoclassical theory has a satisfactory explanation for the altered cyclical pattern (simultaneous acceleration of inflation and deceleration of output growth in the course of the business cycle) or for the long-term (increasing share of price growth in the case of nominal demand changes) development of quantities and prices.

As a result of the slowdown of economic growth and the protracted recession, the work of Schumpeter has been revived, especially his *Theory of Economic Development.* The advanced post-Schumpeterian paradigm intends both to explain this growth retardation and to find a way to regain a balanced growth and move the economy toward full employment. Of primary importance to achieve these goals are the innovating activities of enterprises. Evolutionary or post-Schumpeterian economics has, until now, for the most part, dealt with topics of economic growth and technical progress. It is the object of this chapter to apply this approach to the phenomenon of inflation to integrate the development of prices or inflation and the structure of prices into a theory of evolutionary change. An explanation of inflation starts from two basic principles:

1. The increase of the price level is a permanent phenomenon of economic change, accompanied by cyclical fluctuations around the long-term trend.
2. Inflation is a phenomenon that can be differentiated according to various structural characteristic features. Of special importance is the structure of industrial prices.

To develop an evolutionary approach to inflation, we first deal with the basic elements of evolutionary theory, especially in the Nelson and

Winter version (Section 7.2). In Section 7.3, a short survey of alternative theories of inflation is presented, focusing on cost-based pricing as a price-theoretic, microeconomic foundation and a structure-oriented approach to inflation, including a discussion of the competitive strategy and adjustment behavior of enterprises. Empirical calculations in Section 7.4 emphasize the negative correlation between relative price and productivity growth in the manufacturing sector. To explain observable interindustry differences in productivity growth (and their effects on price growth), some new results in the theory of innovation are presented, also showing sectoral differences in rate and direction (Section 7.5). In this selected interpretation, the interrelation among prices, productivity, and innovation (in the Schumpeterian sense) is the essence of an evolutionary approach to inflation.

7.2   Fundamental ideas of evolutionary theory

Evolution as an ideological concept provides a world view of social and natural sciences (Lewontin, 1968, pp. 202f.). The approach of Nelson and Winter (1982a) and other authors serves in the following to provide a frame of reference for an evolutionary theory of economic change.

The theory of economic evolution describes and explains such phenomena of endogenous change as economic growth, competition through innovations, and adjustment of firms to altered market conditions. Its advocates consider it to be explicitly in the tradition of Schumpeter: "the term 'neo-Schumpeterian' would be as appropriate a designation for our entire approach as 'evolutionary'" (Nelson and Winter, 1982a, p. 39). The attributes of a post-Schumpeterian approach are that it is, among other things, microeconomic rather than macroeconomic, socioeconomic rather than mechanistic, and process-oriented rather than outcome-oriented (Giersch, 1984, p. 105). Rather than neoclassical growth theory, which is equilibrium theory, Schumpeter deals with the dynamic and disequilibrium nature of economic development and provides us with a "'vision' of the capitalist process and the central theoretical structure" (Elliott, 1983, p. 278) and a "vision of the evolutionary process" (Elliott, 1983, p. 295). It is composed of a series of continuous and discontinuous fluctuations, of deviations from a hitherto existing equilibrium and the delayed adjustments and overreactions to a new equilibrium. Economic development not only is an adaptation to exogenous modifications of economic data but also is endogenously caused by the economic process itself, creating in this way new conditions, such as new technologies (creative destruction).

A second cornerstone of the Nelson-Winter evolutionary theory is the behavioral theory of the firm, which is the microeconomic foundation for explaining economic change and development. These authors construct a theory of firm and industry behavior in an enterprise economy characterized by uncertainty and unpredictable technological change. The behavioral theory of the firm deals with the observable process of decision making in large firms in imperfect markets. The overwhelming majority of firm decisions concerning the adjustment to changes in its environment follow simple rules and the application of established methods (Winter, 1971, pp. 244f). "Routine behavior" replaces maximization behavior as a decision rule. Routine behavior is the actual behavior of firms, with their given capabilities and production possibility set. Routine behavior, including the choice of production technologies, rules of price formation, and innovation activity, is characterized by quasi-automated rules of behavior. The applied decision rules are indeed oriented toward realization of profit, but not its maximization, because the knowledge of firms about the decision options and their consequences is limited (bounded rationality): Firms satisfice instead of maximize. Firms' routines can change over time as a result of innovations and new organizational forms (Simon, 1979, p. 502).

Previous contributions to evolutionary economics have dealt with various topics and have not been limited to a special range of applications (Witt, 1987, p. 12). The following criteria characterize evolutionary theory (Witt, 1987, p. 9):

- Explanation of the temporal changes of economic phenomena.
- Application of the idea of historical, irreversible time. Evolutionary changes in firms or industries have an irreversible element.
- Explanation of the endogenous innovation occurring in different economic developments.

A special feature of the Nelson-Winter contribution to evolutionary theory is their synthesis of the post-Schumpeterian paradigm and the behavioral theory of the firm (Gerybadze, 1982, p. 118).

Evolutionary economics deals mainly with explanations of long-run endogenous economic changes. It has not yet been applied to explain the development of prices or inflation nor to explain the structure of prices, although this subject is well to the fore in neoclassical economic theory, and especially industrial organization. The reason for the dominance of the first complex of problems is that in the long run, the gains of an economy from its innovation activity may be greater than those resulting from competitive pricing. In Schumpeterian competition, price competition is relatively insignificant (Nelson and Winter, 1982b, p. 114). Thus, inflation will be interpreted mainly as a long-run phenomenon (price growth), not as a cyclical phenomenon (price adjustment). It is seen as a dynamic event, not an equilibrating event, not as a singular phenomenon, but as integrated into the overall economic development. Thus, the growth of output, wages, and productivity, the innovation activity, and the importance of market structure have to be included (Nelson, 1981a, p. 1060). The differences in the development of prices and their determinants will be examined by a disaggregation of industry.

7.3   Fundamental principles of the theories of inflation

7.3.1   *Definition and conception*

This section describes the fundamental principles of different inflation theories and their underlying microeconomic hypotheses about price formation by enterprises, together with an inquiry concerning the evolutionary elements in inflation. Inflation is defined as an increase of the overall economic price level (Lipsey, 1979, pp. 284ff.). A "general" theoretical explanation of inflation does not exist, but there are competing approaches. Because inflation is seen as an overall economic phenomenon, ideas about it are embedded within the framework of macroeconomic theories.

The macroeconomic view must be supplemented by a microeconomic foundation of price formation, such as marginal or average cost pricing, enriched by considerations of the impact of market structure. Attention also must be given to the explanation of wage-rate changes in the labor market. Whereas price theory attempts to explain individual prices and their structure, inflation theory explains the development of the price level.

The growth of the overall price level results from the weighted price developments in the different sectors of the economy, which probably will not be uniform. The overall economic rate of inflation is, in part, the consequence of the interplay of sectoral price and wage developments. The focus is on manufacturing – the core of a market economy, and the sector that is least subject to government regulations.

The social and institutional conditions of an economy are inherent to the inflationary process (Parkin, 1978, pp. 43ff.; Streissler et al., 1976, pp. 42ff.). Especially the hypothesis of a struggle among different groups for increased income shares is a noneconomic explanation of inflation.

The fundamental cause of inflation in a socioeconomic context is the fact that overall nominal income expectations rise higher than productive power because of the rivalries and illusions of social groups. It is significant in this connection that for individuals or groups, price stability can be considered a "collective good," which everyone benefits from whether he has made sacrifices or not. . . . The rate of decline in the value of money ultimately depends on the claims society makes on the national product. (Kloten, Ketterer, and Vollmer, 1985, pp. 353f.)

This hypothesis attempts to explain both price and wage developments and the causes of demand and cost changes. Interpretations should be broad, including calculation of the national income and its expenditure and distribution (Turvey, 1951, pp. 534f.). This noneconomic approach will not be reviewed extensively in this chapter.

7.3.2   Demand-pull theories of inflation

Traditional classification yields demand-pull and cost-push theories (Lipsey, 1979, p. 287) or market-force and non-market-force theories of inflation.[1] In the former approach, a distinction between a Keynesian and a monetarist version is common (Gordon, 1976, pp. 186f.). The Keynesian theory is not an independent theory of inflation, but it treats price adjustment and inflation within the scope of its theory of output and employment (Kregel, 1979, p. 189). With the wage level given, the price level and its change are determined by the laws of production: With rising marginal and average costs resulting from increases in output and employment, the entrepreneurs simultaneously, or with delay, raise their output prices to cover costs of production. An increase in demand results, at the same time, in quantity (output, employment) and price adjustments (output prices and wages, the latter in the absence of money illusion of wage earners).[2]

Assuming full employment and full utilization of capacity, the Keynesian theory of employment can be generalized or extended to a theory of inflation: "The notion of deficient aggregate demand has been advanced to explain the unemployment problem [and] the notion of excessive aggregate demand was subsequently advanced to explain the phenomenon of inflation" (Mulvey and Trevithick, 1975, pp. 15f.). Unemployment and inflation, in a symmetrical manner, are the results of deflationary and inflationary gaps. If wage earners are subject to

[1] For critiques, see Laidler and Parkin (1975, pp. 742f.) and Addison and Burton (1980, p. 189); for a favorable view, see Rahmeyer (1983, pp. 148f.).

[2] For a modification of Keynes's hypotheses regarding price formation and development, compared with *The General Theory*, see Keynes (1939, pp. 44f.).

money illusion, an increase in demand will not raise wages (or raise them less than proportionately); the price increase takes an equilibrating course and by the decrease in the real wage rate closes the inflationary gap. A permanent price increase can only be the consequence of repeated exogenously occurring excess demand in the output market. However, a complete adjustment of wages to higher prices or to excess demand in the labor market (two-gap model) endogenously causes a lasting increase in prices (assuming that rising prices have no negative feedback on the level of real demand). The shorter the delay between the increases in income and demand, on the one hand, and prices and wages, on the other hand, the faster the price increase accelerates (and vice versa). The wage–price spiral controlled by market forces is the dynamic, persistent element in a Keynesian theory of inflation. The monetary sector is of no explicit importance in the inflationary process; implicitly, an accommodating money supply is always assumed. An increase in the money supply is a necessary but not sufficient condition for inflation.

The monetarist inflation theory is based on a price-theoretic, market-oriented explanation, distinguishing it from sociological or institutional and eclectic theories, in which the monetarists group the Keynesians.[3] The monetarists' criticism of both alternative approaches is directed at the presumed failure to offer a dominant and systematic inflationary impulse. They also criticize the assumptions of the just accommodating effect of monetary factors in explaining inflation and money illusion (or lagged wage adjustment) by wage earners, which accounts for the rising supply curve. Inflation, in the monetarists' interpretation, is entirely a market phenomenon to be analyzed in terms of demand and supply.

The monetarist theory can be represented by a highly aggregated model. In a full-employment equilibrium, the rate of price inflation depends exclusively on the difference between the growth of money supply and full-employment output. There is a proportional relation between the two variables, but there may be a delay in the effect of an increasing money supply on the rate of inflation. In the long run, inflation is solely a monetary phenomenon. The short-run relation between the rate of inflation and the rate of output growth or the rate of unemployment is unknown. The division of a change in the growth of money supply into quantity and price components results from the declining slope of the expectations-augmented Phillips curve (assumption of adaptive expectations): "Ultimately the rate of monetary

---

[3] Laidler (1976, p. 252); Brunner (1974, pp. 181ff.); Brunner and Meltzer (1978, p. 11).

expansion determines the rate of inflation in this model but the Phillips curve plays a very important role in the adjustment process" (Vanderkamp, 1975, p. 117). Price expectations represent the dynamic element in the monetarist model of inflation.

Summarizing, the monetarist theory of inflation determines endogenously actual and expected rates of inflation and the degree of excess demand. The growth of the money supply and the full-employment output are given exogenously. The model is demand-determined, extended by the role of expectations, being demand-determined themselves. Inflation is always the result of exogenous disturbances (e.g., a monetary expansion in excess of real output growth, or the monopoly power of the unions), not of endogenous disturbances of the market system. The causality in the monetarist model runs only from money supply to inflation, not in the other direction, as assumed by Keynesian authors (e.g., in the case of monetary accommodation of an autonomous wage or price increase).

7.3.3   Cost-push theories of inflation

The demand-oriented Keynesian theory of inflation received unfavorable criticism when in the economic recessions of the 1950s in the United States, the (mild) increase in the price level continued in spite of a rise in unemployment and a decrease in output growth. In previous business-cycle recessions, the price level either decreased or was unchanged (Thorning, 1975, p. 99). The criticism is directed at the assumption of the exclusiveness of market determinant factors in price and wage formation and marginal analysis as the heart of the neoclassical theory of the firm. The later elaborated cost-push or supply-oriented theory of inflation claims that the primary reason for triggering and disseminating an increase in the overall price level is the active behavior of the market participants, who, as a result of their market power, have ample scope for discretionary price and wage setting. In detail, the criticism is based on empirical observations that firms face conditions contrary to the assumptions of marginal analysis:

1. Under imperfect competition, firms have a certain degree of price-setting discretion, in cases of both demand and supply changes. The reasons are the degree of market concentration, lack of knowledge about the market, and the heterogeneity of the products. The firms face a falling demand curve and make decisions about quantities and prices; so their behavior is not strictly determined.

2. Firms make decisions with incomplete information about their economic environment (e.g., wages, prices, and changes of demand

and supply). They are unable to get adequate knowledge to determine their marginal revenue and cost curves in an environment of continuous change (Gordon, 1948, p. 277). The degree of uncertainty is assumed to be greater in the case of future demand (regarding the distinction between local and overall economic changes, on the one hand, and transitory and permanent demand changes, on the other) than for production costs, and thus greater for marginal costs than for average costs.[4] To escape this uncertainty, the firms will adjust their prices as far as possible to known indicators or to the least unsafe business indicators. Increasing labor and/or material costs will affect all enterprises to the same extent (modified by their structure of production costs) and trigger a price-increasing tendency, thereby reducing the uncertainty of the firms concerning the reactions of their competitors. In addition, cost changes (e.g., contract-based wages) are regarded as lasting longer than demand changes; so prices will adjust to the former more rapidly and to a greater degree. To sum up, the result is a preference in price formation for cost-based pricing as a more often applied rule compared with competitive pricing.[5] In the normal (or standard) version, price setting results in a markup on normal costs. It is independent of short-run demand and actual cost fluctuations (Coutts, Godley, and Nordhaus, 1978, p. 60). If the cost curve within the relevant production range is horizontal, short-run demand fluctuations cause (given the markup) variations in sales and profits, though not in prices. Also, the level of output can be stabilized by demand-buffering strategies such as variations in inventories and the levels of orders or delivery periods (Hay and Morris, 1979, p. 136). Furthermore, in management strategies in a world of dynamic competition, prices are only one instrument, probably of secondary importance.

The costs of price adjustment mean that sticky, inflexible prices also reduce the *buyer's* costs of price information, diminishing search costs regarding the price level and the availability of supply, and furthering continuity and reliability in customers' relationships. Price changes destroy available knowledge about ruling market prices. Stable prices are a service to the customer and promote the actual and long-run business relationships (implicit-contract view) (Okun, 1981, pp. 138ff.). Price increases should be justified by cost increases, not by sales possibilities only. The orientation to average costs is considered a fair pricing rule. "The mark up onto costs becomes a reasonable way

---

[4] "News about the state of aggregate demand is not received as a neat package, but rather as bits of information arriving week after week" (Gordon, 1983, p. 117).

[5] See, for example, Silberston (1973, p. 79), Wied-Nebbeling (1975, p. 149), and Okun (1981, p. 153).

to set a 'fair' price for the services of the firm" (Okun, 1975, p. 363). For the sellers, cost-based pricing helps to avoid price wars in oligopolistic markets, as well as the costs of price changes (e.g., due to reactions of competitors).[6] After all, a delayed price adjustment in the case of demand fluctuations promotes the stability and functioning of an enterprise economy, because quantity and price adjustments mutually cushion their effects on the business cycle (Perry, 1984, p. 406; Streissler, 1980, p. 41).

3. Price formation by the firms is also determined by their objective. The swing away from marginal cost pricing and the assumption of perfect knowledge at the same time means a turning away from the target of short-run profit maximization (Machlup, 1967, p. 12). Different objectives take its place, such as sales maximization or satisficing. The critique of marginal cost pricing can be summarized as follows:

The closeness with which marginal analysis can approximate real prices is bounded by the *rationality* with which the firm seeks to obtain its own objectives and by the *information* available to it to this end. It also depends on how close theory comes to depict those real *objectives* in its assumption about motivation in the firm. All three, rationality, information and motivation, or at least the latter two, are projections of what I shall call in a broad definition the firm's pricing environment, i.e., the structure of its markets, the internal organization and technical production facilities, in the actual pricing period as well as in the future. (Langholm, 1968, pp. 73f.)[7]

The center of the cost-push theory of inflation is the interrelation among changes in wages, productivity, and prices.[8] In a wage–price model, it explains a permanent inflationary process. In open economies, the prices of imports have to be taken into account as well. The wage equation represents the importance of the labor market. The wage-setting process is composed of a cyclical component, usually explained by a version of the Phillips curve, and a wage norm, unrelated to current unemployment, derived from permanent, contractual employment relations between workers and employers.[9] Labor and most other inputs are purchased by explicit and implicit long-term

[6] "Many so-called 'rigidities' in the behavior of wages and prices are genuinely the consequences of optimizing behavior in markets with efficient transactional mechanisms for dealing with heterogeneous products and factors, which involve significant costs of information and transactions" (Okun, 1980, p. 824).

[7] For a summary discussion of whether or not full-cost pricing is consistent with marginalism, see Lee (1984a, pp. 1118ff.).

[8] For this empirical mainline model of inflation, see, for example, Tobin (1972a) and Perry (1978).

[9] See Perry (1980, p. 209), Hall (1980, pp. 91ff.), and Schultze (1985, p. 2).

contracts, rather than in auction markets, because of the presence of firm-specific investments and labor-turnover costs. The length of time of wage contracts determines the degree of nominal and real wage flexibility (Kahn, 1984, pp. 156f.).

The price equation, based on a variant of the cost-based pricing hypothesis, represents the product market. It describes the direct connection among prices, different kinds of costs, and demand, in cases differentiated by indicators of market structure. The determinants of supply and demand are not explained, but taken as given. Neither the labor market nor the product market is in accordance with the model of an instantaneous market clearing. Prices are not set mainly to clear markets and to allocate resources optimally, but rather with a view to feasible profits or a financial long-run objective (e.g., maintaining the ability to invest and to cover production costs),[10] in that way enabling the firm to survive and grow. Wages and prices respond with delay, and to different extents, to demand fluctuations: Quantity adjustments dominate wage and price adjustments in the short run as (according to Okun's model) a result of long-term relations in a world where information is costly and shopping entails nonnegligible transaction costs.[11] However, changes in demand perceived as permanent will cause changes in wages and prices. Productivity is useful as a basis for calculating normal costs.

An inflationary process, once released, by either excess demand or an autonomous wage or price push, provokes a permanent wage–price spiral relatively independent of the state of demand and supply, given a price- and fairness-oriented wage increase and a cost-oriented price increase.[12] Deep-seated inflationary expectations and given behavioral patterns of the market participants may keep the momentum alive, even in the case of a transitory demand decrease:

Persistence effects are vital to an understanding of the inflationary process. The inflation rate today depends on last period's level of output, and, therefore, on last period's unemployment. And the inflation rate also depends on the expected rate of inflation, which is likely to change only slowly over time. It is these persistence effects which make it difficult to reduce inflation without affecting the unemployment rate. (Dornbusch and Fischer, 1978, p. 403)

[10] See Wiles (1973, p. 386), Lee (1984b, p. 158), and Gordon (1948, p. 284).
[11] For a discussion of inertia in price and wage adjustment, see Gordon (1981, pp. 493ff., 1982a, pp. 1087ff., 1982b, pp. 13ff.). For a critique and modification of Okun's model concerning wage and price setting in an international comparison, see Gordon (1982b, pp. 40f.).
[12] For an analysis of the inflationary process, see Okun (1981, pp. 231ff.).

Whereas neoclassical or monetarist economists are primarily concerned with the proximate causes of inflation, assuming its roots in the behavior of political institutions,[13] Keynesian authors are much more interested in the fundamental causes of wage and price inflation, such as a wage and profit push, an increase in import prices, social conflicts (the so-called bad-actor approach to inflation) (Wachter and Williamson, 1978, p. 550).[14] The money supply is regarded as a more or less endogenous variable, determined mainly by the wage–price mechanism of wage earners and firms establishing a core rate of inflation and inflationary shocks. The consequences of cost-push factors for output, employment, and inflation depend on the degree of monetary accommodation and the extent and length of wage indexation as admitted by cost-push proponents.[15] The behavior of the monetary authorities respecting the accommodation of the existing rate of inflation, on the one hand, and the wage earners and firms in the wage-bargaining process allowing for real wage fluctuations, on the other hand, will not be constant with the passing of time, but may depend on the level and variability of the rate of inflation.

7.3.4   Structure-oriented approach

The demand-pull and cost-push theories of inflation have to be supplemented with structure-oriented hypotheses. These hypotheses stress the importance of the structure both of labor and product markets and of overall economic aggregates for the development of the price level. This still incoherent approach is appropriate for explanation of a creeping inflation and an inflationary basis, but not for runaway, double-digit, accelerating inflation. It is grounded on the following observations (Frisch, 1980, p. 137):

- Different rates of productivity growth in the individual sectors and a relatively stable interindustry wage structure.
- Asymmetrical wage and price flexibility in the case of demand fluctuations.
- Interindustrial dispersion of excess demand and supply in labor and product markets: "Dispersion is inflationary" (Tobin, 1972b, p. 10).

[13] For a discussion of the "vote-maximizing government," see Parkin (1977, p. 47) and Brunner and Meltzer (1977, p. 154).

[14] For this distinction, see Addison, Burton, and Torrance (1980, p. 147).

[15] For an analysis of policy responses to supply shocks, see Gordon (1984, pp. 38ff.).

- Differences in market structure, foreign-trade structure, and cost structure among the industry branches.

The basic pattern of industry prices is the result of the wage and productivity developments (supply-side explanation). The wage structure within the manufacturing sector is relatively constant, the consequence of nearly equal wage increases in all branches. There are two main reasons: First, the development of the wage rate is, to a large extent, determined by overall economic variables such as inflation and unemployment. It takes into account industry-specific peculiarities only to a negligible extent. Second, the trade union's hierarchy (wage-wage effects) and the long-term labor contracts have resulted in a relatively stable wage structure. Relative wages are an important argument in the utility function of wage earners (Lipsey, 1981, p. 553; Trevithick, 1976, pp. 327f.).

The dispersion of productivity growth is greater than that of wage growth. Accordingly, the growth of unit labor costs as a central determinant of price growth is different in all manufacturing branches.[16] The result is that the economic necessity to increase productivity growth varies among firms and industries. Prices, on average, change inversely with productivity, but not proportionally, especially if alterations of the demand structure face rigidities in the pricing process and the production facilities.

If, in the process of overall economic growth and structural change, enterprises successfully strive for corporate growth and survival, they will have to match costs and earnings in the adjustment process by price and nonprice competition, as well as attaining long-run competitive advantages. Alterations in market conditions generally occur unexpectedly and therefore will not trigger uniform and immediate phases of adjustment of all market participants. In a world of economic evolution and continuous endogenous change, the adjustment and competitive processes take place under conditions of incomplete information and adjustment costs and at different speeds of the variables concerned.[17] Because the changes of wages and prices of intermediate input, just like the trend of the market, are given for the single firm, they are considered as an adjustment and competition instrument to a limited degree only. A first step in efforts to reduce production costs is the substitution of inputs whose prices have increased relatively and/or factor-saving technical progress (process innovations,

---

[16] See, for example, Nelson and Winter (1977, p. 38, 1982a, pp. 247, 287).

[17] For a discussion of the hierarchy of quantity adjustments and price adjustments, see Winter (1984, p. 290); for details, see Grönberg and Rahmeyer (1985, p. 241).

e.g., production and process engineering), both increasing productivity growth. Technological progress favors different branches of the manufacturing sector to different extents, accordingly resulting in large interfirm and intersectoral differences in the growth of productivity, unit costs, and prices. Productivity growth is an economic instrument for cutting production costs and maintaining price competitiveness. Quantity adjustments of the firms (capital intensification) lead, other things being equal, to declines in employment.

A second strategy of adjustment is to increase output prices; this negative feedback will reduce demand and output: "The main function of prices is not to be resource-allocators but cost-coverers" (Wiles, 1973, p. 386). To improve proceeds relative to costs, restructuring the product mix of an enterprise or an industry in the direction of higher-valued products is also of use (product innovation). The price–unit-cost relationship determines the growth opportunities of a firm (Nelson and Winter, 1982a, p. 287). Industrial restructuring may be a management strategy preferable to price competition to accomplish lasting competitive advantages. Indeed, the uncertainty regarding the market success of new products is probably higher than in the case of new processes (Nelson and Winter, 1982a, p. 266). Which strategy the enterprises or industries choose depends particularly on the relative trends of their demand and output, but also on the technological opportunities for factor substitution, innovating, and launching new products and processes on the market: "there [is] a tangle of causations, from R&D to productivity growth, from productivity growth and lowered prices to growth of output, from growth of output in the presence of scale economies to productivity growth, from expansion of the industry to greater incentives for R&D, and so on" (Nelson and Winter, 1977, p. 45).

In the course of economic growth and structural change, the overall economic price level will increase if firms or industries with above-average productivity growth do not (relatively) reduce their prices proportionately, but instead use it to allow additional wage or profit increases, whereas sectors with below-average productivity growth are forced to (relatively) raise their prices (or, alternatively, to reduce sales, output, and employment), because wages increase to about the same extent in all economic sectors ("productivity inflation") (Frisch, 1973 p. 14). In the case of asymmetric wage and price flexibility, the allocation of goods and productive factors occurs through differences in wage and price increases.

Besides differences in interindustry productivity growth and the asymmetry of wage and price flexibility, the differentiation of the national economy into sectors with competitive and with administered pricing is well to the fore in the structural theory of inflation.[18] Competitive markets are characterized by instantaneous price adjustment in the case of demand fluctuations, leading always to their clearance, as well as (nearly) homogeneous products and free market entry. Administered markets show the existence of large-scale enterprises, a high or medium degree of market concentration, and barriers to entry and consequently market power of firms. Accordingly, they dispose of a behavior space (e.g., price formation) as cost-based pricing. The industrial process of price formation and inflation may therefore be portrayed as the simultaneous existence of marginal and cost-based pricing. Excess demand directly causes a price increase in competitive markets; this effects an increase of unit material costs in administered markets and, with a delay, also price increases. In the next step, these lead to additional wage increases in both markets ("real-wage resistance") that accelerate the price increase (price–wage spiral). If the administered sector exceeds the competitive sector in productivity growth, it will also be able to raise wages more than the latter. As a result of trade unions' wage policy, this level will be enforced in the competitive sector as well. The consequence will be an above-average rise of unit labor costs in competitive markets, resulting in additional overall price increases. A permanent price increase can also be triggered by way of an autonomous rise in wages and/or prices of intermediate inputs in administered markets, as well as by import price shocks.

In the case of excess supply, the price increase will last for the present as a result of continuing cost increases, especially unit labor costs (due to inflationary expectations and contractual relations in the wage-formation process). A deceleration of inflation will occur analogously to the phase of acceleration, in competitive markets first. Together with a diminishing cost pressure (especially wage costs), the price increase in the administered sector also will decelerate.[19] In this interpretation, the overall economic inflationary process is characterized "as a 'process with a life of its own' . . . a process 'with a significant element of inertia'" (Ackley, 1978, p. 494). The level of the rate of inflation depends on (among other things) the relative sizes of the com-

---

[18] See Nordhaus (1976, p. 59), Guger (1978, pp. 124ff.), and Okun (1981, pp. 135ff.).

[19] "Sluggish price adjustment may emerge . . . if firms wait for price cuts by suppliers before feeling that it is safe to cut prices substantially in response to a perceived dip in aggregate demand, while suppliers wait to cut prices until their assessment of the current aggregate demand situation is confirmed by a reduction in orders from final goods producers" (Gordon, 1983, p. 117).

petitive and administered sectors, the extent and speed of the propagation of inflation between the sectors, and the momentum of the price–wage spiral, which itself depends on the relation between demand and supply in the overall economy and its different markets.

7.3.5 Interim result

To what extent may the different inflation theories be labeled as evolutionary? First, they all deal with temporal changes of an economic phenomenon, in this case, price growth as opposed to output growth. Inflation is interpreted as a dynamic process showing both equilibrating and disequilibrating phases. Second, the existence of (adaptive) inflationary expectations and a wage–price spiral, leading to inertia inflation, are elements of all inflation theories, representing their historical, irreversible character. Third, the hypotheses concerning the process of wage and price formation of enterprises as the cornerstone of cost-push theories may be interpreted within the meaning of evolutionary theory as a routine application of established rules. Decision routines are not rationalized by reference to optimization, but are subject to the firm's history and evolution. Therefore, the microeconomic foundation of the cost-push approach is in accordance with the theory of economic change.

Finally, the pivotal question of evolutionary theory is the explanation of endogenous innovation activities as a new combination of existing routines. Is this criterion applicable to the theory of inflation? There are two suggestions to handle this question. On the one hand, innovations include the carrying out of organizational innovations; as an example, Schumpeter ([1934] 1964, p. 101) mentions the creation and breakup of monopolies. The evolution of a new or altered institutional setting and behavioral pattern of the market participants (including the government) may be interpreted as an innovation. For example, a persistent and perhaps accelerating inflation may lead to a reduction in the duration of nominal contracts and other forms of adjustment in collective bargaining in the labor market, changes in the extent and amount of wage indexation, changes in the degree of real wage resistance of unions, shifts in the wage norm (e.g., from expanding wage premiums to wage-concession bargains in a period of disinflation), and variations in union membership, in strike activity, and in the political and legal balance between trade unions and management.[20] All these institutional and behavioral innovations will in the

---

[20] See Fischer (1982, pp. 169ff.), Mitchell (1985, pp. 575ff.), and Wachter (1986, p. 243).

long run trigger feedback mechanisms to the inflationary process, accelerating or decelerating its speed. The course of the inflationary process may also lead to modifications in the strategy of stabilization policy (e.g., the extent of accommodating an exogenous cost increase or a general change in the policy regime) (Friedman, 1984, pp. 382ff.; Taylor, 1984, pp. 206ff.), thereby influencing the degree of downward wage and price flexibility in a business recession. Behavior patterns of market participants change only slowly. Regime shifts in monetary and fiscal policy, if occurring,[21] will take some time to be recognized as permanent and taken seriously. In this case, even a credible anti-inflationary policy will result in output losses (Gordon and King, 1982, pp. 224ff.). According to historical studies, the inflation–output relation is not sensitive to the policy regime (Perry, 1983, p. 602), even if the disinflation period 1981–4 is included in the estimated price equation (Gordon, 1985, p. 279). The endogeneity of the institutional structure and the behavior of the market participants in the inflation process provide, if further extended, a socioeconomic theoretical approach that is in acccordance with evolutionary theory.

On the other hand, *product and process innovations* (Schumpeter, [1934] 1964, p. 100) show a tendency to accelerate the output and productivity growth of a firm or an industry and at the same time curb their price growth. The interrelation between price and productivity growth and the innovation activity is in this framework the heart of an evolutionary approach to inflation. Both approaches suggested are undoubtedly nonexclusive; rather, they may serve as supplements. Adjustments in the institutional setting of an economy, the behavior patterns of workers and firms, and the policy regime of the government will probably make only a small contribution in explaining the rate and variability of inflation. Beyond that, they occur only sluggishly in the inflation process, if at all. More important, they do not vary among the individual industrial branches and therefore fail to explain inter-industry differences in price and productivity growth. To explain this phenomenon, as well as inflation, process and product innovations may be of vital importance. Next we confine ourselves to the product and process aspects of innovation.

After the presentation of some empirical results on the relations among price, productivity, and output growth across industries, the determinants of sectoral productivity growth and the nature of the innovation process will be studied to gain a somewhat broader perspective on the evolutionary theory of inflation.

---

[21] "Permanent shifts in policy regime are by definition rare events" (Sims, 1982, p. 118).

7.4   Determinants of industrial pricing

7.4.1   Determinants of sectoral price development

Wage and price developments are the focus for explaining a lasting inflationary process (Sawyer, 1983, p. 12). We assume that the price trend depends on the level of demand or the rate of change and the growth of production costs (flexible cost-based pricing). Given annual data, the use of actual instead of normal costs seems to be appropriate. A uniform econometric approach of price setting does not exist (Earl, 1973, p. 83). The majority of the price equations are defined according to general assumptions concerning the behavior of the firms and the presumed pricing factors (Eckstein, 1972). Demand fluctuations may raise prices both indirectly by changes in production costs (in particular wages) and directly through changes in the markup, as well as by price increases in competitive markets. A clear-cut answer to the expected influence of demand on the development of prices is not available. Frye and Gordon (1980, p. 8) and Gordon (1982c, pp. 96f.) view this applied question as follows: "The equation is openly a convenient characterization of the data rather than an attempt to describe structural behaviour."

The following questions concerning industrial pricing will be analyzed:

- Do the demand indicators used influence prices directly or indirectly through production costs?
- What are the differences in the pricing factors in a sectoral comparison?
- Does the degree of market concentration influence industrial pricing?

Our empirical analysis of price and wage determinants is based on 29 two-digit industrial branches of the manufacturing sector in the Federal Republic of Germany for the period 1961–80. The price index of gross output used is a practical approximation of market or firm prices, based on industrial producer prices (for a critique, see Helmstädter, 1982, p. 61). The development of prices is presumed to depend on industry-specific (not overall) economic or industry factors.

Table 7.1 shows the results of estimated price equations for the total processing industry[22] and four subsectors of individual industries (time

[22] Unlike the manufacturing sector, the processing industry does not include power and water supply, mining, and construction.

Table 7.1. *Determinants of price development in manufacturing in the Federal Republic of Germany, 1961–80*[a]

Sectors	Coefficients					R^2	DW
	A0	A1	A2	A3	A4		
Processing industry	0.31	0.19		0.63			
	$(1.82)^b$	(5.34)	—	(18.17)	—	0.98	2.00
Primary and	0.18	0.17		0.71	−0.08		
producer-goods industry	(0.74)	(3.23)	—	(23.43)	(−2.09)	0.98	1.84
Capital-investment-	0.50	0.17		0.45	0.21		
goods industry	(4.20)	(7.24)	—	(14.91)	(7.49)	0.99	2.28
Consumption-	0.34	0.21		0.64			
goods industry	(1.78)	(5.12)	—	(17.07)	—	0.97	2.39
General and	−0.25	0.26		0.66			
luxury-foods industry	(−0.73)	3.75)	—	(7.19)	—	0.88	2.02

[a] Estimating equation: PGP = A0 + A1 · ULC + A2 · ULC′ + A3 · UMC + A4 · UMC′.
PGP = price index of gross output, annual rate of growth.[23]
ULC = unit labor costs, annual rate of growth.
UMC = unit material costs, annual rate of growth.
[b] t statistics.

series). Both unit labor and unit material costs control prices without any lags, as could be expected. On the other hand, demand indicators are not significant; neither is the level or the rate of change of capacity utilization. The estimates for the individual industries do not show a discernible regular pattern of demand determination of prices. Prices adjust without delay; the lagged endogenous variable is not significant. A division of unit labor costs into wage and productivity components shows a positive sign for wages and a negative sign for productivity. The coefficient of wages is considerably less than unity (in the processing industry, 0.45); so wage changes are shifted onto prices only to a limited extent because of the cost-reducing function of productivity growth.

[23] The annual rates of growth have been calculated as logarithmic first differences.

Table 7.2. *Determinants of wage development in manufacturing in the Federal Republic of Germany, 1961–80[a]*

Sectors	Coefficients						R^2	DW
	A0	A1	A2	A3	A4	A5		
Processing industry	1.44 (0.65)[b]	2.34 (2.04)	0.99 (2.64)	—	0.32 (1.60)	—	0.42	1.78
Primary and producer-goods industry	0.84 (0.29)	2.17 (1.53)	1.07 (2.12)	—	0.32 (1.68)	—	0.32	1.81
Capital-investment-goods industry	0.56 (0.28)	1.84 (1.68)	1.00 (3.00)	—	0.38 (2.38)	0.33 (1.98)	0.58	1.97
Consumption-goods industry	2.34 (1.19)	2.05 (1.87)	0.84 (2.45)	—	0.26 (1.42)	—	0.40	2.04
General and luxury-foods industry	1.90 (1.41)	3.26 (4.13)	0.88 (3.64)	—	−0.14 (−0.76)	—	0.62	2.46

[a]Estimating equation: LS = A0 + A1 · (1/AQ) + A2 · CPI + A3 · CPI' + A4 · YBR + A5 · YBR'.
LS = wage rate, gross, annual rate of growth.
AQ = rate of unemployment (percent).
CPI = consumer price index, annual rate of growth.
YBR = labor productivity, annual rate of growth.
[b]t statistics.

Table 7.2 shows the results with a conventionally used wage equation. The development of wages depends on both industry-specific (productivity) and overall economic variables (rate of unemployment, consumer price index). Sociological factors such as union power or strike activity are not included. Remarkably, the (inverse of the) unemployment rate as a demand indicator in the labor market is positive and significant, and prices are completely shifted onto wages (in the case of the processing industry, 0.99); so, unlike prices, demand influences wages directly and therefore prices indirectly (Eckstein, 1984, p. 217; Sylos-Labini, 1979, p. 163). The productivity variable is insignificant. The danger of a simultaneous-equation bias in wage equations is reduced by employing the consumer price index, whereas in the price equation a price index of gross output is used.

Breaking down the manufacturing industry into a highly concentrated sector (CR3 > 0.25) and a less concentrated sector (CR3 < 0.10),[24] we obtain the following results (Rahmeyer, 1985, pp. 315ff.). In the processing industry:

$$PGP = 0.31 + 0.19ULC + 0.63UMC,$$
$$\quad (1.82) \quad (5.34) \quad\quad (18.17)$$
$$R^2 = 0.98, \quad\quad DW = 2.00$$

Highly concentrated sector:

$$PGP = 0.11 + 0.05ULC + 0.11ULC'1 + 0.66UMC,$$
$$\quad (0.48) \quad (1.07) \quad\quad (2.72) \quad\quad\quad (18.29)$$
$$R^2 = 0.96, \quad\quad DW = 1.81$$

Less concentrated sector:

$$PGP = 0.15 + 0.26ULC + 0.60UMC,$$
$$\quad (0.83) \quad (6.95) \quad\quad (13.31)$$
$$R^2 = 0.96, \quad\quad DW = 2.55$$

Unit material costs have a positive influence on prices in all three sectors. Their weight in the cost structure is the highest (about 60 percent); their shift onto prices is more uniform than in the case of unit labor costs. Differences in direct demand determination of prices between the sectors of high and low concentrations have not been detected using this rough estimate.

7.4.2   Structural interrelations of wages, productivity, and prices

In a second step, the relations among the average growth of wages, productivity, and prices are analyzed using a cross-sectional method covering 31 two-digit manufacturing industries, and breaking down the period under examination into subperiods to obtain further insight regarding the determinants of price and productivity growth.[25] Fundamental to an explanation of the (relative) growth of gross value-added prices are its negative correlations with productivity (Table 7.3; equation 1) and output growth (equation 2) and its positive correlation with the growth of unit labor costs (equation 3). In all three cases it is much stronger for 1972–82 than for 1961–71. The relation of prices to productivity is stronger than to output (and still stronger to unit labor

---

[24] Cumulative share of industry sales accounted for by the three largest firms.
[25] For analysis of U.S. data, see Houthakker (1979, pp. 241ff.) and Kendrick and Grossman (1980, pp. 61ff.).

Table 7.3. *Interrelations among relative growth of prices, productivity, and wages in manufacturing, Federal Republic of Germany, 1961–82*

Period	Coefficient			
	A0	A1	A2	R^2
1. PBW/YBR[a]				
1961–82	5.96 (12.54)	−0.61 (−5.57)	—	0.52
1961–71	4.82 (6.08)	−0.37 (−2.44)	—	0.17
1972–82	6.08 (8.82)	−0.67 (−7.73)	—	0.67
1976–82	5.09 (19.86)	−0.59 (−8.49)	—	0.71
2. PBW/BWR				
1961–82	4.41 (14.09)	−0.29 (−3.87)	—	0.34
1961–71	4.12 (7.56)	−0.22 (−2.39)	—	0.16
1972–82	4.41 (16.10)	−0.37 (−3.87)	—	0.34
1976–82	3.90 (13.71)	−0.31 (−3.74)	—	0.33
3. PBW/LK				
1961–82	−0.48 (−0.79)	0.93 (6.82)	—	0.62
1961–71	0.78 (1.05)	0.58 (3.26)	—	0.27

Period	Coefficient			
	A0	A1	A2	R^2
1972–82	−0.02 (−0.04)	0.85 (8.21)	—	0.70
1976–82	0.90 (2.48)	0.63 (8.08)	—	0.69
4. PBW/LK/BWR				
1961–82	0.42 (0.49)	0.79 (4.88)	−0.10 (−1.47)	0.64
1961–71	1.82 (1.73)	0.47 (2.48)	−0.13 (−1.38)	0.31
1972–82	0.19 (0.25)	0.82 (5.81)	−0.03 (−0.38)	0.70
1976–82	0.16 (0.25)	0.76 (6.14)	0.13 (1.39)	0.71
5. PBW/YBR/BWR				
1961–82	5.82 (12.08)	−0.50 (−3.51)	−0.10 (−1.24)	0.54
1961–71	4.96 (6.29)	−0.25 (−1.46)	−0.14 (−1.38)	0.22
1972–82	6.11 (16.40)	−0.68 (5.35)	0.02 (0.17)	0.67
1976–82	5.35 (19.50)	−0.78 (−6.91)	0.18 (2.06)	0.75

Table 7.3 (cont.)

Period	Coefficient A0	A1	A2	R^2
6. PBW/LS				
1961–82	10.34 (3.84)	−0.83 (−2.55)	—	0.18
1961–71	5.09 (1.53)	−0.24 (−0.63)	—	0.01
1972–82	12.14 (4.02)	−1.04 (−2.71)	—	0.20
1976–82	7.65 (2.57)	−0.61 (−1.42)	—	0.06
7. YBR/BWR				
1961–82	2.83 (8.17)	0.38 (4.51)	—	0.41
1961–71	3.37 (5.84)	0.30 (3.10)	—	0.25
1972–82	2.48 (8.70)	0.57 (5.69)	—	0.53
1976–82	1.87 (6.46)	0.64 (7.45)	—	0.66
8. LS/YBR				
1961–82	6.80 (32.73)	0.35 (7.34)	—	0.65
1961–71	7.20 (23.25)	0.29 (4.90)	—	0.45
1972–82	7.04 (40.91)	0.25 (5.41)	—	0.50
1976–82	6.51 (35.99)	0.12 (2.41)	—	0.17
9. B/BWR				
1961–82	−2.69 (−7.52)	0.61 (7.04)	—	0.63
1961–71	−3.05 (−5.08)	0.67 (6.78)	—	0.61
1972–82	−2.47 (−8.63)	0.43 (4.25)	—	0.38
1976–82	−1.48 (−6.30)	0.35 (4.09)	—	0.37
10. YBR/KIB				
1971–82	0.53 (0.54)	0.55 (3.68)	—	0.32
1961–71	2.13 (2.09)	0.38 (2.85)	—	0.22
1972–82	−1.89 (−2.08)	0.95 (5.77)	—	0.53
1976–82	−0.65 (−0.73)	0.91 (4.17)	—	0.37

11. YBR/BWR/KIB

1961–82	0.70	0.30	0.38	0.54
	(0.86)	(3.72)	(2.85)	
1961–71	1.35	0.25	0.31	0.39
	(1.42)	(2.80)	(2.54)	
1972–82	−0.97	0.41	0.69	0.77
	(−1.43)	(5.24)	(5.32)	
1976–82	0.12	0.53	0.51	0.75
	(0.21)	(6.55)	(3.31)	

[a]PBW/YBR means PBW = A0 + A1 · YBR; analogously, PBW/LK/BWR means PBW = A0 + A1 · LK + A2 · BWR.

PBW = gross value-added price, average rate of growth.

YBR = labor productivity (= BWR/B), average rate of growth.

BWR = gross value added, average rate of growth.

B = number of persons employed, average rate of growth.

LK = unit labor costs, average rate of growth.

LS = gross wage rate, average rate of growth. KIB = capital intensity, average rate of growth.

227

costs), because in the individual industrial branches, an above-average output growth goes along with an above- or below-average productivity growth that by itself effects a decrease or an increase in relative price growth. In a multiple regression, only unit labor costs (equation 4) or productivity (equation 5) remain significant; output does not. The structure of wages shows a negative (but only weak) correlation with prices (equation 6). Splitting unit labor costs into wage and productivity components, we find that the negative productivity effect dominates the positive wage effect in 1961–82 and 1961–71, whereas in 1972–82 the effects equalize. Industries showing above-average productivity growth are characterized by above-average output growth (and vice versa) (equation 7). In detail, there are groups of industries with strong and slow growth in output and productivity, and another group marked by strong productivity and slow output growth, where the effect of the former dominates. Output growth and productivity growth are, on the average, mutually reinforcing (demand effect). Besides, by way of price changes, productivity growth is passed on to wage increases (equation 8), even if to a smaller degree (especially in 1972–82). Strongly growing industries are at the same time characterized by above-average growth in employment. For 1961–82 and 1961–71, the relation is tighter between output and productivity growth, whereas the reverse holds true for 1972–82 (equation 9). So the link between output and employment has weakened. Strong-growth industries show above-average growth in both productivity and employment: "employees need not fear working for firms in technologically progressive nonfarm industries since output generally expands sufficiently, as a result of relative price declines or new product development, to offset the productivity advance" (Kendrick, 1983, p. 34).[26] So a decreasing relative price growth in industries experiencing strong output and productivity growth favors a cumulative causation of economic growth (supply effects).

Furthermore, there is a positive correlation between the average growth of productivity and capital intensity (equations 10 and 11). Above-average capital intensification is the result of rapid, investment-promoting economic growth and creation of additional employment, thereby provoking an above-average increase in the capital-output ratio in three of five strongly growing industries. On the other hand, it is the effect of poor investment activities and an above-average decline

[26] On the interrelations among the growth of output, productivity, and prices, see the discussion of the Verdoorn theorem, summarized in the *Journal of Post-Keynesian Economics*, Vol. 5 (1983), No. 3.

in employment in slowly growing industries (defensive productivity growth).

The results of the competitive and adjustment processes of industries measured by return on capital employed (gross profit/fixed capital investment, valued at replacement prices) and gross unit profits (gross profit/gross output, in constant prices) do not show a consistent picture. Both the subsectors with strong and slow output and productivity growth include branches that have a relative increase or decrease in success indicators.

Summarizing, we may conclude that relative productivity growth is the most important determinant of relative price growth, where causality may run the other way as well (Clark, 1982, pp. 149ff.), but there is no proportional relation between the variables. The above-average or below-average productivity growth is not, in general, passed on into a corresponding below- or above-average price increase. The direct effect of relative output growth on the relative growth of productivity and prices is weak, although significant, in both cases. This result may be interpreted as pointing to the fact that in view of economic structural change, the strain of competition and economic adaptiveness through productivity and price adjustments will show pronounced interindustry differentials. Strong growth industries are able to afford above-average wage increases without increases in their relative prices. The price-curbing effect of productivity growth on unit labor costs outweighs the price-increasing effect of wage increases. But the positive correlation with wages weakens the price-curbing role of productivity growth. The structure of wages is an important variable affecting the setup of the economy. A significant correlation with the pattern of employment could not be detected. So the interindustry pattern of prices determines its respective pattern of quantities, but not that of wages.

7.5 New developments in the theory of innovation

The average productivity growth in the Federal Republic of Germany shows large interindustry differences. In the period 1961–80, it ranges from 1.9 percent (musical instruments and toy industries) to 9.8 percent (business office machines and data-processing industries); with regard to the industrial subsectors, the range is from 2.8 (general and luxury-food industry) to 5.0 percent (primary and producer-goods industries). According to the structural approach, these different productivity growth rates are the deep-rooted, fundamental causes of the long-term rate of price growth. Moreover, they affect the interindustry price structure and provide different growth opportunities for the branches of industry. Long-range productivity growth constitutes an attribute differentiating the economic setup.

An interindustry determinant of productivity growth going beyond the structure of output (scale effects) and capital intensity does not exist (Kendrick and Grossman, 1980, pp. 100ff.). The earlier explanation of the differences in interindustry productivity growth, referred to by Nelson and Winter (1977, p. 42) as "the differential productivity growth puzzle," and based on the substitution of productive factors (capital intensification) and factor-saving technical progress, is not sufficient. The rate of technical progress is not exogenously given; rather, its generation and diffusion must be explained in the institutional setting of an enterprise economy using a broader theoretical approach.

Nelson (1981a, p. 1029) and Link (1983, pp. 19ff.) criticize recent research in productivity growth on three points:

- Inadequate research on the microeconomic determinants of productivity growth, such as the importance of large-scale enterprises as complex social organizations.
- Inadequate research on the generation and diffusion of new technologies.
- Inadequate research on the importance of overall economic factors affecting productivity growth (e.g., the rate of inflation and its interindustry variability).

Interindustry differences in productivity growth may be regarded as indicators of different rates of technical progress and innovation activity among firms, just as much as levels of R&D expenditures. We summarize some new results concerning the dynamics of technological advance:[27]

1. Technological development is to a large extent characterized by uncertainty and even chance regarding its technical and market results. Firms, therefore, prefer an incremental strategy in their innovation activity.

2. Technological development in enterprises and industries usually takes place as a continuous, cumulative process, as "technological trajectories," determined, above all, by the technology of the past, but not mainly by major innovations. From this, a higher degree of appropriability of its returns follows. So new technologies have both a private and a public component.

---

[27] See Nelson (1981a, pp. 1045ff., 1984, pp. 6ff.), and Nelson and Langlois (1983, pp. 814ff.).

3. The process of innovation itself develops very differently in enterprises and industries (e.g., regarding the dominance of product and process innovations, the generation and spreading of new technologies, the importance of R&D expenses). So there are "important structural differences among economic sectors, which determine who does the R&D, the relative roles of R&D and learning by experience, and the mechanisms by which new technology is carried into widespread use" (Nelson, 1981a, p. 1051).

4. The innovation process, guided by competitive market forces, may, on the one hand, lead to a less than optimal amount of R&D expenses in fields in which the private appropriation of the returns of new technologies is incomplete. On the other hand, it may also lead to a greater than optimal amount in cases where private appropriation is possible to a greater extent and where large and increasing profit expectations exist. The latter is the result of rivalry among enterprises in the R&D race, promising the winner booming profits, and their search activity along the line of existing technical knowledge ("to cluster around the same broad opportunity," Nelson, 1981b, p. 107). Both characteristic features may lead to duplication of research and an inadequate diversification in the innovation process. The structure and temporal course of innovation activity also matter. Thus, competition in the innovation process may result in suboptimal R&D allocations.

This new understanding of the innovation process has removed previous shortcomings (Rosenberg, 1976, p. 77): limiting research to major innovations while disregarding minor technological improvements; fostering discontinuous instead of incremental evolutionary change; emphasizing scientific research as the origin of new technological knowledge while underestimating the importance of construction and application methods; investigating only the first phases instead of the innovation process as a whole.

For success in inventive activity and technical progress, factors on both the demand and supply sides are decisive. On the demand side, strong growth industries with corresponding profit expectations and, on average, decreasing relative prices show a high intensity of R&D, innovating offensively mostly in products to stimulate and extend existing markets or to open up new markets. Slow-growth industries are, on average, characterized by increasing relative prices and a below-average R&D intensity. The economic necessity to control production costs permanently induces defensive innovations in processes, thereby reducing the labor force. Process innovations are a distinctive feature of stagnant markets and industries. But there is no uniform relation between the level of R&D expenses and productivity growth

(Terleckyj, 1980, pp. 55ff.); it varies subject to market structure and also organizational peculiarities of firms. On the supply side, the existence of technological constraints and opportunities is decisive for the rate and direction of inventive activity. The costs and the feasibility of inventive activity differ between commodity classes or industries, together with scientific knowledge. For example, the capability of carrying out product innovations is limited in the consumption-goods industry compared with the capital-investment-goods industry. The sectoral pattern of inventive activity and thus relative productivity (and correspondingly also price) growth – although the interrelation will undoubtedly not run in a straight line – reflects both the technological scope of the industries to increase productivity and the pressure of economic competitiveness and adjustment to realize feasible gains in productivity. This model of the dynamics of technological advance provides "an account of productivity growth that is consistent with what is known about the process of technological change" (Nelson, 1981a, p. 1060).

7.6   Concluding remarks

An interpretation of the long-run inflationary process and its interindustry differences in the spirit of evolutionary theory and its incorporation into a theory of evolutionary economic change seems to be of great promise. An evolutionary theory of economic change might be improved if enlarged by a detailed explanation of the determinants of the price level and relative sectoral prices. Sectoral price development is supposed to improve or worsen the long-term growth prospects of an industry (allocation function of prices). As a microeconomic foundation of industrial pricing, the behavioral theory of the firm is recommended; it is able to explain the cost-oriented price formation of firms and industries, relatively independent of the state of demand. Thus, there results a compatibility with the Nelson-Winter approach to economic growth referring to the underlying theory of the firm. On the overall economic level, the existence of inflationary expectations and a wage–price spiral are capable of explaining a persistent inflationary process, based on the given structural features of industrial markets. Likewise, the growth of industrial productivity as the most important determinant of relative price development may (within the scope of the entrepreneurial competitive and adjustment process) be partly explained in the spirit of the behavioral theory of the firm. It is an instrument of cost cutting that the firms may use to different degrees depending on the state of demand and their ability to shift costs onto prices. The results are interindustry productivity differences.

The interindustry differences in productivity growth are finally the result of the demand and supply of innovations. New studies on innovative activities have led to the conclusion that individual firms and industries are able to appropriate product and process innovations to very different degrees, subject to different conditions of technological opportunity and appropriability. If, along with Schumpeter, innovations also include organizational changes, then the level, acceleration or deceleration, and duration of the inflationary process may also induce modifications in the institutional setting of the economy and the behavior of the market participants (firms, workers or unions, government agencies) that themselves have retroactive effects on the level of inflation. The explanation of endogenous innovative activities as a consequence of absolute and relative price changes and their reactions on level and structure of price changes is the focus of interest of an evolutionary approach to inflation.

References

Ackley, G. (1978). *Macroeconomics: Theory and Policy.* New York: Collier Macmillan.

Addison, J., and Burton, J. (1980). "The Demise of 'Demand Pull' and 'Cost Push' in Inflation Theory." *Banca Nazionale del Lavoro Quarterly,* 133:187–203.

Addison, J., Burton, J., and Torrance, T. (1980). "The Causation of Inflation." *Manchester School of Economic and Social Studies,* 48:140–56.

Brunner, K. (1974). "Monetary Management, Domestic Inflation, and Imported Inflation," in R. Aliber (ed.), *National Monetary Policies and the International Financial System.* (pp. 179–208). University of Chicago Press.

Brunner, K., and Meltzer, A. (1977). "The Explanation of Inflation: Some International Evidence." *American Economic Review, Papers and Proceedings,* 67:148–54.

(1978). "The Problem of Inflation," in K. Brunner, and A. Meltzer (eds.), *The Problem of Inflation. Carnegie-Rochester Conference Series on Public Policy,* Vol. 8 (pp. 1–15). Amsterdam: North Holland.

Clark, P. (1982). "Inflation and the Productivity Decline," *American Economic Review, Papers and Proceedings,* 72:149–54.

Coutts, K., Godley, W., and Nordhaus, W. (1978). *Industrial Pricing in the United Kingdom.* Cambridge University Press.

Dornbusch, R., and Fischer, S. (1978). *Macroeconomics.* New York: McGraw-Hill.

Earl, P. H. (1973). *Inflation and the Structure of Industrial Prices.* Lexington, Mass.: D. C. Heath.

Eckstein, O. (ed.) (1972). *The Econometrics of Price Determination.* Washington, D.C.: Board of Governors of the Federal Reserve System.

234   Fritz Rahmeyer

(1984). "Foundation of Aggregate Supply Price." *American Economic Review, Papers and Proceedings,* 74:216–20.

Elliott, J. E. (1983). "Schumpeter and the Theory of Capitalist Economic Development." *Journal of Economic Behaviour and Organization,* 4:277–308.

Fischer, S. (1982). "Adapting to Inflation in the United States Economy," in R. E. Hall (ed.), *Inflation: Causes and Effects.* University of Chicago Press.

Friedman, B. M. (1984). "Lessons From the 1979–82 Monetary Policy Experiment." *American Economic Review, Papers and Proceedings,* 74:382–7.

Frisch, H. (1973). *Die Inflation der Gegenwart und ihre Ursachen.* Wien: Verlag der Technischen Hochschule Wien.

(1980). *Die neue Inflationstheorie.* Göttingen: Vandenhoeck & Ruprecht.

Frye, J., and Gordon, R. J. (1980). *The Variance and Acceleration of Inflation in the 1970's: Alternative Explanatory Models and Methods.* NBER Working Paper Series, No. 551.

Gerybadze, A. (1982). *Innovation, Wettbewerb und Evolution.* Tübingen: J. C. B. Mohr/Paul Siebeck.

Giersch, H. (1984). "The Age of Schumpeter." *American Economic Review, Papers and Proceedings,* 74:103–9.

Gordon, R. A. (1948). "Short-Period Price Determination in Theory and Practice." *American Economic Review,* 38:265–88.

Gordon, R. J. (1976). "Recent Developments in the Theory of Inflation and Unemployment." *Journal of Monetary Economics,* 2:185–219.

(1981). "Output Fluctuations and Gradual Price Adjustment." *Journal of Economic Literature,* 19:493–530.

(1982a). "Price Inertia and Policy Ineffectiveness in the United States, 1890–1980." *Journal of Political Economy,* 90:1087–117.

(1982b). "Why U.S. Wage and Employment Behaviour Differs from that in Britain and Japan." *Economic Journal,* 92:13–44.

(1982c). "Inflation, Flexible Exchange Rates, and the Natural Rate of Unemployment," in M. Baily (ed.), *Workers, Jobs and Inflation* (pp. 89–158). Washington, D.C.: Brookings Institution.

(1983). "A Century of Evidence on Wage and Price Stickiness in the United States, the United Kingdom, and Japan," in J. Tobin (ed.), *Macroeconomics, Prices, and Quantities.* Oxford: Basil Blackwell.

(1984). "Supply Shocks and Monetary Policy Revisited." *American Economic Review, Papers and Proceedings,* 74:38–43.

(1985). "Understanding Inflation in the 1980s." *Brookings Papers on Economic Activity,* 16:263–99.

Gordon, R. J., and King, S. (1982). "The Output Cost of Disinflation in Traditional and Vector Autoregressive Models." *Brookings Papers on Economic Activity,* 13:205–42.

Grönberg, R., and Rahmeyer, F. (1985). "Preis- und Mengenanpassungen in den Konjunkturzyklen der Bundesrepublik Deutschland 1963–1981." *Jahrbücher für Nationalökonomie und Statistik,* 200:239–61.

Guger, A. (1978). "Der Inflationsprozess bei administrierter Preisbildung und das Problem der Vollbeschäftigungspolitik," in H. Frisch and H. Otruba (eds.), *Neuere Ergebnisse der Inflations-theorie.* Stuttgart: Gustav Fischer.

Hall, R. (1980). "Employment Fluctuations and Wage Rigidity." *Brookings Papers on Economic Activity,* 11:91–123.

Hay, D., and Morris, D. (1979). *Industrial Economics. Theory and Evidence.* Oxford University Press.

Helmstädter, E. (1982). "Ordnungspolitische Probleme der Strukturberichter-stattung," in B. Gahlen (ed.), *Strukturberichter-stattung der Wirtschafts-forschungsinstitute.* Tübingen: J. C. B. Mohr/Paul Siebeck.

Houthakker, H. S. (1979). "Growth and Inflation: Analysis by Industry." *Brookings Papers on Economic Activity,* 10:241–56.

Kahn, G. A. (1984). "International Differences in Wage Behaviour: Real, Nominal, or Exaggerated." *American Economic Review, Papers and Proceedings,* 74:155–9.

Kendrick, J. W. (1983). *Interindustry Differences in Productivity Growth. A Study in Contemporary Economic Problems.* Washington, D.C.: American Enterprise Institute for Public Policy Research.

Kendrick, J. W., and Grossman, E. S. (1980). *Productivity in the United States: Trends and Cycles.* Baltimore: Johns Hopkins University Press.

Keynes, J. M. (1939). "Relative Movements in Real Wages and Output." *Economic Journal,* 49:34–51.

Kloten, N., Ketterer, K.-H., and Vollmer, R. (1985). "West Germany's Stabilization Performance," in L. Lindberg and C. Maier (eds.), *The Politics of Inflation and Economic Stagnation.* Washington, D.C.: Brookings Institution.

Kregel, J. (1979). "A Keynesian Approach to Inflation Theory and Policy," in D. Heathfield (ed.), *Perspectives on Inflation. Models and Policies* (pp. 189–216). London: Longman.

Laidler, D. (1976). "Inflation – Alternative Explanations and Policies: Tests on Data Drawn from Six Countries," in K. Brunner and A. Meltzer (eds.), *Institutions, Policies and Economic Performance. Carnegie-Rochester Conference Series on Public Policy,* Vol. 4 (pp. 251–306). Amsterdam: North Holland.

Laidler, D., and Parkin, J. (1975). "Inflation – A Survey." *Economic Journal,* 85:741–809.

Langholm, O. (1968). "Industrial Pricing: The Theoretical Basis." *Swedish Journal of Economics,* 70:65–93.

Lee, F. (1984a). "The Marginalist Controversy and the Demise of Full Cost Pricing." *Journal of Economic Issues,* 18:1107–32.

(1984b). "Full Cost Pricing: A New Wine in a New Bottle." *Australian Economic Papers,* 23:151–66.

Lewontin, R. C. (1968). "The Concept of Evolution," in D. Sills (ed.), *International Encyclopedia of the Social Sciences,* Vol. 5. New York: Macmillan.

Link, A. (1983). *Measurement and Analysis of Productivity Growth: A Synthesis of Thought.* Washington, D.C.: U.S. Department of Commerce.

Lipsey, R. (1979). "World Inflation." *Economic Record,* 55:283–96.

   (1981). "The Understanding and Control of Inflation: Is There a Crisis in Macro-Economics?" *Canadian Journal of Economics,* 14:545–76.

Machlup, F. (1967). "Theories of the Firm: Marginalist, Behavioral, Managerial." *American Economic Review,* 57:1–33.

Mitchell, D. (1985). "Shifting Norms in Wage Determination." *Brookings Papers on Economic Activity,* 16:575–99.

Mulvey, J., and Trevithick, C. (1975). *The Economics of Inflation.* London: Martin Robertson.

Nelson, R. R. (1981a). "Research on Productivity Growth and Productivity Differences: Dead Ends and New Departures." *Journal of Economic Literature,* 19:1029–64.

   (1981b). "Assessing Private Enterprise: An Exegesis of Tangled Doctrine." *Bell Journal of Economics,* 12:93–111.

   (1984). *High-Technology Industries. A Five-Nation Comparison.* Washington, D.C.: American Enterprise Institute for Public Policy Research.

Nelson, R. R., and Langlois, R. N. (1983). "Industrial Innovation Policy: Lessons from American History." *Science,* 219:814–18.

Nelson, R. R., and Winter, S. G. (1977). "In Search of Useful Theory of Innovation." *Research Policy,* 6:36–76.

   (1982a). *An Evolutionary Theory of Economic Change.* Cambridge, Mass.: Harvard University Press.

   (1982b). "The Schumpeterian Tradeoff Revisited." *American Economic Review,* 72:114–32.

Nordhaus, W. (1976). "Inflation Theory and Policy." *American Economic Review, Papers and Proceedings,* 66:59–64.

Okun, A. M. (1975). "Inflation: Its Mechanics and Welfare Costs." *Brookings Papers on Economic Activity,* 6:351–90.

   (1980). "Rational-Expectations-with-Misperceptions as a Theory of the Business Cycle." *Journal of Money, Credit and Banking,* 12(2):817–25.

   (1981). *Prices and Quantities. A Macroeconomic Analysis.* Oxford: Basil Blackwell.

Parkin, M. (1977). "Inflation without Growth: A Long-Run Perspective on Short-Run Stabilization Policies," in K. Brunner and A. Meltzer (eds.), *Stabilization of the Domestic and International Economy. Carnegie-Rochester Conference Series on Public Policy,* Vol. 5 (pp. 31–68). Amsterdam: North Holland.

   (1978). "Alternative Explanations of United Kingdom Inflation: A Survey," in M. Parkin and M. Sumner (eds.), *Inflation in the United Kingdom.* Manchester University Press.

Perry, G. (1978). "Slowing the Wage-Price-Spiral. The Macroeconomic View." *Brookings Papers on Economic Activity,* 9:259–91.

   (1980). "Inflation in Theory and Practice." *Brookings Papers on Economic Activity,* 11:207–41.

   (1983). "What Have We Learned about Disinflation?" *Brookings Papers on Economic Activity,* 14:587–602.

(1984). "Reflections on Macroeconomics." *American Economic Review, Papers and Proceedings,* 74:401–7.

Rahmeyer, F. (1983). *Sektorale Preisentwicklung in der Bundesrepublik Deutschland 1951–1977.* Tübingen: J. C. B. Mohr/Paul Siebeck.

(1985). "Marktstruktur und industrielle Preisentwicklung." *IFO-Studien,* 31:295–330.

(1986). "Der Zusammenhang zwischen Lohn-, Produktivitäts- und Preisstruktur." *Zeitschrift für Wirtschafts- und Sozialwissenschaften,* 106:467–93.

Rosenberg, N. (1976). *Perspectives on Technology.* Cambridge University Press.

Sawyer, M. (1983). *Business Pricing and Inflation.* New York: Macmillan.

Schultze, C. (1985). "Microeconomic Efficiency and Nominal Wage Stickiness." *American Economic Review,* 75:1–15.

Schumpeter, J. [1934] (1964). *Theorie der wirtschaftlichen Entwicklung* (4th ed.). Berlin: Duncker & Humblot.

Silberston, A. (1973). "Price Behaviour of Firms," in Royal Economic Society, Social Science Research Council (eds.), *Surveys of Applied Economics,* Vol. 1. London: Macmillan.

Simon, H. (1979). "Rational Decision Making in Business Organization." *American Economic Review,* 69:493–513.

Sims, C. (1982). "Policy Analysis with Econometric Models." *Brookings Papers on Economic Activity,* 13:107–52.

Streissler, E. (1980). "Kritik des neoklassischen Gleichgewichtsansatzes als Rechtfertigung marktwirtschaftlicher Ordnungen," in E. Streissler and C. Watrin (eds.), *Zur Theorie marktwirtschaftlicher Ordnungen.* Tübingen: J. C. B. Mohr/Paul Siebeck.

Streissler, E., et al. (1976). *Die Relativierung des Zieles der Geldwertstabilität.* Göttingen: Otto Schwartz.

Sylos-Labini, P. (1979). "Review Article: Industrial Pricing in the United Kingdom." *Cambridge Journal of Economics,* 3:153–63.

Taylor, J. B. (1984). "Recent Changes in Macro Policy and Its Effects: Some Time-Series Evidence." *American Economic Review, Papers and Proceedings,* 74:206–10.

Terleckyj, N. E. (1980). "What do R & D Numbers Tell Us About Technological Change?" *American Economic Review, Papers and Proceedings,* 70:55–61.

Thorning, M. (1975). "Cyclical Fluctuations in Prices and Output in the United States, 1920–1970." *Economic Journal,* 85:95–100.

Tobin, J. (1972a). "The Wage–Price Mechanism: Overview of the Conference," in O. Eckstein (ed.), *The Econometrics of Price Determination* (pp. 5–15). Washington, D.C.: Board of Governors of the Federal Reserve System.

(1972b). "Inflation and Unemployment." *American Economic Review,* 62:1–18.

Trevithick, J. (1976). "Money Wage Inflexibility and the Keynesian Labour Supply Function." *Economic Journal,* 86:327–32.

Turvey, R. (1951). "Some Aspects of a Theory of Inflation in a Closed Economy." *Economic Journal,* 61:531–43.

Vanderkamp, J. (1975). "Inflation: A Simple Friedman Theory with a Phillips Twist." *Journal of Monetary Economics,* 1:117–22.

Wachter, M. (1986). "Union Wage Rigidity: The Default Settings of Labor Law." *American Economic Review, Papers and Proceedings,* 76:240–4.

Wachter, M., and Williamson, O. (1978). "Obligational Markets and the Mechanics of Inflation." *Bell Journal of Economics,* 9:549–71.

Wied-Nebbeling, S. (1975). *Industrielle Preissetzung.* Tübingen: J. C. B. Mohr/ Paul Siebeck.

Wiles, P. (1973). "Cost Inflation and the State of Economic Theory." *Economic Journal,* 83:377–98.

Winter, S. G. (1971). "Satisficing, Selection and the Innovating Remnant." *Quarterly Journal of Economics,* 85:237–61.

   (1984). "Schumpeterian Competition in Alternative Technological Regimes." *Journal of Economic Behaviour and Organization,* 5:287–320.

Witt, U. (1987). *Individualistische Grundlagen der evolutorischen Ökonomik.* Tübingen: J. C. B. Mohr/Paul Siebeck.

Discussion

RAPHAEL VALENTINO

First and foremost, I would like to congratulate our society and Professor Fritz Rahmeyer for the imaginative bridge his chapter tries to build between productivity growth and the fight against the inflationary process. Even Schumpeter, in dealing with inflation in a little-known article dated June 1948, did not develop his intellectual constructions to this point. What we are trying to achieve through this approach is a cure for inflation by productivity growth, or, if that is too ambitious in certain cases, by "growthflation," as I termed the phenomenon in my thesis on inflation in Brazil (Valentino, 1979). In fact, the cure for inflation must be revival of the economy, not its death. Salazar, in Portugal, succeeded in achieving the transformation of an economy without currency into a currency without economy, thus creating the risk, through repression, of paving the way, when social explosion cropped up, to the final outcome of a country without economy and without currency. Fortunately, this catastrophe was averted.

But before going into the specific issues of this chapter, let us make a quick "review of the troops" of Schumpeter's thoughts about inflation near the end of his life, when he devoted more specific attention to the problem. As it emerges from his 1948 article, inflation, for him, was not only a microeconomic process but also a macroeconomic process. He even came close, in that article, to some monetarist ideas. In the last analysis, this is not singular in the intellectual biography of eminent economists. The Keynes of *A Treatise on Money* is not the same as the Keynes of *The General Theory* and of Bretton Woods. It is well known that John Maynard was born anew every morning; for this reason, his colleagues at Bretton Woods commented that he was too intelligent to be consistent. With reference to two of his colleagues in the British delegation, one was considered too consistent to be intelligent, and the other (an unfair joke) neither consistent nor intelligent. Schumpeter, if he was inconsistent, had the inconsistency of intelligence in the quest for truth. It is in this light that I attempt to interpret his explicit and implicit ideas on inflation.

In dealing with the inflations that ran their courses during and after World War I in Austria, France, Germany, and Italy, he wrote:

The inflations were simple processes. All of them were the results of war finance and could have been stopped within a year or two. But they were not stopped because the people who counted politically did not want to stop them. (Schumpeter, 1948, p. 331)

And he added:

Any cure will inevitably produce what is more unpopular still, a temporary depression, because, so soon as inflation ceases, there will be readjustments in prices and production that will mean losses and unemployment, though neither need be serious. Everyone feels this and is afraid of it, especially in an election year. So inflation runs on by common consent. (Schumpeter, 1948, p. 34)

After having discussed the causes of inflation and distinguished among incipient, advanced, and wild inflation, he approaches the bridge we are now discussing, but he gives us no more than a hint when he writes that "the best remedy for inflation is [an] increase in production" (Schumpeter, 1948, p. 89). Here, he should have written an "increase in productivity," which is what he really implies, as becomes evident from the explanation that follows his general statement on production increase:

However, if this increase in production is to have any positive effect, the volume of credit must not rise in the same proportion. In other words, an increase of production that is to counteract inflation involves more hours and *better quality of work*. It has been argued that our production is at or near its practical peak and that hence no significant increase in output can be expected from an increase in hours of work. But production is at or near its peak only relative to the actual labour conditions. With more work available, *different and more productive arrangements* of processes would be possible, and any shortage of equipment or raw materials that might obstruct increase of output would be quickly eliminated. (Schumpeter, 1948, p. 89)

In these passages, Schumpeter is less monetarist than in the core of the article, and he gives us a fertile hint on the possibilities of building a theory of productivity as an arm against inflation on the basis of his fruitful ideas on innovation as the main source of development.

Evolutionary economics and inflation

Professor Rahmeyer starts by stating that "evolutionary economics deals mainly with explanations of long-run endogenous economic changes" and adds that "it has not yet been applied to explain the development of prices or inflation nor to explain the structure of prices." In this connection, I have two suggestions to improve the quality of the analysis developed in this chapter. First, I would implement the construction of the argument by historical evidence, as Schumpeter did through the business cycles with regard to *The Theory of Economic Development*. The analysis is conceived too much in terms of the symbol-based economy, with little attention, if any, to the real-based economy, which would befit a purely Keynesian analysis, at some stages of Keynes's thought, but definitely not a Schumpeterian analysis. Second, I would enquire in depth about the possible relations between inflation and stages of growth, in a more precise assessment of long-run endogenous economic change. Accordingly, the concept of self-destructive inflation, as developed by Arthur Lewis (1972) in *Theory of Economic Growth*, would be a very helpful framework for this inquiry.

In Professor Rahmeyer's chapter, inflation appears mainly as a past problem, because he confines himself, in the constructive part of his chapter, to the correlation between productivity and output growth in a noninflationary economy (i.e., that of the Federal Republic of Germany). If we were to write a book on contemporary inflation in Germany, it would be one of the slimmest books in the world, much like the history of football in Venice or the history of Mussolini's democratic ideas. But if we look at the history of past inflation in Germany, especially after World War I, our book will put on a lot of weight. Unlike Schumpeter, Professor Rahmeyer's careful analysis of the theories of inflation and of correlations between productivity increase and output growth is silent about the evolutionary path that made it possible to achieve this positive correlation.

It is Schumpeter himself who provides us with the key to the desired construction, and I believe that it is hidden in his *Theory of Economic*

Development in the chapter on business cycles, where he points out that in the course of development, the "secular" price level must fall, as evidenced by the history of prices in the nineteenth century (Schumpeter, [1912] 1974, p. 235). In explaining the "race for means of production" in a period of prosperity, Schumpeter then anticipates an evolutionary approach to inflation, as well as the concept of self-liquidating inflation. In fact, he points out that the appearance of the results of innovations by new enterprises "leads to a *credit deflation,* because entrepreneurs are now in a position, and have every incentive, to pay off their debts; and since no other borrowers step into their place, this leads to a disappearance of the recently created purchasing power just when its complement in goods emerges, and which can henceforth be repeatedly produced in the manner of the circular flow" ([1912] 1974, p. 233). Although Schumpeter makes some qualifications to this description of the process, he discerned very clearly, as early as 1911, the two elements of what would later be called self-destructive inflation: credit as the catalyst of innovation, and liquidation of debts by successful enterprises (i.e., those embodying innovations) (Schumpeter, [1912] 1974, p. 234). If we compare this description to Lewis's concept of "inflations for the purpose of creating useful capital [which] are on the contrary self-destructive" (Lewis, 1972, p. 217), we realize that Schumpeter was fully aware, at the beginning of the century, of the sources that would nourish inflation in the years ahead, especially when he wrote in *The Theory of Economic Development* that "in the modern economic system in which interest has penetrated even into the circular flow, credit may even remain permanently in circulation" (Schumpeter, [1912] 1974, p. 234). He does not make it explicit, but it flows from his thought that both private enterprises and the state may resort to inflationary or self-destructive credit. It is in this light, I believe, that we must read his statement, written many years later in the 1948 article, that inflation may be due to many causes "but the only [one] we need to consider is government expenditure financed by newly created 'money' such as the greenbacks of the Civil War" (1948, p. 34). But Schumpeter did not envisage the state as a successful manager of self-destructive inflationary credit, at least not in his lifetime.

Furthermore, Schumpeter was not an advocate of inflation. The mechanism of the inflationary process he describes makes it clear that he looks at the phenomenon as a transitory and undesirable way of expelling obsolete firms from the innovating economic environment, in a boom of prosperity:

At the beginning of the boom costs rise in the old businesses; later their receipts are reduced, first in those businesses with which the innovation competes, but then in all old businesses, in so far as consumers' demand changes in favor of the innovation. ([1912] 1974, p. 232)

In order to achieve this kind of result, it is not enough to discuss monetary mechanisms to curb inflation. Here, much more than anywhere else, it is of prime importance to study the phenomenon we are dealing with as a *process*, as Professor Rahmeyer points out, by focusing on the dynamic and disequilibrium nature of economic development. As Alfred Marshall felicitously emphasized, perhaps inspired by John Stuart Mill, we can easily reconstruct the physical capital of a nation if its structure of human resources is left untouched, but the opposite is not true.

In this connection, I would suggest that Professor Rahmeyer give special attention to the problems of developing countries. I believe that it is one of our tasks in this society to develop the consequences of Schumpeter's works for the challenges that confront the developing countries. I cannot accept that creative destruction would be taken literally as an answer to this question in the sense that development should entail the destruction of the developing countries in order to reinforce the position of the developed countries, although this seems sometimes to be the guiding principle in the solution of at least some issues in North–South relations. It is a one-sided intellectual satisfaction to find the negative correlation between the (relative) growth of prices and productivity and output growth, because the theory of economic development in Schumpeter's wake must give us the genealogical explanation of the stage at which the developed countries arrived that allowed them to generate this negative correlation. It seems to me absolutely essential in an evolutionary approach to inflation to inquire about the stages of inflation in their correlations to the stages of growth. From which stage is a country able to use productivity growth as an arm against inflation? At the present time, this is a crucial question. When Schumpeter wrote, the "third world" did not exist as an identifiable group of nations, and he was one of those men who think that realistic governments, intelligent men, and beautiful ladies have always the right to change, especially when the world changes.

The necessity for a theory of inflation

Professor Rahmeyer argues that a "general" theoretical explanation of inflation does not exist and that, on the contrary, there are competing approaches. He writes also that the Keynesian theory does not present an independent theory of inflation, because its central theme is a theory to explain the level of output and employment. Thereafter, Professor Rahmeyer provides us with a thoughtful summary of both theories – the monetarist and the structuralist.

Professor Rahmeyer himself points out very appropriately that, assuming full employment and full capacity utilization, the Keynesian theory of employment can be generalized or extended to a theory of inflation. This is a very felicitous interpretation of the Keynesian theory with regard to inflation, insofar as it does not share the view that Keynes is responsible for the contemporary explosion of inflation in many countries, because he released the tiger from jail and destroyed the awareness that the world is finite with his antirecession theories. First of all, as Professor Michio Morishima stresses, the *General Theory* was conceived to cure the British disease. Keynes was too relativist to construct universal theories. Second, as Professor F. A. Hayek, who is not exactly an admirer of Keynes, rightly points out, the author of the *General Theory* was aware of the inflationary risks of his constructions, as he recognized in conversation with Professor Hayek. But Keynes believed that such risks could materialize in the future, and when the situation became threatening, he would use his same ethic of persuasion to defend a nonexpansionist economic strategy. His unexpected death prevented him from changing his mind once again, but if we scrutinize his theory very accurately, we conclude that even in his antirecession emphasis, it was not inflationary at all. In fact, if we keep in mind the well-known Keynesian aggregate function, which is a backward L, we will remember that when there is idle capacity in the economy and a large number of unemployed workers, the increase in demand causes little or no rise at all in prices. The economy then responds by increasing production, not by higher prices. But if demand continues to expand, the economy will approach its full capacity. There will not be idle machines and workers, and the economy will be unable to satisfy further demand by producing more. The end result will be higher prices. At the full-employment level, further increases in demand generate inflation.

If we come back to the backward L, we can agree with Professor Rahmeyer that the main emphasis of the Keynesian theory is the segment *BA,* along which an increase in aggregate demand leads to an increase in real national product. But the chart has two movements; when the segment *BA* reaches the point of full employment, it turns up to form a backward L, in which the segment *AB* indicates that an increase in aggregate demand leads to inflation. Although we agree with Professor Rahmeyer's main argument, we must introduce the qualification that Keynes's emphasis on the segment *BA* was due to historical reasons, as pointed out earlier.

Like the Keynesian theory, which exhibits, as we have seen, two "movements" (to borrow a musical metaphor), the two visions of inflation Professor Rahmeyer discusses in his chapter are also different interpretations of the same "Inflation Symphony." To go along with the metaphor, we would say that monetarists and structuralists play the same symphony, but at different tempos. Schumpeter, once again, offers us a conciliation between the two approaches in his 1948 article (i.e., when the theories did not yet exist explicitly). His definition of inflation is predominantly monetarist: "We have inflation whenever means of payment increase more rapidly than the total output of goods and services" (1948, p. 34). From this general definition, he goes on to elaborate on the causes of inflation and the levels inflation may attain under the pressure of different factors. Like Keynes, once again, he is relativist and points out that measures to stop or to mitigate inflation differ according to the phase the process has reached. "Measures that promise success at a given moment" – he underlines – "may be futile a few months later."

As an experienced statesman, although for a very short period, he was aware that making structural adjustments takes a long time and that inflation makes public administration more costly. This is another paradox of inflation that he puts in a nutshell when he writes in the same article that curtailment of public expenditure is the most ortho-dox of all means to fight inflation, but it is also the most difficult to adopt because of the obstinate opposition it encounters, not compa-rable to that for any other measure, and because inflation fatally increases the cost of public administration.

Schumpeter ends, in the summary of that article, by yielding to the argument that it is not possible to stop inflation in its tracks without creating a depression that may be too much for the political system to withstand. In the face of this obstacle, he points out that it is possible to make the inflationary process die out, and in such a way as to avoid a depression of unbearable proportions.

After rejecting direct controls as futile, except as temporary mea-sures, and reduction in the quantity of money by Stalin's method or by a capital levy, he reinforces his case for credit restriction chiefly directed against consumers' credit and mortgage credit on housing, underlining that the best remedy for inflation is an increase in production.

Schumpeter's prudent recipe confirms a current saying in Latin America that a monetarist is a structuralist in a hurry, and a structur-alist is a monetarist without policy-making responsibility. In the wake of Schumpeter's evolutionary approach, we can endeavor to overcome the limitations of the structuralist school, which views inflation as stemming predominantly from exogenous factors, as well as we can avert the painful demand bloodshed of the monetarist school without an infusion of adjustments on the supply side.

The potential seeds of a third option lie in Schumpeter's works: education for innovation. Alternatively, there is an expression I would suggest to enrich the vocabulary of the evolutionary approach: monetary correction of human resources, the supreme form of quality innovation. We have been too much concerned with the quality of innovation of products and too prone to forget the source of innovation – human resources. When, in my country, indexation was abolished on the grounds that it was the cause of inertial inflation, I suggested replacing the former monetary correction by an age correction of human resources, a plan that I shall not discuss here, because it would go beyond the limits of this intervention. What I would like to stress, however, is the necessity for reassessment of the role of human resources in the field of invention and innovation. There is nothing new without new men, and the newness of men is not measured by age. I fully realize that it is difficult to measure human innovative abilities in economics, as would be desirable. This would be the subject of another paper, but I am convinced that it is essential to stress this point in dealing with the topic under analysis. The Federal Republic of Germany has achieved its present level of productivity, as underlined by Professor Rahmeyer, because of the innovational abilities of its human resources. I believe that Professor Rahmeyer's chapter would be particularly enriched if it devoted greater attention to this point, which is par excellence the source of productivity increases.

Inflation: an unfinished biography

In his summary of inflation theories, Professor Rahmeyer discusses a wide spectrum of causes of inflation. It is entirely understandable that within the limits of this chapter it would be very difficult to exhaust the subject. However, some causes that have been omitted for the sake of brevity should be included. One is the size of the public sector. It is well known that it is harder to curb inflation in an economy with a large public sector, because, among other reasons, the velocity of circulation of money is higher in the public sector, which, furthermore, is a powerful lobby in opposing cuts in public spending. This is an antagonism inside the state that confronts democracy with bureaucracy and does not always achieve a final decision in favor of greater productivity. Although the discussion of the causes of inflation in Professor Rahmeyer's chapter must necessarily be succinct, I also believe that an evolutionary approach to inflation in Schumpeter's wake must encompass genealogical analysis (i.e., the stages through which an economy consolidates the bridge between anti-inflation strategies and productivity growth). This point is of prime importance with regard to the implications of Schumpeter's theory of economic development for developing countries. In this connection, I would enthusiastically encourage Professor Rahmeyer to enlarge on his theoretical biography of inflation, because its end is still far from being in sight, at least in many developing countries, and I am convinced that one of the main tasks of this society is to develop new analyses of Schumpeter's works from the viewpoint of the developing countries. When he wrote, the third world did not exist as such, and only by the end of his life did some hints of the problems of development of the new emergent nations start cropping up as theoretical concerns. In my view, it would be an amputation of Schumpeter's magnificent constructions to circumscribe them exclusively to the developed world.

Incidentally, Professor Rahmeyer observes in his chapter that the differentiation of the national economy into sectors with competitive and with administered pricing is well to the fore of a structural theory of inflation. In actual fact, the environment of his chapter is predominantly a "fixprice" environment, despite the rather structuralist character of the chapter. I think that the two-sided structuralist vision of the national economy could have been a good point of departure for Professor Rahmeyer's inclusion of the case of the developing countries, especially if we take into account that developed countries are predominantly "fixprice" and developing countries have, at least, larger layers of "flexprice zones" that offer substantial room for international comparisons in productivity gains.

At the present time, my country, Brazil, a developing nation, offers a counterexample to the last part of Professor Rahmeyer's statement that the inflation rate also depends on the expected rate of inflation, "which is likely to change only slowly over time." Here, there is the basis for what could be regarded as a missing chapter in *Capitalism, Socialism and Democracy,* concerning developing countries. In fact, Brazil succeeded in dropping from an inflation rate of 15 percent per month in February to less than 1 percent in August, by creating a new currency in the country and thus reversing expectations. The political marketing of the operation was remarkably successful, and its apparently miraculous character owes a lot to the expectations that followed the transition from authoritarian to democratic rule. An important element was that the introduction of the new currency was accompanied by a price freeze and price controls supervised by the population itself, in a spontaneous form of democratic sanction. We do not discount the fact that problems still may be in the offing, especially those related to shortages. But the success over the last few months substantiates our contention that developing countries have a consistent contribution to offer to the evolutionary approach we are dealing with here. In the Brazilian case, I believe that the next challenge to be overcome has much to do with the real sector, an area that I would have liked to see developed more in Professor Rahmeyer's chapter. The symbol-based economy has been an admirable contribution to economics, especially with the features the Keynesian theory gave it. It is an excellent start for a battle against inflation and for productivity, but it is not self-sufficient; it needs support from the "things-based economy."

Furthermore, I would like to add some points to Professor Rahmeyer's unfinished biography of inflation. It is a well-known epistemological obstacle to deal with the reasons why things do not happen. Apparently, we have the same economic instruments at the disposal of the developed and the developing countries, but they fail very often in the latter. If we go further in this direction, we will be confronted with the problem of the "efficiency of inflation," which has been accurately discussed by Thirlwall and Barton (1971) on the basis of an in-depth empirical study. In their conclusion, they point out that the poorer the country, the lower the growth–inflation ratio. In the period 1954–68, we have the following ratios for some countries: Germany, 2.38 percent; United Kingdom, 0.96 percent; United States, 1.81 percent; Japan, 2.78 percent.

These observations lead us into an inevitable assessment of the international constraints imposed on the relationship between inflation and productivity growth on the domestic scene. As Professor Thirlwall points out, when the alliance of inflation with growth has good domestic conditions in which to operate, the only potential threat to growth from inflation comes from the balance of payments if foreign exchange is a scarce resource. But if all countries are inflating, or if foreign exchange is not particularly scarce, the balance-of-payments worries of an inflation are less serious (Thirlwall and Barton, 1971, p. 72).

In an evolutionary approach to inflation, such as we are taking now, international economic rhythms should not be neglected. In Brazil, a developing country, the fight against inflation that succeeded in the middle of the sixties did take into account domestic productivity factors in line with the international environment. For instance, the wage policy had as a basic principle readjustments by the average, not by the peaks, plus an increase in labor productivity. Favorable international conditions, coupled with a rational recipe to fight inflation, paved the way for the "Brazilian miracle." But the success was not to last, first, as I pointed out in my thesis (Valentino, 1979), because of the insufficiency of consensual elements in the pact between growth and inflation, which I termed "growthflation," and, second, because international conditions changed adversely.

On the other hand, in dealing with inflation in developing countries, although not advocating it as a recipe for development, we must inquire whether or not it plays, when its level is moderate, the role that Marxists attach to "primitive accumulation," as a prerequisite of development. I devoted great attention to this phenomenon in my thesis on the Brazilian "growthflation." My regressions have shown that it would be false or premature, to say the least, to argue that inflation has been the source of growth in Brazil in the so-called miracle years (1968–73). When I mention growth in this case, I include productivity growth, because it did occur in the country in those years. In fact, the phenomenon that I termed "growthflation" was present at the launching of the "drive to maturity" in Brazil and at the "miracle years," but it was not their cause, although it had been present at their origin. As a consequence, we are confronted with different stages of the evolutionary approach to inflation, and at some of them, moderate inflation, oddly enough, may be an ally of productivity growth. I would not expect Professor Rahmeyer to exhaust the analysis of all these additional aspects I mention, as someone who has studied economic theory in the developed world and lives it now in the developing world. But even from the angle of the developed world, I think the study of the roles of the state and of the tertiary sector in productivity growth should be expanded somewhat.

By way of conclusion, I wish to stress the merits and the dangers of the evolutionary approach by suggesting that Professor Rahmeyer, in future developments of his provocative theory, draw inspiration from the remarkable book by Professors Richard R. Nelson and Sidney G. Winter (1982), which deservedly has often been quoted at this seminar; the chapter I suggest is 16 ("The Evolution of Public Policies and the Role of Analysis"), and the development I would add would be an analysis of mechanisms and actors of inflation in the light of the model provided by the book. This would save the study of inflation from the temptation of a compelling evolutionism that would impose solutions not transferable from one country to another, especially from developed to developing countries, and would avoid the opposite radical temptation to neglect the lessons of history that are impossible to neglect.

I must apologize for having taken so long, but it was for lack of time to be brief. I believe that the rule of my namesake (Valentino, the couturier) for skirts is the best rule for speeches too: to be long enough to cover the matter and short enough to be interesting. With inflation, however, it happens that the longer they are, the more exciting they become to theoreticians, and the more disastrous to people they affect.

References

Lewis, Arthur W. (1972). *Theory of Economic Growth*. London: George Allen & Unwin.

Nelson, R. R., and Winter, S. C. (1982). *An Evolutionary Theory of Economic Change*. Cambridge, Mass.: Harvard University Press.

Schumpeter, Joseph A. [1912] (1974). *The Theory of Economic Development* (translated from the 2nd German edition). London: Oxford University Press.

(1948). "There Is Still Time to Stop Inflation." *Nation's Business*, 36(June):33–5, 88–91.

Thirlwall, A. P., and Barton, C. A. (1971). "Inflation and Growth – The International Evidence." *Banca Nazionale del Lavoro Quarterly Review*, 98(September):263–75.

Valentino, Raphael (1979). *Growth with Inflation in Brazil (1968–1973): Its Causes, Origins and Consequences*. University of London, Institute of Latin American Studies.

Discussion

ROLF-DIETER POSTLEP

The approach in Dr. Rahmeyer's chapter refers to *elements of an economic theory of evolution*, on the one hand, and, on the other hand, attempts to connect the macroeconomic phenomenon of inflation and the microeconomic analysis of firm behavior, especially by including *economic structure*. Both conceptional starting points characterize a promising way to enrich inflation theory. An evolutionary analysis that examines the conditions of growth and change in the economy seems advantageous in explaining a long-term economic phenomenon like long-term inflation. The structural approach permits incorporation of the differences between economic segments in productivity movements, price levels, and so forth, that necessarily are hidden in macroeconomic analysis.

The microeconomic and structural arguments in the chapter concentrate on the industrial sector as such and especially on that part where large-scale enterprises are regarded as dominating. Of course, it is always a problem to discuss a nationwide economic problem like inflation by focusing on one (though important) sector of the economy. Some remarks concerning this point will be made later, after the approach itself has been discussed.

Comments on the given model

As representative firm behavior, "a routine application of established rules" is assumed. "Firms satisfice instead of maximizing." This implies a cost orientation to pricing policy complemented by a markup to ensure long-term firm growth. Short-term deviations of actual demand from expected demand are adjusted to by variation of current output. When long-term changes occur, production capacity is increased or decreased. According to this microeconomic approach, a firm or a segment of industry can grow (1) if demand increases, either exogenously caused (rising income, etc.) or self-induced (product innovation, advertising), or (2) if the firm's cost situation improves relative to that of competitors. This can occur especially through productivity increases (above all, process innovations), and to a lesser degree through reduction of input prices, especially wages. Wages vary less between firms or economic sectors than does productivity.

Inflation is explained conceptually by referring to the existence of (adaptive) inflationary expectations and the wage–price spiral. Wage increases, if they do not differ substantially between segments of industry, can be absorbed, though to differing degrees, through productivity increases. Such increases lead to different price reactions, if a cost-oriented price policy is assumed. Sectors with above-average productivity grow because they attract demand through their improved relative prices, and the reverse is true for segments with low productivity. The conclusion is drawn that "the overall economic price level will increase if firms or industries with above-average productivity growth do not (relatively) reduce their prices proportionately, but instead use it to allow additional wage or profit increases, whereas sectors with below-average productivity growth are forced to (relatively) raise their prices (or, alternatively, to reduce sales, output, and employment), because wages increase to about the same extent in all economic sectors."

Two questions might be asked with respect to this "productivity inflation" approach:

1. Is the microeconomic assumption of "routine behavior" *a necessary condition* in the framework of the approach presented? To put

it differently: Could not the same macroeconomic conclusions, based on the wage–price spiral and the adaptation of inflationary expectations, also be gained under the assumption of profit-maximizing behavior?

The principle of "routine behavior" describes an empirically observable type of business behavior that has to be analyzed in its macroeconomic inflationary effects. In principle, only that price or markup can be realized that is allowed by demand. If the price set for the desired quantity of production is too high, production has to be reduced, and in the extreme, a retreat from the market becomes necessary. But this conclusion applies to profit-maximizing behavior as well as to markup behavior. Under both behavioral assumptions, a cost increase leads to the desired level of output only if monetary demand increases correspondingly. If the latter remains constant, a selection among producers takes place in both cases.

2. The second question, still arguing within the confines of the approach: Do differences in productivity developments among economic sectors, combined with increasing wage cost (which in the industrial sector accounts for only a quarter of the overall cost), *have to* result in inflation? One can also consider (and observe empirically) price reductions occurring in some sectors, while price increases and stable prices occur in other sectors, so that, on the average, the price level might remain constant. Under the assumption of a cost-oriented price policy, inflationary processes can be explained only if downward price inflexibility can be assumed in those segments where productivity increases are greater than wage increases. To explain such behavior, a separate theoretical approach is necessary, as the chapter indicates. One could think of oligopolistic markets, where price reductions could be understood as a signal for a price struggle. One could also give up the assumption of a strictly cost-oriented price policy and assume price adaptation to increasing demand in these segments.

In addition to these theoretical points, one might refer to some empirical observations. There have always been price reductions in some economic sectors, but on the whole inflation came out arithmetically, because the weighted price increases were higher than the weighted price reductions. But this picture can change, as seen in the recent past in the Federal Republic of Germany. Structural differences in the dynamics of development, thus, are compatible with differing movements of the overall price level. From this it follows that some reference is necessary to a specific historical situation and the relevant economic conditions given at that time (productivity development of the different economic sectors, wage development, monetary policy, etc.). That way, the structural approach can more easily be given empirical relevance.

Inclusion of the nonindustrial economic sector

The theoretical and empirical considerations in the chapter by Rahmeyer are explicitly restricted to the secondary sector (industry). This means that the approach explicitly is based on only one sector of the economy. Industry is still of the greatest importance, but might lose further momentum if the three-sector hypothesis holds; and it has lost importance in the past, as the empirical results show. This leads to the question to what degree the microeconomic approach and the structural and macroeconomic consequences can still be taken as a basis, if the nonindustrial sector is incorporated.

If only the *firm policy* is analyzed, several considerations might follow:

1. In transportation (as well as in electricity production, which is part of the secondary sector) there are many *public enterprises.* They set their prices according to different rules and may also take into account targets like employment or national-safety interest.
2. In contrast to the industrial sector, in the tertiary sector relatively *small-scale enterprises* dominate. Their pricing behavior may be different again, and the same is true of the *professions* that are often allowed to ask legally approved fees.

The *characterization of structure* also has to be modified if the nonindustrial segments of the economy are to be included. For the industrial sector as such, growth industries are characterized by an increase in demand, by high rates of productivity growth, and by relatively low price increases. As to the tertiary sector, different features apply:

1. The demand for services increases; thus, they are to be regarded as a growth sector.
2. Productivity growth rates are relatively low; in the industrial sector this characterizes a stagnating branch.
3. Price increases are relatively strong, which in the industrial sector is also typical of a stagnating branch.

This picture differs from that of the industrial sector. As the demand increase seems to be greater than the negative effect of low productivity growth, this sector enlarges its part in the economy, so that the explanation of the national rate of inflation can less and less rely on the industrial sector alone.

The role of the money supply

In Rahmeyer's chapter, it is implicitly assumed that the money supply increases endogenously to the necessary degree so that inflation can be financed without a decline in employment. But, of course, the policy of the central bank must be considered separately. If the central bank tries to increase the money supply only by the expected rate of real-output growth, as has occurred in the recent past in the Federal Republic of Germany, a long-run inflation seems to be improbable. Thus, it is necessary to take into consideration to what extent the central-bank policy and the economic policy of the government are balanced out. Even if one is not inclined to regard increases in the quantity of money as the *conditio sine quam* in the framework of explanations of inflation, it cannot be denied that in any case it is a *conditio sine qua non*.

Looking at the chapter in an overall perspective, it points convincingly to the central role that overall economic productivity development and the contributions of the different economic sectors should play in the analysis of long-term inflation. Thereby, a link is established between growth and inflation. It could be a matter of further investigation to find out how far the approach can be extended to take into account the question why, in the long run, the average productivity growth could decline. Together with increasing cost pressure, or with increasing claims to GNP, a slowdown in productivity growth indeed generates an inflationary potential.

The chapter is a promising starting point for trying to explain inflation in an evolutionary perspective, and further steps in this direction should certainly be encouraged.

CHAPTER 8

Fiscal pressure on the "tax state"

HORST ZIMMERMANN

8.1 Schumpeter's "Crisis of the Tax State" as a reference point

Joseph Schumpeter's article in 1918 on "The Crisis of the Tax State" ([1918] 1954) was written for a particular reason at a particular point in time. Partly it was an answer to Rudolf Goldscheid's contention that the tax-financed capitalist state could not levy sufficient taxes to cover its necessary expenditures and therefore would incur increasingly higher debt, which would then lead to fiscal crisis (Goldscheid, [1917] 1976). As the financing of World War I had left very high indebtedness, such a scenario could be considered imminent in 1918. Schumpeter devoted much of his effort to showing that the fiscal consequences of the war could be handled by the tax state. The fact that the major tax states survived the transition after two world wars proves that his conclusion was correct, and therefore this issue is not dealt with here.[1]

"The Crisis of the Tax State," although it takes up important issues of the period, also contains generalizing sections. In the latter, a fiscal crisis is defined, a historical crisis is described in detail, and some ideas are presented as to what a future crisis might be like. These are discussed here.

A fiscal crisis, as Schumpeter viewed it, occurs when the available types of revenue become permanently insufficient to finance the level of expenditure considered necessary. This conclusion can be inferred from his example, which describes the transition in Austria and Germany from dues to taxes as the main source of revenue (Schumpeter, [1918] 1954, pp. 8–16).

According to Schumpeter's interpretation, the expenditure needs of the princes in those countries grew rapidly from the fourteenth to the

This chapter was written during a sabbatical term at the Department of Geography of the University of Cambridge in the spring of 1986. The support of the Department of Geography and of Deutsch Forschungsgemeinschaft is gratefully acknowledged.

[1] The Marxist interpretation of fiscal crisis (especially by O'Connor, 1973) and a critique of it have been discussed earlier (Musgrave, 1980, pp. 361–81).

255

sixteenth centuries. One reason was that courts were increased in size in order to tie the increasingly independent country nobility to the court. The main reason was the rising cost of warfare, as mercenary armies became necessary to keep the country nobility in line and to meet the threat of the larger armies fielded by the invading Turks. Thus, the changing structure of society and external forces raised the level of expenditure that was regarded as unavoidable.

The existing sources of revenue – dues from the prince's peasant-serfs, regalia from mint, market, mining, and so forth, with taxes in some towns being an exception – were insufficient to finance this expenditure. Because the forces behind this change were both deep-rooted and permanent, this change should be seen as a crisis of the financial system as such (Schumpeter, [1918] 1954, p. 14), not just a transitory failure due to mismanagement. The crisis was surmounted when, after an interim period of large indebtedness, taxes were established as a new form of revenue. In its later stage, the feudal state thus underwent fiscal pressure because it had not found access to a new type of revenue out of the same GNP. Wherever taxes had been levied already, this new way of making claims on the GNP proved to be successful in fiscal terms and apparently did not put an unbearable burden on the GNP.

This leads to the conclusion that it is not the higher level of expenditure that is crucial in the definition of a crisis, but the temporary lack of an adequate type or technique of revenue. Thus, if a present-day state, in which the public sector is mainly financed by taxes, were to experience a fiscal crisis, this would mean that the amount of necessary expenditure would be regarded as given and would not be decided simultaneously.

The amount of expenditure may be thought of as determined by general consensus, as it has been, a posteriori, presumed to be for social policy until about 1975 (Halberstadt, 1918, p. 30). If taxes do not yield enough revenue to finance these expenditures, this then seems to imply that the type of fiscal crisis described earlier exists or is imminent. The welfare state as being "in the most immediate sense of limit" in crisis because of "a limit in what can be raised in taxation" for this purpose (Glazer, 1981, p. 240) seemingly fits this pattern.

8.2   Fiscal pressure on the tax state

8.2.1   *The notion of fiscal pressure*

For certain more recent types of fiscal problems in tax-financed high-income countries, it is difficult, if not impossible, to separate the pressures due to an exhausted type of revenue (taxes) from the pressures that result from the total of all revenues. Several people have argued that public budgets have increased the amount of public withdrawals from GNP to levels difficult to sustain (Glazer, 1981, p. 240; Halberstadt, 1981, p. 29; Thurow, 1980, chap. 1). An OECD discussion (1981) of the welfare state in crisis ascribes much of the cause to the sum of public (or publicly induced private) flows that the different policies absorb. The typical tax-financed state is seen as facing lasting fiscal problems.

The first question, then, might be whether or not this again constitutes a fiscal crisis. It appears, however, as if all important basic forms of public access to GNP are already in use. Therefore, if taxes are regarded as too high, other existent types of revenue can hardly be drawn on to finance major shares of public expenditure.

Fees and charges,[2] technically, can be applied to only some public services, because of the public-goods character of the other services, and even there, applicable fees often are limited by contravening objectives; some reserves, though, may still be found here (see Section 8.4). Certainly, prices for market goods are no way out; direct participation of the state in the production of private goods increases rather than alleviates the need for budgetary revenue, as the history of nationalized industries shows. Public debt is, in the long run, determined by the fiscal capacity to carry debt service, which itself is related to future tax revenue. Central-bank financing is limited again by contravening objectives, especially the desire to prevent inflation.

This list of possible sources of revenue is drawn up for a market-oriented economy. Different forms of access to GNP exist in non-market-oriented economic systems. But there, "public," "private," and "tax" no longer have the same meanings, and possibly no discernible meaning at all. The inclusion of such economic systems involves more than a discussion of sources of public revenue and is therefore not pursued here, although such a wider discussion certainly was intended by Schumpeter. He tied the tax state to private enterprise ([1918] 1954, p. 38), and later the income tax in particular to a competitive economic system ([1929–30] 1985, p. 120). In general, he saw a particular type of revenue as tied to a particular organization of society (Andic and Andic, 1985, p. 460). Whether or not and when a society might be "growing beyond private enterprise and tax state" (Schumpeter, [1918] 1954, p. 38) will not be pondered here, the more as such a Schumpe-

---

[2] Social security contributions contain elements of taxes and of insurance premiums, depending on the degree to which contributions and receipts correspond by insurance standards.

terian crisis cannot occur "so long as remedies can be found within the system" ([1918] 1954, p. 13). The following considerations are based on the assumption that the observed fiscal problems, although of a new kind, are not caused by a transformation of the economic system and thus can be tackled by adjustments within the system.

The new quality of the fiscal problem arises from the fact that because new sources of public revenue from given GNP apparently are not to be found, the effects of a high level of taxes and the effects of a high level of expenditure can no longer be separated. The situation is similar to that which Schumpeter described for the late middle ages insofar as the necessary level of expenditure is suddenly difficult to finance. In the earlier situation, a new type of revenue was found, and the tax state was created, whereas now it seems difficult to envisage a state financed predominantly by any new source of revenue.

Instead, the fiscal problems seem to originate in a context shaped by the size of public withdrawals from GNP, by the technique of these withdrawals (the revenue structure), and by the effects of public revenues and expenditures on GNP (and thus on future revenue). Taxes, as one type of revenue, play an important but only partial role. Because no change in the economic system is considered here, nor is the tax the only object of the fiscal problem, Schumpeter's term "fiscal crisis" should be eschewed; instead, the term "fiscal pressure" is used.

It is difficult (and I do not attempt it here) to define "fiscal pressure" in precise terms (i.e., as a dependent variable in an explanatory model).[3] It is sufficient for the present to assume that the difficulties in financing the volume of expenditures existing in many high-income countries are increasing.

8.2.2   Formation of fiscal pressure

If we agree that fiscal pressure exists, the first question is why it has not occurred earlier. The fact that lasting fiscal pressure on the tax state has occurred only recently has been attributed to slow (or even negative) economic growth and thus revenue growth (Halberstadt, 1981, p.

---

[3] In his comment on this chapter, H.-D. Wenzel points to possibilities of measuring fiscal pressure explicitly. If it were defined as a situation in which budget-induced marginal GNP became negative, this would first have to be based on knowledge of the effects of the total budget on GNP, which was not intended as part of this chapter. Second, and possibly more important, one would have to know the amount of "necessary" expenditure at that future point in time, because that figure, compared with obtainable revenue, must enter any definition of fiscal pressure. Third, the direct (i.e., non-growth-related) effects of the budget on future taxes are omitted, if fiscal pressure is seen only in relation to GNP.

30; Thurow, 1980, chap. 1). One consequence would be more distributional struggle in a "zero-sum society" (Thurow, 1980). This means that it is not the absolute size of the public budget nor the rate of increase alone that brings about fiscal pressure, but the relation of the budget to GNP. First, as long as revenue rises as GNP rises, additional expenditure can be financed without increasing tax rates and/or raising new taxes. Rising expenditure need not increase the "burden" on GNP, expressed as share of revenue in GNP. Second, growth in GNP for a long time also seemed to allow (or at least to ease) increases in the tax burden. They became necessary because the additional expenditure automatically made possible through economic growth apparently was not considered sufficient. Higher tax burdens were therefore imposed, for instance, by increasing tax rates and rate escalation ("bracket creep").

When lower growth rates produced less revenue, tax-rate increases could, of course, have prevented expenditure cuts.[4] However, not only were rate increases opposed, but instead tax cuts were advocated and often made. It may have been about the time of the recession in 1975 that a need was recognized to consider the amount and technique of public withdrawals from GNP and the relation of the budget to growth. Such a reassessment of total fiscal activity was the more warranted because public budgets had, over the decades, become large with respect to GNP, so that their effects on GNP had to be great.

Large revenue constitutes a burden on the economy, but can be thought of, in the long run, as being offset and consequently justified by a higher contribution to growth through the expenditure side, thus financing the necessary additional revenue. There are indications, however, that these budgetary effects are, on the whole, probably less GNP-enhancing than in the earlier period. Thus, additional taxes are less justifiable by additional expenditures (and their growth effects), and this also holds for a retained budget level in times of negative growth rates. Even more important is the fact that future GNP determines, with a given revenue structure, future revenues.[5] Consequently, less growth inducement per average budget dollar increases the tendency to future fiscal pressure.

---

[4] Deficit spending would have been appropriate only to the degree that a lack in aggregate demand was considered the underlying reason for the unsatisfactory economic performance.

[5] GNP serves two purposes here. First, it measures economic growth, and in that function it reacts to budgetary effects. Second, it is a broad indicator for that part of economic activity that forms the base for taxes, especially the income tax, omitting the shadow economy. As to the relation among national accounting, shadow economy, and tax base, see Feige (1985).

In this context, the following part of the chapter addresses only one particular question: Along which paths, which may or may not work through future GNP, has the public budget during the last two or three decades affected its own future revenues (mainly taxes)?[6] To the degree that such effects, some of which may be positive and others negative, do exist (in the sense of a feedback), the tax state itself increases or decreases the chances for the fiscal pressure it may undergo.[7]

The presumption that a budget can and should have such effects on economic objectives would have been farfetched at a time when the main objective of tax policy was to raise revenue. As these effects emanate from all elements of a budget, we have to trace possible contributions of budgetary policy to fiscal pressure on the tax state not to taxes alone but to all types of revenue and expenditure.

8.3   Budget-induced effects on future tax revenue

8.3.1   Types of effects

The budget-induced effects on future revenue, mainly taxes, can be divided into two groups: those influencing economic growth and those that are independent of growth.

Direct effects (independent of growth): There are several direct relations between current expenditures or revenues and the future tax revenue (from given tax bases):

1.   Irrespective of any reaction of taxpayers, the tax base is

---

[6] A much wider view is indicated in R. A. Musgrave's discussion of this chapter. In an ideal case, a budget increase would be self-financing. To estimate this empirically, one would have to specify the contribution of each budget item on growth numerically, which would not be possible given the state of the art in this field. But such a self-financing budget expansion could serve as a very useful reference point, if fiscal pressure were to be analyzed theoretically in a rigorous fashion. Then, it would, in addition, be necessary to include the "direct" effects (see Section 9.3.1), because they also determine the possible occurrence of fiscal pressure (see footnote 3). Any such reference point, where the budget increase would be harmless in its effect on GNP, could also be taken as a thought of, but unknown, reference point of this chapter, if one assumes that "we may be moving away from it" (R. A. Musgrave, in the oral presentation of his discussion), because the effects of the changes in size and structure of the budget on future GNP and thus revenue are the focus of the following section of this chapter as far as the "indirect" effects are concerned.

[7] The resulting contributions to fiscal pressure can, in addition, be divided into those resulting from government actions (particular taxes and expenditures) and those due to outside influences (changing age structure).

affected. If, for instance, pensions are taxed when the contributions are made, then an aging population will yield less tax revenue in the future.

2. The taxpayer reacts to budgetary influences by giving up taxable activities or by engaging in expenditure-attracting activities. For instance, reducing the hours of work because of rate escalation and dropping out of the labor force in order to receive unemployment benefits are examples.

3. Finally, taxpayers can change their activities to similar activities that avoid taxation or attract expenditures, such as a transition to the shadow economy. The difference from item 2 can be seen in the effect on GNP versus aggregated welfare aspects. If an activity is given up entirely, the goods or services are not produced at all. If the activity is only transferred to the shadow economy, the country may be equally well off, but measured GNP will be reduced, and so will public revenue.

Indirect effects (through economic growth): If GNP determines public revenue to a major degree (with given tax laws), and if the public budget strongly influences GNP growth, then the government itself produces some of the factors that may contribute to fiscal pressure. Methodologically this is more difficult to assess, because the effects on revenue through growth have to be evaluated against all the factors that induce economic growth.

Empirical efforts to break down growth by contributing factors seem not to have incorporated public-sector effects on the private sector directly (Denison, 1979, pp. 2, 91–121; Kendrick, 1981), but they appear among the further possible influences behind the unexplained share of growth (Denison, 1979, pp. 127–33). In addition, we can draw on the literature concerning the effects of individual budgetary activities on individual factors related to growth. However, no final conclusions can be drawn, because other growth-relevant factors were left out, not least the nonbudgetary public activities such as (de)regulation.

This view of budgetary effects on growth, based on effects on future revenue, is narrow in the sense that expenditures and revenues are examined only as to their "productive" effects on GNP. Many aspects of "efficiency" are thereby left out.[8] But if GNP matters for the fiscal pressure on the tax state, this may seem warranted.

With these different types of effects in mind, expenditures and rev-

---

[8] For a wider perspective on efficiency, for which "the loss of GNP is not the proper measure of social cost," see Musgrave (1985, p. 263).

enues are briefly reviewed. Much of this review is in terms of hypotheses and should be regarded as a way of thinking about these relationships, rather than as a quantitative appraisal.

8.3.2   Revenue effects of public expenditures

For the budget[9] to produce positive effects on growth, expenditures have to exert a noticeable positive effect, because revenues, though they may have some incentive effects (e.g., through income reduction and growth-targeted tax expenditures), usually produce disincentive effects. Among expenditures, transfers to individuals and to business and expenditures for purchases and personnel are useful to examine because of differing impacts.

Transfer payments:[10] Transfers to individuals and families or equivalent tax expenditures are given for children's support, income maintenance, old age and disability, and so forth, and usually are not aimed at strengthening growth. Exceptions are, for instance, income-maintenance payments during periods of qualifying for other jobs. Otherwise, these payments are, at best, neutral to growth,[11] and the literature on the pertinent effects therefore deals with "disincentives" to, for instance, labor-force participation and saving.

Among these transfers, those to support people after their working lives (for age or disability) are large and (in Germany certainly) of heavily increasing weight. It is therefore important that payments for these purposes have less disincentive effects compared with many other budget items (Okun, 1975, p. 107). A recent survey of previous studies (Atkinson, 1985, pp. 168–76) has shown that there are marked effects on retirement age (Aaron, 1982), which, however, may be politically desirable as long as high unemployment exists, and can be growth-relevant insofar as the shrinking of unproductive industries is

---

[9] As the total budgetary effect on GNP is under discussion here, the budgets of all layers of government and the social security systems should be included.

[10] Only transfers to the private sector are discussed here. The effects of intergovernmental transfers on growth have been dealt with before (Zimmermann, 1983).

[11] It is also argued that they help to keep the social peace and thus form an indirect prerequisite to growth. This may very probably be assumed for early stages of the welfare state. For additional expenditures on top of an already considerable level, the validity of the assertion would have to show up in a correlation between the amount of such transfers (per capita or in relation to GNP) and some indicator for social (un)rest, for instance, frequency of strikes or votes for radical parties.

eased and the younger people tend to be more productive than the retirees. The effects on savings are thought to be significant by some authors, and negligible by others (Atkinson, 1985, pp. 195–204), and the disincentives to work appear to be rather low.

Similar considerations probably apply to public expenditure for children's support. In Germany, it might appear that the increasing expenditure for old age is almost equaled by decreasing expenditure for the younger generation. However, this does not reduce the potential for fiscal pressure very much. This "cost of the younger generation" is still borne to a large degree privately (Wissenschaftlicher Beirat für Familienfragen, 1979) and thus does not lead to disincentives to work, to save, and so forth. Therefore, its reduction does not alleviate the need for that public revenue necessary to finance the large non-benefit-related part of German pensions.

Besides effects through growth, there are also direct effects of old-age support on future public revenue. They occur through taxability of contributions and/or pensions. For equity reasons, either contributions or pensions should be taxed, so that this income flow is, in the end, fully taxed, as any other income is. At what point in time it is taxed is important for the flow of tax revenue over time (Wissenschaftlicher Beirat beim Bundesministerium der Finanzen, 1986, pp. 63–5). If fiscal pressure is estimated to be higher in the future, at least within this segment of budgetary policy (including the social security systems), then taxation should occur when pensions are received.

The second large group of transfers to individuals is made up of income maintenance, including welfare and unemployment payments. In addition to a possible effect on savings, the influence on labor supply is important here. These effects are to be considered even in times of widespread unemployment in the economy as a whole, because there are always sectoral and regional segments of the labor market in which labor supply is less than satisfactory and constitutes a growth bottleneck. The closer an economy moves to full employment, the more often these cases occur. Empirical evidence shows that some disincentives to work may exist, but their size probably depends very much on the design of the system, like marginal withholding, duration of benefits, and so forth (Danziger, Haveman, and Plotnick, 1981, pp. 995–9), so that existing disincentives could be widely reduced.

Payments and tax expenditures for business and agriculture also have to be examined. Most of them are long-term subsidy programs, which tend to reduce the necessary changes from old to new forms of production and the movement away from sectors of the economy that need not be as large as they are, like agriculture.[12] This leads to direct effects on future revenue, because subsidized sectors usually produce less than average tax revenue. At the same time, this is part of the opportunity cost of forgone growth that might have been achieved if the change had been encouraged, particularly during periods of full or nearly full employment.

Similarly, there have been some payments, especially tax concessions, extended to business, particularly over recent years, that may have been conducive to growth. Without trying to gauge their effectiveness (many of these payments may merely have substituted for private funds), it suffices to say that, at least in Germany, their positive effects could hardly compensate for the growth-obstructing effects of the major part of the transfers to business and agriculture.

Expenditures for purchases and personnel: Public purchases and employment exert influences on growth in two ways. First, the expenditure induces income that appears in GNP; a similar effect would have occurred if the money had been left with the private sector and spent there. Second, and primarily, the expenditure is made for public-service functions like transportation and education, and growth considerations have to be related to the policy fields that make large use of public purchases and personnel. This is certainly not the place to consider extensively the growth contributions of all publicly provided goods and services, but some tendencies should be pointed out:

1. Social policy (including social insurance systems) accounts for a probably increasing share of purchases and investment, for instance, to public financing of old people's homes, and certainly of personnel, because many social services are highly personnel-intensive. What holds for transfers and growth also applies to this share of purchases and personnel.
2. Defense, as another major part of many budgets, has some growth-promoting side effects, but they probably are not large relative to the sizes and effects of other expenditures.
3. Education expenditures as percentages of GDP have increased over the past 20 years in many countries (OECD, 1985, pp.

---

[12] In the Federal Republic of Germany, only 15 percent of federal subsidies and tax concessions in 1986 were specified as growth-oriented, the rest being meant for "adjustment" or openly for "preservation" (Bericht der Bundesregierung über die Entwicklung der Finanzhilfen, 1985, p. 31), though political pressure is already leading toward shifting as much as possible to the more acceptable heading of growth orientation.

48–52). Considering the qualitative demand that structural change in the economy exerts on the labor market, much of this outlay may prove to be a growth prerequisite. The expansion of education in Germany since the 1960s has provided more people with formal education and created a better-educated middle tier of the work force,[13] which can more easily cope with structural change.

4. Physical infrastructure with (often regional) growth effects probably has been reduced as a share in the budget. Certainly, in Germany, the decreasing share of investment in public expenditure can be taken as a symptom (from 11.6 percent in 1976 to 8.3 percent in 1985) (Bundesministerium der Finanzen, 1981, p. 18; 1986, p. 68).

8.3.3   Revenue effects of public revenues

Public revenues, if taken by themselves, always tend to reduce growth, because they withdraw funds from the private sector. Taxes are the most important source.[14] They include, here, social security contributions from employers as well as from employees. Only insofar as these contributions correspond directly, in the sense of an insurance premium, to later individual receipts and are perceived that way will the negative aspects disappear, but this has been increasingly less the case over time.

The direct effects on future revenues are most important, meaning that through the taxation process itself, future revenue is impaired. These effects result from two types of adjustments in the private sector, as mentioned in Section 8.2.1.

First, if a tax is raised (or an existing tax is perceived as a greater burden than before), this may lead to avoidance of part or all of the taxed activity, thus resulting in diminished revenue. Examples include a reduction in the purchase of goods following taxation of these goods, and a reduction in working hours because of income taxation. These effects, given the same structure of the tax system, possibly have become more acute with higher tax burdens, in particular when taxes are progressive and lead to high marginal rates.

---

[13] The lower tier is made up of the "dual system" of apprenticeship and vocational schools, and the higher tier of university education, both of which had been important before.

[14] Tax expenditures were already included in the discussion of expenditures, which they often resemble in their effects.

Second, taxed activity may be transferred to the untaxed sectors, such as household production or the more or less illegal segments of the invisible economy. For the private household, the underlying wedge can be expressed in the difference in incomes before and after taxes, and this is especially important in situations where taxed and untaxed income elements, as well as uses of time, exist side by side.

To show how far-reaching this case is, examples may be most useful if they do not come from the well-researched core area of the "shadow economy" (for a recent overview, see Schneider, 1986), but rather fall in the difficult borderline area between the shadow economy and true household production. This particular borderline with the private sphere probably will always be respected by the fisc, so that activity that is transferred there is definitely lost for taxation. The borderline is clearly crossed when market services are replaced by do-it-yourself activity, as in many areas of house maintenance. Often, however, it is not a full service that is substituted, but some element for which the private household can use its own time as input: furniture and equipment delivered unassembled, or a longer trip to reach the large cash-and-carry establishment (which can thus utilize economies of scale) instead of buying from the shop at the next corner. Only the working time contained in the market price is taxed, whereas the customer's time enters the final product untaxed. The cost that has to be charged for an hour of work in the market, if full cost is to be passed on in the price of a service or a good, includes, among other items, the pre-tax income of employees, social security contributions of employees and employers, and any other taxes and public levies usually passed on. These public revenues work as a wedge between the market price to be asked and the private nonmarket activity replacing or complementing it.

To evaluate the future effects of high taxation, it is important to judge the underlying reasons for the substitution of taxed activity in general and the increase in the shadow economy in particular. It has been argued that the shadow economy grew in the United States most strongly when marginal tax rates decreased, and that it should be attributed more to a change in cultural mores than to taxation (Thurow, 1981, p. 140). To a degree, this is true, and changes in life-style also contribute to a larger tax base in other areas, as the rise in "eating out" among consumer expenditures indicates. However, the great advantage to private households of using untaxed time and other untaxed inputs (such as acquiring special skills to substitute for market inputs in the household production function) is simply a fact. This substitution is becoming more important because of the increase in nonworking time in many countries, time-sharing, and so forth. The use of this mounting reserve of time becomes increasingly attractive as taxes rise higher, and if the fiscal advantage is consistent with life-style habits, it is the worse for future tax revenue. Because the effects result not from a particular tax but from the combination of the many shifted taxes, the tax state has to cope with these effects.

These tendencies also affect GNP growth and thereby lead to indirect effects on future revenues. A reduction in taxed activity or a transfer to untaxed activity means that measured GNP decreases (or increases less). For a more comprehensive welfare indicator, including all private nonmarket activities, it is crucial whether the activity is given up or just replaced.

Future GNP and thus future revenue are also affected if high taxation, besides increasing tax avoidance, reduces the private prerequisites for growth, such as the incentives to work, save, and invest. As for the labor supply, income and substitution effects work contrary to each other and lead to mixed empirical results (Bosworth, 1984, pp. 141–6; Hausman, 1981). The same is true for private saving (Bosworth, 1984, pp. 94–6), whereas a tax reduction for new investment increases investment demand by about the size of the revenue loss (Bosworth, 1984, p. 128). In sum, there are negative effects on growth, but the magnitude is difficult to assess.

Finally, an influence on growth can be seen in the fact that wage earners may be so successful in shifting their taxes fully by wage-rate bargaining (in trying to maintain net real income in the face of inflation and "bracket creep") that they squeeze profits, which are a major prerequisite for investment and further growth (Bacon and Eltis, 1978).

8.4 A tendency toward self-induced fiscal pressure through the tax state?

A quantitative analysis of the factors in the preceding section would have to develop measures of direct effects and of growth-related effects on revenue. These measures would then be applied to the various expenditure and revenue items. If this were done in a time series, the weighted changes would show in quantitative terms whether changes in the level and structure of the budget by themselves increased or decreased the tendencies of fiscal pressure.[15] In this chapter, however,

---

[15] Whether or not fiscal pressure finally develops will also depend on other factors, such as the effects of additional growth or political decisions on the level of expenditure.

it is possible only to sum up the previous rather qualitative statements and see if together they allow for some conclusions.

Looking first at the expenditure categories, transfers to individuals and households seem to contain few positive growth elements, and the main parts of these transfers show some (though not very large) disincentives; "perverse effects" (Glazer, 1981, pp. 242–3), whereby people are actually induced to engage in growth-deterrent behavior, are certainly the exception. Transfers to business and agriculture are mainly adverse to growth in the long run, and again some specific incentives exist. Taking transfers together, it is probably fair to say that this large and (in many countries) growing part of the budget (OECD, 1985, pp. 48–52) is at best neutral to growth, but probably slightly adverse.

Outlays for purchases and personnel are more difficult to assess. They may, on the average, still be at least indispensable prerequisites for growth, if not actually growth-promoting. But this would have to be investigated in much more detail, drawing on work in education economics, health economics, and so forth. The tendency may be that people in high-income societies demand many services of a high-consumption quality from their state, such as in health, recreation, or environment, which, though they increase welfare, do not increase future GNP and thus future revenue. The contributions of these and other fields of policy to ensure adequate ability to work probably could be provided by a much lower level of service than that provided today.

If transfers are regarded as being at best neutral to growth, and if purchases and personnel probably still, on the average, contribute to it, then a very general indicator for the growth contribution of expenditures over time could be the share of transfers in the budget or in GNP. In the United States, the share of transfers almost doubled between 1960 and 1977 (from 5.7 percent to 10.7 percent), whereas total expenditures rose much less proportionately (from 28.2 percent to 36.5 percent) (Musgrave, 1980, p. 376).

Taking expenditure and revenue effects together, revenue necessarily exerts negative effects on growth, and growth-inducing elements in taxation can only help to reduce this negative effect. Over time, the total negative effects of revenue changes probably have increased because of a heavier tax burden, and especially because of higher marginal rates. Therefore, changes on the expenditure side would have to be more growth-inducing than before if, over time, they were to offset the worsening revenue effects and to end up with at least an equal effect of the budget on future revenue, be it through growth or through the direct effects. Probably not much can be said about the total influence of the complete budget at a given time, and therefore the focus here is on the effects of changes in budgetary level and structure. Looking at the tendencies discussed, such as the higher share of transfer expenditures, the often high taxation of investment and profit, and the high advantageousness of tax avoidance, it would appear that the additional positive effects of the budget must be very high to at least offset the additional negative budget influence, aside from other possible inhibitions that may occur through regulation or "social rigidities" (Olson, 1982). If this conclusion seems acceptable, then recent changes in public budgets probably have tended to contribute to fiscal pressure because of their reduced contribution to GNP and future revenue, but also through direct effects like tax avoidance.[16]

Finally, the question is raised whether or not there is an underlying major reason for the ongoing changes in the budget and whether or not from that we can gain some insight on possible ways to reduce the tendency toward fiscal pressure. There could, of course, be a scenario in which there is no reason to be concerned at all. If private-sector activity is geared to growth and is supported by regulations and a general atmosphere favorable to growth, and if this actually leads to sustained satisfactory growth rates, then the budget may be concerned with other objectives than growth alone, and the resulting negative direct effects on future revenue might also turn out to be compensated by growth-induced high revenue. The question, however, is what country can really ignore the growth effects of its budget, and to what degree, arguing that the other growth determinants are sufficient.

So most countries will be concerned about their budgets' effects on growth. If it is true that for a longer period the share of growth-enhancing expenditure has decreased and growth-retarding revenues have probably increased, the main underlying reason could be the increasing orientation toward equality. That would explain the rise in transfer expenditure, and it is often the rationale behind higher and/or restructured taxation. Until the mid-1970s, growth was taken for granted (Blinder, 1974, p. 1); so equality seemingly could be attained with little efficiency cost in the sense of forgone growth.[17]

This leads to possible conflict between equality and growth. It probably does not stem so much from a higher or lower degree of inequal-

[16] This conclusion even leaves out the effect of budget deficits (as offsetting private savings under income-determination aspects). They tend to vary more than the share of other budget elements and were left out of this medium-term consideration.

[17] A. Okun's book *Equality and Efficiency* contains chapters on the reasons and policies for equality, whereas the disincentives to work, save, and invest appear only as "leakages" in the "bucket" to be filled for equalization purposes (Okun, 1975).

ity, as comparisons of high-income countries have shown (Thurow, 1981, p. 138; Williamson, 1979, p. 253); rather, it could be due to the instruments used to further equality: high transfers financed by high and more progressive taxation. If this is true, fiscal pressure is, to this extent, due to a redistribution policy that is not sufficiently matched with growth provisions.

Growth provisions, some of which could also reduce the possible conflict between equality and growth, could take several forms, some related to the size and others to the structure of the budget:

1. The total of budgetary and other policies should be checked to assure that the total of envisaged private and public uses of GNP is matched by the size of GNP that can reasonably be expected. Here the discussion borders on that of the size of the public sector (Musgrave, 1981).

2. A major task could be the restructuring of taxation. Schumpeter ([1929–30] 1985) proposed a growth-oriented tax reform (for a proposal using some of his objectives, see Seidl, 1984), and new efforts are being made in several countries. They aim at reduced marginal rates of the combined taxes and thereby directly at growth incentives.

3. Because much of the fiscal pressure results from the total sum of fiscal flows involved in equalization, the same degree of equalization (if politically desired) should be pursued with smaller and more effective flows. Alternatively, because a reduction in inequality cannot be regarded as equal to a reduction in poverty (Danziger, Haveman, and Plotnick, 1981, p. 1018; Musgrave, 1981, p. 114), efforts could be concentrated on the needy. This would permit much lower taxes and would render tax avoidance less advantageous. To continue the previous equalization-oriented budget policy would otherwise mean to use more and more budget flows, "as most easy gains have already been made" (Danziger, Haveman, and Plotnick, 1981, p. 1019).

4. Much of the desired support for the needy would be achieved through private initiative, with possibly some public financing, as some current social services for the elderly show. This again would reduce the fiscal flows to be financed publicly.

5. The individual instruments of any policy of equality (including contingency policies aimed at equal access without income limitation, as in the old-age and health policy) should be designed so as to minimize negative side effects on growth. This would be of particular importance in Germany, where the worsening age distribution will require much larger expenditures to finance pensions and age-related health needs. One instrument could be stronger use of benefit-related financing, for instance, in social security.

6. Besides equalization-oriented expenditures, other expenditures could be restructured, for instance, transfers to business and agriculture, which, if they cannot be reduced, can at least be linked to incentives to innovate.

If restructuring expenditures and/or revenues does not prove feasible, and if expenditures should rise again in relation to GNP in the future, with additional expenditure probably being less growth-enhancing than before, then taxes will have to rise again, with their growth-deterring effects probably increasing. As a consequence, it may be that "the egalitarian philosophy hits a median-voter barrier, and future redistribution, for the time being, comes to a halt" (Musgrave, 1980, p. 389; see also Bös, 1982), or observers might return to Schumpeter's assertion that society has by that time been "growing beyond private enterprise and the tax state," not through fiscal crisis or pressure, but because "private enterprise will lose its social meaning through the development of the economy and the consequent expansion of the sphere of social sympathy" (Schumpeter, [1918] 1954, p. 38). But this conclusion depends on Schumpeter's definition and version of socialism (1950), under which not only the tax state is at stake, but also the market-oriented economy as such, with all its achievements.

References

Aaron, H. J. (1982). *Economic Effects of Social Security*. Washington, D.C.: Brookings Institution.

Andic, M., and Andic, S. (1985). "An Exploration into Fiscal Sociology: Ibn Khaldun, Schumpeter, and Public Choice." *Finanzarchiv,* 43:454–69.

Atkinson, B. (1985). "Income Maintenance and Social Insurance: A Survey," in A. J. Auerbach and M. S. Feldstein (eds.), *Handbook of Public Economics,* Vol. 2 (quoted from the version in Discussion Paper No. 5, "The Welfare State Programme," ST-ICERD, London School of Economics).

Bacon, R., and Eltis, W. (1978). *Britain's Economic Problem: Too Few Producers* (2nd ed.). London: Macmillan.

Bericht der Bundesregierung über die Entwicklung der Finanzhilfen des Bundes und der Steuervergünstigungen für die Jahre 1983 bis 1986 gemäss §12 des Gesetzes zur Förderung der Stabilität und des Wachstums der Wirtschaft (StWG) vom 8. Juni 1967 (Zehnter Subventionsbericht) 1985. Bundestagsdrucksache 10/3821.

Blinder, A. S. (1974). *Toward an Economic Theory of Income Distribution*. Cambridge, Mass.: M.I.T. Press.

Bös, D. (1982). "Krise des Steuerstaats," in G. Bombach, B. Gahlen, and A. E. Ott (eds.) *Möglichkeiten und Grenzen der Staatstätigkeit* (pp. 354–93).

Tübingen: J. C. B. Mohr/Paul Siebeck [an expanded version of Bös, D. (1981). "Crisis of the Tax State." *Public Choice,* 38:225–41].

Bosworth, B. P. (1984). *Tax Incentives and Economic Growth.* Washington, D.C.: Brookings Institution.

Bundesministerium der Finanzen (1981, 1986). *Finanzbericht.* Bonn.

Danziger, S., Haveman, R., and Plotnick, R. (1981). "How Income Transfer Programs Affect Work, Savings, and the Income Distribution: A Critical Review." *Journal of Economic Literature,* 19:975–1028.

Denison, E. F. (1979). *Accounting for Slower Economic Growth.* Washington, D.C.: Brookings Institution.

Feige, E. L. (1985). "The Meaning of the 'Underground Economy' and the Full Compliance Deficit," in W. Gärtner and A. Wenig (eds.), *The Economics of the Shadow Economy* (pp. 19–36). Berlin: Springer.

Glazer, N. (1981). "Roles and Responsibilities in Social Policy," in *The Welfare State in Crisis* (pp. 240–55). Paris: OECD.

Goldscheid, R. [1917] (1976). "Staatsozialismus oder Staatskapitalismus," in R. Hickel (ed.) *Rudolf Goldscheid, Joseph Schumpeter. Die Finanzkrise des Steuerstaats* (pp. 40–252). Frankfurt/M: Suhrkamp.

Halberstadt, V. (1981). "An Economist's Viewpoint," in *The Welfare State in Crisis* (pp. 28–32). Paris: OECD.

Hausman, J. A. (1981). "Labor Supply," in H. J. Aaron and J. A. Pechman (eds.), *How Taxes Affect Economic Behavior* (pp. 27–83). Washington, D.C.: Brookings Institution.

Kendrick, J. W. (1981). "International Comparison of Recent Productivity Trends," in W. Fellner (ed.), *Essays in Contemporary Economic Problems. Demand, Productivity, and Population.* Washington, D.C.: American Enterprise Institute.

Musgrave, R. A. (1980). "Theories of Fiscal Crises: An Essay in Fiscal Sociology," in H. J. Aaron and M. J. Boskin (eds.), *The Economics of Taxation* (pp. 361–90). Washington, D.C.: Brookings Institution.

(1981). "Leviathan Cometh – or Does He?" in H. F. Ladd and T. N. Tideman (eds.), *Tax and Expenditure Limitations* (pp. 77–120). Washington, D.C.: Urban Institute Press.

(1985). "Perspectives on and Limits to Public Finance for the Financing of Social Policy in Market Economies," in G. Terny and A. J. Culyer (eds.), *Public Finance and Social Policy* (pp. 261–70). Detroit: Wayne State University Press.

O'Connor, J. (1973). *The Fiscal Crisis of the State.* New York: St. Martin's Press.

Okun, A. M. (1975). *Equality and Efficiency.* Washington, D.C.: Brookings Institution.

Olson, M. (1982). *The Rise and Decline of Nations: Economic Growth, Stagflation and Social Rigidities.* New Haven: Yale University Press.

Organisation for Economic Co-operation and Development (OECD) (1981). *The Welfare State in Crisis.* Paris: OECD.

(1985). *The Role of the Public Sector.* Paris: OECD.

Schneider, F. (1986). "Das Ausmass der Schattenwirtschaft in den OECD-Staaten: Ein Versuch der Erklärung." *Wirtschaftswissenschaftliches Studium*, 10:503–8.

Schumpeter, J. A. [1918] (1954). "The Crisis of the Tax State," (translated from German) in W. F. Stolper and R. A. Musgrave (eds.), *International Economic Papers*, 4:5–38; first published as "Die Krise des Steuerstaats." *Zeitfragen aus dem Gebiet der Soziologie*, 4:3–74.

[1929–30] (1985). "Was vermag eine Finanzreform?" in W. F. Stolper and C. Seidl (eds.), *Joseph A. Schumpeter. Aufsätze zur Wirtschaftspolitik* (pp. 112–23). Tübingen: J. C. B. Mohr/Paul Siebeck; first published in *Der deutsche Volkswirt*, 4:75–80.

(1950). *Capitalism, Socialism and Democracy* (3rd ed.). New York: Harper.

Seidl, C. (1984). "The Tax State in Crisis: Can Schumpeterian Public Finance Claim Modern Relevance?" in C. Seidl (ed.), *Lectures on Schumpeterian Economics* (pp. 89–110). Berlin: Springer.

Thurow, L. C. (1980). *The Zero-Sum Society. Distribution and the Possibilities for Economic Change*. New York: Basic Books.

(1981). "Equity, Efficiency, Social Justice, and Redistribution," in *The Welfare State in Crisis* (pp. 137–50). Paris: OECD.

Williamson, J. G. (1979). "Inequality, Accumulation, and Technological Imbalance: A Growth-Equity Conflict in American History?" *Economic Development and Cultural Change*, 27:231–53.

Wissenschaftlicher Beirat beim Bundesministerium der Finanzen (1986). *Gutachten zur einkommensteuerlichen Behandlung von Alterseinkünften*. Bonn: Stollfuss.

Wissenschaftlicher Beirat für Familienfragen beim Bundesminister für Jugend, Familie und Gesundheit (1979). "Leistungen für die nachwachsende Generation in der Bundesrepublik Deutschland," in *Schriften des Bundesministers für Jugend, Familie und Gesundheit*. Stuttgart: Kohlhammer.

Zimmermann, H. (1983). "Grants to Communities in Their Relation to National Growth," in D. Biehl, K. W. Roskamp, and W. F. Stolper (eds.), *Public Finance and Economic Growth* (pp. 297–313). Detroit: Wayne State University Press.

Discussion

RICHARD A. MUSGRAVE

Professor Zimmermann has presented us with a thoughtful and imaginative analysis of fiscal pressure. Seen from the economist's perspective, the problem is one of taxable capacity or, as Zimmermann rightly stresses, of budgetary capacity. This extends Schumpeter's own view of the tax state and its limits, but also narrows his frame of reference.

Let me therefore begin with a brief look at that broader framework, which is where Schumpeter's own genius emerges: his vision of economic institutions floating, as it were, as integral particles in the dynamics of social forces, and indeed the logic and foibles of human nature.

In my first exposure to Schumpeter, at Harvard in the spring term of 1935, he filled the board with Walrasian equations, but that was not his real forte. His forte, rather, was in the tradition of grand social theory – in the style of Marx, Goldscheid, and Weber – that must have characterized the Vienna of his youth. Whereas Marx viewed capitalism as exploitation of the masses, Schumpeter viewed it as a triumph of rationality and progress. Yet their modes of thinking ran parallel, if with opposite signs, and their views of the outcome – the inevitable self-induced fall of the system – did not differ greatly. Both saw progressive taxation as a potential instrument of capitalist destruction – the one with delight, and the other with sorrow.

There are three contexts in which Schumpeter addressed the tax theme: first in "The Crisis of the Tax State" ([1918] 1954), then in several contributions to the *Deutsche Volkswirt* in the late 1920s, and finally in the 1946 edition of *Capitalism, Socialism and Democracy*. In his 1918 essay, Schumpeter, as Professor Zimmermann notes, viewed the tax state as an institution that emerged to fill the gap left by the decline of the feudal system and its revenue sources. The rise of the tax state precisely met the needs of liberal capitalism as it emerged. Beginning in the nineteenth century, and still in the early twentieth, the income tax, in particular, became its most suitable expression. Viewed at this early stage, as the appropriate payment that the bourgeois household would offer the state for services rendered, the income tax was a public-sector reflection of the market system. It served as a quasi price, a quasi fee or benefit tax, but it did not continue in this status. With the expanding size of the public sector and the rise of progressive rates, the income tax was transformed into an instrument of social policy, and therewith its relation to the market system changed. What had once been an expression of the capitalist spirit now became hostile to it.

Marx, in the *Communist Manifesto,* had urged that progressive income taxation be expanded, so as to hasten the fall of the system. Schumpeter similarly viewed its role as a destructive force, not so much as the product of working-class design, but as the inevitable and self-defeating outcome of utilitarian motivation and intellectual hostility to the market. But though inevitable in the end, Schumpeter thought the decline of the system premature and indeed postponable.

The system should be given the chance to continue and to raise the level of income before, as he put it somewhat mystically, "enterprise will lose its social meaning through the development of the economy and the consequent expansion of the sphere of social sympathy." As a contribution to such a postponement, he suggested that the income tax be replaced by an expenditure tax, as Fisher had suggested; or, to smooth Keynesian sensibilities, as Schumpeter put it, the income tax might be replaced by a tax that would exclude income that was invested. Schumpeter's thoughts on tax reform thus fit well into the framework of modern discussion and fit well with the growing popularity of an expenditure tax among the younger generation of fiscal economists. Given this option, I would question Professor Zimmermann's comment that feasible revenue sources have by now been exhausted.

Nor do I share the perspective, be it à la Marx or Schumpeter, that the tax state has become an inherently destructive force. As has become evident over the years, both were too hasty in predicting the downfall of the capitalist system; and they were mistaken, as I see it, in diagnosing the role of the welfare state, including the rise of progressive taxation. Far from destroying the market, use of the public sector to smooth its rough edges has created a setting in which capitalist institutions can be sustained and continue to flourish. The combination of the spirit of the Beveridge Report and the failure of socialism in the Soviet bloc has come to disprove the prognosis of capitalist demise. Such deterrence to capitalist incentives as resulted was outweighed on the whole by the more secure and stable social environment that was created. This is not to deny that the welfare state, in turn, has developed its own defects (What institution would not?), but these are not beyond repair. Indeed, its current critique, as in the United States, seems to be loudest where its extension has been least. As to tax reform, I am not sure that a transition to a Schumpeterian consumption-plus-hoarding tax would perform quite the same function in stabilizing the social environment as did the income tax. It would not do so, in my view, unless bequests were included in the base or unless the expenditure tax were matched by a substantial system of death duties. Otherwise, excessive inequality in the distribution of wealth (even if accompanied by a corresponding leveling of consumption) might well lead to precisely the conditions that a hundred years ago invited the Marxian prognosis.

Let me now leave the heights of grand design and turn to Professor Zimmermann's more down-to-earth analysis of fiscal pressure. Professor Zimmermann does not offer a precise definition, but more generally interprets fiscal pressure as a situation in which it becomes increasingly difficult to meet the level of expenditures that society demands. The underlying concept is thus one of taxable capacity and the economy's limited ability to sustain a rising ratio of tax revenue to GNP. If so, just how is this difficulty and its increasing severity to be measured?

Among various possible approaches, Professor Zimmermann focuses on the effects of the budget on the level of income or income growth. Given a balanced budget, the increase in budget (B) equals those in expenditures (E) and in income (Y). Fiscal pressure (FP) may thus be positive, zero, or negative, depending on the effects of the budget (B) on income (Y), that is, on whether $dY/dB \gtreqless 0$. With dY/dB equal to zero, so is the level of fiscal pressure. Budget expansion leaves income unchanged and reduces disposable income by the increase in B. If dY/dB is positive, fiscal pressure turns into leverage. Income will rise, and disposable income will fall by less than the increase in B. If dY/dB is negative, income will decline, and disposable income will fall by more than the gain in B. The net effects of an increase in B on Y may then be viewed as the sum of the effects of a presumably positive expenditure (E) and presumably negative tax revenue (T). The relationship is complicated, however, because effects on income, especially with regard to revenue, depend on the *rate* of tax t as well as on the *amount* of revenue obtained on T. The rate of tax required to obtain a given revenue in turn depends on the level of income, and hence on the expenditure effects thereon. The two sides of the equation are thus interrelated and must be determined simultaneously. Suppose, for instance, that the elasticity of income with regard to E equals unity. In that case, the required increase in revenue can be obtained without raising the rate of tax, and detrimental effects thereof are avoided. But such will hardly be the case. Given a balanced-budget requirement, an increase in E is likely to require an increase in t as well, and depressing effects on income may result.

Professor Zimmermann then proceeds to suggest a law of rising fiscal pressure. A variety of factors, social, economic, and political, have made for an increase in B, with B rising faster than Y, as suggested by Wagner's law. As B/Y increases, the effects of budget expansion on income will become less favorable and exert increased pressure. This prognosis is based primarily on the presumed impact of budget expansion on capital formation. If the share of public-capital formation in the marginal expenditure dollar is less than the savings share in the marginal tax dollar, budget expansion will retard growth. On the expenditure side, the weight of investment may well fall relative to consumption outlays, especially if the rising importance of transfers and the ambiguous role of defense outlays are considered. On the revenue side, the prognosis is less evident, because a rising tax share may well imply increased reliance on consumption taxes.

However this may be, effects on savings and investment are not the entire story. Effects on labor supply, innovation, and the efficiency of resource use must also be allowed for. Taking a more sophisticated approach, the focus might be on the balance between the deadweight loss incurred on the revenue side and the efficiency gain derived from the provision of public services.

Nor is this the entire story, as distributional considerations cannot be left out. A given change in total income may carry different implications with regard to welfare gains or losses, depending on associated changes in the state of income distribution. Finally, it is not sufficient to think of fiscal pressure in the context of a classical, full-employment model only. This leaves out macroeconomic effects on the level of income that may result from alternative budget policies or, for that matter, from alternative mixes of fiscal and monetary restraints. In the more realistic context of a neoclassical model, the detrimental taxation effects on growth have to be balanced against the potential encouragement to investment afforded by the easier monetary policy that the tax tightening permits. What first seems a problem of fiscal pressure now becomes one of stabilization effects.

The concept of fiscal pressure is thus complex, especially if seen in the broader frame of Schumpeterian analysis. Economic effects, so he would have argued, transcend such bloodless concepts as savings and investment coefficients or measures of deadweight loss. No matter how attractive their theoretical sophistication, they do not go to the heart of the matter. More important than all this, so he might have argued, is the impact of the fiscal system on the animal spirits that underlie capitalist advance and that may be the primary victim of fiscal pressure. But as I noted earlier, the health of these very spirits also presumes a social environment that is not threatened by excessive inequality and insecurity, especially for those who are passive members rather than conquering heroes of the system; and here the supporting role of the fiscal system is of vital importance.

References

Schumpeter, J. A. [1918] (1954). "The Crisis of the Tax State," (translated from German) in W. F. Stolper and R. A. Musgrave (eds.), *International Economic Papers*, 4:5–38; first published as "Die Krise des Steuerstaats." *Zeitfragen aus dem Gebiet der Soziologie*, 4:3–74.

[1929–30] (1985). "Was vermag eine Finanzreform?" in W. F. Stolper and

C. Seidl (eds.), *Joseph A. Schumpeter. Aufsätze zur Wirtschaftspolitik* (pp. 112–23). Tübingen: J. C. B. Mohr/Paul Siebeck; first published in *Der deutsche Volkswirt*, 4:75–80.

[1942] (1950). *Capitalism, Socialism and Democracy* (3rd ed.). New York: Harper.

Discussion

HEINZ-DIETER WENZEL

I am glad to have the opportunity to comment on this very interesting and most stimulating chapter by Horst Zimmermann. In two senses, however, this is by no means a simple task. First, most of the decisive aspects have already been mentioned and discussed in Richard Musgrave's comment. I shall do my best not to repeat them. Second, I have the impression that the way in which the subject at stake has been dealt with and presented shows indeed the spirit of Schumpeter. This is to say that the initiating concept underlying the subject was given preference over the elaboration of all the analytical, definitional, and technical details that would be required to offer a sound basis for such a methodical approach. One is, therefore, easily tempted to agree with the author in all major aspects and to consider any critique of the details presented as rather unimportant. However, I shall try to withstand this temptation and instead stress some specific aspects of this chapter, because I think that they deserve to be discussed more intensively.

One important point in this connection seems to me the task of an appropriate restructuring of taxation that is induced by fiscal pressure. In his 1929–30 article, Schumpeter had already proposed a growth-oriented tax reform, as mentioned by Zimmermann. In 1984, Christian Seidl succeeded in linking this concept with the results of modern fiscal theory.

Another aspect that I deem most essential concerns the basics of the presented concept of "fiscal pressure on the tax state" (Section 8.2). I would like to raise the question whether or not the GNP-growth-oriented procedure as ·emphasized here has the decisive relevance as a criterion for the crisis or pressure concepts used here.

Let me start with the latter. Taking Schumpeter's "Crisis of the Tax State" ([1918] 1954) as a reference point, Zimmermann introduces the notion of fiscal pressure in Section 9.2. Fiscal pressure is a central point in this framework. It seems to me, however, not to be defined

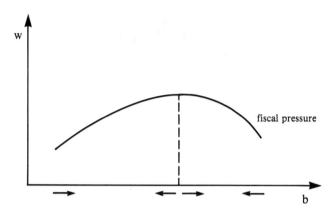

Figure 8.1

clearly. Therefore, I would like to try to formalize my understanding of it in a simplifying first step, and I hope that Zimmermann can agree with it. In analytic terms, fiscal pressure might be expressed in the following way: The growth rate of the GNP is a concave-shaped function of the size of the public budget relative to GNP, assuming a given tax structure. I would like to illustrate this using some simple equations and figures. With the definitions T = taxes, G = government expenditures, Y = GNP, B = budget, and w_Y = growth rate of GNP, assuming $w_Y = F(T, G, Y, \ldots)$ and simplifying,

$$w_Y = f(T/Y, G/Y, \ldots$$
$$=: t \quad =: g$$

we get the total differential

$$\Delta w_Y = f_t \Delta t + f_g \Delta g + R$$

with a remainder R, with $G = T (=: B)$. We assume a balanced budget, and with $b := B/Y$, it follows that $\Delta t = \Delta g (=: \Delta b)$ and

$$\Delta w_Y = (f_t + f_g) \Delta b + \tilde{R}$$

Let us further assume that

$$f_t < 0, \quad f_g > 0$$
$$f_{tt} < 0, \quad f_{gg} < 0$$

Then, w_Y can be approximated by the function given in Figure 8.1. In general, this will mean selecting two intersecting hyperplanes in an n-dimensional context (Figure 8.2). Further differentiation of the expen-

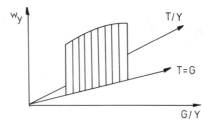

Figure 8.2

diture effect into the two components of productive $(f_{g\text{pr}})$ and transfer $(f_{g\text{tr}})$ effects and $f_g = f_{g\text{pr}} + f_{g\text{tr}}$ would be interesting, but I shall not stress it further here. In other words, the GNP-enhancing effects of public-budget growth diminish because the negative influence of higher tax revenues, expressed as the share of revenue in GNP, rises, and the growth-stimulating effect of higher public expenditures drops.

Zimmermann argues that fiscal pressure occurs when lower growth rates (of GNP) produce less revenue, and problems arise in financing a given expenditure level. However, as long as growth rates of GNP remain positive, revenue will continue to increase, provided that the tax structure remains unchanged. Therefore, primarily, there is no fiscal problem or fiscal pressure. The expression "fiscal pressure" seems of relevance to me only where an increased budget share of GNP leads to negative growth rates of GNP, because in this case a *burden* is evident. It would be very interesting to study this kind of relationship between the growth rate of GNP and the budget share in greater detail. And this seems to me to be the central task in trying to get useful results about pressure or absence of pressure. This would be possible only in the context of dynamic systems, which would be able to reflect the feedback relationships among budget, growth, and future revenue shares. This does not mean introducing "Samuelsonian mechanics," as Professor Helmstädter characterized traditional successfully used dynamic methods, nor abusing ideas of dynamic structures that are characterized only by their vagueness. Therefore, in analyzing economic problems in a Schumpeterian approach, it seems to me of central importance to utilize new tools of qualitative analysis and methods developed in the theory of mathematical chaos and catastrophe. The literature shows that simple applications of catastrophe theory, for example, have already proved very useful in explaining puzzling phenomena in business-cycle situations. In this context, the functional relationship mentioned earlier could describe, in a very simplified manner, equilibrium values for both variables (GNP growth rate and budget share) in a generalized dynamic-growth model, where fiscal activity is a decisive factor for the equilibrium growth rate of GNP. Obviously, the structure of such a curve depends heavily on a given and constant tax system.

In Section 8.3 of Zimmermann's chapter, some examples of dynamic relationships between actual budget variations and future tax-revenue effects are discussed on the basis of plausible economic arguments. Zimmermann distinguishes between direct and indirect effects, the latter influencing growth, and the former assumed to be independent of it. But this differentiation does not seem to be very successful for operational reasons, that is, because the reaction of the taxpayers will nearly always influence growth effects, especially if time paths of adjustment are considered. Therefore, it seems to me, once more, that definite results of fiscal pressure or fiscal-pressure changes in qualitative and quantitative respects largely depend on the availability of analytical models, because only they can provide results in evaluating economic effects that differ in direction, size, and time path.

Furthermore, one may doubt that GNP is an appropriate indicator at all for social benefits, and one may wonder if a growth reduction or a decrease in GNP is a proper measure of social costs, as Richard Musgrave has already mentioned. In this case, the term "fiscal crisis" or "fiscal pressure" even then could not be applied if fiscal activity reduced conventionally measured GNP and at the same time stimulated substitution effects in the direction of activities in nonmarket production (the shadow economy) or household production, as Zimmermann remarked. A more comprehensive indicator for evaluation of tax- and expenditure-induced adjustment processes would therefore seem to be a deadweight loss or a welfare concept, rather than the GNP measures. Some of Zimmermann's remarks can also be interpreted in this way, I think. To conclude, the usefulness of fiscal-pressure indicators only on the basis of conventionally measured GNP seems to me rather modest. This, however, must not mean that the tax state as a concept will prove superfluous. What I mean is that the tax state will not represent the sole and decisive function, because it is only one part of the financial system. Another very important part that has not been considered here is the "debt state," for we know from modern fiscal-growth theory that, especially under efficiency aspects, a pertinent debt policy might even be necessary for utility-maximizing growth.

Fritz Neumark (1984, p. 56) remarks in this context that "The Crisis of the Tax State" would have relevance for the 1990s only if Schumpeter had selected the debt state as the object for his research as well.

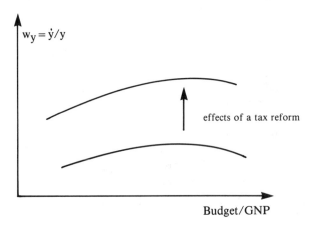

Figure 8.3

These examples seem to be a further indication that by limiting the discussion to the subject of the tax state, we unnecessarily narrow the question at stake and thus weaken the relevance of the results – something that could easily have been avoided.

With that thought, I would like to conclude this point of discussion and turn to another aspect of the appropriateness of a given tax structure and the necessity for thinking about revising the tax structure and aspects of tax reform. These aspects proved to be important in judging the fiscal-pressure concept on the basis of feedback relationships among revenue, budget, and GNP growth in the first part of my comment. If there is such a thing as a functional dependence between GNP growth rate and budget share (relative to GNP), then the characteristics of the existing tax system also determine the course of the curve. To be more precise, if the fiscal pressure increases because we are on the declining part of the concave-shaped graph of the function (Figure 8.3) relating GNP growth rate to budget shares, then an incentive augmenting tax reform, leaving revenue unchanged, can reverse the development of a decreasing growth rate or at least make it temporarily stay the same at otherwise equal parameter constellations. Seidl argues along the same lines: "I am convinced that no crisis of existence of the tax state is imminent, but a frictional crisis instead. The present crisis of the tax state seems also not to be primarily of aggregates but more of a crisis of the tax structure" (1984, p. 109). He develops some suggestions for a reform of our tax system aimed at overcoming the fiscal pressure resulting from the current tax structure. This is not the place to discuss these proposals in detail, particularly because even in the public-finance literature, different opinions exist. Compare, for example, the comments of Fritz Neumark on this subject (1984, pp. 45–65). In concluding my comment, I would like briefly to discuss the crisis-induced possible conflict between equality and growth, as mentioned by Zimmermann. In his opinion, fiscal pressure stems from instruments that are used to further equality, that is, high transfers financed by high and more progressive taxation. However, it has been shown empirically that in high-income countries, there seems to be, in general, no such conflict as discussed in, for example, the articles included in *The Welfare State in Crisis* (OECD, 1981) and especially that by Thurow (1981, pp. 46–51). But if, as is argued by Zimmermann, the conflict stems, properly speaking, from the financing instruments that are used – and here especially from progressive income taxation – the problem of fiscal pressure is again reduced to the problem of finding and using the appropriate tax structure. This important factor is also stressed by Zimmermann at the end of his chapter. Nevertheless, I would like to add at this point that it is not alone a question of tax structure, but in my opinion more a question of revenue structure. I would especially like to point to the necessity not to leave out the debt state when discussing fiscal pressure or the crisis of the tax state.

References

Neumark, Fritz (1984). "Chancen einer Schumpeter Renaissance. Bemerkungen zu J. Schumpeter ordnungs-, konjuhktur-, finanz- und geldtheoretischen Ansichten," in D. Bös and H.-D. Stolper (eds.), *Schumpeter oder Keynes* (pp. 45–65). Berlin: Springer-Verlag.

Organisation for Economic Co-operation and Development (1981). *The Welfare State in Crisis.* Paris: OECD.

Schumpeter, J. A. [1918] (1954). "The Crisis of the Tax State," (translated from German) in W. F. Stolper and R. A. Musgrave (eds.), *International Economics Papers,* 4:5–38; first published as "Die Krise des Steuerstaats." *Zeitfragen aus dem Gebeit der Soziologie,* 4:3–74.

[1929–30] (1985). "Was vermag eine Finanzreform?" in W. F. Stolper and C. Seidl (eds.), *Joseph A. Schumpeter. Aufsätze zur Wirtschaftspolitik* (pp. 112–23). Tübingen: J. C. B. Mohr/Paul Siebeck; first published in *Der deutsche Volkswirt,* 4:75–80.

Seidl, C. (1984). "The Tax State in Crisis, Can Schumpeterian Public Finance Claim Modern Relevance?" in C. Seidl (ed.), *Lectures on Schumpeterian Economics* (pp. 89–110). Berlin: Springer-Verlag.

Thurow, L. C. (1981). "Equity, Efficiency, Social Justice, and Redistribution," in *The Welfare State in Crisis* (pp. 137–50). Paris: OECD.

CHAPTER 9

The role of government in changing industrial societies: a Schumpeter perspective[1]

PETER M. JACKSON

> An enormous influence on the fate of nations emanates from the economic bleeding which the needs of the state necessitates, and from the use to which its results are put. . . . Our industrial organism cannot be understood if this is overlooked. And our people have become what they are under the fiscal pressures of the state.
>
> Fiscal measures have created and destroyed industries, industrial regions even where this was not their intent, and have in this manner contributed directly to the construction (and distortion) of the edifice of the modern economy and through it the modern spirit.
>
> Schumpeter ([1918] 1954, pp. 6–7)

There is a crisis in the modern welfare-tax state. Since 1945, the public sectors of the industrialized nations have grown rapidly, as has the influence of the state. This was for many countries the period of the Keynesian social democratic consensus. Keynesian demand-management monetary and fiscal policies are intended to stabilize the inherently unstable forces of capitalism around a position of nearly full employment and thereby improve the welfare of the citizenry.[2] This was also the period of welfarism. Satisfaction of the demands of welfare-rights groups meant increasing public spending on transfer payments and increasing taxation.[3]

During the early years of the post-1945 period there was a general expectation that the redistributions entailed in the modern welfare-tax

---

[1] The debates described in this chapter are almost wholly confined to the mature, developed economies. For a discussion of the role of the public sector in less developed economies using a Schumpeterian framework of analysis, see Stolper (1983).

[2] In the United Kingdom, the foundations of the postwar economic order were laid in the Beveridge Report (1942), the Education Act (1944), and the Employment White Paper (1944). In addition, the postwar nationalization program brought many key parts of the private sector under public ownership, and other sectors were brought under public control.

[3] For general trends in OECD countries' taxation and public spending, see Brown and Jackson (1986).

285

state would be financed out of economic growth. This was the period that corresponded in many of its features to Schumpeter's vision of the "march into socialism."[4]

The bubble of rosy optimism, however, burst in the early 1970s, and there followed an increase in the strength of the countercurrents against the march into socialism. These countercurrents originating on the right of the ideological spectrum do not seem to have been foreseen by Schumpeter, who regarded intellectual forces as predominantly left-wing. GNP growth rates were inadequate to overcome the resistance to larger tax bills; there were demands to rewrite constitutions in order to constrain the growth of government, and in some cases there were taxpayers' revolts. At the same time, there was disappointment with the performance of the enlarged public sectors, which did not seem to live up to the promises and expectations generated by politicians and their policy advisors. This awareness of the growth of public-sector or government failure was found in almost every area of public policy: Macro and micro policies often were poorly designed, resulting in unintended dysfunctional effects on other parts of the system; policies frequently cost more than originally estimated, and monetary and fiscal policies often failed to contain rising levels of unemployment, or, if they did manage to, their design faults seemed to spill over into rising inflation rates, interest rates, and exchange rates, with inevitable consequences (crowding out and deindustrialization) for private-sector economic activity. Questions were also asked about the impact of rising tax levels and tax rates on work effort, savings, and capital formation, as well as whether or not publicly provided pensions reduced the incentive to save and whether or not unemployment-benefit compensation increased the duration of unemployment. Schumpeter had pointed out as far back as 1918 that the taxing and spending policies of a government have an "enormous influence on the fate of nations." What the countercurrents of the 1970s produced was a deluge of questions about these influences. As the questions poured in, it became very clear that no ready answers were available. What are the impacts of public-sector deficits on employment levels, the money supply, interest rates, and private-sector economic activity? What are the disincentive effects of taxes and social insurance? Who are the net beneficiaries of public spending programs? All of these were unresolved policy issues in search of a solid empirical foundation, and soon they

---

[4] This was the title of Schumpeter's address to the American Economics Association, December 30, 1949, shortly before his death. The address was included as the last chapter in subsequent editions of *Capitalism, Socialism and Democracy*.

appeared on a rapidly growing research agenda – one that is far from complete today.

The countercurrents of the 1970s slowed down the march into socialism, which probably had advanced much further than Schumpeter had ever imagined it would in so short a time. Indeed, in some countries, attempts were made to reverse the post-1945 trends in the public sector. With the election of the Thatcher government in the United Kingdom and the Reagan administration in the United States, policies have been introduced in these countries to privatize parts of the public sector, and deregulation is high on the policy agenda. Among academic economists and political philosophers, the role of government has again become a topic of serious discussion.[5]

9.1   The crisis of the tax state

The role, scope, and limitations of the public sector, or, more generally, the "state," were discussed at length by Schumpeter in his highly perceptive but sadly neglected paper, "The Crisis of the Tax State," published originally in German in 1918. In that paper, Schumpeter set out to examine the sociological and political processes that lie behind the "superficial facts of the budget figures." He called for more attention to be given to fiscal history and fiscal sociology, and he set out to examine "what does failure of the tax state mean? What is the nature of the tax state? How did it come about? Must it now disappear and why?" ([1918] 1954, p. 6). By the "tax state," Schumpeter meant the mixed economy, and the questions he asked in 1918 are as relevant today as they were then. What is the appropriate mix between the public and private sectors, and is there a limit to the scope and role of the tax state in the changing modern industrial economies?

It should be obvious that there cannot be a precise dividing line between what is and what is not an optimal mix of market and non-market (public-sector) resource allocation. There is no absolute calculus that can provide an objective, scientific answer, because much depends on individuals' preferences for the type of society in which they wish to live. Different societies will provide different mixes of liberty, freedom, efficiency, and welfare distributions. No single mix can be considered right or wrong, just or unjust, without reference to the preferences of those who live in that society. Does this mean that the economist or the political philosopher has nothing to contribute to this

---

[5] As recent examples, consider Dasgupta (1986) and Helm (1986). Among political philosophers, see the work of Rawls (1971) and Nozick (1974).

debate? The answer is no. Although the precise dividing line cannot be left to the dispassionate rational analysis of economic and political theorizing, nevertheless, both theoretical and empirical analyses do help to define and to clarify the issues over which there is much political debate and popular misconception. This is a highly charged and passionate debate involving some of the most basic aspects of social life, liberty, freedom, and the relationships between individuals. The contribution of the economist and the political philosopher must be to sort out the many empty political slogans, to identify the possible different costs and benefits associated with alternative social and political structures, and to highlight the probable economic impact of the public sector on the private sector.

These issues are explored in this chapter through what is essentially a Schumpeterian perspective. Taking Schumpeter's vision of the dynamics of a capitalist socioeconomic system, we ask: What is the role of the public sector in Schumpeter's schema? To answer this question, we first need to review, briefly, Schumpeter's views on capitalism, his theory of democracy, and his approach to decision making. Schumpeter's analysis, being in what is nowadays loosely referred to as the Austrian tradition,[6] is concerned with the dynamics of real economics and therefore stands in contrast to the static partial-equilibrium models of Jevons and Marshall or the static Walrasian general equilibrium model, which have frequently been used by welfare economists in support of their defense of state intervention.

The approach adopted is Schumpeterian in another important sense. When considering the question of what role the state should play, we are confronted with the problem of designing efficient forms of public-sector organization and also the grand design of society generally. Few economists today take a broad overview of the organization of society and the design of its institutions (many do not seem to realize that their narrow technical debates are contributing to these meta-issues). To do so requires an investment in reading and understanding a diverse literature drawn from political science, history, sociology, and law. Among those economists who did not shirk from this challenge were Smith, Marshall, Keynes, Friedman, Hayek, and, of course, Schumpeter. The *design* of social institutions to promote efficiency, growth, and improvements in human welfare lies at the heart of much of Schumpeter's writing and is found especially in his *Theory of Economic Development* ([1912] 1934), *Capitalism, Socialism and Democ-*

---

[6] It is an interesting question to what extent Schumpeter's economic analysis is associated with those of other Austrian economists such as Mises, Hayek, and Kirzner.

racy (1942), and *History of Economic Analysis* (1954). It was also central to his article "The Crisis of the Tax State" ([1918] 1954).

What we shall argue is that Schumpeter's analysis does not replace or displace completely the economist's answer to the role of the state as derived from standard neoclassical static analysis. However, a Schumpeterian perspective, with its emphasis on dynamic processes and with an eye on organizational design, forces us to reconsider some of the more extravagant claims made on behalf of the public sector's ability to improve individual welfare, while at the same time forcing a reassessment of where the limits of the tax state may in fact lie.

9.2 Schumpeter's economic thesis[7]

Schumpeter's central ideas were set down in his *Theory of Economic Development* ([1912] 1934) and elaborated in his subsequent writings, culminating in *Capitalism, Socialism and Democracy* (1942). In contrast to much of the economics being written in the early twentieth century, Schumpeter emphasized disequilibria, decision making, uncertainty, and the concept of economic process as essential elements of any analysis of real capitalist economics. Unlike the static economic physics of the neoclassical microeconomics or the classical foundations of macroeconomics, Schumpeter's economic analysis stressed the dynamics of capitalism: structural change and adjustment. His was an economics in which real time and economic processes played central roles and was thus far removed from the timeless heuristic fiction of the neoclassical economist's long steady state.[8] During his lifetime, Schumpeter's economics did not sit comfortably alongside the received wisdom of the dominant neoclassical paradigm nor the works of Keynes and Marx, whose ideas rivaled his.

There are two aspects to the Schumpeterian view of economic development, which is essentially historical and institutional. First, prices have an important function. It is important to get prices correct for efficient decision making and resource allocation. Second, economic development involves discontinuous changes in production functions and hence in the price system. In other words, development involves the periodic production of equilibrium.

The periodic destruction of equilibrium is the chief characteristic of

---

[7] In this section I am pleased to acknowledge the influence of Stolper's writing on my understanding of Schumpeter's economics.

[8] Despite all the major advances that have been made in theoretical and empirical microeconomics, economists do not yet have an adequate theory or account of the "competitive process."

the Schumpeterian process: what is now frequently referred to as "creative destruction." All disrupting changes are due to innovations (new products, improvements in quality, new forms of industrial organization, new sources of supply), which compose the "capitalist engine" whose locomotive force propels capitalism (Schumpeter, 1942, chap. 5). For Schumpeter, the innovator is the entrepreneur, the source of all dynamic change.[9] But the entrepreneur is not regarded as a class; it is instead a function. "Entrepreneurs are not capitalists. They are not a permanent group. Their function cannot be inherited." Entrepreneurial activity brings about the repeated destruction of equilibria at nearly regular intervals. Time must elapse while changes in the parameters of production functions work themselves out, and while the succeeding adaptive processes are carried out. Even with flexible prices and wages, adaptive processes cannot occur instantaneously. Thus, flux, change, and adaptation characterize real economies. That is, economies will generally be in a state of disequilibrium, and any equilibrium that might occur will be temporary.

For Schumpeter, the capitalist system is characterized by incentives and penalties (1942, chap. 6). It is more like a game of poker than roulette. Only a few receive big prizes (out of proportion to effort), but it is the existence of these big prizes that propels the capitalist system, because it is the possibility of winning them that motivates entrepreneurs to take action. Thus, through creative destruction, incompetence and obsolescence are gradually eliminated. These incentives in a capitalist system are, according to Schumpeter, more powerful than they would be in a social system that is more just. It is important, therefore, not to destroy the incentives that fuel the capitalist process, because to do so would result in loss of the extra growth that improves the welfare of the masses.

Uncertain decision-making environments were also central to Schumpeter's model of capitalism. Following in the tradition of Cantillon and von Thunen, Schumpeter's entrepreneur made decisions in a world of uncertainty, where profits and losses existed. The entrepreneur was not simply involved in arbitrage, as modern "Austrians" assume. Shumpeter's entrepreneur was willing to assume the uninsurable risks in the system – he would play poker rather than roulette. The returns to the entrepreneur are therefore returns for incurring those risks that no insurance company will cover because it is impos-

---

[9] Blaug (1985) has shown that Schumpeter developed the concept of the entrepreneur as it is found in the works of Smith, Cantillon, and von Thunen.

sible to predict the probability of gain or loss. Such people are inventors and explorers.

9.3   The entrepreneur and the auctioneer: Schumpeter and the neoclassical tradition

Standard neoclassical welfare economics demonstrates that given a set of specific conditions (well-defined preference functions, constant returns to scale, full information, no uncertainty), then a set of competitive markets will produce a Pareto-efficient allocation of resources. Furthermore, a set of competitive markets generates, through price signals, the information required to coordinate the multitude of decisions made by a diverse group of individuals – Adam Smith's "invisible hand." These results are well known. However, it is equally well known that the competitive solution (equilibrium) will be socially desirable or optimal only if there is an appropriate (socially just) initial distribution of resources (property rights). Also, if any, or all, of the initial assumptions of the competitive model are violated, then the outcome need not be efficient, and market failure will occur.

Market failure can occur for a variety of reasons: Information is costly to acquire; information is not distributed evenly across all individuals; it is impacted; individuals play games and adopt strategies to maximize their self-interest and will not reveal their true preferences if it is in their interest not to do so; externalities exist; many production functions display increasing returns to scale; decision-making environments are complex and highly uncertain. For this variety of reasons, competitive markets will, in reality, fail; they will fail to produce Pareto-efficient allocation of resources – they will instead be imperfect – and in cases of high transactions costs, they will fail to exist. The Arrow-Debreu general competitive model requires a well-defined set of futures markets to solve the intertemporal resource-allocation problem, but such markets are, in reality, very expensive to organize, given the existence of uninsurable risks.

The competitive-market model fails in another sense at the macro level. The invisible hand of Adam Smith's set of markets, which coordinated the decisions of the individuals, was given flesh and blood in the Walrasian model in the form of the auctioneer. It is the activities of the auctioneer that play a central role in establishing the Pareto-efficient competitive equilibrium of the neoclassical model. Dispense with the auctioneer and a severe coordination problem results. Information travels slowly across space and time; information transmission is expensive and imperfect; many individuals, being risk-averse and uncertain about the likely responses of other individuals, will be slow to react to new information.[10] In reality, information failures and coordination problems abound, resulting in effective-demand failures. This was recognized by Keynes,[11] who saw that the *ex ante* savings and investment decisions made by different groups of individuals need not be equal if they face different information sets (decision environments) and will, therefore, result in macro disequilibrium.

The neoclassical model, when it includes the concept of market failure, provides a defense for state intervention in the economy. It was Musgrave (1958), in his seminal treatise on public finance, who gave the clearest account of the public sector's role. The allocative function of government arises from those market failures due to externalities, public goods, and imperfect competition. The government can correct the market failures by (1) using taxes in order to adjust price signals, as in the case of externalities; (2) supplying public goods; (3) regulating monopolies, nationalizing industries, and introducing antitrust/ monopoly legislation. Correction of effective-demand failures is the government's stabilization function. Monetary and fiscal policies may be used for aggregate-demand management.

Finally, the public sector has a role in redistributing incomes (welfare) in response to a recognition that initial endowments of resources are not necessarily distributed among the members of a community according to the principles of social justice. In the absence of nondistortionary lump-sum taxes, which are not in practice feasible, given the information costs that they entail, the taxes raised to finance a government's distributional policies are likely to conflict with achievement of its allocative function. These problems are developed later.

Public-sector or state intervention, however, does not necessarily mean the destruction of the price mechanism. Rather, state intervention should mean a modification of the price mechanism in response to recognition that a capitalist system of economic organization has its failures, shortcomings, and limitations and that the price mechanism, moderated by public-sector intervention to improve its efficiency, is the best form of economic organization in terms of improving general

[10] In the absence of an auctioneer, Schumpeter's entrepreneur is given the opportunity to bridge the information gap through his/her activities. The arbitrage function performed by the entrepreneur will result in a movement toward a new temporary equilibrium.

[11] These ideas of effective-demand failure have been developed by Clower (1969) and Leijonhufvud (1968).

economic welfare and human well-being – what Schumpeter called the "tax state."

Although recognizing that the state has legitimate economic and social roles to play, a growing band of individuals wonder if the state has not grown too large and powerful relative to the rest of the economy. Does the state intervene in such a way that it is in danger of destroying the enterprise culture of the capitalist system that originally it sought to improve and protect? The fear is that market failures are simply replaced by government failures, with the result that there is no net improvement in welfare, but a redistribution of misery.

Once it is recognized that the public sector has a legitimate role to play in the "tax state," then, in the spirit of Schumpeter, every care must be taken to design an efficient form of public-sector organization that includes an efficient set of intervention policies and instruments. In the final analysis, no form of economic organization is completely efficient. It is degrees of imperfection that are to be compared: systems having differing amounts of market failure compared with systems having different degrees of government failure. In all cases, the objective should be to minimize the amounts of failure, imperfection, and inefficiency. Market failure does not imply, per se, that the public sector should be involved in direct public production of commodities or services; that is only one means of organizing supply. A mixed economy has alternative forms of organizational arrangements that might relate to the public-sector supply of a service, for example, franchising, contracting out to the private sector, or regulating a private supply. The question facing the economist is which form of organization is the most efficient.

Schumpeter would not have disagreed with the market-failure approach to state intervention. He clearly recognized that capitalism was not perfect, that it was unstable and produced undesirable consequences, such as long periods of structural unemployment. It is also clear from his writings that Schumpeter was not against state intervention to correct these problems created by capitalism. Where he did lay emphasis, however, was in defining the limits of state intervention and specifying the dangers involved in transgressing those limits.

One key to understanding Schumpeter's contribution to economic analysis is to contrast the roles played by the auctioneer in the Walrasian system and the entrepreneur in the Schumpeterian world. First, Walras's auctioneer is a heuristic fiction, a device employed to establish a process that will generate equilibrium prices, whereas Schumpeter's entrepreneur is a real agent who either responds to disequilibrium situations by arbitrage, thereby setting up an equilibrating process, or creates the destruction of existing equilibria. Second, the activities of the auctioneer and the entrepreneur are in conflict with one another. The auctioneer is attempting to establish for all time a long-run competitive equilibrium, whereas the entrepreneur's actions disrupt existing temporary equilibria by destroying the parameters of the system.

This conflict between the auctioneer and the entrepreneur can provide some clues to the problem involved in state intervention. If the public sector assumes the mantle of a pseudoauctioneer in its attempt to establish equilibria, then do not the actions of the public sector run the risk of conflicting with those of the entrepreneur? The neoclassical model provides a theoretical framework for establishing the terminal state of the long run. It tells nothing about the economic processes through which an economy must pass in real time, nor does it contain an engine for growth and development. Schumpeter's economics, on the other hand, identifies the locomotive forces that will enhance an economy's level of welfare. State intervention in a changing economy, therefore, must balance those functions necessary to establish an efficient and socially just allocation of resources, while at the same time ensuring that its interventionist policies do not drastically slow down the engines of growth and development by destroying the incentive and penalty systems that face the entrepreneur. This balance means that policymakers need to trade off efficiency, equity, and growth. To design policies that will optimize this trade-off requires that the limits of the state be well defined.

9.4   A Schumpeterian approach to public policy

Although a Schumpeterian approach gives an important role to government, it nevertheless puts microeconomic considerations into long-term perspective at the center of the analysis and builds up the macroeconomic relations from them (Schumpeter, 1946; Stolper, 1983). This is in sharp contrast to the short- term macroeconomic public-policy model that has dominated much of the postwar period in the United Kingdom, at least. An almost exclusive preoccupation with Keynesian and monetarist demand-management macroeconomic policies has resulted in insufficient attention being given to the supply side of the economy. Even in instances in which supply-side policies have been pursued, too little regard has been paid to the microeconomic processes that generate supply; microeconomic analysis has been used to serve macroeconomic policy objectives, rather than macroeconomic budgetary policies being used to service microeconomic policies.

The inherent instability of capitalism was fully recognized by Schumpeter. This was a failure of the capitalist system and was the focus of Schumpeter's extensive analysis of the business cycle (Schumpeter, 1935, 1949). Prior to 1939 there was much popular criticism of capitalism; economists such as Lange offered alternative forms of economic organization as better ways of organizing the allocation and distribution of resources. Those alternatives included collectivism, socialism, and planning. Schumpeter did not go down these routes. Instead, he confronted the problem head-on by recognizing that the process of economic development through creative destruction would undoubtedly be disruptive. There would undoubtedly be adaptations and structural unemployment that could exist for long periods of time and could not be solved, as the classical economists suggested, simply by getting the real wage right.

How, then, should a government react to unemployment? Schumpeter was not insensitive to the social problems caused by unemployment, but he did recognize the problems that some forms of intervention might cause:

The real tragedy is not unemployment, per se, but unemployment plus the impossibility of providing adequately for the unemployed without impairing the conditions of further economic development. (Schumpeter, 1942, p. 70)
... public opinion as soon as it becomes alive to the duty in question immediately insists on economically irrational methods of financing relief and on lax and wasteful methods of administering it. (Schumpeter, 1942, p. 71)

In these passages, Schumpeter is at his clearest in stating his position on public policy to ensure (1) that the public-sector organization is efficient and (2) that the choices of policy instruments and the design of policy, while meeting laudable social objectives, do not destroy the incentives that will generate long-run growth and development – in this case, the creation of new jobs, which will solve the unemployment problem. It is these uncomfortable trade-offs and a government's choice of a position on the trade-offs that are the problems facing modern democracies – how best to trade off the long run against the short run and minimize the social costs of adjustment without sacrificing the benefits of development over the long run.

To provide policymakers with an informed choice would require that the economist know empirically the magnitudes of these social costs and benefits. Unfortunately, the current state of knowledge does not permit this. Political rhetoric fills the empirical vacuum. The empirical evidence that does exist is not conclusive. For example, economists have sought to determine whether or not unemployment compensation acts as a disincentive to job search; evidence regarding the impact of unemployment compensation on the duration of unemployment is mixed, but does, on balance, suggest that the disincentive effects are small.

The duration of unemployment depends on many factors, including the state of the labor market (Are there jobs available?), the level of the reservation wage, personal circumstances (family size, mortgage commitments, etc.), and the level of unemployment compensation. Attempts made in the United Kingdom to estimate the elasticity of unemployment duration with respect to unemployment compensation suggest that the elasticity might be as high as 2.5 or as low as zero.

The upper estimate made by Minford (1983) has largely been discredited by Nickell's reexamination (1984) of Minford's analysis. Reliable estimates are found to be much lower. Narendranathan, Nickell, and Stern (1985) found an average elasticity in the region of 0.30 to 0.35. They also found that the value of the elasticity declined with the age of the unemployed. For teenage males, it was on the order of 0.8, and it fell to zero for those aged 45 years. In a study carried out using U.S. data, Ehrenberg and Oaxaca (1976) found an elasticity of unity.

These studies suggest that for the United Kingdom, the present level of unemployment compensation is not as distortionary to the labor-market process as many fear. Given the size of these elasticities, drastic reductions in unemployment compensation would do little to change the duration of unemployment.

Schumpeter was not against subsidies to private industry in order to help adaptation. But he was not in favor of subsidies if they propped up inefficient practices in order to protect jobs. Whereas government could help the restructuring process, it should not attempt to maintan the old equilibrium by introducing policies that would distort prices (e.g., tariffs). Unfortunately, much of the U.K. government's industrial policy during the 1970s was aimed at subsidizing lame ducks, thereby lengthening the adaptation process.

What is the role of deficit financing (fiscal policy) for the purpose of creating employment in a Schumpeterian world? Schumpeter would look closely at the microeconomic impact of the budget. He would want to know, for example, whether the policy would help or hinder the adaptation of the economy and he would have been in favor of specific targeted public policies, rather than more general measures.

According to Stolper, the objective is to "maintain incomes but not specific jobs" (1984, p. 22).

Though Schumpeter did not specify the problem in terms of tax disincentives or crowding out, he was perfectly aware of these concepts in his 1918 paper on the tax state. Thus, the suitability of a budgetary policy would be judged in terms of (1) the impact of taxes on investments, (2) the impact of deficits on interest rates and exchange rates, (3) the impact of interest rates on private-sector investments, and (4) the impact of exchange rates on sales, expected profits, and, therefore, investments. In each case, the microeconomic consequences of the macroeconomic policy must be considered. But, of course, within a Schumpeterian framework, the emphasis is reversed. Given these microeconomic magnitudes, to what extent is it feasible to pursue macroeconomic objectives such as employment creation?

Policy analysis requires facts, and policy analysis within a Schumpeterian framework is particularly demanding in regard to the volume of microeconomic empirical evidence required. What, therefore, is the evidence currently available?

Whether or not public-sector deficits crowd out private economic activity (expenditures) depends on a number of factors. First, deficit or real-resource crowding out is unlikely to occur at less than full employment. Second, portfolio or financial crowding out will occur only to the extent that public-sector deficits drive up interest rates and private expenditures are interest-elastic. Whether or not public deficits cause interest rates to rise depends in turn on what is happening to the supply of savings, what the authorities are doing to the money supply, and the relative elasticities of substitution between money and bonds and bonds and real capital in private portfolios. Moreover, for small open economies, interest rates are greatly influenced by other factors, such as inflationary expectations over the medium term, the movements in interest rates in other economies, and changes in the exchange rate.

Evidence for the United Kingdom[12] suggests that crowding out has been less of a problem than is frequently thought. The rise in the public-sector deficit in the 1970s was matched by an increase in the volume of savings and a reduction in the private sector's demand for loanable funds caused mainly by depressed expectations arising from the recession and a lack of willingness to get tied into fixed-interest debt (corporate bonds) when the expectation was that inflation would

---

[12] For a survey, see Buiter (1985) and Jackson (1984).

fall. Furthermore, there is little evidence to suggest that private-invest-ment expenditures other than house construction or inventories are interest-elastic. It would seem, therefore, that for the United Kingdom, at least, the budgetary actions of government did not distort the prices generated in capital markets, given the levels of public borrowing and the conditions that prevailed during the 1970s and 1980s.

Problems did, however, arise as a consequence of the design of the U.K. government's monetary policy post 1979. Imposing tight con-trols on the money supply in a period of recession, when firms were involved in crisis borrowing from the banks to finance their rising inventories, forced up interest rates. This not only increased the costs of short-term working capital to the corporate sector but also forced up the sterling exchange rate, which in turn reduced exports and pro-moted further rounds of crisis borrowing.

The U.K. "monetarist experiment" is an example of the problems a government faces when it tries to design a monetary policy. In this case, the experiment failed because it distorted so many prices (Jack-son, 1985).

Ensuring an appropriate microeconomic environment for decision making is one of the main objectives when setting fiscal and monetary policies at the macro level. Governments, when pursuing budgetary policies, should make extensive use of existing markets and not replace them with administered systems of resource allocation, which often are dominated by bureaucratic inertia and inflexibility. A Schumpe-terian demand for market-determined allocation is not a prescription for acceptance of the unfettered workings of imperfect market forces. There is a role for government to set undistorted prices not only for the private-sector decision maker but also when carrying out its own cost–benefit appraisals and economic planning. There is a problem with this: What is meant by an undistorted price? How distorted are the prices in real markets? Industrial economists are currently trying to establish how many firms are required in an industry to produce a perfectly competitive price. The answer could be as low as two. Until these puzzles are resolved, it is difficult for the policy analyst to know how to regulate markets with the objective of establishing prices that will maximize efficiency.

In a Schumpeterian world there must be continuous generation of inventions, new ideas, and new ways of doing things to provide the seed for innovations and for creative destruction. At the same time, there must be a willingness to change. This means that there should be no protectionism. Thus, Schumpeter would ask the following ques-tions of public policies: (1) Do government policies stifle, suppress, and constrain entrepreneurship (creative destruction)? (2) Do government policies distort prices (wage rates, exchange rates, and interest rates)? (3) Do government policies aimed at the macro level to sustain full employment destroy the incentives for change? In other words, do fiscal and monetary policies create the appropriate environment of incentives and penalties that will assist the development process?

The periodic destruction of equilibrium that is the chief characteristic of the Schumpeterian process is carried out through new investments. This increases the productive potential of the economy. Encouragement of investment will therefore be the central-government policy, either through the government's own capital programs or by ensuring that the incentives in the private domain are appropriate.

The public sector will finance capital spending in those areas that naturally fall within the public domain: defense, police, and internal justice. In these cases, the choice of specific capital projects should be influenced strongly by the results of cost–benefit appraisals using appropriate prices. Capital spending might also be carried out by the public sector if capital markets should fail.

Capital markets might fail for a variety of reasons, but the main reason is the existence of uncertainty and uninsurable risks. A number of categories of infrastructure, such as roads and transportation networks, could be provided privately, but the costs of collecting tolls, and so forth, are so high that it is not profitable. Investment in fundamental research that has no immediate commercial payoff is also unlikely to be financed by the private sector. An example of this is the research carried out in government-sponsored university laboratories. Indeed, such research can be so expensive that consortia made up of the governments of many countries are necessary to make such ventures feasible: CERN and the European aerospace programs are examples. Without public-sector investment in basic research (which, once it is produced, has public-good characterisitcs), many entrepreneurs would not have the raw material required for innovation.

The existence of uninsurable risks and the failure of the private sector to take such risks provide the public sector with many roles. First, the Arrow-Lind theorem shows that by pooling risks collectively through the public sector, the members of society can enjoy the benefits of investments that otherwise would not have been pursued by the private sector. Second, the entrepreneurs in small businesses often are unable to finance R&D or expand their activities because they have insufficient retained earnings and insufficient collateral, and the institutions in the financial sector are unwilling to lend to them at reasonable rates of interest because of the risks involved.

Banks and financial intermediaries are reluctant to lend to business-men who have a hunch that they might not succeed. Bankers are sel-dom risk-loving gamblers. This failure of the capital market to take such risks constrains entrepreneurial activity and slows down the speed of development.

In an attempt to overcome this market failure, the public sector could underwrite the risks, or it could act as a financial intermediary and provide the funds directly on reasonable terms. Because the mem-bers of society will generally benefit from economic development through job creation and income generation, it seems reasonable to suppose that they might be prepared to support this kind of public-sector activity. The United Kingdom's Enterprise Allowance Scheme provides financial help of £40 per week for 52 weeks to those people who have been unemployed for eight weeks or more, who have a busi-ness venture in mind, and who have £1,000 to invest in it.

9.5   The limits of the tax state

Although the public sector might attempt to solve market failures and encourage entrepreneurial activity by creating suitable decision-mak-ing environments, there is always the danger that the form of taxation used will constrain enterprise. Schumpeter, in his "Crisis of the Tax State," is aware of the issues of tax-disincentive effects, and in that paper he sets down a Laffer-curve type of argument that concludes that tax revenues will eventually fall at higher marginal tax rates. In his *Deutsche Volkswirt* articles for 1927, Schumpeter defines taxable capacity as that level which can be taxed without interfering with the development process. He is, however, more explicit in his 1918 paper, where he states that "the tax state must not demand from the people so much that they lose financial interest in production or at any rate cease to use their best energies for it" ([1918] 1954, p. 20). But Schum-peter goes further than that and makes a point that seems to have been lost in the more recent tax-disincentive debates. What he essentially does is to point out that whether or not individuals find their tax bur-dens tolerable and whether or not disincentives will occur will depend, in part, on how individuals regard taxation. If they can see the benefits of high taxes, then they will be prepared to pay them. The tolerable burden of taxation, therefore, "is a different amount depending on the manner in which particular people view a particular tax state in a par-ticular historical situation which necessitates the tax. In times of patriotic fervour tax payments are consistent with extreme productive adaptation of strength which *normally* would make production cease altogether" ([1918] 1954, pp. 20–1).

9.6 Do taxes constrain work effort, enterprise, savings, and investment?

The question of the precise nature of the disincentive effects of taxation is one of the most controversial issues in public finance today. No single answer can be given, because these effects will vary from time to time and from place to place, depending on the precise details of the tax system. However, in designing tax systems, it is necessary for policymakers to keep these issues in the front of their minds, as Schumpeter urged. Evidence for the United Kingdom[13] suggests that disincentive effects of the income tax for male manual workers do not exist – there may even be a weak incentive effect. However, for second-income earners in households (e.g., working wives), there may be a weak disincentive effect. When it comes to the impact of taxation on the firm, on technical progress, on entrepreneurial activity, and on the long-term rate of growth of the economy, our empirical understanding in much weaker, and it would be wrong to draw any firm conclusions given the current state of knowledge. However, what is clear is that there do exist tax rates that will destroy incentives for entrepreneurs and risk takers and that will constrain the rate and composition of capital accumulation. Whether or not that state has yet been reached is unknown, given the complexity of our tax systems, with their capital allowances, depreciation offsets, and loss write-offs.[14]

Taxes, interest rates, and exchange rates are not the only constraints that the public sector places on private-sector activity. In their attempts to regulate and control the private domain, governments have set up inflexible bureaucracies that often do not respond quickly enough to the decision-making time frame of the private sector. Many initiatives are delayed because of the lags involved in granting planning permission or in processing a request through the legislative framework. A government seeking to encourage an enterprise culture needs to cut away inessential red tape. The establishment of Enterprise Zones and free-port areas in the United Kingdom are experiments that have attempted to pursue this logic.

9.7 Socialized industries

Many goods and services are produced by decreasing-cost industries that, in some countries such as the United Kingdom, have been brought under public ownership and control through nationalization

---

[13] For summaries, see Brown and Jackson (1986) and Brown (1983).
[14] For summaries, see Atkinson and Stiglitz (1980).

or, as in the case of the United States, have been brought under control through regulation. Schumpeter, as a result of the experience he gained with the German Coal Socialization Commission, advocated an alternative form of economic organization – socialization of the production process.

In 1919, the Austrian socialists wanted to eliminate the capitalists, but not the entrepreneurs. Their view was that the capitalists and the bureaucrats were preventing technical progress and that state organizations were run in the interest of capitalists and public employees. Schumpeter advocated industries *owned* by the people, but independent of government interference in their decision making. Socialization would take the form of a corporation run by entrepreneurial management that was independent of both workers and government. Such corporations were to be run in the interests of society and could be compared to nationalization, which was a form of state capitalism.

It is clear from his 1949 article in the *Journal of Political Economy* remarking on the state-managed economy that Schumpeter had few (if any) good things to say about the nationalization program in the United Kingdom. He distinguished between "labourism" and "socialism." The labor men were thought simply to administer capitalism from their own standpoint:

It would hardly do to accept such measures as the nationalization of the Bank of England . . . or the nationalization of the railroads or the mining or of utilities and so forth as proof positive of socialist intentions. It is true that the socialist aspect has been strongly emphasised. It is also true that the nationalization policy is coupled with an attitude towards private enterprise in general that amounts to sabotage. ([1949b] 1951, p. 298)

Socialization was a theoretical concept that differed from nationalization, and Schumpeter spent little time discussing the problems of implementation. In his discussion of how socialization might work, we see the hallmark of Schumpeter's approach – ensure that the incentive structure within decision making will result in resource allocations that will promote growth and development. This means that the entrepreneurs in socialized industries should be paid a competitive wage (compared to private industry), and profits made by socialized industries should be paid into the budget.[15] Moreover, socialized industries should not be subsidized, because that would distort the prices faced by decision makers and could result in misallocation of resources. Stol-

---

[15] It is not clear from Schumpeter's discussion how the capital spending of the socialized industries would be financed if net profits were not retained but were paid instead to the central exchequer.

per (1983), following the Schumpeterian approach, has questioned the logic of the policies pursued by many governments that, for reasons of social justice, subsidize the prices of public-enterprise outputs while levying taxes in order to finance the subsidies. That type of policy maximizes the amount of distortion to the economy imposed by government.

The concept of socialization, therefore, suggests an alternative to nationalization and regulation. Socialization is only an alternative to the current policies of the new right aimed at deregulation and privatization. Socialization combines the pursuit of efficiency and growth with the objective of distributive justice.

9.8   The distributional function of government

Discussions about the distributional function of government arouse the most intense passions among economists and noneconomists alike. Unlike other Austrian economists, such as Hayek, Schumpeter had little to say about redistributive taxation. He did, however, justify transfer payments on the grounds that entrepreneurial rewards contain an element of economic rent and that it was necessary to pay for the costs of economic development, such as those incurred in structural unemployment. Nevertheless, Schumpeter counseled caution, pointing out that transfer payments should be paid only up to the point where they would affect economic development by giving too much to consumption and not enough to investment.

The market outcome, even if it is efficient, may not be socially just, because it depends on the initial distribution of property rights, individual talents and disabilities, and so forth. Austrian arguments, embodied in the writings of Hayek (1948, 1960, 1976), asserted that the distribution of resources produced by the unfettered workings of the marketplace was socially optimal. This left the state with the minimalist role of night watchman, ensuring that, through its competition policy, the market worked efficiently.

Any redistribution carried out by government was assumed to violate individual liberty and freedom. Drawing on the philosophical work of Berlin (1969), economists of the libertarian persuasion on the new right have argued that market transactions are expressions of "negative freedom" and that to interfere with such transactions through government intervention is to violate negative freedom. By "negative freedom," Berlin meant freedom from coercion, an absence of "the deliberate interference of other human beings (or human agencies) within the area in which [one] could otherwise act" (1969, p. 112). This, of course, included freedom from state interference.

The libertarian position, which if subscribed to would severely constrain government action, has come under severe attack for its ad hocery, its assertions, blind faith, and concentration on a limited notion of liberty (Dasgupta, 1980, 1982). In particular, it ignores Berlin's notion of "positive freedom," that is, the freedom and ability "to be someone, not nobody; a doer – deciding, not being decided for, self directed . . . conceiving goals and policies of [one's] own and realizing them . . . to be conscious of [oneself] as a thinking, willing, active being, bearing responsibility for [one's] choices and able to explain them by reference to [one's] own ideas and purposes" (Berlin, 1969, p. 131). The distinction between negative and positive freedoms and the implications for government action are brought out clearly by Dasgupta:

A person may be assetless and, more importantly, chronically malnourished, lacking thereby motivation and physical capabilities necessary to be employable in a freely functioning labour market, his sole means of escape from the bonds of deprivation. He does not enjoy positive freedom. He is unable to be a "thinking, willing, active being." Such a man does not have life plans, or projects, or "own ideas and purposes." But if he is not prevented by others from seeking and obtaining employment in a freely functioning labour market he is negatively free. In this example, what keeps him in wretchedness, what deprives him systematically of his right to positive freedom, is not the dictates of a person, or an agency but the workings of the free play of market forces. (1986, p. 28)

The promotion and extension of positive freedoms provide the rationale for much public-sector activity, including the provision of subsidized goods and services and redistributive taxation. Dasgupta refers to commodities such as basic shelter, medical care, primary education, and sanitation facilities as "positive-rights goods." Concern with positive freedoms results in state guarantees of positive-rights goods.

The distributional function of government is circumscribed by value judgments. There is no scientific way of determining where a society should lie on the trade-off continuum between redistribution and other objectives, such as allocative efficiency and growth. To proceed down the road of redistribution can mean a heavy price in terms of growth forgone, but that might be a price that members of a community are prepared to pay. So, too, is there a trade-off between positive and negative freedoms. Pushing hard for positive freedoms results in an erosion of negative freedoms: Will individuals be prepared to pay this price? Different societies at different points in space and time will be distinguished by their preferences for different positions on these trade-offs. The membership fee for joining one society rather than another is the opportunity cost of being at one point on the trade-off continuum rather than another. Any individual member of the society who does not agree with the majority choice can express "voice" or "exit" (Hirshman, 1970).

9.9   Conclusions

Choosing those activities that are the legitimate concern of the public domain, and the degree to which they should be pursued, can result in an endless debate. Some of the principal issues have been reviewed in this chapter, which has also attempted to consider them in a Schumpeterian framework, broadly defined.

The vigorous enthusiasm with which some postwar governments pursued the teachings of naive Keynesians gave birth to false hopes that governments could, through their interventionist policies, provide stability and everlasting growth, development, and prosperity. After two decades of comparative stability and prosperity, the stagflationary years of the 1970s and the recessions of the 1980s highlighted in stark reality that the policies that governments had pursued were insufficient, that their payoffs were short-lived and that they contained, in some instances, the seeds of their own destruction. These events brought forth a series of countercurrents: attempts to reassess the appropriate role of government in a changing environment. Schumpeter, unlike the Keynesians, had emphasized the long run in economic policy-making. His theory of economic development showed the importance of supply-side factors, especially investment in new ideas and new forms of organization. More important, he focused attention on the microdynamics of economic life, seeking to establish the motivating forces that would propel an economy through time to higher levels of prosperity. His central concept was that of "creative destruction," and his principal economic agent was the entrepreneur. Schumpeter's economic framework differed in significant ways from that of the dominant neoclassical system of Marshall and Walras. The entrepreneur played a significantly different role from that of the Walrasian auctioneer, and a key to understanding Schumpeter's economics is to contrast these roles. Another important difference between Schumpeter and the dominant model is that he attempted to produce a truly dynamic economics, compared with the timeless, long-run static model of the Walrasian system.

In his "tax state" paper, Schumpeter recognizes the legitimate role of government, a theme that was developed at length in *Capitalism, Socialism and Democracy*. He is, however, quick to point out and stress the limits of the tax state and the problems that are created if these limits are exceeded. Here, he is drawing attention to the disincentive effects of taxation and the strong possibility that public-sector actions will distort the prices that private-sector decision makers face, with the result that they will make inappropriate decisions that will retard growth and development and thereby slow down the transition to greater prosperity.

Determination of the size of the welfare costs of government action has filled the research agenda of public-sector economists for many years now. Do taxes cause disincentives? Do budgets force up interest rates and crowd out private investment? Does regulation constrain profitability and reduce investment? The answers to these questions are mixed, depending on time and place, because the designs of fiscal systems vary so much. Getting the design of policy correct is central to the Schumpeterian tradition. But designing policies that will enhance growth, promote efficiency, and ensure some degree of social justice in complex, changing, and uncertain environments is no mean task, especially given our limited knowledge about the basic economic relationships involved. A Schumpeterian approach to policy does not replace the neoclassical market-failure model; rather, it complements and enhances that model by emphasizing the long-run uncertainty and the nature of the competitive process. Just as there is creative destruction in the world of commerce, so, too, is there creative destruction in the world of ideas. Integrating a Schumpeterian perspective into policy analysis will make the whole venture richer and should lead to development within this area of thought.

References

Atkinson, A. B., Goluka, J., Micklewright J., and Rau, N. (1981). "Unemployment Duration and Incentives: A Preliminary Analysis of the Family Expenditure Survey Data 1972/77." Unemployment Project Working Note No. 6, London School of Economics.

Atkinson, A. B., and Stiglitz, J. (1980). *Lectures on Public Economics.* New York: McGraw-Hill.

Berlin, I. (1969). "Two Concepts of Liberty," in *Four Essays on Liberty.* Oxford University Press.

Beveridge, W. H. (1942). *Social Insurance and Allied Services.* Cmnd. 5404. London: HMSO.

Blaug, M. (1985). *The Entrepreneur in Marx and Schumpeter.* Discussion Paper in Economics No. 35. University of Buckingham.

Brown, C. V. (1983). *Taxation and the Incentive to Work* (2nd ed.). Oxford: Blackwell.

Brown, C. V., and Jackson, P. M. (1986). *Public Sector Economics* (3rd ed.). Oxford: Blackwell.

Buiter, W. (1985). "A Guide to Public Sector Debts and Deficits." *Economic Policy* (November).

Clower, R. (1969). "The Keynesian Counter-Revolution: A Theoretical Appraisal," in F. H. Hahn and F. R. P. Brechling (eds.), *The Theory of Interest Rates.* London: Macmillan.

Dasgupta, P. (1980). "Decentralisation and Rights." *Economica,* 47.

(1982). "Utilitarianism, Information and Rights," in A. Sen and B. Williams (eds.), *Utilitarianism and Beyond.* Cambridge University Press.

(1986). "Positive Freedom, Markets and the Welfare State." *Oxford Review of Economic Policy,* 2(2).

Ehrenberg, R. G., and Oaxaca, R. L. (1976). "Unemployment Insurance, Duration of Unemployment and Subsequent Wage Gain." *American Economic Review,* 66.

Hayek, F. von (1948). *Individualism and Economic Order.* Chicago: Gateway.

(1960). *The Constitution of Liberty.* London: Routledge & Kegan Paul.

(1976). *The Mirage of Social Justice: Law, Legislation, Liberty,* Vol. 2. Longon: Routledge & Kegan Paul.

Helm, D. (1986). "The Economic Borders of the State," *Oxford Review of Economic Policy,* 2(2).

Hirshman, A. (1970). *Exit Voice and Loyalty.* Cambridge, Mass.: Harvard University Press.

Jackson, P. M. (1984). *Macroeconomic Activity and Local Government Behaviour.* PSERC monograph, University of Leicester.

(1985). *Implementing Government Policy Initiatives: The Thatcher Administration 1979/1983.* London: Royal Institute of Public Administration.

Leijonhufvud, A. (1968). *On Keynesian Economics and the Economics of Keynes.* Oxford University Press.

Minford, P. (1983). *Unemployment Cause and Cure.* London: Martin Robertson.

Musgrave, R. A. (1958). *The Theory of Public Finance.* New York: McGraw-Hill.

Narendranathan, W., Nickell, S., and Stern, J. (1985). "Unemployment Benefits Revisited." *Economic Journal.*

Nickell, S. J. (1984). "A Review of *Unemployment Cause and Cure* by Patrick Minford, with David Davies, Michael Peel and Alison Sprague." *Economic Journal,* 94 (December).

Nozick, R. (1974). *Anarchy, State and Utopia.* New York: Basic Books.

Rawls, J. (1971). *A Theory of Justice.* Oxford University Press.

Schumpeter, J. A. [1912] (1934). *Theorie der wirtschaftlicken Entwirklung.*

Leipzig: Duncker & Humblot; English translation, *The Theory of Economic Development,* translated by R. Opie. Cambridge, Mass.: Harvard University Press.

[1918] (1954). "Die Krise des Steuerstaates," (translated as "The Crisis of the Tax State") in W. F. Stolper and R. A. Musgrave (eds.), *International Economic Papers.* London: Macmillan.

(1927a). "Finanzpolitik und Kabinettssytem." *Der deutsche Volkswirt,* 1(April 8).

(1927b). "Finanzansgliech das deutsche Finanzproblem: Reich, Lander und Gemeinden." *Der deutsche Volkswirt,* 1(June 3).

(1935). "A Theorist's Comment on the Current Business Cycle." *Journal of the American Statistical Association, Supplement,* 30(March).

(1942). *Capitalism, Socialism and Democracy.* New York: Harper & Brothers.

(1946). "The Decade of the Twenties." *American Economic Review,* 34(2)(May).

(1949a). "The Historical Approach to the Analysis of Business Cycles." Universities National Bureau Conference on Business Cycle Research (November). New York.

[1949b] (1951). "English Economists and the State Managed Economy." *Journal of Political Economy,* (October):371–82; reprinted in R. V. Clemence (ed.), *Essays of J. A. Schumpeter.* Cambridge, Mass.: Addison-Wesley.

(1954). *History of Economic Analysis.* London: Allen & Unwin.

Stolper, W. F. (1983). "Fiscal and Monetary Policy in the Context of Development: A Schumpeterian Approach," in D. Biehl and W. F. Stolper (eds.), *Public Finance and Economic Growth.* Detroit: Wayne State University Press.

(1984). "The Relevance of Schumpeter's Ideas for Economic Policy." Unpublished mimeograph.

(n.d). "Schumpeter and the German Socialization Attempts of 1918/1919." Unpublished mimeograph.

Discussion

FRIEDRICH SCHNEIDER

The contribution by Professor Peter Jackson raises many important questions concerning the role of government in industrial societies. In his discussion he tries to combine Schumpeter's theories about state behavior with actual public-finance problems in our times. However,

The author would like to thank the participants of the first congress of the International J. A. Schumpeter Society for stimulating comments.

in my opinion, one should give much more weight to Schumpeter's work with respect to the question of what we can learn *nowadays* from Schumpeter's ideas, when analyzing the role of government in our industrial societies. As already stated by Professor Jackson, Schumpeter's main perspective was to place the emphasis on dynamic processes, concentrating on political institutions, so that the public sector is able to improve individual welfare.

In this comment, I shall employ this perspective and, as an example, examine how political institutions can influence the size of social security policies.

The influence of political institutions on social security policies

The purpose of this note is to provide some information on how politicians acting within the framework of different political institutions influence social security policies over time. First I consider a representative-democracy situation, and then I switch to a direct democracy, where I investigate how voters-taxpayers evaluate social security issues when these can directly influence their future development.

Social security policies in representative democracies

One of the basic assumptions of the public-choice approach is that in a representative democracy with discontinuous elections, a government can be considered to be in a special position of power, similar to that of a monopolist. The government has various advantages compared with the opposition party or parties, of which the most important are (1) the opportunity to influence the development of the economy, (2) the possibility of redistributing income, and (3) the possibility of changing laws. Hence, once elected to office, the government has considerable discretionary power that it can use to carry out its ideological programs. In the case of a serious threat to its political survival, the government will undertake a vote-maximizing policy concentrating on securing reelection rather than continuing to pursue its ideological goals. For this purpose, the government will undertake an economic policy that maximizes the chance of being reelected, relying on two facts:

1. The voters' rather "short-sighted" memory and limited knowledge of the functioning of the economy.[1]

---

[1] It is an open question how short the voter's memory actually is. For a detailed discussion, see Schneider and Frey (1987) and the literature cited there.

2. The voters' low incentive to obtain precise information about the government's past record (and future intentions), because the voter knows that he has practically no influence on the election outcome through his vote.

The main conclusion from these two facts is that if a government fears that it may lose the next election, it will switch to a "popular" fiscal policy – one that is clearly preferred by a majority of the voters.[2] Social security policies are, indeed, a good example of such a popular fiscal policy. If the government increases social security payments before an election, it may gain additional votes in all age groups among those entitled to vote:

1. Retired voters benefit immediately without being subject to higher (tax) payments.
2. Voters relatively close to retirement age also benefit by a non-negligible amount that is certainly larger than their additional social security taxes.
3. Voters far from retirement age will not feel the higher tax burden so heavily, because most of them underestimate their tax burden, and, in addition, the insurance argument is frequently used by the government; that is, it will argue that now all contributors are "better insured."

Empirical investigations of the development of social policies confirm these hypotheses for several representative democracies. First, among the economic indicators having an important impact on a government's popularity (the best available indicator for the government's reelection prospects), personal transfer payments (including social security) have a significant and sizable influence on government popularity, besides classical factors like unemployment and the inflation rate. This holds for Australia, the Federal Republic of Germany, and the United States.[3]

Second, the use of social-policy instruments for reelection purposes is well established, as shown by empirical investigations. Bank (1970) and Liefman-Keil (1971) found that for Germany, increases in social security programs are most often undertaken in an election year. The same conclusion was reached by Tufte (1978) for the United States.

---

[2] The particular fiscal policy undertaken differs from country to country and over time. For example, in the United Kingdom and the United States up to the mid-1970s, an expansionary fiscal policy was undertaken when the government/president was afraid of losing the election (Frey and Schneider, 1978a, 1978b).

[3] For a detailed analysis of the results reported here, see Schneider and Frey (1987).

Moreover, if the spending behavior of governments in representative democracies over the last 20 to 25 years is econometrically analyzed, transfer payments are the most frequently and intensively used instruments if a government fears that it will not be reelected.

These empirical results indicate that in representative democracies, governments use social-policy issues for their own selfish purposes, believing that it is very likely that a majority of the voters will support the party in power, because the benefits are clearly visible, and the additional costs (higher taxes) are distributed over the whole electorate and will not be felt very much. Only in recent times, when most Western countries have suffered from a major recession, have the voters come to realize their increasing tax burden. But now, the well-known public-good effect arises: Every government that wants to cut transfer and subsidy programs will face the stiff resistance of the affected voters, because the costs of reduced programs and subsidies are clearly visible and painful, but the benefits of possibly lower tax rates will be spread over almost all voters. Because of this, it is very difficult for a government to undertake cutbacks in transfer programs. In this situation the government faces the dilemma that it can no longer use an increase in social-policy programs for reelection purposes without an increase in the tax burden and/or the public deficit or cutbacks in other expenditures.

Social security policies in a direct democracy

Having discussed why in representative democracies voters have little incentive to be concerned with the development of social policies, especially their financing, we now consider the case of a direct democracy: Switzerland. Here, almost every change in social-policy issues must be approved in a national referendum, and if an increase is proposed, the method of financing must be explicitly stated. Thus, the frequent referenda over various social-policy issues provide an opportunity to investigate the main determinants of the voters in rejecting or accepting a referendum proposal on many policy issues.

A good opportunity to analyze voters' behavior in such a situation was provided by two proposals for a major change in the Swiss social security system. In a national referendum in December 1972, voters could reject both or accept only one. The proposals were as follows:

1. The "PdA initiative," a proposal by a left-wing party (Partei der Arbeit) that involved (a) a drastic increase in social pensions in real terms, (b) an inflation indexation, and (c) an

increase in the personal income tax on people with high incomes to finance the rise.

2. The "counterproposal" of the Swiss government (Gegen-vorschlag des Bundesrates), which involved "only" inflation indexation.

The PdA initiative was rejected with 84.6 percent no votes, and the counterproposal was accepted with 76.9 percent yes votes. From the outcomes of these two referenda it seems to be worthwhile to analyze the electorate's motives that determined these results. At a first glance, and in comparison with the great popularity of increasing the social security benefits in representative democracies, the opposite result should have been expected: a huge majority for the PdA initiative and a rejection of the counterproposal.

Using the public-choice approach, Schneider and Pommerehne (1983) developed hypotheses about the voters' behaviors:

1. The higher the proportion of older voters in a Swiss kanton, the higher (lower) the yes-vote share for the PdA initiative (counterproposal), *ceteris paribus*.
2. The higher the proportion of younger voters in a kanton, the higher (lower) the yes-vote share for the counterproposal (PdA initiative), *ceteris paribus*.
3. The higher the income level in a kanton, the lower the yes-vote share for both proposals, because high-income people would be "net losers" in both proposals because of the redistributional effects.[4]

For the PdA initiative, Schneider and Pommerehne clearly confirmed the foregoing hypotheses. High-income voters and those aged 25 to 34 rejected the PdA initiative, and citizens over 65 were clearly in favor of it. Half of the variance of the dependent variable (52 percent) was explained in a statistical sense. As regards the counterproposal, only the income variable had a significant negative influence on the dependent variable, and "only" 39 percent of the variance was explained in a statistical sense. In sum, these results show that the voters were somewhat influenced by short-term utility-cost considerations, but that these factors were far from being sufficient to explain satisfactorily the voting behavior.

---

[4] That redistributional effects hurt people with high incomes (50,000 Swiss francs and more in 1972) has been shown by Pommerehne and Schneider (1985). A very detailed analysis of this problem is given by Oberhänsli (1982).

Therefore, these two authors extended their approach to include broader and long-term perspectives of a more general benefit–cost calculus (Pommerehne and Schneider, 1985, p. 91):

1. One argument is that voters/taxpayers considered the burden of increased social security tax rates for the next generation, especially if they had children.
2. Another argument is that voters/taxpayers took into consideration the expected negative effects on future economic development. In order to evaluate such long-term aspects, voters needed some knowledge of the working of the economy; therefore, their education was important, and it is hypothesized that voters with a university degree (degree of an elementary school) had the best (an insufficient) education to evaluate the proposed negative consequences on the economy.

The empirical results of the expanded approach show that the argument of the increased future burden on the next generation had a significantly negative influence on the PdA initiative, but not on the counterproposal of the government. The variables for the educational level of the voters influenced the outcome for both proposals. Voters with only an elementary education supported the initiative (and rejected the counterproposal); voters with a high school and/or university degree supported quite strongly the counterproposal and rejected the initiative. This result might be interpreted to indicate that "better-educated" voters were more aware of the possible future negative consequences of the initiative than were the other groups.[5] Including these long-term perspectives, the share of explained variance of the outcome for the PdA initiative rises to over 80 percent, and that for the counterproposal increases from 40 percent to 70 percent. It seems that now the major factors determining the decision process of the Swiss electorate concerning these two proposals have been adequately captured.

Concluding remarks

If we summarize these findings when comparing the development of social security policies in different political institutions, the represen-

---

[5] Another, also very plausible, interpretation is that this "education distribution" reflects quite closely the income distribution, so that the voters with university degrees (the rich) would have been net losers under the proposed changes of the initiative, and therefore they rejected it.

tative democracy and the direct democracy, we find three main conclusions about the role of government in our societies:

1. In representative democracies, government quite often uses social security policies for its own selfish purposes. Elected politicians can do so because the institutional framework within representative democracies gives the government almost a monopolistic position over time. Hence, the government will use this position to carry out ideologically oriented policies, and if necessary it will undertake "popular" policies in order to secure its reelection.

2. In representative democracies, voters are in favor of a widening of social security programs as long as the burden of financing them is distributed over all voters/taxpayers. When the tax burden of increased government activities becomes apparent, for various reasons, no group of voters wants to bear the easily visible and painful reductions in social security activities, especially when the whole electorate will benefit from possible lower tax rates.

3. Contrary to the situation in representative democracies, citizens in direct democracies have greater possibilities for influencing policy questions. For example, in Switzerland, the voters can initiate a referendum over an issue like an increase in social security payments in order to change the current situation. The empirical investigation of two quite different proposals concerning the further development of the Swiss social security system demonstrates that the decision of the electorate to reject a drastic widening of the social security system and instead to accept "only" an inflation indexation was based on various short- and long-term considerations.

Hence, Schumpeter's idea of concentrating on dynamic processes with respect to government activities in different political institutions is a worthwhile approach to analyzing policy questions in our time. A comparison of the development of social security policies between representative and direct democracies provides new insights and possibly new alternatives if drastic changes (e.g., a reduction in social security programs) have to be undertaken.

References

Bank, Hans-Peter (1970). "Die Sozialgesetzgebung der Bundesrepublik Deutschland und ihr zeitlicher Zusammenhang mit den Wahlterminen seit 1949." *Recht und Arbeit,* pp. 101–15.

Frey, Bruno S., and Schneider, Friedrich (1978a). "A Politico-Economic Model of the United Kingdom." *Economic Journal,* 88(2):243–53.

———— (1978b). "An Empirical Study of Politico-Economic Interaction in the U.S." *Review of Economics and Statistics,* 60(2):174–83.

Liefman-Keil, Elisabeth (1971). "Sozialpolitische Entscheidungen," in H. Sandmann (ed.), *Aspekte der Friedensforschung und Entscheidungsprobleme in der Sozialpolitik* (pp. 61–71). Berlin: Duncker & Humblot.

Oberhänsli, Urs (1982). *Einfluss der AHV und der beruflichen Vorsorge auf die persönlichen Ersparnisse in der Schweiz.* Frankfurt: Verlag Haag und Herchen.

Pommerehne, Werner W., and Schneider, Friedrich (1985). "Politisch-ökonomische Uberprüfung des Kaufkraftsinzidenzkonzeptes: Eine Analyse der AHV-Abstimmungen von 1972 und 1978," in E. Brugger and R. L. Frey (eds.), *Sektoralpolitik versus Regionalpolitik* (pp. 75–100). Diessenhofen: Rüegger.

Schneider, Friedrich, and Frey, Bruno S. (1987). "Politico-Economic Models of Macroeconomic Policy," in T. D. Willet (ed.), *Inflation and the Political Business Cycle.* San Francisco: Pacific Institute.

Schneider, Friedrich, and Pommerehne, Werner W. (1983). "Ideologie vs. Eigennutz: Eine empirische Untersuchung der AHV-Vorlage von 1972." Unpublished mimeograph, Universität Zürich.

Tufte, Edward (1978). *Political Control of the Economy.* Princeton University Press.

Discussion

KARL-DIETER GRÜSKE

Professor Jackson presents a chapter on a very interesting part of the Schumpeterian world, namely, the role of the state. This topic is sometimes neglected, because Schumpeter and his successors concentrated on the market and its evolution in changing industrial economies. But considering a state's share of nearly 50 percent in modern economies, the role and the influence of the government cannot be ignored.

In this respect, Jackson gives a comprehensive and impressive overview on Schumpeter's contribution to the relations between the market and the state. However, it is the task of a discussant not only to applaud the speaker but also to criticize and to show some additional or complementary aspects. Primarily, I concentrate on some empirical results that are supplementary to the findings in Jackson's chapter.

Following Schumpeter, Jackson asks many questions concerning the influence of the public sector on other parts of the economic system. Unfortunately, almost none of these questions can be answered definitively, neither empirically nor theoretically. This, of course, is disappointing after about 50 years of more or less intensive research, and it is not the author's failure, but the failure of the analyses in the different fields. The reasons can be found in countervailing factors, such as the income and substitution effects in responding to a tax change, or, frequently neglected, a transfer alteration – apart from an overall view concerning the whole public influence. Other facts are, for instance, the different situations, time, and special laws and regulations that affect the results. In my view, the main reason for this lack of knowledge lies in the lack of consistent empirical studies and dynamic models that would analyze the causes and impact of regulations, of taxes (or, preferably, all revenues), and of all expenditures (not only of transfers) on market behavior in the long run. This would be a scientific task in the Schumpeterian sense.

Because of the absence of such models, one has to look for other ways. I would like to show at least some empirical results from recent research on the different effects that the state produces. Influenced by Schumpeter's work on "The Crisis of the Tax State" ([1918] 1954), Jackson concentrates on the public-revenue side, examining the effects on work effort (incentives), savings, and capital formation (investment, interest rates, crowding out). From my point of view, this seems a little one-sided. Jackson ignores public expenditures and studies only the *traditional* tax effects. But besides inefficiency in the public sector with respect to public goods, there are many additional welfare losses or, at least, resource absorptions connected with taxes. They produce corresponding effects that have been totally neglected.

To give an overview, I present Figure 9.1 as a basis for a new analysis of tax effects (Recktenwald, 1984).

The diagram starts with tax collection, which absorbs resources from the market sector as regular and actual tax burdens that affect income and the growth of the economy. The tax requires political and administrative collection and compliance costs in the public sector. Furthermore, one can analyze at least four additional categories of welfare losses. These are substitution losses (expressed as avoidance burdens and tax evasion), excess burdens, tangible and intangible compliance costs, and losses of efficiency in the shape of opportunity costs caused by a wrong or inappropriate policy of taxation.

Although the individual phenomena of causality are well known both in literature and in practice, they have been analyzed only in isolation, for example, the underground economy or the excess burden in the optimal-taxation theory. In other approaches, they are more or less neglected, as is the case for collection and compliance costs, or have

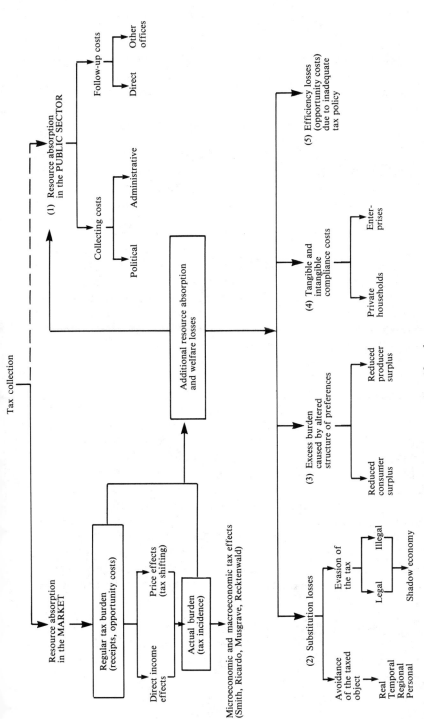

Figure 9.1. Analysis of tax effects: resource absorption and welfare losses.

only been barely recognized, such as efficiency losses due to an incorrect taxation policy. Even approaches to a theoretical or empirical proof or integration are missing.

To demonstrate the empirical importance of these additional costs, I give only examples. In the Institute of Economics at the University of Erlangen-Nürnberg, a research project has been finished recently, supervised by H. C. Recktenwald. It concerns the administrative collection costs for different types of taxes in the public sector, and the compliance costs (red-tape-shifting) of tax laws and other regulations in the private sector (Bauer, 1987; Grüske, in press; Tiebel, 1986). These costs totaled 80 billion DM in 1984, about 6 percent of national income. The distinct regressive distribution of the compliance costs impedes competition and limits market entry, especially for small enterprises. The evidence is that there have been large increases in these additional costs in the last 30 years. Examination of the excess burden in a study of U.S. data by Ballard, Shoven, and Whalley (1985, p. 125) reveals additional welfare losses of 13 to 24 percent of the tax system, whereas Browning (1987, p. 11) indicates 10 to 300 percent; these have to be added to our cost figures.[1] In this respect, Schumpeter's skepticism about public intervention seems to be supported by the empirical data.[2]

Analyses like these represent a starting point, not only for an optimal tax system but also for an efficient system, when looking for ways of minimizing costs on different levels. This also involves concerns about deficiencies inside the public bureaucracies, the political influences, and the failures in the voting mechanisms, which are only briefly mentioned by Jackson, despite the vast literature on this topic.[3]

I use the examples cited to point out that the empirical vacuum on tax effects noted by Jackson can be filled in some respects. This is also true for the redistributive effects of the state mentioned by Jackson, although Schumpeter did not say much about this topic. For instance, in several studies for West Germany, I found that between 1963 and 1978, the redistributive effects of the public budget on personal incomes were relatively constant, despite the fact that the social budget had grown from 41 percent to nearly 50 percent of public expenditures

---

[1] Applying the American findings to West Germany would yield results ranging from 54 to 100 billion DM. For the very problematic application of these figures, see Recktenwald (1986).

[2] Additionally, the size of the shadow economy has to be considered. See H. Zimmermann's discussion of this in Chapter 8. They point in the same direction.

[3] For an overview, see the volumes edited by Hanusch (1983, 1984).

(Grüske, 1985a). Interpreting these results, one finds obvious hints of the ineffectiveness of the public redistributive system.

Evaluations like these lead to an expanded view of the market, compared with the state. From Schumpeter's viewpoint, the essential point is the comparison of allocative market failures and allocative state failures. The distributive side is relatively neglected in this respect. Thus, generally the distributive market criticism – which is in itself unjustified because it is not the task of the market to produce a just distribution – ends with the redistributive duty of the state, without asking whether or not the state fulfills that goal in an efficient and effective way. From this point of view, and supported by empirical and theoretical results, the allocative side has to be complemented by the redistributive side, and the distributive "market failure" compared with the redistributive state failures.[4] Social security systems, based on "uninsurable risks" in the market, should be included. In this respect, Jackson's analysis could also be expanded, because he discusses only such uninsurable risks as "investment risks" (e.g., infrastructure, basic research).

To sum up, the trade-off between efficiency and equity gets an additional variant. Jackson points out how to design policies that will optimize the trade-off between efficiency and equity, but this leads to results, as optimal-taxation theory shows, that are not feasible within the political process. I think it would be preferable to speak of minimizing the failures in the public sector and to establish an efficient system, which can never be optimal, but is second best in its effects on market allocation and distribution.

Public finance contributes the "theory of public waste" to point out the reasons for public inefficiency (including the external effects mentioned earlier on incentives, savings, etc.). If one starts from there, efficient action can be enforced only by connecting self-interest and public interest. In this regard, Schumpeter suggested demonstrating the benefits of high taxes to the taxpayers. In an expanded view, the decisive principle is the economic and political linkup among users, payers, suppliers, and decision makers, wherever possible, if decisions are made concerning the burdens and benefits of public supply (Recktenwald, 1986).

In any event, Schumpeter had recognized that the market outcome is inefficient or inequitable in some respects. This does not allow us to deduce automatically that government intervention will necessarily

---

[4] For details, see Grüske (1985b, p. 363). The analysis should be expanded to dynamic processes of redistribution (dynamic incidence) in the sense of Schumpeter.

lead to improvement. Such a deduction has been compared by Stigler to the situation of an emperor judging a musical competition between two players, who gave the prize to the second player, having heard only the first (Atkinson and Stiglitz, 1980, p. 9).

This does not mean that the government has no way to support the dynamic process of the economy in the Schumpeterian sense. On the contrary, there are many measures, not only taxes and expenditures but also measures establishing conditions that create an appropriate environment of incentives and penalties under free competition, that support technical change and mobility of factors. Jackson does not work out a design of policy in the Schumpeterian tradition in detail, but does give some stimulating suggestions in the perspective of the Schumpeterian world of structural change and creative destruction in the long run.

References

Atkinson, A. B., and Stiglitz, J. E. (1980). *Lectures on Public Economics.* New York: McGraw-Hill.

Ballard, C. L., Shoven, J. B., and Whalley, J. (1985). "The Total Welfare Costs of the United States Tax Systems: A General Equilibrium Approach." *National Tax Journal,* 38:125–40.

Bauer, E.-R. (1987). *Der volkswirtschaftliche Aufwand für die Steuererhebung – Eine empirische Analyse des deutschen Steuersystems.* Research project, University of Nürnberg (Institut für Volkswirtschaftslehre). Göttingen: Vandenhoeck und Ruprecht.

Browning, E. K. (1987). "On the Marginal Welfare Cost of Taxation." *American Economic Review,* 77(1):11–23.

Grüske, K.-D. (1985a). "Redistributive Effects of the Integrated Financial and Social Budgets in West Germany," in A. J. Culyer and G. Terny (eds.), *Public Finance and Social Policy* (pp. 239–57). Proceedings of the 39th Congress of the International Institute of Public Finance (IIPF), Budapest, 1983. Detroit: Wayne State University Press.

(1985b) *Personale Verteilung und Effizienz der Umverteilung – Analyse und Synthese.* Göttingen: Vandenhoeck und Ruprecht.

(in press). *Additional Losses of Taxation: Compliance Costs and Administrative Costs – Some Empirical Evidence.* Proceedings of the 42nd Congress of the IIPF, Athens, 1986.

Hanusch, H. (ed.) (1983). *Anatomy of Government Deficiencies.* Berlin: Springer.

(ed.) (1984). *Public Finance and the Quest for Efficiency.* Detroit: Wayne State University Press.

Recktenwald, H. C. (1984). "Neue Analytik der Steuerwirkungen. *"Wirtschaftswissenschaftliches Studium,* 8:393–400.

(1986). "Kritisches zur Theorie der optimalen Besteuerung – Über Sinn und Widersinn des excess Burden – Prinzips." *Hamburger Jahrbuch für Wirtschafts- und Gesellschaftspolitik,*" 31:155–75.

Schumpeter, J. A. [1918] (1954). "Die Krise des Steuerstaates," (translated as "The Crisis of the Tax State,") in W. F. Stolper and R. A. Musgrave (eds.), *International Economic Papers.* London: Macmillan.

Tiebel, C. (1986). *Überwälzte Kosten der Gesetze.* Göttingen: Vandenhoeck und Ruprecht.

CHAPTER 10

Following and leading

MOSES ABRAMOVITZ

In the great Schumpeterian vision of a developing economy, no ideas are more important than the notions of innovation and imitation, of leadership and followership.

This chapter is, in a sense, an extension of these ideas. Schumpeter's theories were designed to illuminate the growth process within individual nations. In Schumpeter's treatment, innovation and imitation are characteristics of the entrepreneurs and the firms of particular countries. When one considers comparative growth among groups of countries, however, one encounters similar but not identical ideas. In this context, we think of countries as leaders or followers. This extension of Schumpeter's categories carries with it the hypothesis that leading countries, whose innovating activity is limited by the advance of knowledge itself, have a more restricted growth potential than do followers. The latter, at least in principle, can advance not only *with* the frontier of knowledge, but also *toward* the frontier. Moving from Schumpeter's entrepreneurs as innovators to nations as leaders is a step consonant with the idea that innovation is, in part, a social function, not just an individual, heroic action. It is a step farther along the road that Schumpeter himself traveled when he considered the replacement of the entrepreneur-innovator by large-scale corporate management.

Needless to say, this modification of Schumpeter's vision is nothing new. One encounters it repeatedly in studies of economic history, especially when comparisons among countries are attempted. Still more, it is widely believed that the growth potential afforded by the opportunity to catch up was a very important element in the growth booms of the postwar period. Here, the United States was viewed as the leader, with Western European countries and Japan as followers. Next, a weakening of that potential is now often advanced as a partial expla-

This chapter is an abbreviated version of a longer paper recently published in Sweden (Abramovitz, 1986a). See also Abramovitz (1986b). I acknowledge with thanks the critical reading and suggestions of Paul David, as well as the support of the Center for Economic Policy Research at Stanford University.

nation for the sustained retardation in growth since 1973. Finally, there is the impact of the advance of Japan and of the newly industrializing countries on the economies of the older leaders in North America and Western Europe. This impact serves to remind us that the catch-up process is more than acquisition of knowledge by followers from leaders. There are other interactions between the pursuers and the pursued that may affect not only the gaps between them but also their ranks on the international income ladder.

With these thoughts in mind, it seems to me to be of interest to take up again the theme of leading and following in relation to the comparative standings and growth rates of different countries. This chapter has three parts. First, there is a discussion and restatement of the catch-up hypothesis as it bears on the relative growth rates of countries. Second, there is a historical review of the operation of the catch-up process as it has emerged in the experience of the presently industrialized countries. This review is hung on the statistical framework provided by Angus Maddison's (1982) estimates of labor productivity in 16 countries in the industrialized West in a series of key years stretching over the long interval from 1870 to 1979.

Finally, I add some reflections bearing on conceivable tendencies for old leaders to fall behind. These are stimulated by current anxieties about the possible decline of the United States and Western Europe in the productivity scale.

Obviously, these very broad subjects cannot be treated adequately in a single chapter. All I can hope to do is to deal with them somewhat incompletely and suggestively. My object is mainly to arouse interest and to indicate the sorts of questions that arise and some lines of study worth pursuing.

10.1   The catch-up hypothesis

The catch-up hypothesis asserts that being backward in terms of level of productivity carries a *potential* for rapid advance. Stated more definitely, the proposition is that in comparisons across countries, the growth rates of productivity over a long period tend to be inversely related to the initial levels of productivity.

The central idea is simple enough. Imagine that the level of labor productivity is governed entirely by the level of technology embodied in capital stock. In a "leading country," to state things sharply, one may suppose that the technology embodied in each vintage of its stock is at the very frontier of technology at the time of investment. The *technological age* of the stock is, so to speak, the same as its *chrono-*

logical age. In a follower, whose productivity level is lower, the technological age of the stock is high relative to its chronological age. The stock is obsolete even for its age. When a leader discards old stock and replaces it, the accompanying productivity increase is governed and limited by the advance of knowledge between the time when the old capital was installed and the time it is replaced. Those who are behind, however, have the potential to make a larger leap. New capital can embody the frontier of knowledge, but the capital it replaces is technologically superannuated. So, the larger the productivity gap between leader and follower, the stronger is the follower's potential for growth and, other things being equal, the more rapid one expects the follower's growth rate to be. Followers tend to catch up and grow faster if they are initially more backward.

Viewed in the same simple way, the catch-up process should be self-limiting, because as a follower catches up, the possibility of making large leaps by replacing superannuated technology by best-practice technology becomes smaller and smaller.

This is the simple central idea. It needs extension and qualification. There are at least four extensions:

1. Backwardness carries an opportunity for modernization in disembodied, as well as embodied, technology.
2. The same technological opportunity that permits rapid progress by modernization encourages rapid growth of the capital stock. So, besides a reduction in technological age toward chronological age, the chronological age also goes down, and the rate of rise of the capital–labor ratio speeds up. Productivity growth benefits on both counts.
3. Growth in productivity also makes for an increase in aggregate output. A larger horizon of scale-dependent technological progress then comes into view.
4. If countries at relatively low levels of industrialization also contain large numbers of redundant workers in farming and petty trade, there is also an opportunity to raise productivity by improving the allocation of labor.

Besides extension, the simple hypothesis also needs qualification. First, technological backwardness is not usually a mere accident. Tenacious societal characteristics normally account for a portion, perhaps a substantial portion, of a country's past failure to achieve as high a level of productivity as economically more advanced countries have done. The same deficiencies, perhaps in attenuated form, normally remain to limit a backward country from making the full technological leap envisaged by the simple hypothesis. I have a name for these characteristics. Following Kazushi Ohkawa and Henry Rosovsky (1973, chap. 9), I call them "social capability." Having regard to technological backwardness by itself leads to the simple hypothesis about catch-up and convergence already stated. Having regard to social capability, however, we expect that the developments anticipated by that hypothesis will be clearly displayed in cross-country comparisons only if social capabilities are the same. One should say, therefore, that a country's potential for rapid growth is strong not when it is backward without qualification but rather when it is technologically backward but socially advanced.

The trouble with absorbing social capability into the catch-up hypothesis is that no one knows just what it means or how to measure it. In past work, I identified a country's social capability with technical competence (for which, at least among Western countries, years of education may be a rough proxy) and with its political, commercial, industrial, and financial institutions (which I characterized in more qualitative ways). I had in mind mainly experience with the organization and management of large-scale enterprise and with financial institutions and markets capable of mobilizing capital for individual firms on a similarly large scale (Abramovitz, 1979). On some occasions the situation may be sufficiently clear. In explaining postwar growth in Western Europe and Japan, for example, one may be able to say with some confidence that these countries were competent to absorb and exploit the existing best-practice technology. More generally, however, judgments about social capability remain highly problematic.

One important aspect of the matter stems from the fact that social capability develops in part, perhaps in large part, in response to technological opportunity and in the course of exploiting it. People learn to organize and manage large-scale enterprises in the course of trying. Institutions auxiliary to large-scale production arise in response to demand. The content of education is reformed as the needs of new technologies are appreciated.[1]

These considerations qualify the notion that a follower's potential

---

[1] When the Harvard Center for Research in Entrepreneurial History was founded after the war under Schumpeter's inspiration, the issue of institutional responsiveness came to the fore. John Sawyer and David Landes attributed France's perceived growth lag behind Germany in the late nineteenth century and early twentieth century to persistent deficiencies in French business organization that they traced to still deeper characteristics of French society. Alexander Gerschenkron (1962), besides contending that differences in business organization were not pronounced, believed that organization would have responded to opportunity had it existed (Landes, 1949, 1951; Sawyer, 1951, 1952).

for rapid growth weakens as its technological level converges with that of the leaders. This is not necessarily the case if social capability is itself endogenous, becoming stronger as technological gaps close. There is a quasi-technical point with a similar bearing: It is the fact, noticed by Edward Denison (1967) and Irving Kravis et al. (1978), that as followers' levels of income converge with that of the leader, so do their structures of production and prices. That makes it easier for followers to borrow the technologies previously explored by the leaders.

The combination of technological gap and social capability defines a country's *potentiality* for productivity advance by way of catch-up. This, however, should be regarded as a potentiality in the long run. The pace at which the potentiality is realized during any limited period of time depends on still another set of causes that are largely independent of those governing the potentiality itself. There is a long story to tell about the factors controlling the rate of realization of potential. Its general plot, however, can be suggested by noting the topics of the three principal sections of this chapter:[2]

1. The facilities for the diffusion of knowledge – for example, channels of international technical communication, multinational corporations, the state of international trade and of direct capital investment.
2. Conditions facilitating or hindering structural change in the composition of output, in the occupational and industrial distribution of the work force, and in the geographical location of industry and population. Among other factors, this is where conditions of labor supply, the existence of labor reserves in agriculture, and the factors controlling internal and international migration come in.
3. Macroeconomic and monetary conditions encouraging and sustaining capital investment and the level and growth of effective demand.

Having considered technological catch-up, with its several extensions and qualifications, I can summarize by proposing a restatement of the hypothesis, as follows:

Countries that are technologically backward have a potentiality for generating growth more rapid than that of more advanced countries, provided their social capabilities are sufficiently great to permit successful exploitation of technologies already in operation in richer

---

[2] My paper cited earlier (1979, pp. 18–30) describes the operation of these factors in the 1950s and 1960s and tries to show how they worked to permit productivity growth to rise rapidly in so many countries, in concert and for such an extended period.

Table 10.1. *Comparative levels of productivity, 1870–1979: means and relative variances of the relatives of 15 countries compared with the United States (U.S. GDP per man-hour = 100)*[a]

Year	(1) Mean	(2) Coefficient of variation[b]
1870	77 (66)	.51 (.51)
1890	68 (68)	.48 (.48)
1913	61	.33
1929	57	.29
1938	61	.22
1950	46	.36
1960	52	.29
1973	69	.14
1979	75	.15

[a]1870 and 1890: figures in parentheses are based on relatives with the United Kingdom = 100.
[b]Standard deviation ÷ mean.
Source: Calculated from Maddison (1982, Tables 5.2 and C.10).

countries. The pace at which the potential for catch-up is actually realized in a particular period depends on other factors limiting the diffusion of knowledge, the rate of structural change, the accumulation of capital, and the expansion of demand. Catching up tends to be self-limiting, but the strength of this tendency may be weakened or overcome, at least for limited periods, by advantages connected with the convergence of production patterns as followers advance toward leaders or by other endogenous enlargements of social capabilities.

10.2   Historical experience

We now consider the experiences of the 16 countries covered by the improved Maddison estimates of man-hour productivity at nine key years from 1870 to 1979.[3] I have compressed the message of these data into three measures (Tables 10.1 and 10.2):

1.   Averages of the productivity levels of the various countries relative to that of the United States, which was the leading

[3] The 16 countries are Australia, Austria, Belgium, Canada, Denmark, Finland, France, Germany, Italy, Japan, the Netherlands, Norway, Sweden, Switzerland, the United Kingdom, and the United States.

Table 10.2. *Association (rank correlation) between initial level and subsequent growth rate of labor productivity (GDP per man-hour in 16 countries, 1870–1979)*

Shorter periods			Lengthening periods	
Years	(1)	(2)	Years	(3)
1870–1913	−.59		1870–1890	−.32
1870–1890		−.32	–1913	−.59
1890–1913		−.56	–1929	−.72
			–1938	−.83
1913–1938	−.70		–1950	−.16
1913–1929		−.35	–1960	−.66
1929–1938		−.57	–1973	−.95
			–1979	−.97
1938–1950	+.48			
1950–1979	−.92			
1950–1960		−.81		
1960–1973		−.90		
1973–1979		−.13		

Source: Underlying data from Maddison (1982, Tables 5.1, 5.2, and C.10).

country for most of the period. (For 1870 and 1890, I have also calculated averages of relatives based on the United Kingdom.) I calculate these averages for each of the nine key years and use them to indicate whether or not the productivity levels of followers, *as a group,* were tending to converge on that of the leader.

2. Measures of relative variances around the mean levels of relative productivity. These provide one sort of answer to the question whether or not the countries that started at relatively low levels of productivity tended to advance faster than those with initially higher levels.

3. Rank correlations between initial levels of productivity and subsequent growth rates. If the potential supposedly inherent in technological backwardness is being realized, there is likely to be some inverse correlation; and if it works with enough strength to dominate other forces, the coefficients will be high.

The Maddison data are valuable for a variety of purposes, but for those to which I put them, these data have many deficiencies.[4] For the

---

[4] These data have the weakness inherent in any estimates of GDP and man-hours that stretch back into the nineteenth century. Beyond that, my simple measures fail in a

moment, however, I ask, What do the three measures tell us if we accept them more or less at face value?

I first make some observations on long-term development over the whole period of 109 years.

Other countries, on the average, made no net gain on the United States. The average of relatives for 15 countries stood as follows:

1870	77
1890	68 (when U.S. actually became #1)
1979	75

This indication of very limited, or even zero, convergence is really stronger than the figures suggest. That is because the productivity measures reflect more than gaps in technology and in reproducible capital intensity, with respect to which catch-up is presumably possible. They also reflect differences in natural resource availabilities that, of course, are generally favorable to the United States and were far more important to the United States and to all the other countries in 1870 than they are today. In 1870, the agricultural share of U.S. employment was 50 percent; in 1979, it was 3.5 percent. For the other 15 countries, the corresponding figures are 48 and 8 percent on the average (Maddison, 1982, Table C.5). So the U.S. advantage in 1870 depended much more on our favorable land–man ratio than it did in 1979. Putting it the other way, other countries, on the average, must have fallen back over the century in terms of the productivity determinants in respect to which catch-up is possible.

In other respects, however, one can clearly see the influence of the potential for catching up. The variance among the productivity levels

number of respects to isolate the influence of the catch-up hypothesis proper. Because they do not allow for the richness of countries' natural resources in relation to population, productivity levels are imperfect reflections of levels of technology. Labor productivity levels also reflect past accumulations of reproducible capital, both tangible and human, and these may also be independent of technological levels in one degree or another. The measured growth rates of labor productivity will be influenced by the pace of capital accumulation. Although differences in rates of accumulation may themselves be a function of countries' opportunities to make advances in technology, they may in some degree be independent of the potential for technical progress. Countries will also differ in their ability to employ current best-practice technology for reasons other than their social capability. Differences in resource endowment will matter if the path of technological advance has been resource-biased. If best-practice technology is scale-dependent, and if there are obstacles to international trade, political or otherwise, large countries will have a stronger potential for growth than smaller ones. All these deficiencies must work to reduce the inverse correlation between levels of labor productivity and subsequent growth rates that the catch-up hypothesis otherwise predicts.

of the 15 follower countries declined drastically over the century – from a coefficient of variation of 0.5 in 1870 to 0.15 in 1979. Not only that, the decline in variance was continuous from one key year to the next, with only one reversal – in the period across World War II. In the same way, the inverse rank correlation between the initial productivity levels in 1870 and subsequent growth rates over increasingly longer periods becomes stronger and stronger until we reach a correlation coefficient of $-.97$ across the entire 109 years.[5] (Again, there was the single reversal across World War II, when the association was actually – and presumably accidentally – positive.)

I think the steadily declining variance measures and the steadily rising correlation coefficients mean that initial productivity gaps did indeed constitute a potentiality for fast growth that had its effect later if not sooner. The effect of the potentiality became visible to a very limited degree very early. But if a country was incapable of, or was prevented from, exploiting that opportunity promptly, the technological growth potential became stronger, and the country's later rate of advance was all the faster. Though it may have taken a century for obstacles or inhibitions to be fully overcome, the net outcome was that levels of productivity tended steadily to even out, at least within the group of currently advanced countries in our sample – that is, within the group of followers.

This is the big picture. How do things look if we consider shorter periods? There are two matters to keep in mind: the tendency to convergence *within* the group of followers, and the convergence (or lack of it) of the group of followers *vis-à-vis* the United States. As to the convergence within the follower group, the figures suggest that the process varied in strength markedly from period to period. The main difference was that before World War II, it operated weakly or at best with moderate strength. For almost a quarter century following that war, it apparently worked with very great strength. Why was this?

For the period before World War II, I think it is useful to consider

---

[5] Because growth rates are calculated as rates of change between standings at the terminal dates of periods, errors in the estimates of such standings will generate errors in the derived growth rates. If errors at beginning and end years were random and independent, there would be a tendency on that account alone for growth rates to be inversely correlated with initial-year standings. Inverse correlation coefficients would be biased upward. Note, however, that if errors at terminal years were random and independent and of equal magnitude, there would be no tendency *on that account* for the variance of standings about their mean to decline between initial and end years. The error bias would run against the marked and steady declines in variance that we observe. Errors in data tended, however, to decline over time; so this may account for some of the observed declines in variability.

two shorter periods: roughly the decades before 1913 and those that followed. In the years of relative peace before 1913, I suggest that the process left a weak impress on the record for two reasons, both connected with the still early state of industrialization in many of the countries. First, the impress of the process was masked because farming was still so very important, and measured productivity therefore depended heavily on the amount and quality of farmland in relation to population. Productivity levels, therefore, were especially erratic indicators of gaps between existing and best-practice technology. Second, social capability was still limited, particularly in the earlier years and for the more recent late-comers.

As the pre–World War I decades wore on, however, both these qualifying circumstances became less important. One might therefore have expected a much stronger tendency to convergence after 1913. But this was frustrated by the uneven impact of World War I, by the years of disturbed political and financial conditions that followed, by the uneven impact of the Great Depression itself, and by the barriers to international trade that were erected after the war and in the course of the Depression.

The unfulfilled potential of the years 1913–38 was then enormously enlarged by the effects of World War II. The average productivity gap behind the United States increased by 39 percent between 1938 and 1950, and the poorer countries were hit harder than the richer. These were years of dispersion, not convergence.

The post–World War II decades then proved to be the period when – exceptionally – the three elements required for rapid growth by catching up came together (Abramovitz, 1979). The elements were large technological gaps, ample social competence reflecting higher levels of education and enhanced experience with large-scale business, and conditions favoring rapid realization of potential. This last element encompasses several matters. There was on this occasion (the situation was otherwise after World War I) a healthy reaction to defeat in war and to the chance for political reconstruction. The postwar political and economic reorganization and reform weakened monopolies, brought new men to the fore, and focused the attention of governments on the tasks of recovery and growth. Facilities for technological diffusion improved. International markets were opened. Large labor reserves in home agriculture and immigrants from southern and eastern Europe provided a flexible and mobile labor supply (Kindleberger, 1961). Government support, technological opportunity, and stable international money favored heavy and sustained capital investment. The outcome was the great speed and strength of the postwar catch-up process.[6]

The record of the last century amply confirms and illustrates both the power of the catch-up process and its limitations. Its power is illustrated by the steady tendency to convergence within our sample of countries in the face of all but that most powerful of autonomous disturbances, a great world conflict of the magnitude and severity of World War II. Its limitations are illustrated by the very modest degree of convergence recorded for decades when social capabilities were being established or when macroeconomic disturbances and interferences with trade were obstructing the realization of potential.

Beyond these observations, there is a limitation suggested by the very character of the sample of countries in the Maddison tables. All are countries that either were already on the path of industrialization over a century ago or were soon to take that path. It is therefore a sample of countries that already possessed or were soon to acquire the social attributes needed for modern economic growth. It is obvious, but still noteworthy, that all these countries, with the dramatic exception of Japan, are either Western European countries or countries that drew their populations from Europe. Sharing a common culture to such a wide extent, the convergence of economic outcomes that we observe was, in a sense, a foreordained conclusion. Its very occurrence is perhaps less notable than the fact that it required more than a century to be accomplished – much more if we look back to the early nineteenth century, when modern economic growth took its start in Britain.

That the scope of the catch-up process depends on the acquisition of some still vaguely defined set of social attributes is hardly a novel finding. The dependence of the process on social capability, however, is severe. According to a recent study by William Baumol (1985), no evidence of systematic convergence appears in a more comprehensive sample of countries including the countries of the Third World. This, of course, does not mean that the potential for catching up is restricted to the countries of the Maddison sample. It is well known that widening circles of countries in Asia and Latin America are now well launched into the process of catching up. They are separating themselves from the laggards of the Third World and converging toward the productivity levels of the earlier leaders. Indeed, given the degree of convergence that already marks the European–North American cir-

---

[6] For comments on the catch-up process after 1973, see Abramovitz (1986a).

cle, it seems likely that the great potential for economic advance by catching up has now passed to the newly industrializing countries in other regions.

10.3   Moving ahead and falling back

The catch-up hypothesis in its simple form does not foresee changes in leadership nor, indeed, any shifts in the ranks of countries in regard to level of productivity. It contemplates only a reduction in productivity differentials between countries. Yet there have been many changes in ranks and, of course, the notable shift of leadership from Britain to America toward the end of the last century.[7] This was followed by the continuing decline of Britain in the productivity scale. Today there is a widely held opinion that Japan will soon surpass America and that both Europe and America face serious injury from the rise of both Japan and a group of still newer industrializing countries.

Needless to say, I cannot deal with the variety of reasons – all still speculative – for the comparative success of the countries that advanced in rank and the comparative failure of those that fell back.[8] I focus instead on a few matters that serve to reveal the ramifications and limitations of the simple catch-up hypothesis considered earlier.

U.S. leadership and the congruity among resources, scale, and technological progress

Why did the productivity gap between United States and the average of other industrialized countries (Table 10.1) resist reduction for more than a century? Parts of the answer have already been noticed. Many, though not all, of the followers were also latecomers in respect to social capability, and many of them suffered serious reversals or retarded progress during the disturbed years from 1913 to the 1950s.

There is still another, perhaps more fundamental, reason. The path of technological progress that offered the greatest opportunities for advance during most of the century following 1870 was at once heavily scale-dependent and biased in a labor-saving but capital- and land-

---

[7] According to Maddison's figures (1982, Table C.19), the long period from 1870 to 1979 saw Australia fall by 8 places in the ranking of his 16 countries, Italy by 2.5, Switzerland by 8, and the United Kingdom by 10. Meanwhile, the United States rose by 4 places, Germany by 4.5, Norway by 5, Sweden by 7, and France by 8.

[8] The possibility of overtaking and surpassing was considered theoretically by Edward Ames and Nathan Rosenberg (1963) in the closely reasoned article "Changing Technological Leadership and Industrial Growth."

using direction. The United States, with its large population, its high incomes, its continental market, its tolerance for standardized products, its abundant resources, and its capacity to raise capital both at home and abroad, enjoyed great advantages in exploring and developing the possibilities of this preferred technological path.[9]

These considerations have importance beyond their value in explaining the persistence of American leadership. They point to a general qualification to the simple catch-up hypothesis. Followers do not enjoy an unlimited potential for growth by technological borrowing. Their potential, indeed every country's potential, is limited by the degree of congruence between their own resource endowments and their access to economies of scale, on the one side, and the resource and scale biases of the evolving path of technology, on the other.

Interaction between followers and leaders

The catch-up hypothesis in its simple form is concerned with only one aspect of the economic relations among countries: technological borrowing by followers. In this view, a one-way stream of benefits flows from leaders to followers. A moment's reflection, however, exposes the incompleteness of that idea. There are other interactions between followers and leaders by way of the rivalry in trade, and by way of capital flows and population movements. Moreover, the transfers of knowledge are not solely from leader to followers, and the net flow tends to shift as average productivity gaps become narrower. There is space only for brief comment.

First, as to trade, as countries forge ahead, their burgeoning competitive strength damages the laggard industries of rivals. The rise of British factory-made cotton textiles ruined the Irish linen industry during the first industrial revolution. Later, the appearance of cheap American grains depressed European agriculture for decades. Successful industrial competition from America, Germany, and other European countries retarded British growth from 1870 to 1913 and perhaps longer (Matthews et al., 1982, chap. 14, 15, 17). Today, the rise of Japan and the newer industrializing countries is having a serious impact on the older industries of America and Europe, as well as on some of their newer industries.

A question arises whether or not these sectoral shifts in comparative

[9] On the resource and scale biases of technological progress in the nineteenth and early twentieth centuries, see Abramovitz and David (1973). For the American advantage, see Nathan Rosenberg (1981).

advantage have generalized effects on the overall productivity growth of countries. I believe they may have such effects through two channels. There is a Verdoorn effect. It is harder for an industry to push the technological frontier forward, or even to keep up with it, if its own rate of expansion slows down – and still harder if it is contracting. There is also the depressing effect on aggregate demand of an unfavorable trend in the balance of trade. Both those effects and perhaps others deserve more extended discussion than there is space for here (Abramovitz, 1986b).

Next, there are the interactions through population movements. The nineteenth-century migrations were responses to both the appeal of the New World and the pressure of its cheaper farm products on European agriculture. The movement supported productivity growth in the countries of destination in two respects. It helped them exploit economies of scale, and by making labor supply more responsive to increases in demand, it helped sustain periods of rapid growth. Countries of origin suffered mixed effects. They were relieved of the burden of low-productivity workers, but they suffered such scale disadvantages as accompanied slower population growth. Migration in more recent decades from the Mediterranean countries to northern Europe presents a picture of largely similar design and effect.

Needless to say, migrations are shaped by considerations other than relative levels of income and changing comparative advantage. I stress these matters, however, because they help us see the complexities of the catch-up process within a group of connected countries.

As to capital flows, a familiar generalization is that capital tends to flow from countries of high income and slow growth to those with opposite characteristics or, roughly speaking, from leaders to followers. That description, however, applies in the first instance to gross new investments. There are also reverse flows that reflect repayment of old loans. So in the early stages of a great wave of investment, followers' rates of investment and productivity growth are supported by capital imports, while those of leaders are retarded. Later, however, these effects may become smaller or may be reversed, as we see today in the relation between North Atlantic leaders and Latin American followers. The full picture is, of course, far more complicated than this idealized summary. It will hardly accommodate the huge American capital import of recent years, not to mention the Arabian exports of the seventies and their reversal now under way.

Finally, there are the international flows of knowledge. The transfer from leader to followers is, of course, the essence of the catch-up hypothesis. As technological gaps narrow, however, the direction of flow begins to change. Countries still a distance behind in average productivity move into the lead in particular branches and become sources of knowledge for older leaders. Question then arises about the net damage, if any, suffered by old leaders from the advance of latecomers. The more immediate effect may, indeed, be injurious to leaders as the growth of their older industries is restricted by the competition of followers. But the final effect may be beneficial as the latercomers reach the frontiers of technology and begin to contribute to the general advance of knowledge.

Development as a constraint on further advance

When Britain suffered its growth climacteric nearly a century ago, some observers thought its slowdown was due in part to its early lead. Is there a general lesson in this suggestion?

Thorstein Veblen (1915) thought so. His idea, later developed by Charles Kindleberger (1961), was that the capital stock of a country consists of an intricate web of interlocking elements. They are built to fit together, and one cannot replace one part with more modern and efficient equipment without a costly rebuilding of other components. Such decisions may be handled efficiently if all costs and benefits are internal to a firm. When they are divided among different firms and between private and public sectors, the adaptation of old capital structures to new technologies may be a difficult and halting process. This is the kernel of wisdom in the common, but perhaps exaggerated, notion that somehow wartime destruction confers a growth advantage on an injured country. The matter deserves wider study. All advanced industrial countries have large accumulations of capital goods, interdependent in use but divided in ownership among many firms and between private and public authorities. One may assume that the problem so posed varies in its impact over time and among countries and, depending on its importance, may have some influence on the eventual productivity rankings of countries.

There is an analogous and perhaps more important problem in our commitments to human capital, to business organization, and to political institutions. The doctrinal and institutional commitments induced by past development may stand as obstacles to further development, even as the cultural and institutional equipment of preindustrial times served to block or delay the beginnings of modern economic growth.

The United States was the pioneer of mass production, as embodied in the huge plant, the rigid assembly line, the standard product, and the long production run. It was the developer also of massive corporate finance, as embodied in the mammoth diversified conglomerate corporation. The vision of business carried on within such organizations, their indirect, statistical, and bureaucratic methods of planning, consultation, and decision, the distractions of trading in assets rather than production of goods – these mental biases have sunk deep into the American business outlook and into the doctrine and training of young American managers.[10] One may ask how well this older vision of management, organization, and enterprise will accommodate the problems and potentialities of the emerging computer and communications revolution. Will the potentially free and flexible business and financial markets of America spawn appropriate new organizations and doctrines, or will these arise more easily in countries where the overhang of the past is lighter?

Development and catching-up have also brought with them a new outfit of political institutions. The increases in income enjoyed by the entire North Atlantic community, joined to an egalitarian impulse and democratic politics, have permitted people to satisfy latent desires for all kinds of nonmaterial goods, from maintenance in old age and job security to a safeguarded environment, and for much else besides. I cannot and need not describe here the variety and scope of these measures. Nor need I analyze at length the potential conflicts between the business freedom and the structural changes required by technological advance and the new system of protections, regulations, and taxation that makes up the modern "welfare state." A sense that forces of institutional change are now acting to limit the growth of Western countries pervades the writings of many observers who see these economies as afflicted by institutional arthritis or sclerosis or other metaphorical maladies associated with age and wealth. We can all recognize such views as a contemporary variation on the famous Schumpeterian theme of the decline of capitalism.

How much validity there is in all this is still uncertain. Empirical work has not yet yielded consistent and persuasive results. Moreover, the welfare state has positive as well as negative effects on growth. The structural changes involved in development engender conflict, and the welfare state, with its transfers and regulations, is a mode of conflict resolution and a means of mitigating the costs of change that would otherwise induce resistance to growth. The general bearing of the new institutions on the catch-up hypothesis, however, is clear enough. If

---

[10] Criticisms along these lines frequently are suggested by experienced observers of American business. They are summarized by Edward Denison (1985, chap. 3); see also Eli Ginzberg and George Vojta (1985).

the growth-inhibiting forces embodied in the welfare state viewed broadly were endogenous, positive functions of income levels, uniform across countries, that would be another reason for supposing that the catch-up process is self-limiting. The productivity levels of followers would converge toward, but not exceed, the leader's level. But these forces clearly are not uniform functions of income. The welfare state has reached a higher degree of elaboration in Europe than in the United States. Moreover, the objects of government expenditure, the structures of taxation and transfers, the power of labor unions and of business interests, and the responses of markets differ from country to country. The institutional developments that accompany rising incomes, therefore, besides having some influence on growth rates generally, may constitute a wild card in the deck of growth forces. They will tend to produce changes in the productivity rankings of countries, perhaps including even the top rank.

10.4   Concluding remarks

This chapter points in two directions. It shows that differences among countries' productivity levels create a strong potentiality for subsequent convergence of levels, provided that countries share a similar "social capability." It reminds us, however, that the institutional and human capital components of social capability develop only slowly as education and organization respond to the requirements of technological opportunity. Further, the pace of realization of the potential for catch-up depends on a number of other conditions that govern the diffusion of knowledge, the mobility of resources, and the rate of investment.

Long-term convergence, however, is only the general tendency of a group. The growth records of countries, on the surface, do not exhibit the uniformly self-limiting character that a simple statement of the catch-up hypothesis might suggest. Dramatic changes in productivity rankings mark the experiences of individual countries even within a group that otherwise displays a general trend to convergence. Some causes of shifts in rank are exogenous to the catch-up process. The state and development of a country's ability to exploit emerging technology depend on a social history that is peculiar to itself and that may not be closely bound to its existing level of technology. The evolving path of technological advance may be more congruent with the resources and scale of some countries than with those of others. Some shifts, however, are influenced by the catch-up process – as when the competition of advancing latecomers makes inroads on important industries of older leaders. There are also the social and political concomitants of rising wealth itself that may, in some respects and in some circumstances, weaken the social capability for technological advance.

Some of these findings are, manifestly, direct extensions of Schumpeterian themes, and all of them can be accommodated within the range of social phenomena with which he was concerned. Some of them also are now subjects of intense interest and study. I would mention particularly questions related to innovation as it is carried on under the aegis of large business corporations and also the broader subject within which that falls, namely, the relations of science, technology, and business and the various styles and degrees of effectiveness with which these relations are cultivated in different countries. I would express the hope that our new society will be a useful instrument for pursuing these large subjects and for encouraging many others to do the same.

References

Abramovitz, M. (1979). "Rapid Growth Potential and Its Realisation: The Experience of the Capitalist Economies in the Postwar Period," in E. Malinvaud (ed.), *Economic Growth and Resources. Proceedings of the Fifth World Congress of the International Economic Association* (Vol. 1, pp. 1–30). London: Macmillan.

(1986a). "Catching Up and Falling Behind." Fackforeningsvorelsens Institut for Ekonomisk Forskning (Trade Union Institute for Economic Research), Economic Research Report No. 1, Stockholm.

(1986b). "Catching Up, Forging Ahead, and Falling Behind." *Journal of Economic History,* 46(June)(2):385–406.

Abramovitz, M., and David, P. A. (1973). "Economic Growth in America: Historical Parables and Realities." *De Economist,* 121:251–72.

Ames, E., and Rosenberg, N. (1963). "Changing Technological Leadership and Industrial Growth." *Economic Journal,* 73(March):13–31.

Baumol, W. J. (1985). "Productivity Growth, Convergence and Welfare: What the Long-Run Data Show." *American Economic Review,* 76(December)(5):1072–85.

Denison, E. (1985). *Trends in American Economic Growth, 1929–1982.* Washington, D.C.: Brookings Institution.

Denison, E. F., assisted by Poullier, Jean-Pierre (1967). *Why Growth Rates Differ, Postwar Experience of Nine Western Countries.* Washington, D.C.: Brookings Institution.

Gerschenkron, A. (1962). "Social Attitudes, Entrepreneurship and Economic Development," in *Economic Backwardness in Historical Perspective* (pp. 52–71). New York: Praeger.

Ginzberg, E., and Vojta, G. (1985). *Beyond Human Scale.* New York: Basic Books.

Kindleberger, C. P. (1961). "Obsolescence and Technical Change." *Oxford Institute of Statistics Bulletin,* 23(August):281–97.

(1967). *Europe's Postwar Growth: The Role of Labor Supply.* Cambridge, Mass.: Harvard University Press.

Kravis, I., Heston, A., and Summers, R. (1978). *International Comparisons of Real Product and Purchasing Power.* Baltimore: World Bank, Johns Hopkins University Press.

Landes, D. S. (1949). "French Entrepreneurship and Industrial Growth in the Nineteenth Century." *Journal of Economic History,* 9(May):45–61.

(1951). "Business and the Businessman in France," in E. M. Earle (ed.), *Modern France: Problems of the Third and Fourth Republics.* Princeton University Press.

Maddison, A. (1982). *Phases of Capitalist Development.* Oxford University Press.

Matthews, R. C. O., Feinstein, C., and Odling-Smee, J. (1982). *British Economic Growth, 1856–1973.* Stanford University Press.

Ohkawa, K., and Rosovsky, H. (1973). *Japanese Economic Growth, Trend Acceleration in the Twentieth Century.* Stanford University Press.

Rosenberg, N. (1981). "Why in America," in O. Mayr and R. Post (eds.), *Yankee Enterprise: The Rise of the American System of Manufacturers.* Washington, D.C.: Smithsonian Institution Press.

Sawyer, J. (1951). "Strains in the Social Structure of Modern France," in E. M. Earle (ed.), *Modern France: Problems of the Third and Fourth Republics.* Princeton University Press.

(1952). "The Entrepreneur and the Social Order," in W. Miller (ed.), *Men in Business, Essays in the History of Entrepreneurship* (pp. 7–22). Cambridge, Mass.: Harvard University Press.

Veblen, Thorstein (1915). *Imperial Germany and the Industrial Revolution.* New York: Macmillan.

CHAPTER 11

On the coming senescence of American manufacturing competence

MARK PERLMAN

A previous sublime sense of child-like confidence – the conviction that a beneficent God looks after drunks and the United States – having shriveled, our America of the late 1980s differs from the America of the early 1950s, particularly in perception, but also to an increasing degree in fact. A romantic sense of an overhanging black storm cloud has replaced a similarly romantic sunshiny optimism. This metaphor is useful in that it offers a perception of the going set of dominant expectations. Particularly when viewed retrospectively, states of expectations are crucial, because they affect willingness to invest effort, money, and time; all are the sinews of economic strength.

The commonplace that America is losing – indeed has lost – its worldwide industrial manufacturing leadership has more than a modicum of truth, but, as such, it is also overstated. Aggregate American output capacity still remains very large. Yet the handwriting on the wall clearly suggests that certain important portions of our industrial might wither before foreign onslaughts. It is the speed of this decline that is crucial – crucial because it represents the unanticipatedly rapid collapse of certain specific industries (e.g., basic steel, machine tools), industries some consider essential for American and NATO strategic defense. This decline also is worrisome for two quite different reasons: a manifestation of the loss of American competitive adaptability, and a loss of certain kinds of job opportunities. These types of job opportunities are the reservoirs feeding the flows of defense-important surge capacity.

These points deserve both repetition and expansion. Loss of American competitiveness can be seen both on the governmental level and in the private sector. What happens to America's defense capacities (including, particularly, its competence to offer some sort of an umbrella for much of the world) is an obvious consideration. But another aspect, what goes on in the *private sector,* is no less significant. What kind of economic world will it be when America becomes principally a service economy, rather than an industrial manufacturing

343

leader? Will leadership then transfer to other industrial manufacturing countries like Japan and the East Asian LDCs (e.g., Taiwan, Korea, and Singapore), or can a leading service economy replace manufacturing economies as the focus of leadership? This is a new problem; the older pattern, however, is the one with which we are most familiar.

At the end of World War II and for much of the succeeding period, there had been, with the exception of certain strategic materials not domestically obtainable, no doubt regarding America's manufacturing adequacy for defense purposes. A legislative program was developed to meet these needs; it concentrated on the maintenance of adequate stockpiles of 58 raw materials, 49 of them minerals, not readily available from American sources. In 1950, the Congress, intent on avoiding the problems faced during the period 1940–5, enacted such legislation. Although appropriations were regularly made for this stockpile maintenance, they were insufficient as well as laggard and tinged with the suspicion that the interests of the domestic mining industries – as well as national defense needs – were being kept in mind. Professor Raymond F. Mikesell has recently written an evaluation of the 1950 program, as amended (Mikesell, 1986).

More recently, those assessing the history of the maintenance of these stockpiles have become aware of new concerns, including the following needs: (1) to monitor the availability of new materials and industrial processes; (2) to take into account changing political and natural disaster risk functions; (3) to recognize the increasing American strategic defense dependence on foreign production of intermediate and final products; (4) to note the lack and/or disappearance of large numbers of skilled labor cadres, as well as standby physical plant production surge capacity; (5) to compensate for a growing disillusionment about national economic planning, even for something so basic as incentives for creation of private-sector stockpiles; (6) to come to grips with the causes of our foreign trade imbalance and other aspects of our national commercial policy, particularly those associated with loss of international competitiveness in manufacturing.

The United States started rearming in 1939–40. At the time, because of the Great Depression, there was considerable standby manufacturing capacity, as well as stocks of underutilitized disciplined labor, both skilled and unskilled. During the first Reagan administration, rearmament was once more undertaken on a grand scale, but the industrial situation was different. In one of his last publications, Otto Eckstein and his staff put the matter as follows:

Can the United States continue to play the role of guardian of the Western world, with its heavy political, economic, and military burdens, with a weakening manufacturing economy? What are the social problems created by the reduction of job opportunities for blue-collar workers: Will the United States develop the kind of permanent regional disparities in economic well-being that haunt Great Britain, where the industrial heartland is trapped in depression while the service-based London area achieves prosperity? Can – or should – government policies act to reverse the decline of manufacturing industries? (Eckstein et al., 1984)

This chapter has several purposes. The most immediate is to examine the statistical bases of the now common view that the United States has lost its premier role in manufacturing, a *sine qua non* of its established role as the guarantor of Western military superiority. A second, after examining briefly some of the explanations offered in the prolix and growing literature, is to add my own view of how the current situation developed. Finally, I ask whether or not the problem, as such, deserves a high-priority solution and whether or not such an outcome remains possible.

11.1   Looking at the facts

The data

A word about the data is desirable if for no other reason than to show how fragile are the concepts and numbers used in providing the foundations of our analysis.

In any essay there are inevitably certain key words. Here the key words are "manufacturing" and "decline," and these must be identified carefully. "Manufacturing" is really a word of art, as defined by the Bureau of the Census. Although used early in the nineteenth century, its current technical employment stems from developments in the 1930s, when the set of articulated national accounts was adopted. It was a time when the transition from agricultural employment was in full swing, when "manufacturing" clearly referred to industry-specific firms concentrating on the production of related goods, goods produced for sale mostly (but not completely) in the domestic market.

Because the era when all firms can easily be put into one or likely no more than two industrial categories seems to be approaching an end, the term has now lost something of its original vigor. Previously, mergers and acquisitions represented horizontal or vertical integration of firms. Recently, the character of such expansionary moves has changed, bringing about integration of firms in unrelated industries. As a result, overhead costs to the firm are distributed over a varying group of products produced for different industries. The emergence of this new kind of industrial structure has one additional interesting result.

A greater proportion of a firm's employees are now engaged in simple "pecuniary" (to raise Veblen's ghost) activities – activities not resulting in sales of goods and services to customers and/or consumers. It follows, therefore, that the declining industries have changed in form as much as they may have diminished in quantity; this point is significant because it limits comparisons that one inevitably draws.

"Decline" also has a variety of meanings. In some cases, the word conveys simply a relative retrenchment in product output. For example, export markets have been in whole or in part lost, and imports, either as completed goods or as a result of foreign sourcing, have come to replace many domestic manufactures. In some instances, the growth in output that normally accompanies increases in consumption has not occurred. In other cases, there has been or threatens to be loss of substantial production capacity. There is clearly an indifferent ignorance about how the ordering of social priorities affects output.

The data employed here refer mostly to the American gross domestic product and employment. Gross domestic product is a measure of goods and services produced in a year; specifically, it includes the value of domestically produced items, whether they are produced by domestic or foreign capital, and it excludes the value of items (and the profits and other shares received from items) produced abroad by American capital. It is therefore a measure of what is going on "at home" and reflects our on-site economy, not the impact of our imports or income from external holdings. Yet, it is necessary to consider what is imported. Thus, part of our quantitative product analysis shifts from considerations of gross domestic product to include the importance and value of import penetration. We also must consider employment.

"Employment" refers to numbers of people, not to the numbers of hours worked nor, of course, to any level of earnings. "Employment by industry" has become a somewhat more elusive concept, because, as noted earlier, "industry" is a less precise term than it once seemed to be. For instance, the Westinghouse Electric Corporation, once principally (though not entirely) in the electric motor and electric appliance industries, now produces a much wider variety of products and, particularly, *services*. The reporting of employment data is carried out by each of the firm's separate establishments, as well as by the aggregated firm. There can be discrepancies between what the individual establishments produce and classify and what the firm reports, particularly with the allocated division of personnel working in "overhead." There is also another complication. In recent years, there has been an increase in the amount of work that is contracted out; indeed, one area of such contracting involves the purchase of business services, one of the faster growing sub-industrial groups. Large firms, for which Westinghouse serves as an example, are now buying many services that previously they produced "in house." Such shifts, of course, will be reflected in the industry-specific gross domestic product and employment data.

Analyzing output aggregates

We are looking at manufacturing output not only from the standpoint of defense but also in terms of the changing relationships between industrial structures and our social priorities. We want to put changes in manufacturing into the general perspective of changes in the American economy. Two approaches to such analysis come to mind. The first concerns domestic output and the imports related to domestic output or consumption; the second concerns compositional changes in the employment of our labor force.

We start with 1955 because American economic leadership during the decade 1945–55 was abnormal, made so by the vast wartime destruction in all the other major industrialized nations. Table 11.1 provides an overall picture of the profound changes in the American economy, with emphasis on manufacturing. What should be noted first is that there have been marked changes in composition during the almost 30-year period, but these patterns of change have not been consistent during these three decades. Particularly in recent years, the following major sectors have shrunk in relative importance: agriculture, forestry, and fisheries; manufacturing. Others clearly have grown: finance, insurance, and real estate; services (particularly business services and health services); and government.

Second, we explain closely the changes in the manufacturing sector of the economy, because declines here are the focus of our interest. Both the durable and nondurable groups of industries have fallen in overall relative importance. Our data (in percentage terms) are in current prices so as to better show the industrial structure for the time period indicated. Comparisons between time periods reveal changes in the structure of the economy.

Table 11.2 (based on constant 1982 dollars) shows the growth in output for each sector. First, in 1985, the gross product in real terms was 139 percent larger (239 percent of the original) than it had been in 1955. Second, the rates of growth have varied greatly compared with the growth rate for the gross domestic product. Third, in none of the major sectors or the two-digit manufacturing industries (except for leather and leather products and primary metals) has output actually

Table 11.1. *Industry shares (%) of U.S. gross domestic product[a] for selected years, 1955–1985*

Industry	1955	1965	1975	1985
Agriculture, forestry, and fisheries	4.96	3.46	3.56	2.31
Mining	3.10	2.00	2.61	3.10
Construction	4.74	4.96	4.84	4.60
Manufacturing	30.08	28.37	22.60	20.11
Durable goods	17.56	16.93	13.05	11.70
Lumber and wood products	0.97	0.77	0.66	0.58
Furniture and fixtures	0.47	0.43	0.31	0.33
Stone, clay, and glass products	1.12	0.94	0.73	0.62
Primary metal industries	2.85	2.37	1.80	0.88
Fabricated metal products	2.01	1.93	1.73	1.39
Machinery, except electrical	2.60	2.86	2.64	2.39
Electric and electronic equipment	1.91	2.30	1.79	2.04
Motor vehicle equipment	2.93	2.65	1.26	1.27
Other transportation equipment	1.61	1.54	1.06	1.25
Instruments and related products	0.62	0.69	0.65	0.65
Miscellaneous manufacturing	0.55	0.44	0.44	0.30
Nondurable goods	12.50	11.44	9.55	8.41
Food and kindred products	3.42	2.87	2.47	1.77
Tobacco manufactures	0.57	0.47	0.32	0.31
Textile mill products	1.09	0.93	0.64	0.42
Apparel and other textile products	1.07	0.96	0.73	0.52
Paper and allied products	1.12	1.03	0.87	0.87
Printing and publishing	1.36	1.34	1.18	1.31
Chemicals and allied products	2.08	2.06	1.90	1.67
Petroleum and coal products	0.77	0.77	0.63	0.81
Rubber and miscellaneous plastic products	0.64	0.72	0.66	0.64
Leather and leather products	0.37	0.27	0.16	0.08
Transportation and public utilities	9.12	8.95	8.96	9.46
Wholesale trade	6.57	6.69	7.43	7.01
Retail trade	10.07	9.74	9.88	9.48
Finance, insurance, and real estate	12.58	14.14	14.02	15.84
Services	8.70	10.6	12.64	16.16
Business services	0.92	1.52	1.94	3.62
Health services	1.91	2.43	3.66	4.62
Government and government enterprises	9.67	11.18	13.29	12.06
Statistical discrepancy	0.45	−0.17	0.16	−0.14

[a]Gross domestic product: 1955, $403.3 billion; 1965, $699.3 billion; 1975, $1,580.9 billion; 1985, $3,957.0 billion.
Sources: U.S. Bureau of Economic Analysis, *The National Income and Product Accounts of the United States, 1929–82,* and *Survey of Current Business,* 1983–6.

Table 11.2. *Gross domestic product by industry*

Industry	Constant 1982 dollars (billion)					Percentage				
	1955	1965	1975	1984	1985	1955	1965	1975	1984	1985
Gross domestic product	1,485.5	2,070.6	2,665.7	3,447.5	3,548.3	100	100	100	100	100
Agriculture, forestry, and fisheries	69.1	66.7	73.1	85.0	92.2	4.65	3.22	2.74	2.47	2.60
Mining	92.0	109.4	125.6	133.0	130.6	6.19	5.28	4.71	3.86	3.68
Construction	133.3	193.7	149.4	156.7	163.1	8.97	9.35	5.66	4.55	4.60
Manufacturing	327.7	462.5	547.5	760.7	776.9	22.06	22.34	20.54	22.07	21.89
Durable goods	208.5	286.9	325.2	462.0	481.5	14.04	13.74	12.20	13.23	13.57
Lumber and wood products	8.9	14.1	16.4	21.1	20.6	0.60	0.68	0.62	0.60	0.58
Furniture and fixtures	5.4	7.1	7.8	12.8	11.6	0.36	0.34	0.29	0.37	0.33
Stone, clay, and glass products	13.1	17.2	18.7	22.3	22.2	0.88	0.82	0.70	0.64	0.63
Primary metal industries	46.3	51.0	44.0	40.0	34.4	3.12	2.44	1.65	1.15	0.97
Fabricated metal products	27.1	38.3	41.8	55.7	53.2	1.82	1.83	1.57	1.60	1.50
Machinery, except electrical	33.2	48.8	64.1	111.0	134.5	2.23	2.34	2.40	3.18	3.79
Electric and electronic equipment	12.7	27.8	37.6	72.1	76.5	0.85	1.33	1.41	2.06	2.16
Other transportation equipment	25.3	33.5	33.8	39.5	47.1	1.61	1.50	1.26	1.45	1.33
Motor vehicle equipment	23.9	31.3	33.7	50.8	45.2	1.70	1.60	1.27	1.13	1.27
Instruments and related products	6.1	9.7	16.1	24.2	24.3	0.41	0.46	0.60	0.69	0.68
Miscellaneous manufacturing industries	6.5	8.4	11.3	12.4	11.7	0.43	0.40	0.42	0.36	0.33
Nondurable goods	119.2	175.6	222.2	298.6	295.4	8.02	8.41	8.33	8.55	8.33
Food and kindred products	29.1	39.1	48.2	61.0	63.8	1.96	1.87	1.81	1.75	1.80
Tobacco manufactures	5.6	7.5	10.0	7.2	6.7	0.38	0.36	0.38	0.21	0.19
Textile mill products	5.9	9.7	10.6	16.9	15.5	0.40	0.46	0.40	0.48	0.44
Apparel and other textile products	10.1	13.5	16.7	21.6	19.7	0.68	0.65	0.60	0.62	0.56

Table 11.2 (cont.)

Industry	Constant 1982 dollars (billion)					Percentage				
	1955	1965	1975	1984	1985	1955	1965	1975	1984	1985
Paper and allied products	11.9	16.1	20.2	32.1	31.2	0.80	0.77	0.76	0.92	0.88
Printing and publishing	18.8	27.3	32.4	42.9	41.6	1.27	1.31	1.22	1.23	1.17
Chemicals and allied products	14.1	26.1	39.3	63.6	62.6	0.95	1.25	1.47	1.83	1.76
Petroleum and coal products	14.0	20.7	25.1	25.2	25.0	0.94	0.99	0.94	0.72	0.70
Rubber and miscellaneous plastic products	5.7	10.5	15.2	24.4	26.1	0.38	0.50	0.57	0.70	0.74
Leather and leather products	4.0	5.0	4.4	3.8	3.2	0.27	0.24	0.17	0.11	0.09
Transportation and public utilities	112.3	161.5	246.4	312.8	323.3	7.56	7.80	9.24	9.07	9.11
Wholesale trade	75.6	119.8	185.6	254.1	264.5	5.09	5.79	6.96	7.37	7.45
Retail trade	139.4	190.0	247.5	330.6	339.8	9.38	9.18	9.28	9.59	9.58
Finance, insurance, and real estate	160.2	259.8	387.6	512.6	523.9	10.78	12.55	14.54	14.87	14.76
Services	153.0	240.4	352.4	509.5	538.5	10.30	11.61	13.22	14.78	15.17
Government and government enterprises	223.4	284.3	355.6	390.7	399.4	15.04	13.73	13.32	11.33	11.26
Statistical discrepancy	6.2	-3.4	4.2	-1.4	-5.0	0.42	-0.16	0.76	-0.04	-0.14
Residual	-6.6	-14.0	-8.7	3.2	1.1	-0.44	-0.68	-0.33	0.09	0.03

Sources: U.S. Bureau of Economic Analysis, The National Income and Product Accounts of the United States, 1929–82, and Survey of Current Business, 1983–6.

declined. Fourth, when one takes account of differing price changes, analysis shows that prices in manufacturing rose less than in the rest of the economy. Finally, the great output losers in relative terms were as follows: agriculture, forestry, and fisheries; mining; construction; and, strangely, government. The principal gainers were the following: transportation and public utilities; wholesale trade; finance, insurance, and real estate; and services. Relative price changes, again, were responsible for some of the shifts.

Our interest is primarily in manufacturing. Changes in the role of manufacturing, as seen in constant dollars, seem not to have been significant, although, on the whole, durable goods fell slightly (5.8 percent), and nondurable goods rose slightly (6.6 percent). One explanation may be that prices were more volatile for nondurable goods than for durable goods. Within each of these two subcategories, some changes in rank ordering have occurred.

Table 11.3, using all manufacturing as the basis for comparison, identifies the big losers: primary metals; motor vehicle equipment; food and kindred products; apparel and other textiles; and leather and leather products. The major gainers were as follows: machinery; electric and electronic equipment; chemicals and allied products; and instruments and related products. The numerical differences between the two sets of data (one denominated in current dollars and the other in constant [1982] dollars) reflect both different sets of individual price changes and differences in compositional weights. The data based on current dollars are better, but not perfect, indicators of each year's industrial composition; the data in constant dollars are tied to 1982 weights, but do give a picture of the growth of each separate industry.

So much, for now, for the general and specific growth in the American manufacturing economy. What about import penetration? Table 11.4 focuses on two phenomena: the value in 1984 of imported manufactured goods, and the degree of import penetration in the 25 leading four-digit industries with the greatest value of imports. Growth in imports may not reflect abandonment of domestic output so much as the fact that growing consumption draws its increments from production abroad. Such is the difference between two high-import-value industries: motor vehicles and basic steel. In the mid-1980s, the American auto industry was attempting to regain its 1970 production levels, although imports continued to increase, absorbing a greater portion of domestic comsumption. For steel, on the other hand, in what probably is strategically a more critical example, there was an appreciable loss of domestic output: Imports of steel grew, and American total consumption fell.

Table 11.3. Percentages of manufacturing share of gross domestic product by two-digit industry for selected years, 1965–85

Industry	Current dollars (billions)					Constant 1982 dollars (billions)				
	1955	1965	1975	1984	1985	1955	1965	1975	1984	1985
Total manufacturing	100%	100%	100%	100%	100%	100%	100%	100%	100%	100%
Manufacturing (billion dollars)	121.3	198.4	357.3	779.8	776.9	327.7	462.5	547.5	760.7	463.1
Durable goods	58.37	59.68	57.74	58.23	58.19	63.63	62.03	59.40	60.73	62.0
Lumber and wood products	3.22	2.72	2.91	2.96	2.87	2.72	3.05	3.00	2.77	2.65
Furniture and fixtures	1.57	1.51	1.40	1.72	1.66	1.65	1.54	1.42	1.68	1.49
Stone, clay, and glass products	3.71	3.33	3.22	3.05	3.07	4.00	3.72	3.42	2.93	2.86
Primary metal industries	9.48	8.37	7.98	5.23	4.39	14.13	11.03	8.04	5.26	4.43
Fabricated metal products	6.68	6.80	7.67	7.12	6.90	8.27	8.28	7.63	7.32	6.85
Machinery, except electrical	8.66	10.08	11.67	11.41	11.90	10.13	10.55	11.71	14.59	17.31
Electric and electronic equipment	6.35	8.11	7.92	9.69	10.15	3.88	6.01	6.87	9.48	9.85
Other transportation equipment	9.73	9.32	5.57	6.84	6.33	7.29	6.77	6.15	6.68	6.06
Motor vehicle equipment	5.36	5.44	4.70	5.39	6.22	7.72	7.24	6.17	5.19	5.82
Instruments and related products	2.06	2.42	2.85	3.27	3.23	1.86	2.10	2.94	3.18	3.13
Miscellaneous manufacturing	1.81	1.56	1.82	1.54	1.48	1.98	1.82	2.06	1.63	1.51
Nondurable goods	41.55	40.32	42.26	41.77	41.82	36.37	37.97	40.58	39.25	38.02
Food and kindred products	11.38	10.13	10.94	8.53	8.82	8.80	8.45	8.80	8.02	8.21
Tobacco manufactures	1.90	1.66	1.43	1.56	1.56	1.71	1.62	1.83	0.95	0.86

Textile mill products	3.63	3.28	2.83	2.31	2.07	1.80	2.10	1.94	2.22	2.00
Apparel and other textile products	3.54	3.38	3.22	2.83	2.58	3.08	2.92	3.05	2.84	2.54
Paper and allied products	3.71	3.63	3.89	4.41	4.35	3.63	3.48	3.69	4.22	4.02
Printing and publishing	4.53	4.74	5.21	6.36	6.52	5.74	5.90	5.92	5.64	5.35
Chemicals and allied products	6.92	7.26	8.40	8.26	8.28	4.30	5.64	7.18	8.36	8.06
Petroleum and coal products	2.56	2.72	2.77	3.40	4.01	4.27	4.48	4.58	3.31	3.22
Rubber and miscellaneous plastic products	2.14	2.52	2.91	3.14	3.20	1.74	2.27	2.78	3.21	3.36
Leather and leather products	1.24	0.96	0.70	0.47	0.41	1.22	1.08	0.80	0.49	0.41

Source: U.S. Bureau of Economic Analysis, *The National Income and Product Accounts of the United States, 129–85,* and *Survey of Current Business,* 1983–6.

Table 11.4. *Imports for 25 leading four-digit product groups, ranked by value of manufactured U.S. imports in 1984*

Industry	1984 import values ($ billions)[a]	Growth rate[b] (%)		Import penetration ratio[c]	
		1972–84	1980–4	1972	1982
Motor vehicles & car bodies	38.4	15.6	16.0	13.6	26.7
Petroleum refining	21.1	21.2	12.2	7.4	7.3
Motor vehicle parts & accessories[d]	11.4	15.8	24.7	7.6	10.5
Blast furnaces & steel mills	10.1	11.5	11.2	9.8	17.2
Office machines, typewriters, etc.	9.4	26.9	45.7	6.6	8.0
Radio & television receiving sets	9.2	13.9	22.7	34.9	49.5
Semiconductors & related devices	7.2	29.3	22.6	11.5	25.8
Paper mills, except building paper	4.6	12.4	10.4	15.3	13.8
Children's outerwear, n.e.c.[e]	4.1	16.8	24.5	16.3	20.3
Radio & communication equipment	4.0	24.9	19.2	3.2	8.1
Primary nonferrous metals, n.e.c.	3.9	13.9	−5.6	41.4	46.2
Electronic components, n.e.c.	3.1	32.5	31.8	2.7	7.8
Jewelers' mats & lapidary work	3.0	19.5	16.7	68.6	88.2
Photographic equip. & supplies	2.9	19.5	14.6	6.2	12.3
Sawmills & planing mills, general	2.9	7.9	7.4	16.1	15.2
Industrial inorganic chemicals, n.e.c.	2.7	18.3	7.8	8.5	13.5
Furniture & fixtures, n.e.c.	2.5	19.0	22.7	2.7	5.5
Men's & boys' shirts & nightwear	2.5	17.6	15.3	10.7	22.5
General industrial machinery, n.e.c.	2.4	22.1	19.6	4.0	8.9
Miscellaneous plastic products	2.0	16.8	18.9	2.2	2.8
Construction machinery	2.0	21.2	15.5	2.7	5.6
Women's footwear, except athletic	2.0	14.7	27.4	19.0	32.1

Table 11.4 *(cont.)*

Industry	1984 import values ($ billions)[a]	Growth rate[b] (%)		Import penetration ratio[c]	
		1972–84	1980–4	1972	1982
Pulp mills	1.8	11.6	1.5	30.4	29.1
Telephone & telegraph apparatus	1.8	28.9	45.2	2.1	5.0
Tires & inner tubes	1.8	13.7	12.2	7.5	12.5

[a]Imports are valued on a customs basis. Data have been adjusted to ensure comparability between 1972 and 1984.
[b]Compound annual rate of growth in the value of imports.
[c]Ratio of imports to new supply (domestic product shipments plus imports).
[d]Includes imports and exports of automotive products between the United States and Canada, which move duty-free between the two countries; a significant portion is intracompany shipment.
[e]Not elsewhere classified.
Source: U.S. Department of Commerce, Bureau of Industrial Economics, *Industrial Outlook, 1986.*

In one sense, the import penetration data represent changes in both the "money cost" and the "strategic capacity loss" of imports. The money-cost factor affects the balance of payments immediately, and over a few years can lead to capacity loss. But such an impact is far from inevitable. The money cost is affected by the exchange value of the dollar. In 1984, the dollar was overvalued; by 1986, the exchange ratio was less favorable to imports and consequently more favorable to domestic production. But if the dollar remains overvalued for long periods, strategic capacity loss may occur; even if and when the exchange ratio ultimately returns to a level more consistent with domestic production, the production facilities and their labor cadres may have been abandoned, as well as the commitment to domestic research and development.

Although the two are interactives, the distinction between the two factors money cost and strategic capacity loss is useful. For example, note that the import values of motor vehicles and motor vehicle parts (bodies and parts and accessories), petroleum products, and blast-furnace steel products account for about one-third (31.8 percent) of the value of imported manufactures, a sum of no small concern. Yet, of these three, actual import penetration was more than 20 percent only in motor vehicle bodies, and that included some imports from Canada.

When did this import crisis begin? Compare the data on motor vehicles and car bodies with those on blast furnaces and steel mills. In the first case, the growth of imports in the most recent years (1980–4) has been much higher than for the entire period 1972–84. In the second case (blast furnances), the rate of penetration in recent years has been marginally less than it was for the whole period. It is the speed of recent import substitution for the domestic product that identifies areas where losses of employment and productive capacity may yet be reversible. Put another way, we can determine from Table 11.4 what has been happening and infer when it seems to have started; in addition, we can determine how serious individual industry crises are and whether or not it is too late to start considering remedies.

Looking at output in several industries

The crucial fact about import penetration is that it has severely affected a few strategic defense-related industries, especially steel production, nonferrous metal production, and the manufacture of machine tools and cars.

Steel production: This is the bellwether of American strategic defense; it remains at the heart of our capacity to produce the articles of war. Both the army and navy depend on steel goods. Like the cloud on the horizon no bigger than a man's fist, the disassembly of the American steel industry began in the 1950s, when American firms, then producing at capacity, turned over to foreign competitors the production of some of the less profitable lines (e.g., wire production). During the late 1950s, after a steelworkers strike, American automobile manufacturers looked increasingly to foreign sources in order to protect their own production from similar interruptions. To no minor degree, then, the original loss of domestic hegemony was tied up with overutilization of capacity and problems of labor relations. The trouble began with problems of unit costs (productivity considerations), rather than with questions of product quality.

Steel mills, however, produce joint products; one is steel, but others are polluted air and water. Until the mid-1960s there was little concern about the disposition of anything except the steel. In the late 1960s, attitudes, as reflected in legislation, changed. A great deal of invest-

Table 11.5A. *Steel-mill products (million dollars, except as noted)*

Item	1972	1982	1983	1984	1985[a]	1986[b]	1987[c]
Steel-mill product shipments (current dollars)	25,289	43,006	42,660	48,010	49,982	45,983	45,062
Shipments (1982 dollars)	67,755	43,006	42,079	45,684	48,526	45,527	43,750
Imports (current dollars)	2,725	8,861	6,242	10,102	9,462	8,210	8,114
Imports/new supply (%)	9.8	17.2	12.9	17.5	16.8	16.0	16.2
Imports/apparent consumption (%)	10.0	17.8	13.2	n.a.	n.a.		
Exports (current dollars)	627	1,587	994	880	818	785	808
Exports/shipments (%)	2.5	3.7	2.4	1.9	1.8	1.8	1.9

[a]Estimates, except for imports/exports.
[b]Estimates.
[c]Forecasts.
Source: U.S. Department of Commerce, Bureau of Industrial Economics, *Industrial Outlook, 1987,* and internal documents.

ment was legislatively mandated for procurement of pollution-control equipment. Because the price schedule of American firms could not accommodate both the need for pollution control and the need for newer cost- and quality-effective equipment, these were funds that did not go into steel-product modernization. Funds were limited, and funds spent on one need could not be used for the other. Although the industry tried to protect its domestic market by advocating quotas, tariffs, and involuntary restraints, its efforts were not effective. The result was a decrease in general industry profitability. Several firms merged domestically, another merged internationally, at least one went into other industries, and most of those remaining, irrespective of their arrangements, suffered massive annual losses.

In Tables 11.5A and 11.5B, one can see the growing role of imports and the declining importance of exports. Where once the industry was healthy, capable of export competition, currently it is sick, having lost both export and domestic competitiveness. The notable points are as follows:

Table 11.5B. *Steel-mill products (million short tons, except as noted)*

Item	1972	1982	1983	1984	1985[a]	1986[b]	1987[c]
Steel-mill product shipments	91.8	61.6	67.6	73.7	73.0	69.5	68.0
Exports	2.9	1.8	1.2	1.0	0.9	0.9	0.9
Imports	17.5	16.7	17.1	26.2	24.3	20.8	20.2
Apparent domestic consumption	106.6	76.4	83.5	98.9	96.4	89.4	87.3
Exports/shipments (%)	3.2	2.9	1.8	1.4	1.2	1.3	1.3
Imports/apparent consumption (%)	16.6	21.9	20.5	26.5	25.2	23.3	23.1

[a]Estimates, except for imports and exports.
[b]Estimates.
[c]Forecasts.
Source: See Table 11.5A

- The number of tons shipped since 1972 has fallen less (26 percent) than the relevant money value in 1982 dollars (35 percent). Unit prices are down, and/or the more expensive lines have been replaced either by imports or by substitute nonferrous products.
- American export tonnage has fallen by about 70 percent since 1972 (and by 50 percent since 1982).
- The import/new-supply percentage (measured in current dollars) by the mid-1980s was up by 65 to 75 percent above 1972.

In addition to the foregoing reasons for the decline of domestic steel manufacturing are increasing American reliance on imports for raw-steel products and factors that have reduced consumption. The latter include more efficient use of steel in construction, substitution of lighter and/or cheaper products, and smaller cars using less steel.

Motor vehicle production: The loss of international competitiveness in automobiles differs in several ways from the loss in steel. In steel, the change occurred largely for reasons of excessive American unit cost; in autos, the shift reflects the vagaries of derivative oil (gasoline) prices, including the impact of higher fuel prices on consumer tastes for smaller vehicles. It also reflects the consequences of poor decisions in America regarding product design, as well as quality control and subsequent maintenance service. Import penetration in the late 1970s and particularly in the early 1980s initially occurred not only because the

Japanese small cars were cheaper (they were somewhat so) but also because Japanese manufacturers were offering what appeared to be a better product. The traditional troubles associated with owning imported cars (lack of availability of replacement parts and inability to get effective repairs made quickly and reasonably) were minimized to the point that they no longer afforded an edge to American producers. In contrast to the steel industry, the American automobile manufacturers were more successful in fighting back; they tried to reassert control of their traditional home market. To this end they redesigned their product and the ways used to manufacture it. They also relied on trade tactics similar to those employed by the steel industry (e.g., voluntary quotas); in this respect, the automobile industry was more successful. Part of this success, doubtless, was achieved because they used cheaper imported steel. There is more to their switch, however; they also sourced abroad in Mexico as well as in Canada, and these data are concealed by the exclusion of imports from Canada from the import figures.

Tables 11.6 and 11.7 show changes in the auto industry. The numbers of new cars have fluctuated; actually, the peak year was 1973, when over 11.4 million cars were sold. This number was approached again only in 1977, 1978, and 1985. One can also observe the growth of imports, excluding the Canadian portion, in percentage terms – from 7.6 percent in 1972 to 20.6 percent in 1985. The earlier zenith was in 1980. The panel on the value of motor vehicle parts and accessories suggests a lagging variation of the same story; increases in imported replacement parts lag increased imports of autos by a few years. The effort to regain domestic control of the American market shows some success; that success, however, is partially confused by an accounting practice summing domestic American and Canadian production.

In recent years, as the dollar has weakened internationally and as political pressure to buy American-made products has gathered (or has been expected to gather) momentum, some Japanese firms have shifted to assembling their cars within the U.S. continental borders. This shift also beclouds the popular perception of the American side of the industry. Is an American-assembled Chrysler, made in some measure from imported components, more "American" than a Honda or Toyota, similarly American-assembled, that is also made up in some measure of imported components? Is it the "national" ownership of the firm, the trade name of the auto, geographical location, or some varying combination of the three that makes the manufacturer "American"?

Table 11.6. *Automobile industry (billion current dollars, except as noted)*

Factor	1972	1975	1980	1984[a]	1985[a]	1986[b]	1987[c]
Value of motor vehicles and car bodies							
Shipments	41.0	43.4	61.4	$112.4	$115.8	$106.0	$101.0
Shipments (1982 dollars)	79.6	71.9	70.8	107.1	107.7	96.3	89.4
Excluding Canada[d]							
Imports	3.4	4.6	15.5	21.4	26.6	33.5	40.0
Imports/new supply (%)	7.6	9.5	20.1	17.1	20.6	25.5	n.a.
Exports	0.7	2.4	2.9	1.7	2.0	2.4	2.7
Exports/shipments (%)	1.8	5.6	4.7	1.7	2.0	2.3	n.a.
Including Canada							
Imports	6.7	8.9	21.2	38.4	47.7	n.a.	n.a.
Imports/new supply (%)	13.6	16.4	24.8	24.6	n.a.	n.a.	n.a.
Exports	2.2	5.4	6.8	8.1	9.8	n.a.	n.a.
Exports/shipments (%)	5.2	11.9	10.6	6.8	n.a.	n.a.	n.a.
Value of motor vehicle parts and accessories							
Shipments	19.4	23.0	35.6	55.8	58.7	61.6	64.8
Shipments (1982 dollars)	56.6	47.6	48.6	54.7	56.0	57.4	58.9
Value of imports	1.9	2.5	4.7	11.3	12.8	n.a.	n.a.
Imports/new supply (%)	7.6	8.1	8.9	13.5	n.a.	n.a.	n.a.
Value of exports	2.3	3.7	5.9	11.1	9.3	n.a.	n.a.
Exports/shipments (%)	11.3	15.5	15.4	13.3	n.a.	n.a.	n.a.

[a]Estimates, except for imports and exports.
[b]Estimates.
[c]Forecasts.
[d]Excludes imports from Canada, as identified under the 1965 agreement.
Source: U.S. Department of Commerce, Bureau of Industrial Economics, *Industrial Outlook, 1987.*

Machine tools production: Although it is possible to find many industries more disastrously hit by import competition (e.g., clothing and shoes), no *strategic* industry seems to have been *much* more adversely affected by developments within the past few years than machine tools.

The two panels in Table 11.8 make this point in several interesting ways. First, the real value of domestic shipments in both parts of the industry rose until 1980 and has since then fallen markedly. Second, imports in metal cutting have risen to more than one-third of the shipments. Third, exports in both parts of the industry have risen slightly in percentage, but have fallen in absolute terms, since 1980. An indus-

Table 11.7. *Passenger car retail sales (thousand vehicles)*

Year	Domestic[a]	Imported	Total
1972	9,327	1,623	10,950
1973	9,676	1.763	11,439
1974	7.454	1,413	8,867
1975	7,053	1,587	8,640
1976	8,611	1,499	10,110
1977	9,109	2,076	11,185
1978	9,312	2,000	11,312
1979	8,341	2,329	10,671
1980	6,581	2,398	8,979
1981	6,209	2,327	8,536
1982	5,757	2,223	7,980
1983	6,795	2,387	9,182
1984	7,952	2,439	10,390
1985	8,205	2,838	11,042
1986[b]	7,850	3,105	10,955
1987[c]	7,050	3,650	10,700

[a]Domestic includes Canadian units of American manufacture.
[b]Estimates.
[c]Forecasts.
Source: Motor Vehicle Manufacturers' Association.

try spokesman asserted in June 1986 that imports were running at 41 percent of consumption. Finally, employment of these workers, many of them particularly highly skilled, has fallen.

Selected nonferrous metals: In relative terms, import penetration of the domestic American market in the principal nonferrous metal fields has been slightly greater overall; however, in all other ways it has paralleled developments in the steel industry (Table 11.9).

From the standpoint of employment

Another way to see the compositional changes in the economy is to examine what the labor force is doing. Here one finds several critical underlying points. In 1955, there were 50.6 million nonagricultural jobs in the United States; in 1986, there were 100 million jobs, a 98 percent increase. Although this increase in employment opportunities

Table 11.8. *Machine tools (million dollars, except as noted)*

Factor	1972	1975	1980	1982	1984	1985[a]	1986[b]	1987[c]
Metal cutting								
Shipments	1,259	2,406	4,952	4,155	2,815	3,000	3,000	2,700
1982 dollars	3,766	4,781	5,720	4,155	2,696	2,778	2,703	2,348
Imports	105	304	1,237	1,271	1,322	1,690	2,000	1,800
Imports/new supply (%)	7.7	11.2	20.0	23.4	31.9	36.0	40.0	40.0
Exports	190	418	680	654	455	500	510	520
Exports/shipments (%)	15.1	17.4	13.7	15.7	16.2	16.7	17.0	19.3
Metal forming								
Shipments	670	1,026	1,749	1,384	1,363	1,500	1,350	1,300
1982 dollars	2,162	2,198	2,069	1,384	1,315	1,415	1,250	1,171
Imports	35	79	273	234	341	427	510	490
Imports/new supply (%)	4.0	5.9	9.7	9.9	13.8	22.2	27.4	27.4
Exports	124	217	425	372	289	278	320	325
Exports/shipments (%)	18.4	21.2	24.3	26.9	21.2	18.5	23.7	25.0

[a]Estimates, except for imports and exports.
[b]Estimates.
[c]Forecasts.
Source: U.S. Department of Commerce, Bureau of Industrial Economics, *Industrial Outlook, 1987.*

Table 11.9. Selected nonferrous metals: primary aluminum, copper, zinc (million dollars, except as noted)

Factor	1972	1975	1980	1984	1985[a]	1986[b]	1987[c]
Shipments	5,684	6,831	15,115	12,505	13,510	9,677	9,716
Shipments (1982 dollars)	12,303	10,128	13,485	12,082	14,939	9,087	8,964
Imports	732	885	2,133	2,651	2,066	3,127	2,580
Exports	244	372	1,159	556	517	320	349
Imports/new supply (%)	11.4	11.5	12.4	17.5	13.3	24.4	21.0
Exports/shipments (%)	4.3	5.4	7.7	4.5	3.6	3.3	3.6

[a]Estimates, except for imports and exports.
[b]Estimates.
[c]Forecasts.
Source: U.S. Department of Commerce, Bureau of Industrial Economics, Industrial Outlook, 1987.

is one of the great marvels of American social policy during the period, the high-wage (and generally unionized) sectors have lost employment opportunities in relative terms. Moreover, in order to "pay" (as well as to "compensate") for such employment-affecting factors as implementation of affirmative action, environmental improvement, and environmental safety considerations on the job, a great deal of potential productivity growth and, quite possibly, national comparative economic competitiveness were sacrificed. The result is that what had been a source of confidence in a rising living standard (i.e., expansion of employment opportunities and eventually wages in the manufacturing sector) began to go sour.

As noted, jobs in the nonagricultural sectors grew 98 percent during the 31-year period (1955–86). As can be seen from Table 11.10, jobs in construction increased 75 percent, in transportation and public utilities 28 percent, in wholesale and retail trade no less than 100 and 136 percent, respectively, in finance, insurance, and real estate 174 percent, in services a whopping 272 percent, and in government an impressive 157 percent. But during the same three decades, the number of jobs in the manufacturing sector grew only 14 percent, with jobs in durable goods and nondurable goods rising by 19 and 6 percent, respectively. Business services and health services grew between 1965 and 1986 no less than an overwhelming 331 and 217 percent, respectively. The growth in business services doubtless reflects, in part, purchasing from outside sources some services once produced within the firm.

Also of interest are the changes in the rankings of employment during the 31-year period among the various two-digit manufacturing industries. The heavy losers were primary metals, tobacco, textiles, petroleum and coal, leather and leather products, apparel and other textiles (where the absolute numbers actually fell), fabricated metals, transportation equipment, and food and kindred products (where the absolute numbers rose slightly). Within manufactures, there were no great gainers.

In absolute numbers, manufacturing industries that gained were machinery, electrical equipment, instruments, and rubber. However, none of these industries showed an increase in the proportion of the nonagricultural labor force it employed.

On the whole, services are replacing manufacturing as the principal area of employment opportunities. Also, within manufacturing, the relative numbers of jobs for the unskilled are falling. Among the two-digit manufacturing industries there have been some improvements during the past five years. From an overall standpoint, manufacturing job opportunities are relatively less important. The "basket case" is

Table 11.10. *Nonagricultural employment by sector, selected years, 1955–86*

Industry	Number employed (thousands)					Percentage distribution				
	1955	1965	1975	1985	1986	1955	1965	1975	1985	1986
Total	50,641	60,765	76,945	97,699	100,167	100	100	100	100	100
Mining	792	632	752	969	792	1.6	1.0	1.0	1.0	0.8
Construction	2,839	3,232	3,525	4,662	4,960	5.6	5.3	4.6	4.8	5.0
Manufacturing	16,882	18,062	18,323	19,426	19,186	33.3	29.7	23.8	19.9	19.2
Durable goods	9,541	10,405	10,688	11,566	11,345	18.8	17.1	13.9	11.8	11.3
Lumber and wood products	771	654	615	703	727	1.5	1.8	0.8	0.7	0.7
Furniture and fixtures	347	410	417	497	497	0.7	0.7	0.5	0.5	0.5
Stone, clay, and glass products	588	628	614	600	595	1.2	1.0	0.8	0.6	0.6
Primary metal industries	1,267	1,253	1,139	816	768	2.5	2.1	1.5	0.8	0.8
Fabricated metal products	1,221	1,372	1,458	1,472	1,439	2.4	2.3	1.9	1.5	1.4
Machinery, except electrical	1,449	1,735	2,057	2,181	2,082	2.9	2.9	2.7	2.2	2.1
Electric and electronic equipment	1,227	1,615	1,702	2,208	2,169	2.4	2.7	2.2	2.3	2.2
Transportation equipment	1,894	1,873	1,715	1,990	1,984	3.7	3.1	2.2	2.0	2.0
Instruments and related products	382	445	550	724	717	0.8	0.7	0.7	0.7	0.7
Miscellaneous manufacturing industries	396	420	407	376	367	0.8	0.7	0.5	0.4	0.4
Nondurable goods	7,341	7,656	7,635	7,860	7,841	14.5	12.6	9.9	8.0	7.8
Food and kindred products	1,825	1,757	1,676	1,637	1,641	3.6	2.9	2.2	1.7	1.6
Tobacco manufactures	103	87	78	65	61	0.2	0.1	0.1	0.1	0.1
Textile mill products	1,050	926	868	703	709	2.1	1.5	1.1	0.7	0.7
Apparel and other textiles	1,219	1,354	1,243	1,162	1,115	2.4	2.2	1.6	1.2	1.1
Paper and allied products	550	639	642	683	690	1.1	1.1	0.8	0.7	0.7
Printing and publishing	835	979	1,083	1,422	1,479	1.6	1.6	1.4	1.5	1.5
Chemicals and allied products	773	908	1,013	1,042	1,027	1.5	1.5	1.3	1.1	1.0
Petroleum and coal products	237	183	195	177	194	0.5	0.3	0.3	0.2	0.2
Rubber and miscellaneous plastic products	363	471	608	795	801	0.7	0.8	0.8	0.8	0.8
Leather and leather products	386	353	248	175	155	0.8	0.6	0.3	0.2	0.2

Table 11.10 (cont.)

Industry	Number employed (thousands)					Percentage distribution				
	1955	1965	1975	1985	1986	1955	1965	1975	1985	1986
Transportation and public utilities	4,141	4,036	4,542	5,300	5,286	8.2	6.6	5.9	5.4	5.3
Wholesale trade	2,926	3,466	4,415	5,769	5,853	5.8	5.7	5.7	5.9	5.8
Retail trade	7,610	9,250	12,645	17,425	17,978	15.0	15.2	16.4	17.8	17.9
Finance, insurance, and real estate	2,298	2,977	4,165	5,924	6,305	4.5	4.9	5.4	6.1	6.3
Services	6,240	9,036	13,892	21,936	23,072	12.3	14.9	18.1	22.5	23.0
Business services	n.a.	1,139	2,042	4,453	4,909	n.a.	1.9	2.7	4.6	4.8
Health services	n.a.	2,080	4,134	6,267	6,586	n.a.	3.4	5.4	6.4	6.6
Government	6,914	10,074	14,686	16,300	16,735	13.7	16.6	19.1	16.7	16.7

Source: U.S. Department of Labor, Bureau of Labor Statistics, *Employment, Hours and Earnings, United States, 1909–84*, Vols. I & II; *Employment and Earning, 1985* and 1986.

Table 11.11. *Employment in private nonagricultural industry and manufacturing, 1955–86 (thousands)*

	Private nonagricultural		Manufacturing		
Year	All employees	Production employees as % of all employees	All employees	Production employees as % of all employees	Manufacturing employees as % of total private nonagricultural
1955	43,727	85.8	16,882	78.7	38.6
1960	45,836	84.0	16,796	74.9	36.6
1965	50,689	83.4	18,062	74.4	35.6
1970	58,325	82.6	19,367	72.5	33.2
1975	62,259	81.9	18,323	71.2	29.4
1980	74,166	81.7	20,285	70.1	27.4
1981	75,126	81.5	20,170	69.5	26.8
1982	73,729	80.7	18,781	67.8	25.5
1983	74,330	80.8	18,497	68.0	24.9
1984	78,477	81.0	19,412	68.4	24.7
1985	81,404	80.9	19,426	68.0	23.9
1986	83,432	80.9	19,186	67.9	23.0

Source: U.S. Department of Labor, Bureau of Labor Statistics, *Employment, Hours and Earnings, United States, 1909–84*, Vols. I & II; *Employment and Earnings*, 1985 and 1986.

employment in metal production generally, and steel production specifically. Those from Pittsburgh have appreciated this point for some time.

Another interesting change in the American labor force has been the reduction in the number of production workers in general, and those in manufacturing specifically. Table 11.11 shows this change for private nonagricultural workers and for those in manufacturing. The point is that the market for highly paid production workers (largely found in the unionized manufacturing sector) is contracting rapidly. Production workers in services, even when unionized, do not have high wage rates.

Summary

What have we shown?

Decline: As an activity center in the American economy, manufacturing has been slipping. This slippage has occurred as government, services, and finance, real estate, and insurance have grown.

Nonuniformity: The decline in manufacturing has not been uniform. Some sectors, such as textiles and shoes, are bare shadows of what they once were. Others, such as steel and aluminum production and machine tools, are clearly in the process of losing out, with much worse prognoses than their present situations. Still others, such as autos and some electronics, are holding on, but with increasingly less auspicious expectations. On the whole, that portion of manufacturing most identified with the American defense capacity has generally diminished in relative terms, and much of it has diminished in absolute output. Employment is also lower in these industries.

Imports: This domestic decline obviously has occurred because of tremendous growth in imports into the American economy, reflecting better manufacturing management in other MDCs – autos, machine tools, and electronics coming from Japan and Germany. Other factors reflect the vagaries of the American intermediate-product legislation – auto parts coming from modern plants in Canada. The foregoing says nothing of the important and growing role of imports from LDCs, where labor costs are much lower and where, in the nature of things, plants (i.e., the fixed equipment) are newer and better adapted to concerns of current market costs.

Exports: The growth of competitive MDCs, and the LDC foreign-market export capacity, and the recent international impact of the overvalued American dollar have served to shrink the demand for American exports. Some writers have said that the solution to the problem is simply to allow the dollar to fall to some "true equilibrium" level. Would that it were only so!

11.2   Putting the picture in perspective

Explanations

Of these, there are several.

Comparisons of managements over time and space: One of the great achievements of the post–World War II period was the speed with which the two principal defeated industrialized nations, Germany and

Japan, recovered their manufactured-goods competitive capacities. What had been destroyed in the war were older plants; what had not been destroyed were competent, competitive managements and disciplined, skilled labor cadres. This was the situation on which the Marshall Plan and private efforts were built.

If the underlying strength of the German and Japanese economies was unexpected in the period 1945–50, so the fragility of many aspects of management in the American manufacturing sector during 1975–84 was a comparable revelation. In their time of distress, Germany and Japan suffered from destroyed facilities, but they benefited from efficient management and low-cost (efficient) labor. In its time of relative distress, America suffered mainly from outmoded existing plants and high-cost labor, and American management pursued solutions that did not adequately address these considerations. Unwilling and perhaps unable to come to grips with the problems of changing their traditional methods of handling their labor force, and obsessed with the priority of meeting their firms' immediate profit needs, increasingly large numbers of American firms pursued solutions of the Gordian knot type by procuring intermediate-type and even finished goods and services by sourcing out at home or abroad, by transferring operations overseas, and/or by diversification to other industries, industries about which they seemingly know a good deal less. It is hard to identify just what these managements had in mind, if it differed from a rather superficial or very here-and-now commitment to quick profits. This predilection for contracting out, particularly for many business overhead and record-keeping activities, may even explain part of the growth in the American services sector – relevant current data are not easily available.

Sourcing abroad has been only somewhat easier to detect. These facilities not only are likely to enjoy cost and local-market trade advantages in their host countries but also are likely to be used for exports to the United States, as well as to other countries to which the American firms previously shipped. Many LDC host countries, sensing the advantages of such economic hospitality, have made significant efforts to accommodate the absorption of firms that once were almost entirely based in America.

Technology and technological changes: The economics literature is rich in studies showing the impact of invention and innovation on economic progress. R. D. Norton summarizes much of this material particularly well in a recent *Journal of Economic Literature* survey article (Norton, 1986). Drawing on summaries of the various "laws" of industrial growth offered by Simon Kuznets in 1930, Walter Hoffman in 1931, Arthur F. Burns in 1934, Alvin H. Hansen in 1937, and Joseph A. Schumpeter in 1939 and 1942, Norton notes that economic progress often is seen as a concomitant of technological change. He states that the tendencies of national economies and industries toward senescence are associated with the degree of vigor of the factors affecting supply and demand. Each of the theorists mentioned was pursuaded that economic maturity, the immediate forerunner of economic senescence, was a state featuring the interactive impact of a decline in the introduction of technology and a sclerotic flagging of demand. Kuznets, in particular, was intrigued with the effect of competitive efficiency in lowering economic rents, as well as opportunities to use self-governing incentives. Early on, Kuznets had offered the observation that new factories in less developed areas tend to undersell their long-established competitors because of their newer, state-of-the-art technology or their lower labor costs or both.

Norton's discussion also focuses on the product cycle. That cycle has a biological analogy; it suggests regular patterns of differing rates of market acceptance, as well as choices of locations by firms, which are "increasingly footloose" and free to migrate to low-wage, politically receptive locations at home and abroad. The representative writers were Edgar M. Hoover in 1948 and Raymond Vernon in 1966. Hoover stressed declining labor productivity, particularly where firms had a long history of difficult management–worker relationships. Vernon emphasized that American firms, in seeking to penetrate European markets, built state-of-the-art plants in Europe. In the process, they employed more cost-efficient European labor and used the output of these newer plants to undersell their original American establishments. After a time, so Vernon reported, the moves shifted from the once newer European plants to even more modern plants built in the LDCs. Invariably, the mostly recently built plants, because of their technological modernity and the relative cheapness of their labor costs, have managed to undersell previously built plants of their competitors (both American and European).

Norton cites several writers concerned with differing kinds of "maturity," a term chosen for some inexplicable reason to indicate sclerosis. Kindleberger, from 1953 to 1980, wrote of an industrial "climacteric," or what amounts to an inability to "switch and reswitch." Mancur Olson, from 1977 until 1983, extended the analysis (and the metaphor) to the political process.

The complication of a raging inflationary rate is another aspect discussed by Norton. In this context, inflation appears initially as a result of economic sclerosis, and afterward the inflationary rate itself becomes the cause of further sclerotic changes.

The technology of mass production, a form of rationalization largely eliminating the need for highly skilled workers, received a new and speculatively interesting treatment by Michael Piore and Charles Sabel (1984). Accepting the point that MDCs in general, and the United States in particular, can no longer undersell low-cost-labor/mass-production facilities in the LCDs, they argued that a contrary American strategy should be considered. It is possible, they aver, for MDCs to undersell the LDC mass-production factories by offering low-priced, computer-produced, custom-assembled products.

For some time, Dale Jorgenson, to mention but one of many, has argued that American industrial competitiveness has been lost because of policies, both political and economic, serving to starve private investment in the installation of state-of-the-art equipment. To this argument, Eckstein and his group added the absence of public promotion of scientific research and technical manpower training, both depending on an awareness of changes in technology. However, up-to-date knowledge of technology is not sufficient. Implementation and technological change must be predicated on systematic knowledge of the operations of the money-capital, the physical-capital, and the human-capital markets. Effectiveness in the product markets is related to, even, in part based on, an understanding of all aspects of the factor markets.

There are, however, certain other technological developments involving knowledge transmission that affect the ability to integrate inputs, intermediate goods, and product markets. These are sometimes overlooked. In the 1960s, two communications "revolutions" occurred serving to make feasible the thorough worldwide integration of product markets. Jet air travel made it physically (and commercially) possible for almost all national markets to be reached overnight from any point on the globe, thus permitting quick transfer of goods and, when necessary, frequent temporary transfers of repair and managerial personnel. Unless political steps were taken to forestall these movements, the traditions protecting national domestic-market hegemony were eroded. And the global use of satellite telephone and data-transmissions services further destroyed national inaccessibility.

Given these changes, American managements saw the economic savings to their firms in sourcing and building new plants abroad. By way of contrast, more nationalistically oriented modern managements, such as those in Japan, recognized early on how these technological advances could be employed to the advantage of their own home-country-based firms. The initial Japanese choice was not to source or build abroad; rather, it was to use the communications "revolution" to penetrate, on an ever increasing scale, distant foreign markets.

When it ultimately became apparent that countries buying their products were likely to raise trade barriers to imports, many of these firms responded by building plants in host countries. In the international jostling, host countries demanded further concessions. During the past 10 years or so, some LDCs have required "performance contracts" specifying that foreign-owned (e.g., American) firms can sell in a particular national market (e.g., Brazil or Mexico) only if some specified portion of the product is manufactured in the host country. Also, some specified proportion of what is so manufactured is exported in order to give the host country some positive foreign-trade income. In the case of MDCs such as the United States (particularly earlier) and Japan (more recently), the accommodation was to set up joint-venture plants involving host countries' clearly less competitive firms along with the exporting countries' apparently stronger firms.

Market scale and the economics of distribution: Let us start with a discussion of method, if only to put the discussion of policy in some perspective. Economic historians and economic theorists have not traditionally had a harmonious professional relationship. Each group has its own explanation for the disharmony, but the conflict centers on one group's preference for a nominalist approach (essentially relying on cognitive perception) and the other's preference for a realist approach (relying on the search for essences and the application of rules of reasoned thinking). Economic historians, tending to be empiricists first and theorists second, have centered their studies on particularistic growth of nations (and sometimes regions); they have generally been more unwilling to base policy on reasoned models and in practice often have questioned the applicability of policies based on static theory. Their studies have led them to believe that national self-interest creates solutions as well as problems, and on the basis of their findings they occasionally have advocated nationally responsible solutions to such questions as providing work opportunity and pursuing social investment in economic modernization.

On the other hand, in the last 100 years the tendency toward formalism among economists has become almost irresistible (Woo, 1986). By and large, the traditional theoretical test most preferred is one of imminent criticism, and though considerable lip service usually is paid to the importance of data, virtually no economist spends much time examining the quality of the data used. But facts are still said to be important, particularly if, when assembled, they "confirm" one's own theory or "squarely deny" someone else's theory.

We come now to policy. Few economic theories have a record of persuasiveness as great as that for the theory of comparative advantage, the cornerstone of free trade policies. Free trade is the issue that separated Schmoller from Menger; it was the issue that led Marshall to intervene to convey his chair to Pigou rather than let it fall into the hands of Foxwell. Nonetheless, I aver that there are, underlying the free trade question, at least two technical aspects to the difference in emphasis that have been largely overlooked. One is the question of scale. The other is the analytical priority given to the details of supply, rather than to the determinants of effective demand. The dynamics of supply relate to changing technology; long-term changes in effective demand can relate to the opening of markets across political boundaries as well as to more traditionally economic matters such as the size distribution of income.

Neo-classical economics focuses on either constant or decreasing returns to scale. Piero Sraffa's great contribution, to say nothing of his destructive attack on Marshall's influence, has been to suggest that in practice the presence of firms enjoying increasing returns is frequent. More recently, Fellner and others have suggested increasing returns, otherwise seen as economies of scale, as the "source" of the productivity residual, once the Golden Fleece and now the current Holy Grail for those seeking to explain economic progress.

But if there is anything to Malthus's economics, the economics based on demand, it is the specter of economic stagnation, a condition that can be described as the capacity to produce outrunning the capacity to consume effectively. Attention then turns to what makes expanded consumption possible. Obviously, one solution is to increase and possibly to redistribute incomes in such a way as to augment aggregate purchases. Another solution is to broaden the extent of the market. Doing so politically by means of breaking down national tariff barriers can lead to expanded consumption, and that has been the traditional argument for *laissez-faire, laissez-passer.*

Companion to this obvious opinion is another, less obvious opinion. If a firm or even an economy, faced with stagnation, wishes to enjoy economies of scale, it can do so by market segmentation, provided it can keep the segments apart. The traditional way (and the way used so effectively by the Japanese at the current time) is to use a protected domestic market to cover a large portion of the firm's fixed (overhead) costs and to use foreign markets to achieve scale. Positing the presence of decreasing costs, the larger the scale, the cheaper the unit variable costs. That is one way to win the competitive battle in foreign markets.

One may well ask why protection of, and higher prices in, the domestic market is essential to this position. The answer is that *ex post*, it is not, but in a world of uncertainty, from an *ex ante* standpoint, the situation may appear to be thus to the involved entrepreneurs. Richard Cantillon saw this point some 250 years ago when he observed that entrepreneurs committed themselves to known costs and were possible victims of unknown prices when they entered into their activities. The argument runs that industrialists, assured of sufficient domestic demand to cover overhead, fear less and can take greater export chances (Cantillon, [1755] 1964).

As I review the conflict between the two professional groups, what stands out is that there is truly an a priori dependence overlooked by the economists. Full enjoyment of the economies of scale on the production side may require adjustment on the consumption side. What does it avail any entrepreneur to produce cheaply if he cannot find customers? But if there has been a flaw in the economists' presentation, the economic historians have made a similar error. They have failed to see that national economic expansion is not simply the result of producers trying to penetrate markets; the cry for market expansion may well come from a producing nation's consumers objecting to the higher domestic prices used to amortize overhead production costs. What consumers want is that entrepreneurs take even more chances than would otherwise be necessary.

The foregoing, a general explanation of the American system, as advanced by Daniel Raymond (Perlman, 1984), is what Professor Dorfman (1946, p. 534) calls the "Prussian system" (as adapted by Friedrich List), as exemplified more recently by Japan. It explains how market segmentation with protection can be used *even without trade subsidies* to guarantee scale and how foreign markets can be easily captured, particularly if firms are operating under conditions of increasing returns. When (as seems more than likely in the current case of Japan) indirect and even direct trade subsidies are employed, there is little wonder that the American commitment to relatively open domestic markets for manufactured goods leads to contraction for the affected American goods.

Credit arrangements: Public subsidization of exports is a well-established international trade practice, even if its use has seemingly been prohibited by the General Agreement on Trade and Tariffs. Even there, an exception has been made for remittance of the value-added tax, which has resulted (as that tax has become the mainstay of public finance) in American firms paying real estate, payroll, and both gross- and net-profit taxes and having to compete against non-American firms that have their principal tax (the value-added tax) remitted on exports.

There have been, however, other credit arrangements in which American firms should have suffered no competitive penalties. During the Hoover administration, the federal government set up the Export-Import Bank, which gave access to easy credit to overseas (foreign) customers seeking to purchase American goods. Easy credit was possible because the American government guaranteed the necessary loans.

This approach was hardly unique to the United States; other countries have followed identical or similar practices. Many Americans have commented that the Japanese Ministry of International Trade and Industry (MITI), working along with the Japanese banks and the interested Japanese firms to facilitate investment in manufacturing, has developed these practices to a fine art. One variant of this kind of activity is the trading company, a foreign-trade arrangement that permits nonrelated firms to coordinate their trade practices (buying and selling) in foreign markets. American firms have the legal right to do what the Japanese have done; what the Americans seemingly lack is the structure of socioeconomic leadership to undertake it on a massive scale. It may not always have been so; the various river authorities (e.g., the Tennessee Valley Authority, the Columbia River Authority, the Boulder Dam Authority) are examples of the same kind of thing (coordination of financing and production) done on the domestic front.

Exchange rates: The American dollar's tremendously strong exchange-rate relationship from 1982 until 1986 has exacerbated all of these tendencies. But even if the exchange-rate problem had not arisen (as it had not during the Carter administration, 1977–81), most of these tendencies would nonetheless have been strong. Thus, I infer that the exchange-rate problem represents an exacerbation rather than a cause. The principal causes seemingly lie elsewhere.

Planning policy or legislation – a red-herring issue: There are some who see in the leadership differences between the Japanese and American manufacturing industries a contrast between an integrated, planned MITI approach and an ideologically free-market-oriented stance of "no industrial policy." Indeed, part of Norton's comprehensive survey of the recent literature builds on the work of Robert B. Reich (1982, 1983, 1984). Reich, using the kind of data-based position well developed by Eckstein et al. (1984), seeks to stimulate awareness of the need for a "conscious" (deliberately planned) American public industrial policy. Norton builds on just this point, with the add-on that for a time there were within the American camp two principal lines of argument, one stressing *preservationism,* which is concerned with trying to preserve our manufacturing legacy, and the other stressing the *modernist* view, namely, that economies, using political means, cannot effectively stay some forms of the inevitable consequences of the market determination of their competitive strengths. Such elaboration of the different American and Japanese national approaches, particularly as put in any of these terms, misses the critical point: Both nations have profound industrial-development policies that have found expression in legislation.

Norton reports at length (indeed, even synthesizes) the recent American debate between two groups of "economists." One group, the "preservationists" (Lester Thurow, *Business Week* magazine, and Amitai Etzioni), urge social equity as a criterion for making policy; insofar as they urge reindustrialization through industrial product targeting and policies aimed at augmenting savings and investment, they have in mind preservation of job opportunities as well as defense capability as the top priorities. The other group, the "modernizers" (e.g., William H. Branson, Marina von Neumann Whitman, and Robert E. Reich), want to force international competitiveness on the manufacturing sector through a combination of ruthless pruning of moribund firms and encouragement (even subsidies) for those capable of becoming internationally competitive.

The debate was overtaken by events. The events were the decisions taken by the Reagan administration to show its ideological commitment to free-market forces and the international overvaluation of the dollar. The former precluded a kind of deliberate planning; the latter led to hitherto unknown levels of import penetration of the American home market, to further losses of export markets, and to enormous trade deficits.

Despite the assertion that the Reagan administration was against planning or targeted intervention, the true basic difference was not so simple as "plan versus no plan." Rather, the important contrast between the two approaches can best be seen when one identifies the particular priorities legislatively assigned to various underlying national objectives. One should look beyond the instruments selected to achieve objectives, particularly when considered singly, to the results flowing from policies associated with conflicting goals, that is, to the social priorities lying behind the legislation.

What are these goals? Japan seemingly pursues its historical objectives – dominance in East Asia and Southeast Asia through establishment of an economic "co-prosperity sphere." America's objectives during the past three decades have given top billing to affirmative action as applied to employment opportunities, improvement of the environment, reconstruction of the defense competence (the reputation for which was destroyed in Vietnam), and some kind of economic leadership in shaping international economic interdependence.

Competing social priorities: What I see here are two things. First, identifying the list of social goals and their priorities, when viewed retrospectively, suggests that powerful nations like the United States and Japan largely get what they want. In the process, they often must decide between conflicting uses of scarce resources, and what gets the nod is what has been given the higher priority. Second, what these nations (as well as others) achieve in any given time period may later be perceived as having been an error, because of inadequate *ex ante* recognition of the *ex post* costs and social consequences of the assigned priorities.

Explicit examples may be useful. One might refer to a series of recent American choices and their impact on overall productivity growth. Since the 1960s, we in America have assigned high priorities to two social-reform policies: affirmative action in the job sphere and environmental protection. Only more recently have we come to realize what pursuit of these goals has meant in terms of the destruction of our capacity to match other nations' productivity gains.

Even so, the story is not that simple. We entertained other high-priority social goals as well, and they, too, introduced contradictions. The goals of cost-effective, self-contained rearmament and international trade patterns based on simple economic efficiency were contradictory ends. Another American goal, one not mentioned until this point, has been the Reagan administration's commitment to domestic price stabilization, a goal already achieved, although achieved partly at the cost of high interest and adverse exchange rates. Altogether, pursuit of these various objectives has resulted in an America with, on the one hand, fairer employment opportunities, better air and water, and seemingly more fearsome military prowess and, on the other hand, decreased international manufacturing competitiveness in many areas.

The following are some of the more significant social goals that have, at various times, dominated different aspects of our national programs:

- Affirmative-action programs
- Consumers' and workers' environmental safety
- Price stability
- Jobs and employment
- Economic growth
- Restraint in government budget growth
- Moderation of changes in exchange rates and export–import trade balances
- Efficient domestic production of goods and services
- Regaining international military power

Each of these has merit, although any evaluation of such merit will reflect designated importances and self-interests of different groups. The important thing is how the different groups (and ultimately society itself) order the priorities. The Lyndon Johnson "Great Society" state welfare programs put higher priorities on affirmative action, jobs, and consumers' and workers' environment and safety than on price stability and budget control. The Reagan administration has stressed price stability and military power.

By and large, what presidents stress is what they are likely to achieve, although often it is the case that the results will also include some things not intended and probably not desired. For example, there has been an increase in the absolute number of jobs, but the jobs that have been created have been in finance, real estate, insurance, services, and government, generally not in the manufacturing sector. In order to remain competitive, many firms have elected to source abroad (or even source from cheaper American subcontractors rather than try to make their own domestic production lines more efficient). This raises a question: What did pursuit of each of these objectives do to American manufacturing competitiveness?

- An affirmative-action program redirected job opportunities, changing the emphasis from efficiency to facing the need to end a broad history of social inequities for various groups. Not only were hirings and promotions to be based on factors other than merit alone, but also pay scales were to be reconsidered in order that social justice be achieved. When such shifts in pay scales brought about capital substitution, then the government budget was to be the "provider of last resort."

- The legislative and administrative desire to mandate improvements in environment and safety for consumers and workers invariably diverted funds from investment in physical and human capital (plants and educational programs). Because they led to rebuilding and investing in equipment for reasons other than competitive efficiency, programs designed to achieve these social goals worked to the disadvantage of American firms' domestic operations.

- The goal of reducing the rate of price inflation (if not actually introducing price deflation) has been popular with a generally aging population, contemplating life on fixed pensions. In order to achieve this goal, governments have encouraged high interest rates, and firms have relied on shaving costs. Costs have been reduced by contracting out to suppliers who are in low-wage areas (i.e., the "sun belt"), by sourcing abroad (i.e., Singapore, Taiwan, Korea, Hong Kong, and other LDCs), or by trying to achieve economies of scale by reducing the number of varieties of any particular good that is produced.

- Implementation of the socially desirable goal of creating sufficient jobs to provide employment opportunity for the current members and the likely number of new entrants to the labor force led to production inefficiencies. This goal also led to legislation covering those workers who became victims of the efficiency-increasing substitution of capital for labor. This effort to manipulate job opportunity has resulted, at least in part, in a reduced labor-productivity growth rate.

- The goal of maintaining and/or increasing the rate of economic growth nationally (and, if possible, regionally) in order to sustain or improve living standards and achieve a minimum level of political confidence has also been successful. Contrast Singapore (until very recently) with Britain, or New England's economic growth with the senescence in the Great Lakes area. But renaissance has been achieved in part by using policies involving private incentives, purchased with public funds. Tax concessions and state, county, and municipal tax rebates served in the initial years, at least, to subsidize change and implicitly to increase tax burdens on those firms that did not move.

- The perceived need to reduce the rate of growth in government budgets in order to avoid "investment crowding-out" has enjoyed widespread political popularity, even if not yet appropriately implemented.

- A continuing belief that introduction of flexible exchange rates would somehow redress imbalances in foreign trade in the current account and capital account, and in the process allocate efficiently the geographic location of investment, has not worked out as anticipated. These failures may be due in part to employee resistance to real wage reductions, or they could be associated with legislatively mandated programs enacted to smooth transitions, but having the unintended result of frustrating the long-haul benefits. There is a side to the theory involved that is seldom examined: the role of true uncertainty. As Cantillon put it over 300 years ago, entrepreneurs and governments have to make decisions, based on known costs, about likely prices.
- Efficient production of goods and services, as noted earlier, has been frustrated by pursuit of the other objectives.
- The need to keep the collective American mind focused on the critical role its military power plays in all aspects (political and economic, tactical and strategic, moral and idiosyncratic) of the world's system of resolution of international conflict should be paramount.

11.3   Conclusions

The focus of this chapter has been the decline in American manufacturing competitiveness generally, and American defense manufacturing competence specifically. That there have been significant changes in these areas seems to be beyond dispute, although they have been neither universal nor uniform.

Some have asserted that this deterioration has followed some scientific historical law, usually perceived in terms of a biological analogy, and Schumpeter's phrase "creative destruction" often is cited as an amplification. On reflection, I think that Schumpeter's concept is intuitive, an exemplar of a Hegelian kind of evolutionary contradiction. It is the kind of thing that has more appeal to pure intellectuals than to practicing economists.

The more conventional economic explanations relating to technology, extent of the market, economies of scale, and foreign-exchange rates have their prior importance, but ultimately they are based on sets of chosen social values. Therefore, I assert that a more plausible set of reasons concerns conflicts in national priorities and a preference for abstract principles (the Ricardian theory of comparative advantage and the more modern perception of international economic interdependence), rather than a later Malthus-like appetite for facts and empirical findings. I hasten to add that the Ricardian theory of international comparative advantage is a short-run theory, not a long-run theory, and many particularly competent trade economists (e.g., John Stuart Mill and Jacob Viner) have long seen that free trade can be demonstrated to be better than no trade. To prove that it is better than protected trade would require more specifications, such as the impact of retaliation and determination of which social group's interest is dominant (the consumer's interest or some producer's interest).

It is not difficult to hear numerous voices crying out about the evils of protectionism, but there is another and possibly more neutral and clearly methodological way to phrase the issues: Why is Japan, a country obviously breaking the rule of established international trade theory (the seemingly immutable law of comparative advantage), apparently doing so well? In what ways and to what extent in measurable output has the de facto American commitment to international economic interdependence, so admirable in theory and yet so disappointing to America's own competitive capacity and its allies' military defense, been self-destructive in the long term? So phrased, the emphasis is not on the policy, but on the scientific ways of thinking.

The question of the existence of overriding international interest is not easy. Many seem to assert that what is good for all nations must be good for each; such an argument may have a zero-sum theoretical validity, but it lacks empirical and non-zero-sum theoretical validity. Yet it is the position most economists prefer to argue.

Not so to some sophisticated political scientists. Sir Isaiah Berlin makes the point that overcommitment to abstraction (I have in mind here "internationalism") comes easily to intellectuals and that such abstractions advanced by Marx and Rousseau compare poorly with the intellectual reform programs offered by Disraeli and Moses Hess when the record comes to be examined. Berlin's acceptance of the significance of group (e.g., national) interest swallows hard in this modern world. But swallowing hard does not make it irrelevant.

In the end, I conclude that the conditions that gave us such a long period of relative economic growth (1946 until now) were derived from a general recognition of the lessons of two world wars and an agreement regarding the institutions set up after World War II. These institutions reflected above all else that era's set of American social-goal priorities. Translated, they stressed economic growth in many countries rather than one. The Berlin argument noted earlier identifies the weakness of such altruism. It is satisfying to live in a time when the costs of altruism are not realized; later, when the costs have to be paid, it is comforting, yet important, to recall the dreams.

References

Berlin, Isaiah (1981). *Against the Current: Essays in the History of Ideas.* Oxford University Press.

Burns, Arthur F. (1934). *Production Trends in the United States since 1870.* New York: NBER.

Cantillon, Richard [1755] (1964). *Essai sur la nature de commerce en général* (translated by Henry Higgs). New York: Augustus M. Kelley.

Dorfman, Joseph (1946). *The Economic Mind in American Civilization, 1606–1865,* Vol 2. New York: Viking Press.

Eckstein, Otto, Caton, Christopher, Brinner, Roger, and Duprey, Peter (1984). *The DRI Report on U.S. Manufacturing Industries.* New York: McGraw-Hill.

Hansen, Alvin H. (1939). "Economic Progress and Declining Population Growth." *American Economic Review,* 29(March)(1):1–15.

Hoffman, Walther G. [1931] (1955). *British Industry, 1700–1950.* New York: Augustus M. Kelley.

Hoover, Edgar M. (1948). *The Location of Economic Activity.* New York: McGraw-Hill.

Jorgenson, Dale W. (1981). "Productivity and Growth: Retrospect and Prospect," in *Dimensions of Productivity Research: Proceedings of the Conference on Productivity Research* (Vol. 1, pp. 5–25). Houston: American Productivity Center.

Jorgenson, Dale W., Christensen, Laurits R., and Cummings, Dianne (1980). "Economic Growth, 1947–73: An International Comparison," in J. W. Kendrick and B. N. Vaccara (eds.), *New Developments in Productivity Measurement and Analysis. National Bureau of Economic Research Studies in Income and Wealth* (Vol. 44, pp. 595–691). University of Chicago Press.

Jorgenson, Dale W., Kuroda, Masahiro, and Yoshioka, Kanji (1984). "Relative Price Changes and Biases of Technical Change in Japan." *Economic Studies Quarterly,* 35(August)(2):116–38.

Kindleberger, Charles P. (1953). *International Economics.* Homewood, Ill.: Richard D. Irwin.

(1961). "Obsolescence and Technical Change." *Bulletin of Oxford University Institute of Economic Statistics,* 23(August):281–97.

(1962). *Foreign Trade and the National Economy.* New Haven: Yale University Press.

(1973). *The New York Times* (letter), March 1.

(1974). "An American Economic Climacteric?" *Challenge,* 16(January-February)(6):35–44.

(1978). "The Aging Economy." *Weltwirtschaft Archiv,* 114(3):407–21.

(1980). "The Economic Aging of America." *Challenge,* 22(January-February)(6):48–9.

(1983). *"On the Rise and Decline of Nations."* [Review of Olson]. *International Studies Quarterly,* 27(1).

Kuznets, Simon (1930). *Secular Movements in Production and Prices – Their*

Nature and Their Bearing Upon Cyclical Fluctuations. Boston: Houghton Mifflin.

Mikesell, Raymond F. (1986). *Stockpiling Materials: An Evaluation of the National Program.* Washington, D.C.: American Enterprise Institute for Public Policy.

Norton, R. D. (1986). "Industrial Policy and American Renewal." *Journal of Economic Literature,* 24(March)(1):1–40.

Olson, Mancur (1977). *The Causes and Quality of Southern Growth.* Research Triangle Park, N.C.: Southern Growth Policies Board.

——— (1982). *The Rise and Decline of Nations: Economic Growth, Stagflation, and Social Rigidities.* New Haven: Yale University Press.

——— (1983). "The South Will Fall Again: The South as Leader and Laggard in Economic Growth." *Southern Economic Journal,* 49(April)(4):917–32.

Perlman, Mark (1984). "L'audience de Malthus aux Etat-Unis comme économiste," in A. Favue-Chamoux (ed.), *Malthus hier et aujourd'hur* Congrès international de démographic historique CNRS, mai 1980. Paris: Centre National de Recherche Scientifique.

Piore, Michael, and Sabel, Charles (1984). *The Second Industrial Divide.* New York: Basic Books.

Reich, Robert B. (1982). "Industrial Policy: Ten Concrete, Practical Steps to Building a Dynamic, Growing and Fair American Economy." *New Republic,* 186(March):28–31.

——— (1983). *The Next American Frontier.* New York: Penguin Books.

——— (1984). "Small State, Big Lesson." *Boston Observer,* 3(July)(7):32.

Schumpeter, Joseph A. [1942] (1962). *Capitalism, Socialism and Democracy.* New York: Harper & Row.

Sraffa, Piero (1926). "The Law of Returns Under Competitive Conditions." *Economic Journal,* 36:535–50.

Vernon, Raymond (1966). "International Investment and International Trade in the Product Cycle." *Quarterly Journal of Economics,* 80(May):190–207.

Woo, Henry K. H. (1986). *What's Wrong with Formalization in Economics? – An Epidemological Critique.* Newark: Victoria Press.

Discussion

FRANZ GEHRELS

The changes in the structure of American industry so well documented in the Perlman chapter may lead different readers to different interpretations. Do they indicate a declining ability of the world's leading nation to play its economic and political role in the world? Or are we witness to shifts common to all advanced industrial countries? In the case of iron and steel, all countries are plagued by worldwide oversupply, induced partly by demand shifts to other materials, and partly by the worldwide slowdown in economic growth. To be sure, American steel has lagged behind in modernization and is plagued by high labor costs compared with other sectors (this last is also true in Western Europe). One can argue that comparative advantage has been distorted by these high relative wages. Similar things can be said about the U.S. automobile industry, but I cannot think of equally good arguments in the case of the machine tools industry.

On the other hand, the spectacular developments in electronics, computers, communications, and space technology give reason to be optimistic for the future. Are we not witnessing another great technological revolution that almost inevitably will leave some industries in its backwash? And if we think of defense capability, are not these new industries more crucial than the old ones?

The apparent slowdown in productivity in the United States may look different when examined more closely. For one thing, the labor force has changed, with more young workers and women possessing, on the average, less training and entering into low-productivity jobs. Coupled with this is the rapid expansion of the service sector, which, to a greater extent than manufacturing, provides just that kind of employment. Roughly speaking, manufacturing provided about the same total employment in the early seventies as in the mid-eighties, and the expansion of employment by about 22 million took place in the service sector.

Another aspect of the slowed productivity growth in the United States is the growth in the supply of capital compared with that of labor. The United States is a country with a relatively low savings rate and rapid growth of the labor force (to be sure, the negative trade balance also adds to the supply of savings). By comparison, West Germany and Japan have high savings rates (but positive trade balances, which subtract from the supply of real savings), and Germany, at least, had an employment contraction. German output per worker rose in excess of 2 percent per year, while U.S. output per worker rose less than 1 percent. The growth of capital per worker, with the associated more rapid modernization of equipment, was probably an element in this difference between the two countries.

Not to be excluded as a possible element in the slower growth of U.S. productivity than in some other countries is the quality of the labor force. One author puts Switzerland, Germany, and Austria in one group, with their tradition of training skilled labor, and France, Great Britain, and the United States in another, lower group. Presumably Japan would belong to the first group. The ability to produce and to adapt to new technology is the greater, the better trained is the labor force.

Perlman expresses some pessimism about the effectiveness of the price mechanism in correcting the huge negative balance of trade for the United States. This came about, in part, through consumers' growing appetite for imported goods, for which U.S. industry in its inflexibility was unable to produce good substitutes. I do not, however, share his pessimism about the price mechanism as a corrective. On the one hand, he rightly sees the European practice of levying a compensating duty for the domestic value-added tax as, in effect, a barrier to trade like any other duty. But its deterrent to imports is by means of raising the supply price. If this is effective, then so, too, should be price reduction by means of the exchange rate. To be sure, the short-term effect may be weak, especially as firms commonly hold the foreign-currency price of exports stable. But, in the long run, price adjusts to the exchange rate, and buyers respond to relative price, both in the United States and in the rest of the world. This is the more strongly true when domestic substitutes are present.

If indeed such a correction takes place, the supplement to domestic savings from the trade deficit will disappear, and the low rate of savings will become a greater problem. This presupposes that we shall return to full employment – in a recession, there is no shortage of savings.

Discussion

WOLFGANG F. STOLPER

Perlman's chapter establishes the relative losses of American manufacturing industries, relative, that is, to (a) the development of service industries and (b) imports. There are "basket cases," such as basic steel, and other cases in which increases in production have been combined with even larger imports – and thus have led to only a relative deterioration of the American position, both in the domestic American market and in third markets.

I accept all the explanations cautiously advanced by Perlman. The case of the basic steel industry is well known. An obsolescent industry whose management for years has refused to see the writing on the wall undoubtedly bears an enormous share of the responsibility for the decline of this once mighty industry. A few years ago, when the steel industry finally decided to ask for technical help from Japan, the head of U.S. Steel stated that on a scale from 1 to 10, the American basic steel industry rated about a 3.

I mention this for two reasons. There is, in theological terms, the sin of pride, and we know that pride comes before the fall. There was a refusal to acknowledge developments elsewhere in the world, a belief that "we" knew everything best – in Schumpeterian terms, a mistaken belief in one's leadership position when, in reality, leadership had passed to someone else because remedial action was not taken in time.

There are, of course, many special cases in steel, as anywhere else. In steel, there are the so-called minimills, now accounting for about 20 percent of the market, that are successfully competing with the cheapest of foreign competition. There are new competitive products, as in aluminum, itself an industry under foreign pressure. There have been technical changes elsewhere that have diminished the relative demand for steel, and there is the fact of a worldwide overcapacity in basic steel.

But the last point, in particular, raises the question why it should be precisely the American industry that has had to reduce its capacity, rather than the foreign competition. Both our Canadian neighbors and the Europeans are under the same international pressures as the American steel industry; yet they seem to do much better than their American competitors, and surely not because wages are so much lower. The most serious competition in U.S. trade in general does not come only from low-wage countries. Japan alone accounts for one-third of our trade deficit. It surely has ceased to be a low-wage country, and indeed lower-wage countries like Korea are breathing down its neck. The Germans have also succeeded in maintaining both an export surplus and their position in third-world markets.

I could give a similar example from our automobile industry, which is finally mending its ways (whereas basic steel seems to prefer to die an inglorious death) and is producing better and cheaper cars.

On the other hand, the American industry rejected a system invented in Pittsburgh that allows much greater engine efficiency with much lower pollution – a system that was bought by the Japanese industry. All these cases are management failures. A third case is textiles, somewhat different. Here, when the international value of the dollar was low, the American industry competed successfully with Asian imports. But recently that industry has experienced difficulties because of the high value of the dollar. I expect that as the dollar falls in value, textiles will again become internationally competitive. It is true that a market once lost can be regained only with difficulty. But that argument goes only so far; after all, a market lost was once a market owned. Things can change either way, depending on the reactions of the participants.

All the explanations given by Perlman are correct and important.

The first two explanations are industry-specific and can be categorized as failures or successes of management and innovation. The last one highlights a point that Perlman does not consider specifically, a point that I would like to consider: the relationship between general government policy, specifically budgetary policy, and the deteriorating balance of payments, and particularly the deteriorating position of manufacturing in international trade.

As a preliminary point, let me emphasize that at least since Colin Clark's *The Conditions of Economic Progress* (1940), certain facts have been quantitatively established, of which the theories of stages of the nineteenth century (limited and impressionistic) are examples: namely, that in the course of growth, economies undergo certain changes in their productive structures. Agriculture loses its relative importance; industry increases up to a point, but then also loses its relative importance; tertiary industries keep growing in relative importance. More refined findings of this type have been published, for example, by Chenery (1960). The relative decline of manufacturing can therefore be accepted as normal. But a relative decline is quite consistent with absolute growth. If others grow richer, we need not therefore grow poorer.

Second, agriculture and manufacturing are, of course, too crude as categories. Within them there must be substantial changes taking place. In agriculture we are aware of some of the changes, at least since Thuenen. In manufacturing, Walter Hoffman, for one, has established logistic growth paths for individual industries. Continuing growth of the manufacturing sector thus requires continuous introduction of new industries as well as the renewal of old industries in rather radical ways. Old industries that increase their output (e.g., agriculture) can do so only by continuous technical change, implying a steady decrease in employment. A former head of the United Automobile Workers pointed out in a discussion that the automobile industry would go the way of agriculture: efficiency, high output, and low employment.

Growth of industries depends in part on innovative activities, but also, in part, on governmental policies, not only and perhaps not primarily with respect to international trade. However, "creative destruction," which does not seem to please Perlman as an explanation in specific cases, must have proceeded far enough to give new processes a chance. I sympathize with Perlman, for "creative destruction" does not refer primarily to industries, but to specific processes. And although slide rules may become hopelessly outdated by calculators – except in the most backward of regions, where neither batteries nor electricity are to be had – there is really no reason that Keuffel and

Esser, well-known makers of the slide rule, could not switch to other products that still remain salable. Also, there is no reason that obsolete methods of producing steel cannot be replaced by more up-to-date methods, thus maintaining the industry.

Just as in the basic Keynesian model trade must be taken into account, thus modifying the model considerably, so must the basic Schumpeterian model be adapted to a multimarket environment.

Perlman mentions an early study by E. M. Hoover, Jr. (1948) and the later studies by Vernon concerning the product cycle (1966), that is, how specific industries or sub-industries move from market to market in the process of innovation, development, and imitation.

I should mention here Loesch's analysis of how in the process of growth new industries become feasible that can efficiently produce for the domestic market (and later perhaps for export) goods that were previously imported. Protective and import-substituting policies have used this fact to justify their position, quite wrongly I believe, by reversing cause and effect. One does not become rich by import substitution, but import substitution in specific industries is a natural consequence of becoming richer.

In fact, Gustav Stolper had already advanced the idea of the product cycle when he argued in the mid-1920s that technology tends to diffuse internationally very quickly. In other words, other countries will acquire the new technical processes quickly, and after innovations become equalized internationally, the situation will revert to one of international competitive advantage to those same factors previously operative under the theory of comparative advantage.

I come now to the main point of my remarks. For 1986, the American GNP in current prices is estimated to be $4,207 billion. Total gross domestic investment is estimated to be $684 billion, or about 16.3 percent of GNP. Nonresidential investments are $459 billion, or 10.9 percent. Although these figures will undoubtedly be somewhat changed when the next estimates of the Department of Commerce are published, this is irrelevant for my purpose. Gross domestic savings are estimated at $579 billion, or 13.8 percent of GNP. Now, residential construction plus inventory change is $225 billion. Subtracting this from total gross domestic savings leaves available to domestically financed nonresidential investments $354 billion, or about 61 percent. In any case, about 2.5 percent of GNP or about 18 percent of all gross domestic investments must be financed directly or indirectly from abroad.

The gross domestic savings ratio is thus not quite sufficient to finance gross domestic nonresidential private investment. Go a step further. About 20 percent of this gross investment must be direct replacement; so only about four-fifths of GDPS is available to add to productive capacity. For 1985, the total renewable capital of the nation is estimated at about $12,027 billion. Assume (somewhat unrealistically) that about half of this is productive plant and equipment, or about $6,000 billion. A gross investment in nonresidential investment of $256 billion means a renewal of the industrial structure in 23 years.

Now, if we assume that the savings rate is 25 percent of GNP – which is approximately what it is in Japan or the Federal Republic of Germany – the calculations will look as follows. Total available domestic gross savings would be $1,052 billion. After deducting $225 billion to finance residential construction and inventory accumulations, $827 billion would remain. Gross domestic savings of $827 billion would suffice to renew the whole nonresidential ("productive") industrial structure of about $6,000 billion every 7.3 years!

Obviously, my calculations are meant to make a point, to focus on what I consider to be the main problem, not to reflect reality in every point. Obviously, there would be a decline in domestic consumption that would be reflected partly in more investments and partly in a change from an import to an export surplus. I made a similar calculation about 30 years ago, on the basis of Walter Hoffmann's German figures, that suggested that the Bundesrepublik was renewing its industrial structure every five years or so.

Also, there would be other changes that would be germane. In the first place, the rate would increase. If we have a consumption-led boom, we require ever growing increases in consumption just to stay even. This follows an acceleration principle. Also, a consumption-led boom (that is, precisely, a boom fired by increasing deficits) does *not* lead to adequate increases in productivity. American productivity has not increased very much even in manufacturing industries, explaining why the mighty American industry has fallen behind in relative terms. The current income tax reform, which shifts an increasing burden to corporations and away from individuals and which does not include consideration of increased-consumption taxes, cannot help increase consumption. This will be good in the very short run, but it does not bode too well for savings and productivity increases even in the medium term.

Thus, I conclude, first, that the big budget deficits and inadequate domestic savings are the major cause of the enormous import surpluses that threaten American competitiveness in international markets. By contrast, I believe that cutting the deficits would very quickly reduce the import surplus.

Second, renewing the American capital structure every 20 to 25 years means, in effect, capital consumption. The first effect has been to convert the United States from the biggest creditor to a big debtor nation in the world. American policy in recent years has been primarily a consumption boom at the expense of maintaining the domestic capital structure and of future developments.

Third, if the United States renews it capital structure only every 20 to 25 years, it lags in the accumulation of capital (which, I believe, has really been capital consumption) and, more directly relevant to a Schumpeterian theme, in having less embodied technical progress compared with countries that renew their capital structures every five to seven years.

Fourth, this puts enormous stress on *all* American manufacturing industries. It must be remembered that the American expansionary fiscal policy was accompanied by a tight monetary policy expressed in high interest rates. The short-run explanation is that high interest rates were necessary to fight inflation. But increasingly they have become necessary to keep foreign capital flowing into the United States to finance the deficits that show no sign of abating. The alternative is not merely a rebirth of inflation but a further decline in the external value of the dollar. What the United States faces is a clear application of Chenery and Bruno's two-gap model (1962). Domestic savings and capital imports are substitutes for each other, which is really a very old insight.

Fifth, after an unreasonable increase in the international value of the dollar, we now have a very sharp decline. This decline has not yet led to improved export performance, but it is expected to do so within half a year or so. The reason for both events was that non-American industries, when the dollar rose, instead of reducing dollar prices, increased their domestic prices, and now, with the declining value of the dollar, instead of increasing dollar prices, they reduce their domestic prices. Thus, we have seen an asymmetry: The strong dollar did not lead to reduced dollar prices of imports, but to higher foreign profits, aided and abetted, incidentally, by the foolishness of voluntary export controls in exporting countries, which the decline of the dollar is whittling away. The dollar prices of imports have just begun to increase, and exports will increase. However, although this will bring some relief to American manufacturing and will at least halt and perhaps even reverse the process of deindustrialization, I fear that the real cause of the trouble, the enormous budget deficit, is not adequately dealt with.

Sixth, I agree with Perlman that there is not much to the senescence theory that industries age and fall victim to arteriosclerosis, unable to compete with industries elsewhere that are using newer equipment. Industries are not people. There is no natural law that says that this aging must take place. If we save 10 percent of GNP, it surely will happen. If we save 20 to 25 percent, it will happen only if other factors determining comparative advantage dictate the shift to different industries.

Seventh, these other factors include wage rates, but also technical innovation. Whereas the United States saves 10 percent and has instituted a tax reform that will not stimulate savings, German and Japanese policies do stimulate savings. Hence, their productivity progress is likely to remain faster than that of the United States, thereby frustrating the declining value of the dollar, or rather forcing it to a level below where it would be with more savings. This implies not only slower growth, with pressure on manufacturing, but also slower innovative progress in old and new industries – until interest rates come down not because of insufficient demand for funds at the present but because of an increased supply of savings. Even the stock market will one day wake up to this. The cure for premature senescence is to increase capital formation by greater domestic savings.

A protectionist policy would be exactly the wrong policy to pursue. With a fluctuating exchange rate, it makes no sense at all as a general policy. With fixed exchange rates, tariffs and the like are second or third best substitutes for devaluation and for cutting real wages without appearing to do so. Devaluation does so directly and without discrimination among industries. With luck, exports absorb idle capacity and unemployed labor without raising money wages. This still leaves real wages declining, an inevitable consequence of having to reduce balance-of-payments deficits.

With free fluctuating exchanges, tariffs and quotas can be "defended" only as a method of destroying the price system in favor of particular recipients. There are immediate inherent and large costs on other domestic industries, and these policies are likely to be ineffective even in the short run. They can be defended as giving an industry some breathing space while it adjusts to new technologies and new competitive situations, but they place a direct burden on nonprotected industries.

Perlman quotes the late Otto Eckstein: "Can – or should – government policies act to reverse the decline of manufacturing industries?" My answer is an unequivocal yes to both parts of the question. But this is best done not by questionable "industrial policies," and certainly not by protectionist policies, but by policies that stimulate domestic savings and increases in domestic productivity. The central policy is tax policy. The rest, I believe, will solve itself as a consequence.

As I have built up my argument, I have chosen not to react to specific questions, but I should like to add one.

It is true that we can prove that some trade is better than no trade, but not that free trade is the best of all policies. But this is not an argument that can be used in the present context, for the potential gains from protection consist of the fact that we get *more imports* for fewer exports. This is the opposite of what protectionists desire: fewer imports and more exports. This argument for protection has always been a chimera.

Nor can it be argued that import restrictions will, without reducing real wage levels, create employment. It was estimated a few years back that the creation of one job in the automobile industry by import restrictions cost between $50,000 and $75,000, and in steel as much as a quarter of a million dollars.

Even if employment in the automotive and steel industries should be increased, which is dubious, this would be at the expense of other industries where these sums would then not be spent. Because most industries are less capital-intensive than steel or automobiles, there must be a *loss* of employment. One has to be aware of the fallacy of composition in these matters. The loss of employment and ouput to imports caused by falling international competitiveness is a real problem. Protection in its many variants is the worst possible solution to that very real problem. The real solution is an increase in domestic savings, and that requires a different budgetary policy.

References

Chenery, H. (1960). "Patterns of Economic Growth." *American Economic Review,* 50(September):624–54.

Chenery, H., and Bruno, M. (1962). "Development Alternatives in an Open Economy: The Case of Israel." *Economic Journal,* 72(March):79–103.

Clark, C. [1940] (1957). *The Conditions of Economic Progress* (3rd ed.). London: Macmillan.

Hoover, E. M. (1948). *The Location of Economic Activity.* New York: McGraw-Hill.

Vernon, R. (1966). "International Investment and International Trade in the Product Cycle." *Quarterly Journal of Economics,* 80:190–207.

Name index

Aaron, H. J., 262
Abramovitz, Moses, 5, 16, 129, 323, 326, 332, 333n6, 335n9, 336
Ackley, G., 218
Addison, J., 209, 215n14
Aftalion, A., 12, 13
Akerman, J., 155, 164, 170, 174, 176
Albach, H., 93n2
Albrecht, J., 184n20
Ames, Edward, 334n8
Andic, M., 257
Andic, S., 257
Arrow, Kenneth J., 147, 153, 183
Ashton, T. S., 170
Atkison, A. B., 262, 263, 301n14, 320
Avery, Clarence, 99
Axell, B., 176–7

Bacon, R., 267
Ballard, C. I., 318
Bank, Hans-Peter, 310
Barton, C. A., 247
Bauer, E. R., 318
Bauer, Otto, 58
Baumol, W. J., 24, 333
Becker, B. S., 24
Bergholm, F., 184n20
Berle, Adolf A., Jr., 140, 141
Berlin, Isaiah, 303–4, 381
Birdzell, L. E., 169
Blaug, Mark, 290n9
Blejer, M. I., 202
Blinder, A. S., 269
Blum, Reinhard, 145
Blume, Lawrence, 13, 14
Böhm-Bawerk, Eugen von, 49, 55, 56, 58
Borchardt, Knut, 17, 18
Bosworth, B. P., 267
Branson, William H., 376
Braudel, F., 169
Brown, C. V., 285, 301n13
Browning, E. K., 318
Brunner, K., 210n3, 215n13, 233
Bruno, M., 390
Buiter, W., 297n12

Burch, Phillip H., Jr., 141
Burns, Arthur F., 370
Burton, J., 209n1, 215n14

Cantillon, Richard, 290, 374, 380
Carlsson, B., 151, 161n7, 170
Catephores, George, 2, 23, 53, 54, 56, 58, 60–2, 64, 68, 160, 188
Chen, E. K. Y., 161n7
Chenery, Hollis, 15, 16, 387, 390
Christensen, Laurits R., 382
Clark, Colin, 16, 387
Clark, J. B., 58
Clark, John M., 12, 13, 171
Clark, P., 229
Clemence, R. V., 71n1
Clower, R., 292n11
Cohen, K., 182
Coutts, K., 212
Cowling, K., 200
Cummings, Diane, 382

Dahmén, Erik, 151, 155, 166
Danziger, S., 263, 270
Darwin, Charles, 96
Dasgupta, D. S., 6, 87n28, 183, 287n5, 304
David, P. A., 335n9
Day, R. H., 156
Denison, E. F., 261, 338
Diamond, P., 181, 182
Disraeli, Benjamin, 381
Doody, F. S., 71n1
Dorfman, Joseph, 374
Dornbusch, R., 214
Douglas, Donald, Sr., 108
Duijn, J. J. van, 86n26
Dye, Thomas R., 139

Earl, P. H., 233
Eckstein, O., 221, 223, 344, 345, 371, 376
Edgeworth, Francis Y., 23n1
Ehrenberg, R. G., 296
Eisenstein, E. L., 169

393